# OVERWHELMED

# OVERWHELMED

## WORK, LOVE, AND PLAY WHEN NO ONE HAS THE TIME

### BRIGID SCHULTE

BLOOMSBURY
LONDON · NEW DELHI · NEW YORK · SYDNEY

First published in Great Britain 2014

Copyright © 2014 by Brigid Schulte

The right of Brigid Schulte to be identified as the author of this work has been asserted
by her in accordance with the Copyright, Designs and Patents Act 1988

No part of this book may be used or reproduced in any manner whatsoever without
written permission from the publishers except in the case of brief quotations
embedded in critical articles or reviews

Bloomsbury Publishing Plc
50 Bedford Square
London
WC1B 3DP

www.bloomsbury.com

Bloomsbury is a trademark of Bloomsbury Publishing Plc

Bloomsbury Publishing, London, New Delhi, New York and Sydney
A CIP catalogue record for this book is available from the British Library

ISBN 978 1 4088 2668 3

10 9 8 7 6 5 4 3 2 1

Designed by Abby Kagan
Printed and bound in Great Britain by CPI Group (UK) Ltd, Croydon CR0 4YY

MIX
Paper from
responsible sources
FSC
www.fsc.org
FSC® C020471

*To Liam and Tessa,*
*that your horizons may be clear and wide,*
*and to Tom, always*

# CONTENTS

## PART FIVE: TOWARD TIME SERENITY

# PART ONE

## TIME CONFETTI

# 1

# THE TEST OF TIME

Time is the soul of this world. —Pythagoras

It is just after 10 a.m. on a Tuesday and I am racing down Route 1 in College Park, Maryland. The Check Engine light is on. The car tax sticker on my windshield has expired. The cell phone I'd just been using to talk to one of my kids' teachers has disappeared into the seat crack. And I'm late.

I screech into the crowded University of Maryland parking garage and wind ever higher until I at last find a spot on the top deck. My palms are sweating. My breath is shallow. My heart races and I feel slightly sick. I throw the car into Park, fumble ineptly with the parking ticket machine, and race down the stairs.

Only later, in revisiting this frantic day in my memory, will I realize that the sky had been that poignant shade of autumn blue and the leaves tinted with red. But as I live it, the stress hormones coursing through my veins tense my entire body and collapse my vision into a narrow, dizzying tunnel. Because I am filled with dread.

This is the day I have been avoiding for more than a year. Today, I am meeting with John Robinson, a sociologist who for more than a half century has studied the way people spend their most precious, non-renewable resource: time. Robinson was one of the first social scientists in the United States to begin collecting detailed time diaries, counting the hours of what typical people do on a typical day, and publishing scholarly tomes summing up the way we live our lives. For his pioneering work, his colleagues call him Father Time. And Father Time has challenged me to keep a time diary of my own.

He told me that his research proves that I, a hair-on-fire woman struggling to work a demanding full-time job as a reporter for *The Washington Post* and be the kind of involved mother who brings the Thanksgiving turkey for the preschool feast and puts together the fifth-grade slide show, have thirty hours of leisure time in a typical week.

Today, he is to dissect the mess of my time diaries and show me where all that leisure time is. I feel as if I am a bug, pinned on a specimen tray, about to be flayed and found wanting.

Because this is how it feels to live my life: scattered, fragmented, and exhausting. I am always doing more than one thing at a time and feel I never do any one particularly well. I am always behind and always late, with one more thing and one more thing and one more thing to do before rushing out the door. Entire hours evaporate while I'm doing stuff that needs to get done. But once I'm done, I can't tell you what it was I did or why it seemed so important. I feel like the Red Queen of *Through the Looking-Glass* on speed, running as fast as I can—usually on the fumes of four or five hours of sleep—and getting nowhere. Like the dream I keep having about trying to run a race wearing ski boots.

And, since I had kids, I don't think I've ever had a typical day.

There was the morning my son tae kwon do roundhouse kicked me when I went to wake him up, which sent my coffee splattering over every single book on his bookshelf. I hurriedly wiped the pages dry so they wouldn't stick together and render the entire library useless. Which of course made me glaringly late for work and threw my plans for the day into the shredder. My sister Mary has these kinds of days, too. She calls them Stupid Days.

There was the day when my husband, Tom, was overseas again and I flew in late to a meeting with school officials to discuss why our then-ten-year-old son, who knew more about World War II than I ever will, was floundering in fifth grade. I dragged along our second grader, still in her pajamas and slippers because she'd stayed home sick. And I nervously kept an eye on my BlackBerry because I was in the middle of reporting a horrific deadline story about a graduate student who'd been decapitated at an Au Bon Pain.

Then there was the time when the amount of work I needed to do pressed so heavily on my chest that I'd said no when my daughter asked, "Mommy, will you please come with me on my field trip today?"

We'd been through this before, I told her. I couldn't come with her on every field trip. Then her big blue-gray eyes started to water. I felt all the breath drain out of me. I thought, at the end of my life, would I remember whatever assignment it was that seemed so urgent—I don't even recall it now—or would I remember a beautiful day in the woods with a daughter who had been struggling with unexplained stomach-aches, was socially wobbly since her best friend moved away, and who still wanted me to be with her? I went. I spent three hours in the woods with her, guiltily checking my BlackBerry, then, after putting her to bed that night, went back to work for another four.

I have baked Valentine's cupcakes until 2 a.m. and finished writing stories at 4 a.m. when all was quiet and I finally had unbroken time to concentrate. I have held what I hope were professional-sounding interviews sitting on the floor in the hall outside my kids' dentist's office, in the teachers' bathroom at school functions, in the car outside various lessons, and on the grass, quickly muting the phone after each question to keep the whooping of a noisy soccer practice to a minimum. Some appliance is always broken. My to-do list never ends. I have yet to do a family budget after meaning to for nearly twenty years. The laundry lies in such a huge, perpetually unfolded mound that my daughter has taken a dive in it and gone for a swim.

At work, I've arranged car pools to ballet and band practice. At home, I am constantly writing and returning e-mails, doing interviews and research for work. "Just a sec," I hear my daughter mimicking me as she mothers her dolls. "Gimme a minute." She has stuck yellow Post-it notes on my forehead while I sit working at the computer to remind me to come upstairs for story time.

My editors can recount every deadline I've blown. My son, Liam, once recited every single one of the handful of honors assemblies or wheezy recorder concerts I'd missed in his entire life. I was even failing our cat, Max. I asked someone at the pet store what I could do to make him stop scratching up the carpets. "He thinks you're his mother. He's showing he needs more attention from you," she'd said. "Can't you find time to play with him every day?"

"Can't I just squirt water at him instead?"

At night, I often wake in a panic about all the things I need to do or didn't get done. I worry that I'll face my death and realize that my life got lost in this frantic flotsam of daily stuff. Once, my sister Claire told me that when you smile, it releases some chemical in the brain and calms anxiety. I have tried smiling. At 4 a.m. In bed. In the dark.

It didn't work.

On some level, I know that who we are depends very much on how we choose to spend this ten minutes or that hour. I know from all those bumper stickers that this is my one and only life, and from the Romans that time flies. And I know from the Buddhists that we should embrace the moment. I wake with every good intention of making the most of my day—to do good work, to spend quality time with my children, to eat less trail mix, to stop driving off with my wallet on top of the car. But then one of the kids throws up, or the babysitter calls in sick, or the kitchen faucet starts gushing water, or some story breaks and everything collapses.

I fast-walk across the University of Maryland campus like it's Judgment Day. I'm hoping these hectic, tardy, and chaotic little scraps of time that I've been tracking will add up to a meaningful life. But as I rush into the sociology building where Robinson works, I'm more afraid they'll show anything but. I'm terrified that all the mess that I usually keep stuffed behind a friendly, competent, professional, if harried, veneer will come spilling out.

"Sorry to be late," I apologize breathlessly. John Robinson just shrugs. He is, I would soon find out, no slave to the clock. He is seventy-four years old. Tall, thin, and stooped, he wears khaki pants, a canary yellow polo shirt, and sensible shoes. His long, wispy gray hair is styled in a Beatles mop top. Robinson leads me into a conference room, saying he'd rather meet here than in his office. (I would later discover why.)

We sit. I reach into my backpack and pull out two little black Moleskine notebooks, $3\frac{3}{4}$ inches wide by $5\frac{1}{2}$ inches long, crammed with crazy scribbles. Robinson had challenged me to track my time fully a year and a half earlier. I had been part of an internal work group at the *Washington Post* researching why so few women were reading the newspaper. "Maybe we should just hire them all babysitters," one male editor had joked. But it was serious business. In previous eras, women were always among the most faithful newspaper subscribers. But these days, only women of a certain age in retirement seemed to have the time. We began talking to women between the ages of eighteen and forty-nine and heard responses that all sounded something like this:

"I read the paper, typically at midnight, in bed . . . I have no time in the morning. I do everything in the house. I pay all the bills, take out the trash, I've got the dry cleaning in the car. So in the morning, when my husband is reading the paper, I'm in constant motion getting the girls to school and getting ready for work. Men are different. They could read the newspaper with piles of laundry all around them. I can't."

One woman confessed that she canceled the paper because the unread stack became a nagging reminder of all the things she hadn't been able to get to. "It's just one more thing to feel bad about."

The internal working group, many of us mothers and caregivers frantically grabbing scraps of time to read the newspaper we worked for ourselves, soon learned that market researchers call our demographic "frenetic families." It was my job to get the time-use data showing how busy and time-starved women are, particularly mothers. Not knowing where to start, I Googled "time busy women," and up popped John Robinson.

When I called him, I told him we thought women were stretched too thin to read the newspaper.

"Wrong," Robinson interrupted.

"Women have time," he said. "They have at least thirty hours of leisure every week. It's not as much as men, but women have more leisure now than they did in the 1960s, even though more women are working outside the home."[1]

I blinked. Hard. I felt like I'd been clonged on the head with a frying pan.

I quickly ran through what I could remember of the previous week. I'd been up until some ungodly hour the night before making my son finish a homework project. I did have a day off for having worked a weekend shift, but I spent it avoiding doing the taxes by cleaning the oven, and on the phone with Apple customer service trying to figure out why all the icons on the Mac had turned into question marks. The only activities that, with some stretching, I would consider "leisure" were our usual Family Pizza Movie Night on Friday, a seventy-five-minute yoga class on Saturday morning, and a family dinner at a friend's house with the kids in tow. There were the few minutes each night when I struggled to keep my eyes open long enough to read more than the same paragraph of a book. But *thirty* hours?

"I don't know what you're talking about," I finally managed to sputter. "I don't have thirty hours of leisure time every week."

"Yes, you do," he'd said. "Come and do a time study with me, and I'll show you where your leisure time is."

I put it off for months. Part of me wanted to prove Robinson was wrong. Some days I felt so overwhelmed I could barely breathe. But honestly, I was more afraid than angry. What if Father Time was right? What if he found that I was *squandering* my time? Frittering away those precious Buddhist moments? Wasting my one and only life? What if I *did* have thirty hours of leisure and was simply too stressed out, disorganized, neurotic, or *something* to notice?

Truthfully, I've never been good with time. A friend once stole my watch as we traveled through Asia after college and set it ten minutes ahead, so we wouldn't keep missing our trains. Another, shaking his head as I crammed writing seven incomplete term papers into the last week of college, told me, "You, my dear, spend time as if you had a discount." As a kid, I constantly ran out the door with shoes and toothbrush in hand to get to school or to church.

Working and becoming a mother had just pushed me over the edge.

So I had to wonder, was it just me? Were other people more focused, better organized, or just plain better at figuring out how to make time to do good work, be a good parent, fold the laundry and, as our Declaration of Independence spells out, pursue happiness in their abundant leisure time?

I asked friends. They asked their friends. I sent out queries to Listservs and on social media. "Looking for moms with leisure time." I got answers back like this one:

"If you find her, I think I'd probably put her in a museum, next to Big Foot, a Unicorn, a Mermaid and a politician who doesn't play dirty. I honestly think the only moms who have leisure time also have 'staff.' I manage about 5 hours a week for working out, but that's not really leisure—just less expensive than psychotherapy."

One friend counted fifteen hours of leisure a week. Another, stretched between her work as a psychotherapist in New York and caring for her busy toddler and her dying mother-in-law, didn't even try. "What I would give for a bunch of Mormon sister wives or a few Muslim harem mates," she e-mailed. "So tired I cannot speak." My friend Marcia reminded me that our husbands made time for their monthly neighborhood Del Ray Dads' beer-drinking outings in the neighborhood, but that our attempts for a similar Moms' night fizzled. Everyone was too busy. And, she said, even when she did have the occasional night out, her husband and kids continually called asking her where they needed to be or where they could find their stuff. "I feel like I never sit down," said one mother of two who had recently quit her job as an attorney. "Except in the car." Another mother said that if she found herself with a free moment, she spent it anxiously asking herself what she was forgetting. "I can't seem to get myself to just relax and enjoy the moment," she said. "I have to find something, anything, to do, because that's what I'm usually doing—something."

When I read that some social scientists thought the time crunch was really an indulgent "yuppie kvetch," I asked a friend who works with working-poor immigrant families if I could come to one of their monthly evening meetings. A group of about fifty people gathered in the cafeteria of the local high school. As I went from table to table, many explained how they cobbled together two or three part-time, low-paying jobs to pay the rent. They lived in apartments with two and sometimes three other families. They couldn't afford child care and shuffled their kids from an *abuela* to a neighbor to a TV set somewhere or hauled them along to work. They spent their time worrying about homework they didn't understand and were too afraid to ever ask for time off to care for a sick child or meet with a teacher. Standing in front of the group, I asked them if they felt rushed and could never do in a day all the things they wanted and needed to do. All fifty hands shot up. I asked if they ever had time for leisure, to relax. They stared at me in silence. Finally, one woman responded in Spanish. "Maybe at church," she said. "Or when I sleep."

As I began to think more about leisure time, I realized that I kept putting it off, like I was waiting to reach some tipping point: *If* I could just finish picking all the weeds, chopping the invasive bamboo, cleaning out the crayons and shark teeth and math papers and toys and bits of shells and rocks and too-small clothes in the kids' closets, buy more cat food, fix the coffeepot, complete this story assignment, pay these bills, fill out those forms, make that phone call, send this wedding present five months late—*then* I could sit down and read a book. As if leisure was something I needed to earn. Even when I seemed to have some free time, it was often for such a short period that I was at a loss for what to do with it. So I just went on to the next item on the to-do list.

As a kid, I remember losing myself for hours in imaginary worlds, playing with marbles or LEGOs or dolls or in the woods behind our house in Oregon. I remember playing the piano and long hours spent splayed across my bed reading. But I also remember that my mother, usually with a basket of laundry in hand, would come across me and sigh, "I wish I had the time to do that." Did I somehow absorb the idea that becoming an adult, a mother, meant giving up time for the things that give you joy?

I talked to mothers who said they both loved and dreaded the holidays. They both longed for and loathed vacations. "So much work," they said. And even when it appeared on the outside as if they were all having fun—going to the pool or taking a family bike ride—on the inside, they said, they were often preoccupied. They were thinking about the car pool they needed to set up, worrying about the homework that was due, the groceries to buy, and all the while, taking emotional temperatures and making sure everyone else was happy. Their brains whirred in perpetual logistics mode.

I thought of the stressed-out working mom Tina Fey played in *Date Night*. Her leisure fantasy? To be in a hotel room with clean sheets, completely alone, drinking a Diet Sprite.

This is certainly not how the ancient Greek philosophers envisioned leisure. To them, living a life of leisure was the highest aim of a human being. True leisure, the Greeks believed, free from the drudgery of work, not only refreshed the soul but also opened it up. It was a time and a space where one could be most fully human.[2] I thought of my daughter, Tessa, whom I found one day sitting in a chair, hugging herself and smiling. "I just love feeling my soul," she said. "Don't you?"

Most days, honestly, I felt like I didn't have the time. If, as Ovid said, "In our leisure we reveal what kind of people we are," what kind of person did that make me? It's not that I didn't *want* to refresh my soul. I just always felt too busy to get to it.

"Ah," Ben Hunnicutt, a leisure scholar at the University of Iowa, told me, when I made that confession to him. "One of the seven deadly sins."

I'd called him one morning to ask about leisure and found him playing a Mozart divertimento. He'd taken an hour-and-a-half walk after lunch with his wife and granddaughter the day before and chuckled fondly at the memory of the poem they wrote about it. He was preparing for his evening singing group. He wasn't sure how many hours he spends at leisure, but he makes time for it every day.

I was still stung by his opening comment. "Busyness is a sin?" I asked.

"In the Middle Ages, the sin of sloth had two forms," he said. "One was paralysis, the inability to do anything—what we would see as lazy. But the other side was something called *acedia*—running about frantically. The sense that, 'There's no real place I'm going, but by God, I'm making great time getting there.'"

To Hunnicutt, people in the modern world are so caught up in busyness they have lost the ability even to imagine what leisure is. He told me to read Walt Whitman's "Crossing Brooklyn Ferry," where the poet enjoins people to hit the road and "Let the paper remain on the desk unwritten, and the book on the shelf unopen'd! / Let the tools remain in the workshop! let the money remain unearn'd!"

But all I could imagine was the house going into foreclosure if the mortgage "remained unpaid" and the faces of two crestfallen children running after me on that open road crying, "Mommy! Mommy! Come back!"

"Well, then," he persisted, "what does leisure look like to you?"

I paused. "A sick day."


I'd started keeping my time diary in the little black Moleskine notebooks because my time was too unruly to shove into the orderly rectangles of the time diary template John Robinson had given me. His Excel spreadsheet seemed simple enough: "What Did You Do?" and gave me a choice of about eleven different activities, like "Paid Work," "Sleep," "Housework," and "Leisure." But every activity seemed to bleed into every other one. And, because I always seemed to be doing more than one thing at a time, I had to create my own category: "Doing Anything Else?"

I'd called Robinson in despair. I was at work. I was eating lunch at my desk. I was talking to him on one line and on hold with the pharmacy on the other line trying to refill my son's EpiPen prescription. I was working on a story on one computer screen. And on another, I was surfing the State Department website trying to figure out how to get a death certificate for my brother-in-law, who'd died in China.

"What the hell kind of time is that?" I'd asked. "Work? Housework? Child Care? Personal Care. All four?"

Robinson told me to just keep a diary and he'd figure it out.

The little black books, then, became confessionals, not only of what I did with my time but also how I felt about it.

Sitting in the university conference room with Robinson, clutching my time diaries, I am seized by a sense of inadequacy. I wish the books showed that I got to bed early, flossed regularly, did exemplary work, never yelled at my children, and had finished scrapbooks for them. I wish they showed I lived the kind of wise, meaningful life that young girls would want to emulate rather than run screaming from. Instead, the little books are pockmarked and scrawled in different colors of ink, the result of being hauled around for more than a year from work to home to the sidelines of hockey and baseball games, wrestling car pool, neighborhood parties, Girl Scout camping trips, and flute, drum, and ballet lessons. One went through the dryer. They have been dragged to Target and to Starbucks, where I noted once with envy, *Who ARE these people sitting around drinking coffee in the afternoon?*

The notebooks dutifully chronicle such embarrassments as the late bills and the time spent on the phone in crisis management mode because I put something off too long. They report the tedious hours spent dangling, on hold, waiting for the phone guy, the cable repairman, the plumber, or the man who promised to finally fix the dishwasher so ineffective we'd dubbed it the Delicate Flower. They noted the days I spent unshowered, in my workout clothes, meaning to get to the gym but never making it there.

I had even recorded a session with a tarot card reader that my friends egged me into seeing at a neighborhood Halloween party.

Spirit Card: Stagnation. Hmm. You're looking for something and you're feeling stuck. Draw a card and see what you can do about it.
Setback.
Oooh. Draw another.

Hermit.

You need some time for yourself to be quiet. What can you do to give yourself that kind of time? Can you get up earlier?

In tracking my time, I now know exactly how many minutes it can take to break your heart: seven. That's how long it took for my daughter to tell me, in angry tears as I finally cut her too-long fingernails in the bathroom one evening, that I was always at the computer and never spent enough time with her. And that, when she grew up, she wanted to be a teacher. "Because then at least I'll be able to spend time with my kids."

In the conference room, hand still on my little black notebooks, I think of confetti. That's how my life feels. Like time confetti—one big, chaotic burst of exploding slivers, bits, and scraps. And really, what does a pile of confetti ever amount to?

John Robinson looks at me quizzically.

I hold my breath and reluctantly slide the notebooks across the table.

He squints at my spidery handwriting.

"What's this word?"

I look.

"Panic," I say, reddening. "Wake in a panic."

I glance at the passage from Sept. 16.

2 am–4 am Try to breathe. Discover that panic comes in the center of the chest—often in one searing spot. Fear in the belly. Dread just below that. The should haves and self-recrimination oddly come at the left shoulder. Worrying about money. Angry with myself that we can't or don't figure it out. Worried that I don't spend enough time with my kids. That they're growing so fast before my eyes, yet I'm missing it.

Alarm off at 6 am. Up. Thankfully. Finally put the comforter cover on—it's been crumpled up, clean, at the bottom of the bed for days.

Robinson sighs.

"Do you have anything less stream-of-consciousness?"

John Robinson has been getting under people's skin for decades. Studying how people spend the 1,440 minutes in a day, Robinson has developed some very fixed notions about human behavior. He insists that although most Americans *feel* they're working harder than ever, they aren't. The time diaries he studies show that average hours on the job, not only in the United States but also around the globe, have actually been holding steady or going down in the last forty years. Everybody, he says, has more time for leisure.[3]

Instead, Robinson maintains that we "exaggerate" our work hours to show how important we are. His studies find that we sleep more than we think. We watch too much TV. And we're not nearly as busy as we seem to feel. Overworked Americans? Mothers coming home from work to the exhausting "second shift" of housework and child care? Children overscheduled? Everyone too busy for leisure time? Wrong. Wrong. Wrong. And wrong.[4]

If we don't feel like we have leisure, Robinson maintains, it's entirely our own fault. "Time is a smokescreen. And it's a convenient excuse," he'd told me. "Saying, 'I don't have time,' is just another way of saying, 'I'd rather do something else.' Free time is there. It's just what you want to do with it."

What Robinson does not dispute is the fact that people *feel* that they have less time and lead frenetic, harried lives. He was the one, after all, who came up with a way to measure that perception—a ten-question "time crunch scale" that researchers all over the world now use. One question asks whether you feel your spouse doesn't know you anymore. Another, if you just don't have time for fun. His studies have consistently found that those who feel the most crunched for time are women.[5]

"It's very popular, the feeling that there are too many things going on, that people can't get in control of their lives and the like," he told me. "But when we look at people's diaries, there just doesn't seem to be the evidence to back it up. I'm not saying that people are lazy, but the numbers do not match up between what they say and what the diaries show. It's a paradox. When you tell people they have thirty or forty hours of free time every week, they don't want to believe it."

In his 1997 book, *Time for Life*, Robinson likens modern American culture to the aimless whirl of ants whose anthill has just been stomped on. The brainless rushing about makes us feel time starved, which, he writes "does not result in death, but rather, as ancient Athenian philosophers observed, in never beginning to live."[6]

Robinson's specialty, the science of measuring how people use time, is barely a century old. For most of human history, people noted the passing of time by the transit of the sun, the chores that got done by sundown, the tides, the changing of the seasons. But with the rise of the clock and the coming of the industrial age, time-and-motion studies on factory floors to boost the productivity of "stupid" manual workers became all the rage.[7] Time became money. It could be earned, spent, or wasted. In the 1920s, the U.S. Department of Agriculture studied what farm wives did with their time and offered advice on how to do it more efficiently. The former Soviet Union was the first country to extensively use time diaries to measure collective-farm output and worker productivity as part of their central-planning efforts.[8]

Robinson began measuring time in the 1960s. In 1972, he took part in a groundbreaking effort to collect time diaries in twelve developed countries around the globe. That's when he got his first taste of how perceptions about time can be not only powerful but also powerfully wrong. Everyone assumed that American housewives, with all their time-saving appliances, would be freed from the drudgery of housework. Instead, the time diary comparison showed that they spent just as much time cleaning as did women without them, in Bulgaria.[9]

Hooked, he started running small-scale time-use studies himself. One was funded by AT&T because executives wanted to know how much time people were spending on the phone. (A lot.) The U.S. Environmental Protection Agency funded another in the 1990s to find out how much time people spent outdoors. (Not much. Less than 8 percent of their time, a statistic, he says, that they used to push for cleaner indoor air quality standards.)[10] But people were skeptical of the value of studying time. In the 1970s and '80s, when his research was funded by the National Science Foundation, Robinson said his work was scorned as a waste of taxpayer money.

But over time, as Robinson and others were able to show that time diaries could describe patterns in human behavior in a way that other surveys and economic indicators could not, academics and governments began collecting diaries and analyzing time as a matter of routine. The International Association for Time Use Research now boasts upward of twelve hundred members diligently combing time diaries collected in more than one hundred countries.[11] And since 2003, economists at the U.S. Bureau of Labor Statistics have collected diaries from more than 124,000 people for the American Time Use Survey, an annual $5 million-plus effort to track what Americans do with their time.[12]

Some findings are obvious: Mothers, even those working outside the home for pay, still do twice the housework and twice the child care as fathers.[13] If I didn't already know that intuitively, that phenomenon was certainly showing up in my time diary: *Saturday, 9–10:30 pm, Clean up after 11-year-old's birthday party while husband smokes cigar on back patio.* Other discoveries reflect what different cultures value or the forces that shape their lives: Robinson has found that people spend the most time walking in Spain, relaxing in Italy and Slovenia, and watching TV in Bulgaria. In the United States, people spend more time on computers than those in other countries, volunteer more, and spend the most time taking care of children and aging adults.[14]

Some time studies are now making their way into important policy discussions. Feminist economists have argued for years that unpaid housework and child care—the invisible "labor of love" known as women's work—has intrinsic value. That domestic labor of women, they argue, has, for centuries, freed men to concentrate solely on paid work, kept economies humming and civilizations propagating. If time is money, they say, then documenting how much time women spend caring for children, the elderly, and the sick, driving car pools, overseeing homework, picking up dirty socks, washing dishes, and the like is one way to show its value.[15] In 2012, Colombia became the first country to pass a law to include a measurement of unpaid household work in their System of National Accounts.[16]

In the University of Maryland conference room, John Robinson pronounces my little black notebooks unreadable and slides them across the table back to me, unanalyzed. I had meant to type up the contents and analyze them myself first. But it was such a laborious process that I'd had time to make it through only one week. I pull out the sheets of neatly typed paper for the week of September 29 through October 5. Robinson takes them, pulls out a yellow highlighter, and hunts for leisure.

He highlights every run, every 6 a.m. DVD workout in the bedroom with the sound off so I won't wake the kids, every yoga class. *Leisure*.

"Exercise is leisure?" I ask. "That feels more obligatory." And, I want to add, it took nine years, Lexapro, a wicked bout of stress-induced eczema, and thirty extra pounds to figure out how to squeeze it into my day in the first place.

"Exercise is leisure."

Every time I read the newspaper he swipes it with the highlighter.

"But that's my job."

"Reading is leisure."

He finds an hour at midnight Wednesday when I was farting around on the computer, beating it roundly in a game of backgammon (okay, busted), downloading photos and e-mailing them to family, answering e-mails, and arranging for a cleaning service to come to my friends' Jeff and Molly's house because Jeff was battling stomach cancer and Molly was busy working to support the family while trying to figure out how to save Jeff's life. *Screeeeech* goes the highlighter.

Lying in bed for twenty minutes one particularly exhausted morning listening to NPR while trying to get *out* of bed. Leisure.

"What? I was trying to get up! Shouldn't that be somewhere between sleep and personal care?"

"Listening to the radio is leisure."

Friday Pizza Movie Night with the kids. Visiting my sick friend with the kids. Talking to a friend on the cell phone about her leisure time while taking my son's bike to the shop for repairs with the kids. Leisure. Leisure. Leisure.

To John Robinson and his yellow highlighter, Sunday, October 4, was a day filled with leisure for me.

This is what it felt like to live: I'd spent the morning taking care of Jeff so that Molly and her kids could go to church. With minutes to spare to get my daughter to the *Nutcracker* audition she'd been begging to do, I pulled up to the house and discovered she wasn't ready to go. "We couldn't find her tights," my husband said.

"THEY'RE IN THE DRYER!" I'd yelled. "I TOLD YOU THAT BEFORE I LEFT!"

Then, after grabbing the tights out of the dryer, flinging them at my daughter to put on in the car, and barely making her audition on time, on the way home, the car died. I'd glided into a grassy median strip and called a tow truck. My daughter and I played tic-tac-toe and hangman while we waited. For two hours.

*Screeeech* goes the highlighter.

"Wait a minute," I say. "Waiting for a tow truck is leisure?"

"Oh, you were playing with your daughter," Robinson corrects himself. "That's child care."

"So if I were broken down on the side of the road by myself, that would be leisure?"

"Yes."

Robinson does not highlight the best ten minutes of the day. I'd gone in to check on my then eleven-year-old son after family story time, like I do every night. It's my favorite part of the day, when the storm systems of homework and chores and the craziness of the waking hours have convulsed, spent their energy, and passed. I lay down and he snuggled into my shoulder.

"Mom, if you could have any superpower, what would it be?"

"Hmm. I think I'd like to fly," I said. "You?"

"I'd change into anything I wanted," he said as he drifted dreamily off to sleep. "If I wanted to fly, I could change into a bird. I could be a deer. Or a crocodile."

Those fleeting and lovely minutes, Robinson classifies as child care.

In the end, Robinson finds about twenty-eight hours of what he calls leisure for the week.

"But they didn't *feel* very leisurely," I protest.

"I just measure time." Robinson shrugs. "I'm not a chronotherapist."

I'd been afraid I not only had no leisure time, but that Robinson would find that I didn't work enough. Instead, we found I typically worked more than fifty hours a week, often at weird hours and in chopped-up chunks. (I get paid for working 37.5.) I slept an average of six hours a night, when you factored in longer weekend sleep time. If you counted worrying and yanking out gray hairs at red lights, I spent almost every waking hour multitasking.

We found that I somewhat obsessively "tidied" in scraps of time—picking up the muddy shoes under the kitchen table, the jackets left on the floor, the junk mail that pours in—that added up to nearly an *hour* every day. And my guilt that I wasn't spending enough time with the kids? One week, when both they and the babysitter were sick and I worked at home, out of the seventy-three hours that my children were awake that week, I spent all but *seven* in their presence. It wasn't all quality time, mind you. ("I love you. I'm working. Shut the door and go away.") But I was there.

I began to question everything I assumed was true about my life. Why did I feel I never did enough work? Why did I worry that I never spent enough time with my kids? Did I really need to keep the house so tidy? Why did I feel I didn't deserve to relax until the to-do list was done? Why did every conversation I had seem to start with, "How are you?" "Fried." "You?" "Same." Were we, in proclaiming our frantic busyness, as Robinson insisted, just showing off?

Why was my husband smoking a cigar while I was clearing up birthday party stuff? Why did I feel he had a career while I just tried not to get fired? When we started out, Tom and I promised we'd be equal partners, and yet somehow we both automatically assumed that *I* was the parent who should take the kids to the doctors' appointments, go on field trips, volunteer at the school book fair, and stay home when they were sick. Why? Why did I feel so guilty about working? Was it hormones? The way my brain was wired? Because I was defying the natural order? Or was I trying to prove to all the people who'd said, "Well, *I'd* never let anyone else raise *my* child," that even though I used child care, I *was* raising my children, too?

Robinson and I stroll over to the campus dining room for lunch. He never does much of anything in a hurry. Halfway through the meal, waiters come over to say the dining room closes at 2:30 and it's 2:45. "I'm in no rush," Robinson says. Oblivious of the waiters who are.

I ask if he knows people who have found a way to knit scraps of time together into longer, smoother stretches to do meaningful work, spend quality time with their kids, partner, and family, and have found the space to refresh their souls. I thought of the psychologist Erik Erikson, who said, "The richest and fullest lives attempt to achieve an inner balance between three realms: work, love and play."

Where could I go to find that? I ask. Sort of a "Work, Love, Play" for the rest of us?

He shrugs. He says that while he had always wanted to spend time with people in order to understand the "personal cosmologies" of the modern American family, he's never done it. He smiles wanly. "I'm better at crunching numbers."

He thinks.

"You know," he says. "If you really want to find out, you should come to the next IATUR conference."

"IATUR?"

"The International Association for Time Use Research. It's in a few months."

"Where?"

"Paris."

# 2

# LEISURE IS FOR NUNS

"Blorft" is an adjective I just made up that means "Completely overwhelmed but proceeding as if everything is fine and reacting to the stress with the torpor of a possum." I have been blorft every day for the past seven years.          —Tina Fey, *Bossypants*

Paris in July is hot. Swelteringly hot. I have come straight from the airport this morning to sit in a stew of sweat in the Amphithéâtre Jean Moulin in the Institut d'Études Politiques building by rue Saint-Guillaume. I nod off in a heavy haze of hunger, jet lag, and heat, listening to droning presentations on "time and squared time" and other incomprehensible technicalities of time study at the International Association for Time Use Research's annual conference. I am shaken from my drooling stupor when one speaker begins rattling off the results of a survey of two hundred working parents and time stress.

Two-thirds of the working parents felt they didn't get everything done in a day that they'd wanted to.

Fifty-seven percent worried they didn't spend enough time with their families.

Nearly half felt trapped every day.

If they needed more time, 60 percent said they cut down on sleep.

And 46 percent said they had no time for leisure, even though it was what they most enjoyed.

I assume she's talking about workaholic, overachieving America. But she throws up a PowerPoint slide. This is Australia.[1]

Then there's Canada. The presenter, Helen Perkins, a social psychologist from Griffith University in Australia, says that in Canada, a survey of more than thirty thousand workers and working families found that nearly 90 percent reported moderate to high levels of "role overload"—meaning they were trying to do too many things at once to meet the demands of both work and life. Never mind play.

This time pressure has enormous cost. In a massive government report, *Work-Life Conflict in Canada in the New Millennium*, Health Canada found that growing numbers of people are straining on the brink of role overload. More are depressed and anxious. As work weeks get longer and leisure time shrinks, people are becoming sicker, more distracted, absent, unproductive, and less innovative. All of that time strain cost businesses and the health-care system an estimated $12 billion a year in 2001 alone. "The link between hours in work and role overload, burnout, and physical and mental health problems," according to the report, "[suggests] that these workloads are not sustainable over the long term."[2]

I sit up straight and begin furiously taking notes. I had, as John Robinson suggested, come to Paris to the IATUR conference. I had slapped together a hash of babysitters and overnights for the kids because Tom was overseas again, pulled out the thankfully not-quite-maxed-out Visa and, with a sense of exhilarated disbelief that I was really doing it, jumped on a plane to Paris. I was on a quest to find out if other people live in a frenetic shower of time confetti, or whether I, as John Robinson maintained, was just a nut. More, I wanted to find if anyone, anywhere, had figured out how to have time for all the elements of the Good Life. Who was doing meaningful work he or she loved, had ample time for a rich life and deep human connections outside of it, and refreshed their soul with leisure time? Who had work, love, and play wired?

I page through the IATUR program, "The Timing of Daily Life," and find strange comfort. I quickly see that I'm not the only one trying to get a handle on the contours of the crazy jangle of modern life, a state of being so intense that I had come to think of it as the Overwhelm. I know it's not grammatically correct; Tina Fey's "blorft" isn't either. But that everything-all-at-once feeling that you're burning the candle from both ends and out the middle was just more than an adjective could handle. It demanded its own noun.

In session after session, time researchers from around the globe reported on rising levels of role overload for both women and, increasingly, men, the sense that life is speeding up at a breakneck pace and that, though they yearn for it, many people can't seem to find an elusive moment of peace. "This is *the* hot topic in time research right now," said Kimberly Fisher, a sociologist who studies time at Oxford. "A lot of researchers are struggling with role overload in their own lives. There's great interest in trying to understand why time pressure is going up."

A whole new generation of time researchers has emerged, Fisher explained, and they no longer see time in the clean, well-lit rectangles of distinct activities that John Robinson has. Time is murky. Porous. It has no sharp edges. What often matters more than the activity we're doing at a moment in time, they have found, is how we *feel* about it. Our perception of time is, indeed, our reality.

A number of time researchers even had lives that seemed a lot like mine. Janice Compton, a time-use researcher at the University of Manitoba, confessed she'd had trouble reading an e-mail I'd sent her "with my six-year-old jumping around trying to tell me about his latest Spider-Man battle."

In their presentations, social scientists were seeking to understand why so many people, Americans in particular, work such long hours, why women still do so much more housework and child care than men, even when they work full-time, and why women around the globe have yet to reach anything near parity in leadership in virtually every field, from academics and business to science and politics, even though they make up half the workforce in many countries, are increasingly more educated than men, and often outperform them. They lined up different countries to see if the overwhelm differed between social democracies with supportive family policies and those without them. Researchers puzzled over tallies that showed that even with such long work hours, parents—American parents in particular—are spending more and more time with their children. And they wanted to know why so few people around the world—women in particular, American women especially—report feeling they have so little time for leisure. One scholar even described women's leisure as "minute vacations"—those fleeting moments to daydream or gaze at a sunset, perhaps, or as I did one night searching for my son's bike helmet, to notice that the moon was uncannily beautiful.[3]

A whole new field of research is beginning to look into why the overwhelm matters. At what point does role overload lead to burnout and fatigue at work? When does it begin to tax the family system? How much of it is required before a physical or emotional breakdown occurs? Some researchers are taking workers' blood and saliva samples throughout the day to measure the telltale spike in the stress hormone cortisol when time pressure squeezes the body and mind. Entire presentations laid out the inverse relationship of increasing role overload and declining birthrates all over the world, which means many societies will soon have a worrisome surplus of old people and fewer young workers to support them. In the United States, the fertility rate began falling when the economic crisis hit in 2008, but it had already dropped among those with a college education to what some social scientists call the "crisis" level.[4] Steven Philip Kramer, a professor of strategy at the National Defense University, warns that countries that fail to address gender equity, redefine traditional families, reform immigration, and pass government policies that help men and women more easily combine work and family "do so at their own peril."[5]

The overwhelm, I was finding, was about so much more than just getting Mom a gift certificate to a spa to calm down or telling her to breathe deeply at stoplights (the advice I got). This was about sustainable living, healthy populations, happy families, good business, sound economies, and living a good life.

At coffee breaks, some women researchers, who struggled with role overload of their own, shared stories of their young daughters or female students who proclaimed to want anything but their own crazy busy lives. Although Facebook chief operating officer Sheryl Sandberg would soon tell them to *Lean In* to their careers and not throttle back on their ambition out of fear there wasn't enough time to have both a career and a family, the researchers worried that many young women they knew already had. "My daughter decided to become a teacher. Not that she's passionate about it, but she doesn't see any other way to have time to work and have a family," one researcher confided. "And she doesn't even have a boyfriend yet." I myself would soon get an e-mail from a talented colleague, frazzled with two young children, a demanding job, and a husband who routinely didn't get home until 9 or 10 p.m. She announced she'd had it and was quitting to stay home with her kids. Her e-mail subject line: "Leaning Out."

As I pored over the time studies searching to understand why the feeling of being overwhelmed was on the rise, one central truth emerged clearly: When women began working in a man's world, their lives changed completely. Yet workplace cultures, government policies, and cultural attitudes, by and large, still act as though it is, or it should be, 1950 in Middle America: Men work. Women take care of home and hearth. Fathers provide. A good mother is always available to her children. But obviously, life isn't so sharply divided anymore. And until attitudes, however unconscious, catch up with the way we really live our lives, the overwhelm will swirl on. Nowhere is that disconnect between expectations and reality more apparent than when a woman has a child. Time studies find that a mother, especially one who works outside the home for pay, is among the most time-poor humans on the planet, especially single mothers, weighed down not only by role overload but also what sociologists call "task density"—the intense responsibility she bears and the multitude of jobs she performs in each of those roles.[6] That's the no-win feeling of overload Anne-Marie Slaughter captured so perfectly when she wrote about resigning as director of policy planning at the State Department to be more available to her children. Her 2012 article in *The Atlantic*, "Why Women Still Can't Have It All," became one of the most-read articles in the long, august history of the magazine and unleashed a torrent of pent-up rage and frustration around the world.

But time studies are showing that more men, too, now want to Have It All—meaningful career and rich family life—and are finding out just how hard that is. Fathers are beginning to feel as much time stress as mothers, and in some cases, more.[7] The General Social Survey, a project of the National Science Foundation, which since 1972 has tracked the shifting opinions of Americans, has shown a steady rise in the number of both men and women who say they "always" feel rushed. But by far the biggest change has been among fathers of young children. Mothers in these intensive years of diaper changing, Cheerio flinging, and losing bottles under the seats until the car smells like a goat, have always been harried. When asked if they often had time to spare in 2004, exactly zero percent of mothers with children under six said yes. But the number of fathers who felt harried nearly *doubled* from 1982 to 2004, and a negligible 5 percent of fathers felt they often had time for leisure—far fewer than in previous years.[8] "I think you might have hit on a new diagnosis: OBL," Tom Smith, director of the General Social Survey at the University of Chicago's National Opinion Research Center, said as I combed through the findings with him. "Overwhelmed by Life."

Technology spins that overwhelm faster. At the conference, researchers sought to unravel how the explosive speed and sheer quantity of information, and the rapid and mystifying shifts in the economy and politics, and the uncertainty about the future, are swamping everyone.

All those stolen glances at the smartphone, the bursts of addictive texting and e-mail checking at all hours with the iPhone, Android, or BlackBerry by the bed, the constant connection—even taking electronic devices into the toilet to shop[9]—don't show up in time diaries. Yet that activity splinters the experience of time into thousands of little pieces. And living in an always-on technological haze leads to mental exhaustion. "People don't have as much mental space to relax in a work-free environment. Even if something's not urgent, you're expected to be available to sort it out," Oxford's Kimberly Fisher explained one afternoon over coffee in a Paris bistro. "So even though checking your smartphone and other gadgets at 11 p.m. doesn't take up that much actual *time*, you feel you've never quite gotten away from work and had a chance to wind down."

In the United States, the time strain is intense.

In their studies of the changing workforce, the Families and Work Institute, a nonpartisan research organization, has found that nearly 40 percent of the American workers they surveyed, from the top to the bottom of the socioeconomic ladder, report feeling overworked. They work among the longest hours and the most "extreme" hours of any industrialized country in the world.[10] Nearly one-quarter of those in the "golden years" generation, those sixty-two and older and thought to be basking in leisure, said they still felt flattened by all the tasks they needed and wanted to do in a day.[11] "Overwork is just our reality," Ellen Galinsky, director of the institute, told me. "There's this feeling of never-ending responsibility."

Half of the workers they surveyed in 2008 felt there were too many tasks to complete in a typical workweek. Two-thirds said they didn't have enough time for themselves or their spouses, and three-fourths felt they didn't spend enough time with their kids. (This, even though both American mothers *and* fathers, including those who work full time, spend more time with their kids than parents in many other countries.[12]) Many said they worked on vacation, or failed to take it at all. The United States is the only advanced economy that doesn't guarantee workers paid time off. Nearly one-quarter of all American workers get no paid vacation, most of them low-wage and part-time workers. And those whose companies do offer paid vacation get about fourteen days a year, far fewer than the twenty to thirty-day minimums, plus paid national holidays, for workers in other industrialized countries. Even so, nearly six in ten American workers say they don't take all the vacation they've earned, putting the United States simultaneously at the bottom of the global list for vacation time offered and at the top of the list for workers who throw those vacation days away.[13] An increasing number of workers reported feeling overwhelmed, in poorer health, overworked, depressed, angry at their employers for expecting so much, resentful of others they thought were slacking off, and being so exhausted that they were prone to making mistakes and doing lower-quality work.[14]

Even mothers who've opted out of the workforce to take care of home and children feel pressed for time. "I've interviewed a lot of moms who had quit working because they thought life would be much more leisurely. It wasn't," Galinsky said. "For women these days, your to-do list is always going . . . It's being overwhelmed by everything you have to do and having that tape running in your head about it all the time."

That mental tape-loop phenomenon is so common among women it even has a name. Time-use researchers call it "contaminated time." It is a product of both role overload—working and still bearing the primary responsibility for children and home—and task density. It's mental pollution, one researcher explained. One's brain is stuffed with all the demands of work along with the kids' calendars, family logistics, and chores. Sure, mothers can delegate tasks on the to-do list, but even that takes up brain space—not simply the asking but also the checking to make sure the task has been done, and the biting of the tongue when it hasn't been done as well or as quickly as you'd like. So it is perhaps not surprising that time researchers are finding that, while "free time" may help ease the feeling of time pressure for men, and in the 1970s helped women a little, by 1998 it was providing women no relief at all.[15]

Relief from the overwhelm is exactly what the time researchers, ultimately, are looking for. As they tallied minutes, analyzed international time diaries, and talked "segmented regression analysis," what the re-searchers in Paris said they hoped to discover were the keys to trans-forming the modern squeeze of endless, fractured work hours, frantic family time, and crappy bits of leisure time confetti into a blissful-sounding state they called . . . time serenity.

Steeled with the knowledge that I am not alone, I eagerly head to a seminar about time stress and working families in the Netherlands, hoping to find some answers.

In both the Netherlands and the United States, about 75 percent of all mothers with school-age children work outside the home.[16] But the majority of the mothers in the Netherlands work part-time, while the United States has among the highest proportion of mothers who work for pay full-time, and who return to full-time work within six months of having a child.[17] I'm curious to see if part-time work is the answer to the overwhelm. At least that's what many stressed-out American mothers would like to think. The Pew Research Center found that 60 percent of the working mothers they surveyed in 2007 said part-time work would be their ideal job situation, and that number held fairly steady after a bruising economic recession.[18] (Not so for fathers, how-ever. Fully 75 percent continue to say full-time work is their ideal.[19])

So I am expecting Marielle Cloin, a researcher with the Institute for Social Research at the Hague, to report that these Dutch mothers work-ing part-time have it all figured out.

She found, however, that people with more education felt more time stress than those with less education. She found that women felt more time stress than men. And those part-time working mothers? It turns out they felt the most time pressure of all.

They worked fewer hours in paid work than men but more than made up for it in hours put in on the unpaid job of taking care of the children and the household. Leisure for part-time working mothers was, like mine, scattered, and often interrupted by work, housework duties, or children. Men had more total leisure and enjoyed it in longer stretches of unbroken time.[20]

"I'm afraid the 'one and a half' work model for families preferred in the Netherlands comes across quite badly when it comes to time pres-sure," she confesses to the group, referring to the prevailing family structure of a full-time working father breadwinner and part-time working mother. I catch up with Cloin in the lobby after her presentation. I ask her why she doesn't think part-time work is the answer that leads to time serenity.

"It's role overload," she explains. "It's the constant switching from one role to the next that creates that feeling of time pressure." When all you're expected to do is work all day, you work all day in one long stretch, she says. But the days of the mothers she studied were full of starts and stops, which makes time feel more collapsed: You have to get the kids out the door on time for school, you watch the clock at work to make sure you get home in time to give them lunch, you get them back to school, you return to work, you're back for pickup, shuffle them to their activities, shop for groceries, do chores, catch up on a little more work, help with homework, work some more, make dinner. "It's exhausting," she said.

"Time for leisure?" I ask.

Cloin shook her head.

"Much of a mother's leisure was spent with her children," she says. "We see over and over that the very first thing to suffer for mothers is 'me time.'"

## Work

Over the course of the next few days, as I sat in session after session, cornered researchers, and pored through reports, what I discovered was, by turns, fascinating, frustrating, contradictory, puzzling, and enraging. More than anything, I was struck by how ignorant I was of the forces that had shaped my own life. I soon realized that I could never begin to understand why leisure time feels so elusive until I had a better sense of time pressure in the other two arenas of life that always squeezed it out: work and love.

I didn't understand how John Robinson and others could insist that leisure time was increasing because work hours were going down,[21] contradicting Juliet Schor, who, in *The Overworked American*, reported that Americans were working a full month longer in the 1990s than in the 1960s. Polls also reported that most Americans felt they had, at most, sixteen and a half hours of leisure a week.[22]

What's really happening is that work hours and leisure time in America are dividing. If you have an education and a high-paying career, chances are you're working an insanely high number of hours and have little leisure time. If you're poor or uneducated, you're having trouble finding enough work at all, and your "leisure" is often just blank hours of worry about how to pay the rent. Robinson's number is misleading, because it averages these two very different trends. Sociologists Kathleen Gerson and Jerry Jacobs argue in their book *The Time Divide* that the split in workers' time began in 1938, when the U.S. government passed the Fair Labor Standards Act. That law, which is still in force today, created two classes of workers: hourly and salaried. The law didn't limit the number of hours workers could work a week, as a number of other countries do. But it did protect hourly workers from overwork by mandating that employers pay them overtime after putting in forty hours on the job. Salaried workers received no such overwork protection.[23]

As the decades passed, by the 1970s, high-paying hourly manufacturing jobs that required only a high school diploma disappeared overseas. The service economy, with a huge appetite for college-educated salaried workers, expanded. The number of salaried professionals, who in 1938 comprised only one in every seven workers, doubled by 1995, and continues to grow. In the crudest sense, then, U.S. law allows employers to work these professionals to death without paying them overtime or being forced to hire more workers—which would require costly benefit packages—to share the load. Now, nearly 40 percent of American men and 20 percent of American women with a college education report putting in more than fifty hours a week on the job.[24] As do an astounding 32 percent of professional single mothers.[25]

But to truly understand why the overwhelm has been building, it is better to study what has happened to *families*, argue sociologists Michael Hout and Caroline Hanley. That, they say, is the only way to capture the enormous shape-shifting that both the workplace and family have undergone. In the late 1960s, about 38 percent of American mothers with young children worked outside the home, many working part-time. By the 2000s, 75 percent did, many of them working full-time. The researchers found that working parents combined put in thirteen more hours a week on the job in 2000 than they did in 1970. That's 676 hours—about 28 days—of additional paid work a year for a family. And that's on top of all the unpaid hours spent caring for children and keeping the house together. So if harried working families feel they're working more now, they wrote, it's because they are.[26]

## *Love*

In our many conversations, John Robinson had proudly told me that men and women were coming closer to egalitarian "time androgyny," as men do more housework and child care than in previous decades and more women work outside the home. In fact, his big presentation in Paris outlined what he called an international time "convergence."

It's true, total paid and unpaid workloads for fathers and mothers *aren't* that different. In dual-income couples, fathers average sixty-seven hours a week, mothers seventy-one.[27] But, I came to see, what's important is not the total time but *where* the time is spent. Fathers spend more time at work, about thirteen hours more a week than mothers.[28] Mothers, even when they're employed, are still doing twice the housework and child care, just as the sociologist Arlie Hochschild outlined in 1989 in her groundbreaking work *The Second Shift*. And those fewer working hours are a big reason why they still lag behind men in pay, promotions, corner offices, and leadership roles in virtually every profession.

When it comes to housework, the drudgery that Simone de Beauvoir so aptly described as "more like the torture of Sisyphus . . . the clean becomes soiled, the soiled is made clean, over and over, day after day," women are still doing the bulk of it. Though women are clearly doing far less now than in the 1960s and men are doing more, women still spend about twice as much time scrubbing and polishing. Fathers increased their weekly housework hours from four in 1965 to ten in 1985, before backsliding to a little more than nine hours in 2003. And they haven't put in a minute more since.[29]

In a study of housework in Britain, researchers found that men tended to do the chores they enjoyed, like cooking or shopping. But women slogged on, getting stuff done whether they liked it or not.[30] One-quarter of Italian men do no housework at all. Men in Japan and South Korea spend less than an hour a day on chores.[31] In South Africa, women do three times the amount of housework and child care that men do, even when the women work and the men are unemployed.[32] New research finds that the amount of housework a woman does depends to a great degree on her *own* earnings. The more a woman makes, the less housework she does.[33] It's not so much that her partner does more, but she either lets it slide or has the ability to pay someone else to do it.

Researchers call this time imbalance between paid work and unpaid domestic chores the "gendered division of labor" and, they say, it's been stalled for years. In a study of German couples, Berlin economist Miriam Beblo explained to me, even when more egalitarian-minded couples decide to live together—before marriage, before children— women spend more time doing housework while men enjoy more leisure time. For couples who marry, the scales are tipped even farther,[34] and farther still when the first child arrives. Through the years, I have seen an increasing number of fathers strapping on BabyBjörns and taking the baby for a walk, shopping for groceries, taking kids to school, and doing the ballet pickup. Surveys are showing that fathers are feeling more time squeeze than mothers. Still, time-use researchers report that the ratio of mothers' childcare time to fathers' ranges from 2:1 in the United States, Canada, the Netherlands, and Norway, to more than 3:1 in Estonia, Austria, France, and Palestine, to nearly 10:1 in South Africa.[35]

I met with Lyn Craig, a sociologist and time-use researcher from Australia, who has been puzzling over the overwhelm for years. In America, much like in other developed countries, men have nearly tripled the amount of time caring for their children, from two and a half hours a week from 1965 through 1985 to about seven hours in 2003.[36] But that increase is "trivial," she said, compared to mothers who still put in twice the hours. And, in carefully looking at what fathers are actually *doing*, Craig found in a time study of Australian parents that fathers are still largely the "fun" parent. Though the role of fathers continues to evolve, her most recent studies show they are the ones playing, wrestling, and goofing around, while the Mom is still the "default" parent in charge of everything else. "A higher proportion of men's housework and childcare is done with the spouse present. So the men are *helping*," Craig explains. "This is not tag-team care. They are being delegated to, which doesn't free up a mother's time or lighten her load."[37]

But the finding that really made my head spin was this: In America, mothers today spend *more time* taking care of their children than mothers did in the 1960s, even though so many more are working, and working full-time, outside the home. Mothers, on average, spend about fourteen hours a week caring for their children, up from ten hours in 1965, and they've almost tripled the amount of time they spend in high-quality "interactive care," reading to and playing with their children.[38] The more education a parent has, the more time he or she spends with the children.[39]

And still, UCLA time-use researcher Suzanne Bianchi told me, most parents don't feel like it's enough. Panic-inducing headlines on studies linking mothers' employment to childhood obesity, slower learning, lower test scores, and risky behavior may have something to do with it,[40] she said, along with ever-rising expectations about what it takes to be a "good" mother, and, increasingly, an "involved" dad. "There has been a real ratcheting up in what we think we need to do for our children," she told me. "And that's reflected in these increasing hours with children."

It seems an almost impossible time conundrum. How can mothers spend more time on the job *and* more time with their kids? Bianchi said mothers tend to choose jobs that are not always on the career fast track so they can reduce or flex their time. They don't do as much housework, either living with dust bunnies and overflowing junk drawers, or hiring someone else to handle it. They don't spend as much time taking care of themselves and have less time with their spouses and partners. They sleep less. One researcher in Paris remarked, "Employed mothers talking about sleep is like a hungry man talking about food."

And mothers have given up time to play.

## *Play*

One evening at the Paris conference, I tag along with Lyn Craig and, over dinner in the university district, press her on leisure time. There was a time, she says, that the mostly male time researchers coded housework and child care as leisure.[41] The men had to work all day, she says, and they thought staying home with the kids sounded like fun. Once a newer group of mostly female researchers came of age and insisted housework and child care were *not* the same as leisure, they discovered that women's leisure is different from men's leisure in both quantity and quality.

While leisure time for men and fathers remained relatively unchanged until recently, once mothers went to work, they sacrificed virtually every scrap of what had once been personal leisure time in order to spend it with their children. Gone is the "pure" leisure of the adults-only coffee klatches, bridge parties, and cocktail and dinner parties of the 1960s. Gone, too, is much of the civic volunteering. Weekend activities often center on kids' sports, cheering on the sidelines, or educationally enriching activities, like trips to the museum or zoo or schlepping them to cello lessons. More than ever, families socialize together: Going out to dinner usually means bringing the whole family along. Mothers' time to themselves and time with adults both dropped by about seven hours a week from 1975 to 2000. Employed mothers' drops in pure leisure were even steeper: They had nine hours of pure leisure and fifteen hours of total free time.[42]

Men tend to enjoy longer, unbroken stretches of time in any activity, whether it's time to concentrate on work or to fully sink into the time-out-of-time experience of "pure" leisure on their own—on the golf course, on the fishing boat, or on the sofa watching the ball game all Sunday afternoon. Italian men, for instance, enjoy nearly an hour and a half more time for uninterrupted leisure *every day* than Italian women do.[43] Women's leisure tends to be fragmented and chopped up into small, often unsatisfying bits of ten minutes here, twenty minutes there that researchers call "episodes."[44] That's the dangling "in-between time" I found in my own time diaries, hanging between the end of one activity and the beginning of the next that's too short for anything other than a quick item on the to-do list.

Mothers' leisure, Craig says, tends to be more interrupted, contaminated by mental noise, and "purposive." "It's all about meeting the family's needs," Craig says, even monitoring everyone's emotional temperature. "It's like she has host duties—she's making sure everyone's having a good time. On the whole, it's good to be with the family and there is pleasure in that, but it's stressful. You may be at the pool. That's coded as leisure, but you're constantly looking out the side of your eye to watch your child. You're not really relaxing. I see it as like being on call in a fire station. You go up and down the pole. You train. You are always on alert. Always ready."

(Rachel Connelly, a labor economist at Bowdoin College, took the same time diaries that John Robinson analyzed, subtracted all the leisure time when mothers have that *feeling* of being "on call," and came up with a vastly different result. "I actually have women with no leisure at all," she told me later.)[45]

After dinner, Craig and I walk the darkened streets of Paris puzzling about finding a way out of the overwhelm. Craig, a wiry woman with shoulder-length brown hair, has a wicked wit and both a scholar's impartial curiosity and an advocate's passion. "What's missing from this talk about 'having it all,'" she says, "is the recognition that if it's left for women to work out for themselves, like it is now, they can't have it all. You can't add work and do more child care without getting enormously time stressed. You can't have it all unless other things shift in other people's behavior—unless men actually reduce their working hours and increase their time doing housework and child care, unless cultures change and we're prepared to give social support to parents. Women have made all the changes unilaterally that they really can. I don't see what else they can do."

There is one outlier, she says, as we walk through the silent streets. Mothers in Denmark, where more than 80 percent are employed, most of them full-time, not only have about as much leisure time as Danish fathers, they also have more "pure" leisure time to themselves than mothers *and* fathers in any other country she's studied.

That, I thought, I've got to see.

After analyzing my time diary a few months before, John Robinson was convinced that I was such a hopeless case that he needed to give me personal lessons in leisure, telling me, "If you can't go to Paris and have fun, then there's something really wrong with you." On the last day of the Paris conference, John Robinson grabs my arm and says it's time for a final lesson.

He wants to take me to lunch. I'm wearing jeans, a sweaty green $5 T-shirt from Target, and flip-flops, and my feet and ankles have swollen uncomfortably in the heat. Robinson is wearing his sensible rubber-soled shoes and a wrinkled green short-sleeved knit shirt in need of a washing. He's carrying a crinkly plastic bag. I envision a casual little bistro.

We duck into a taxi and Robinson directs the driver to take us to the Place de la Concorde, at the foot of the Champs-Élysées. We get out at the Hôtel de Crillon, a glorious five-star hotel, built as a palace in 1758. Here, Benjamin Franklin signed a treaty with the French in which they recognized the Declaration of Independence. Out front, about where I am standing, Louis XVI lost his head in the French Revolution. The hotel looks like Versailles. And the people coolly floating in and out in smart tailored suits, micro-miniskirts, and impossibly high heels with unswollen ankles look like they do not shop at Target. *Ever.*

With mounting mortification, I follow Robinson inside, my flip-flops thwacking noisily on the polished marble floors. The elegant waitstaff, not blinking an eye, usher us graciously into a gilded, mirrored, and near-empty dining room. Robinson has brought along Jonathan Gershuny, another time-use éminence grise from Oxford, to school me in the ways of leisure. Under the soft light of nineteenth-century crystal chandeliers, the men order the *quails ballottine* with chardonnay vinegar and I the sea bream and julienne vegetables with nori leaves and rocket salad juice. The two men are at work on a new study showing how everyone in every profession overestimates the amount of time they really work.[46] Slackers all.

To John Robinson, making time for leisure is the key to the good life. And an act of will. Once, he kept his own time diary. He was in the middle of a huge project, working at the office until 11 p.m. every night. "I figured I was working one hundred hours that week. But when I measured it, it was only seventy-two. That's when I got skeptical about people's perceptions about time." He decided to change. "I was not living the kind of life I wanted." So he began to travel and to go out every night. "A day without live music," he likes to say now, "is like a day without sunshine." Divorced with two grown children and living alone, Robinson will sometimes hop the Metro in D.C. with *The Washington Post*'s Weekend Section and no idea where he's going. He gets off when he feels like it and sets off for adventure. He watches late-night TV because he can and runs two miles every day. He spends winters at a condo in Berkeley, is a proud member of BURP, a Belgian beer-tasting society, and makes an annual pilgrimage to Burning Man, the wild, no-holds-barred free-for-all that culminates in a fiery conflagration in the Nevada desert.

A few days earlier, Robinson had given me the first of his "leisure lessons"—to just have fun—taking me to a cheap secondhand wedding apparel store near the train station. I had dutifully shuffled along behind him as he scoured racks of clothing, until my head began to hurt and I just wanted to sit down.

"You know what?" I said. "I hate shopping."

"Oh," he said, genuinely surprised. "And here I figured this is what we'd be doing all afternoon."

In another lesson, Robinson said that to make time for leisure, other priorities have to fall away. Like cleaning. Like cleaning one's (read: his) office. He finally let me in once after I attended a time studies class he teaches. "We'll have to crawl in," he warned as he opened the door. With papers, books, boxes, charts, files, photos, and piles of debris strewn all over the furniture and the floor and burying what at one time must have been a desk, his office looked like the bottom of a hoarder's trash chute after being hit by a hurricane. "I meant to clean it up," he said, shrugging and, with his arm, sweeping piles of paper off a portion of the red velvet couch to find a spot for me to sit.

At the Hôtel de Crillon, as we wait for the food to arrive, Robinson tells me that if I, or other women, feel imprisoned by housework, we have only ourselves to blame. Why do women still do more cooking and cleaning than men? Why do we have less time for leisure? Our standards are too high. "Do you *have* to be able to do open-heart surgery on your kitchen floor? How clean do the dishes have to be? As long as you're not spreading disease, that's clean enough," he chides. "Women are their own worst enemies." (He has not seen my sticky kitchen floor. Nor does he seem to understand that when everything else feels like it's coming apart at the seams, at least having the house tidy somehow helps you breathe.)

The leisure lesson today, apparently, as we sit, sweat-soaked, underdressed, and out of place in this room dripping with prestige, privilege, and power, is to *just do it*. Make time for leisure when the spirit seizes you, no matter what you happen to be wearing.

For this final lesson, Robinson asks Jonathan Gershuny to give me a grand disquisition on the history of leisure since the dawn of humanity and why these days, leisure, too, is suffering from the time squeeze. Gershuny tucks into the artfully arranged plate set before him and begins. Early humans needed one another to survive, so they worked cooperatively, he says. They hunted and gathered and shared what food was to be had. Life was hard, to be sure, but they still found time to paint on cave walls. Leisure time, in fact, was critical for progress:

Innovations like the wheel and tools sprang directly from idle hours. But as soon as survival became assured, the value of the work of men and women diverged. Women did the uneventful, industrious, and boring work like hoeing the garden and pounding roots, he says, while men became associated with "exploit," high-status activities that required prowess and intelligence, and were a lot more fun, like hunting, sports, the priesthood, and war. Leisure, he says, is just another version of exploit. It implies activities involving intelligence, soul-stretching passion, skill, and mastery. "So the start of the leisure class is with the leisure sex," he says. "Men."

Over time, the farther a man could distance himself from that drudge work, the higher his status. With the rise of class, social caste, and the feudal system in Europe, the "superordinate class"—the aristocracy—showed its power by being idle and holding sway over a large retinue who could also afford to while away the time as everyone else of lower status toiled in lives of unending drudgery. The American upper class of the 1890s, the captains of industry, though they themselves were often busy, likewise maintained large retinues in "conspicuous idleness" to show off their position.

The strawberry tarts and chocolate fingers with banana ice cream and coffees have come and gone. I put down my notebook.

"You know, this is all really fascinating," I say. "But what you have given me is a history of leisure for men. What I want to know is whether there has ever been a history or an expectation of leisure for women. John thinks there's something wrong with women if they feel they don't have leisure time. But have they ever? I think of the old saying, 'A woman's work is never done.' And all the images I grew up with—Grandma from *The Waltons* was always ironing. I don't think I ever saw her with her feet up, like Grandpa, sitting on the front porch reading the newspaper."

Gershuny pauses and leans back in his delicate silk armchair.

"Yes. Well. Women," he muses, looking up at the crystal chandelier, stroking his beard and frowning, appearing stumped by the question. Historically, he begins, women's leisure—the ladies who lunch—was purely a reflection of the status of the men around them.

"Women," he says finally, "have always rather been in the *laboring* class."

Gershuny points me to the seminal work on leisure by Thorstein

Veblen, who, in 1899, wrote *The Theory of the Leisure Class*. When I later got around to reading it, there it is, *bam*, right on page 2: "Manual labour, industry, whatever has to do directly with the everyday work of getting a livelihood, is the exclusive occupation of the inferior class," Veblen wrote. "This inferior class includes slaves and other dependents, and ordinarily also all the women."

When we return to the conference, I seek out Kimberly Fisher, who, as the secretary of IATUR, carries in her head a near-complete archive of all time studies ever done. I ask her about the history of leisure for women. If the idle ladies who lunch were merely reflections of their husbands' status, what kind of leisure have women ever experienced for themselves?

Fisher, a woman with wavy red hair and big glasses and who moves in a fast-talking whirl, stops short. She cocks her head, as if surprised I'd even had to ask the question.

"That's why women became nuns."

After a few short, hot days in Paris, I'd had time to step out of my own swirling overwhelm just long enough to begin to see its form and pressure and how it consumes everyone. But I still had no answers for what to do about it.

So many places I'd looked suggested the only way out of the overwhelm was hiring help—nice if you could afford it—or dropping out. John Robinson, trying to be helpful, loaned me a video of a 1994 PBS special *Running Out of Time*, showing how one stressed-out couple solved their time crunch by moving to a farm.[47] The protagonist in the novel *I Don't Know How She Does It* quit her job, moved to the country, and spent the day splashing in puddles with her child. Hoping for a more realistic answer, when I finished, I threw the book, hilarious as it was, across the room.

What if you like your work, or at least some form of it? What if you can't quit your job or wouldn't know what to do with yourself on a farm? What if you can't afford help or if just scraping together your mortgage payment every month pretty much taps you out? Is dropping out really the only way out?

What if you wanted—or needed—to find time to do good work *and* splash in puddles with your child? Could you ever allow yourself a moment of peace? I began to wonder how ordinary people like me could make their lives work right here, right now, right where they are.

I decided to look for stories of imperfect people who had at least begun to see their own time confetti and were struggling to find their way toward time serenity. Perhaps they were clearing a path for other flawed souls like me. If, as Erik Erikson wrote, the keys to the good life are having enough time for three great arenas: work, love, and play, I would scour all three asking two questions: Why are things the way they are? How can they be better?[48] I would look for bright spots in the frantic gloom.[49]

# 3

# TOO BUSY TO LIVE

It will not seem futile for young people to dream of a brave and new and shining world . . . Science and technology, labor-saving methods, management, labor organization, education, medicine—and not least, politics and government. All these have brought within our grasp a world in which backbreaking toil and longer hours will not be necessary . . . The material things that make life interesting and pleasant will be available to everyone. Leisure, together with educational and recreational facilities, will be abundant, so that all can develop the life of the spirit, of reflection, of religion, of the arts, of the full realization of the good things of the world.

—President Dwight D. Eisenhower's acceptance speech at the 1956 Republican convention

Jane Vangsness Frisch is busy. She's getting her Ph.D. She just got married. She works all the time for a state agency that prizes face time in the office. With the main office five hours from her home, she's on the road 80 percent of the time. Her "alone time" is when she's studying. Or in the car. It's a harried lifestyle she feels compelled to lead in order to be successful. What's lost in the busyness? "Family," the twenty-eight-year-old says. "My husband and I have chosen not to have kids, because there's no time."

Vangsness Frisch is the first speaker at a focus group on the busyness of modern life.[1] She says her only time for leisure is when she goes for a run with a friend, which she considers efficient multitasking: socializing and exercise. "But I hate running."

Across the table, Josh Malnourie, a thirty-two-year-old IT worker for an insurance company where people routinely put in seventy-hour workweeks, says he and his wife have just had a baby and he volunteers on a number of charity boards. "I never get everything done that I need to do," he says, adding that he was double-booked at the moment and really should be at another meeting. "I guess I could sleep less."

Travis Kitch works two jobs for two different and demanding bosses. His wife works full-time, and they are struggling to raise two special needs kids. "We are in a state of constant busyness," he says. And leisure sometimes just feels wrong. "The Protestant work ethic is very strong here. The whole 'Idle hands are the devil's workshop' thing is very big. I'd love to canoe more, but . . ."

At the head of the table, Betsy Birmingham, fifty, says she juggles raising five kids with being an associate dean and professor at the local university. "The last time I felt like I had a moment to myself, to breathe?" She pauses. "Last week. When I went to my doctor's office for my annual mammogram."

Just then, a tall, trim woman with short gray hair cut into a stylish bob bursts in, apologizing for being late. She introduces herself as Deb Dawson and launches into a rushed explanation about her dog, the dog's "intestinal issues," a trip to the vet, and squeezing in another meeting at the library. She takes a breath. "Then I got stuck in traffic!"

I look out the window. From our perch in the bar of the eighteen-story Radisson Hotel, the tallest building in town, I see a handful of cars lined up at one of the few stoplights. Acres of cornfields stretch as far as the eye can see beyond that. We are not in New York, Washington, Boston, Chicago, or L.A.

We are in Fargo, North Dakota.

Fargo. Population 107,000. On the broad, flat Great Plains bordering Canada. Here, old-time farmers still have dinner at midday and supper in the evening, a heavy-duty tractor manufacturer is one of the biggest employers in town, and the local fair on the street below is serving deep-fried battered cheese curds and pork chops on a stick.

"Life is stressful in Fargo," the focus group organizer, Ann Burnett, had told me. And she didn't mean the occasional life-threatening traumatic stress of the Red River that winds through town overflowing its banks and swamping entire neighborhoods like it has in recent years. She meant ordinary, everyday life. "People are going nuts."

As I began my search for bright spots in the overwhelm, I had first turned to rural America. With visions of bucolic country vistas, church suppers, and porch sitting, I assumed life would perhaps be less chaotic, the breathing a little easier. Then I came upon Burnett's research on busyness and what she calls the "great speed-up" of modern life. Burnett, fifty-four, is a professor of communication and director of the Women and Gender Studies Program at North Dakota State University in Fargo. And all of her subjects live in small towns in the Midwest.

I'd called her up, incredulous.

"People are busy in Fargo?"

"Oh, honey," she'd said, guffawing. "You want to meet some overwhelmed North Dakotans? I can arrange that."

As the fried cheese poppers and Diet Cokes arrive, Burnett asks the group she's convened what drives their busyness. Being busy makes them feel productive and important, they say. Admitting you take time for yourself is tantamount to a show of weakness. The thought of leisure time makes them feel . . . guilty.

"It's like everything has to have a purpose," muses Dawson, fifty-nine, marveling at how the leisure of so many retired people she knows sounds so exhausting, all the golf they make a point of telling her they play, the traveling they do. "Maybe it justifies how you spend your time. When you're busy, you're saying, 'This is who I am. I'm doing something important. I'm not just taking up space on Earth.'"

Dawson has five children, has written a memoir, made a film, runs a charity for orphans in the Sudan, and travels to Africa. She used to go to the massive stone Presbyterian church downtown, as did her parents, grandparents, and great-grandparents. It's only a block from her condo. She wonders if she might feel a little calmer if she went, "being in a place of God where you can regain perspective about your place in the world," she says. "Yet I don't seek it out. Because I'm too busy."

Ann Burnett, a petite woman with straight dark blond hair that hangs to her shoulders, speaks slowly and deliberately. She began studying busyness one December several years ago. As a scholar of how the language we use creates our reality, she'd been noticing people increasingly talking about being "strapped" for time.[2] Terms like "time-starved" and "time famine" had become common. With time pressure on her mind, Burnett opened the annual holiday letters that had begun to arrive in her mailbox. "I began to count how many times people said, 'We're busy.' 'We've had a busy year.' 'We're busy, busy, busy.'"

Intrigued, she began to collect holiday letters, keeping her own, asking friends and colleagues for redacted copies of theirs. Soon, as word spread that she was analyzing the language in these annual "brag sheets," people began sending her letters from all over. Her stash, which now numbers in the thousands, dates back to the 1960s. They serve as an archive of the rise of busyness.

She pulls thick files out of the cabinets in her cramped office and we begin to page through sheaves of letters adorned with candy canes and Christmas trees. It quickly becomes apparent how previous heartfelt "blessings of the season" are quickly dispensed with so writers can dive headfirst into the jumble of their lives. "Our schedules have always been crazy, but now they're even crazier!" writes one. "We've had an action-packed year!" enthuses another. "I don't know where my time goes," writes a mother who juggles a job and three kids. "But it seems that I work hard all the time and never seem to accomplish anything."

Throughout the festive letters, Burnett has circled words and phrases that appear with astonishing frequency: "hectic," "whirlwind," "consumed," "crazy," "hard to keep up with it all," "on the run," and "way too fast." Days are full. Time races past. "Ever faster the planets spin," writes one. One letter has even turned the joy of the season into another to-do list: "Set up Dickens Village. Check. Make caramels, flatbread, chex mix and krumkake. Check." One family confessed they'd been too busy to make a Christmas deadline: "We hope you'll consider this our VALENTINE to you."[3]

The more Burnett read, the more she saw that people seemed compelled to be, or at least portray their lives as being, busy. Some writers even appeared to be *boasting* about their busyness, living life "constantly on the go," as if showing off their near superhuman ability to cram an ever-greater number of activities and achievements into a finite amount of time. One letter bragged about a Memorial Day weekend not of lazy barbecues but of a "whirlwind trip to Arkansas, Louisiana, Mississippi and Alabama." Another family was not just busy, but *so* busy schlepping kids around to activities that the mother boasted driving "a hundred miles a day."

One letter writer, making fun of the holiday one-upmanship of busyness, wrote sarcastically of accepting a Nobel Prize in physics, building three start-ups into *Fortune* 500 companies, and sailing around the world, where the family "learned to communicate with dolphins and discovered a new region of deep-water volcanoes." That, Burnett said, is when she realized "My God, people are *competing* about being busy. It's about showing status. That if you're busy, you're important. You're leading a full and worthy life." There's a real 'busier than thou' attitude, that if you're not as busy as the Joneses, you'd better get cracking."

Burnett began to think that what people were really communicating was that they'd earned a "badge of honor" for living in fast-forward. *Time* is not what changed as the holiday letters became increasingly frantic through the decades. It still takes twenty-four hours for Earth to spin on its axis. What changed is the cultural imperative not just to *have* it all, but to *fit* it all in on the fast track, packing in a multitude of work, activities, and obligations until life feels, as one researcher put it, like an exhausting "everydayathon."[4] Somewhere toward the end of the twentieth century, Burnett and other researchers contend, busyness became not just a way of life, but *glamorous*. Now, they say, it is a sign of high social status.[5]

Burnett points out a fairly typical missive:

> I'm not sure whether writing a Christmas letter when I'm working at the speed of light is a good idea, but given the amount of time I have to devote to any single project, it's the only choice I have. We start every day at 4:45 AM, launch ourselves through the day at breakneck speed (the experience is much like sticking your head in a blender), only to land in a crumpled heap at 8:30 PM, looking something like the Halloween witches impaled spread-eagle on front doors, wondering how we made it through the day.

Tick tick tick. The letters are often single-spaced, multipage laundry lists of lives lived dangerously fast: Activities. Achievements. Awards. Trips. Guitar lessons. Cheerleading camps. Basketball teams. Kindergarten flag football. Tae kwon do belts. Hip replacements. Heart surgeries.

Back surgeries. Graduations. Anniversaries. Births. Deaths. Check. Check. Check. The handwriting often snakes up the sides of the letters into the margins of the decorative garland of stockings and tinsel stars.

We put the letters aside for a moment and Burnett calls two colleagues on Skype to catch up on their ongoing research on busyness. They've studied how living fast and busy frays relationships. Couples they've interviewed lament that they have no time for each other. "I can't honestly tell you when actually we had the last real conversation," one told her. They likened their lives to living on a "speeding train," a "roller coaster," and a "carousel and there's no way to get off." In just trying to hold on, the couples put work and kids first. Their relationships, they said, fell to the "bottom of the family food chain."[6]

Burnett and her colleagues' current project examines women and busyness. They're deep in the process of analyzing the language women have used in interviews to describe their lives. "One woman we interviewed said, 'It's not the kind of cars you drive anymore, it's how busy you are, how many activities you're in, the bumper stickers on your car—that shows status,'" Burnett's colleague, Becky DeGreeff, says over Skype. Another woman admitted judging people for taking time off. "We assume that if people aren't always busy, then they must be lazy," she told them. "I don't know how people would *not* be busy," sniffed another. "I'm so tired. I need a sabbatical," one woman said, before quickly vowing she'd never take one, as if that would be admitting a lack of stamina to keep up.[7] DeGreeff says she overheard two mothers who'd dropped their daughters off at a dance class and were busy grocery shopping before the class let out. "One mother sighed that she had all these report cards to sign and give back to the teacher. Like, 'I'm busier. I win.' Then the other mother snorted and said, 'Yeah, but I have two more kids than you.' Like, 'No, *I* win.'"

Busyness is now the social norm that people feel they must conform to, Burnett says, or risk being outcasts. "No one is writing 'Time stands still' or 'I have nothing to do.' There's no way people are going to show they're not meeting the bar of being busy," she says. But people either aren't aware of, or aren't admitting the toll busyness is taking. "People don't say, 'My house is a pigsty, the laundry's really piling up,' or 'We're all completely overweight because I don't have time to cook a decent family meal.' There is a real downside to busyness. But these letters don't show it."

Burnett is finding an odd paradox. Some people assert that the busy lifestyle is a personal choice they'd made in order to get ahead or give their kids an edge for the future. Others are resigned, saying they feel obligated to live superbusy and fast, as if swept away on a fast-moving tide. "As if you don't get to choose, busyness is just there," Burnett says. "I call it the nonchoice choice. Because people really *do* have a choice." Some even seem to create the perception of a breathlessly busy lifestyle—like a traffic jam in Fargo—even when it may not necessarily be so. Why, she wonders, is there such a compulsion for busyness when, her research clearly shows, no one is happy about it?

It's a question that Edson Rodriguez, a sociologist who studies frenetic families in L.A., has been puzzling over. To Rodriguez, the drive for busyness has become a powerful cultural expectation. The human urge is to conform to it. "Culture is more powerful than the individual people who partake in it," he told me.

The urge for humans to conform to the social norm of the group can be irresistible. In lab experiments first conducted in the 1950s, psychologists surrounded a test subject with others who purposefully gave the wrong answer to a question—in one case, the length of a set of lines. Even though it was obviously wrong, three out of four subjects couldn't resist choosing it, as well. Gregory Berns, a professor of psychiatry and behavioral sciences at Emory University, more recently has gone a step further in exploring the human urge to conform. Putting his subjects into brain scanners, he studies what the pressure to conform looks like. He showed his subjects two different three-dimensional shapes on a computer screen and asked them to decide whether the shapes were alike or different. He followed that with photos of other people and the answers they supposedly offered. The results were intriguing: When a subject was shown that everyone else in a group disagreed with his or her answer, the amygdala, the fear center of the brain, went wild. Not only that, when the group all gave the wrong answer, the perceptual circuits in the subject's brain lit up—*not* the forebrain that deals with conscious decision making and monitoring conflicts. So strong was the urge to conform, Berns concluded, that the brain actually *changed* what the subject saw.[8]

"As a culture, we have translated speed into being a virtue. If you are busy, if you get things done quickly, if you move quickly throughout the day, it expresses success. You're achieving," Rodriguez said.

"We're validated by those around us living the same way and sanctioned if we aren't following this cultural expectation. The feeling is, if I'm not busy today, something's wrong."


Everywhere, even in rural America it seems, people strive to be busy.[9] They tell pollsters they're too busy to register to vote.[10] To look busy and important—or because they can't help themselves—people obsessively check their smartphones every ten minutes.[11] In surveys, people say they're too busy to make friends outside the office,[12] too busy to date,[13] too busy to sleep, and too busy to have sex.[14] Eight in ten Britons report being too busy to eat dessert, even though four in ten say dessert is better than sex.[15] We're in such a rush that the typical sound bite for a presidential candidate has been compressed from forty seconds in 1968 to 7.3 seconds in 2000.[16]

Remember those unused vacation days? People say they're too busy to take a vacation[17] and too busy for a lunch break.[18] That's prompted retailers like McDonald's to launch "It's Your Lunch. Take It" ad campaigns. The travel site Orbitz has been trying to get people to make a pledge to take all their vacation days. And the Las Vegas Convention and Visitors Authority has mounted a "Take Back Your Summer" ad blitz, showing a harried office worker climbing on top of her desk and, Norma Rae–style, holding up a placard reading VACATION NOW.[19]

One physician has said the modern drive toward fast-paced busyness is a pathology. He dubbed it "time sickness."[20] Others said it was more a psychological mania. They called it "chronophilia."[21]

Psychologists write of treating burned-out clients who can't shake the notion that the busier you are, the more you are thought of as competent, smart, successful, admired, and even *envied*.[22] It's the new epidemic, psychiatrist Ed Hallowell has said.[23] In his book *CrazyBusy: Overstretched, Overbooked, and About to Snap!*, Hallowell maintains that in addition to showing status, busyness is a new kind of high. I was hearing it in interviews. "There is a certain rush," one young man told me, "when you're going a thousand directions at once and getting it all done."

Being superbusy has become so normal that it's now a joke. The actor Casey Wilson explained in an interview that her character, Penny, on the TV Show *Happy Endings*, abbreviates her words, like "hilar" for hilarious and "appresh" for appreciate, because she's just too busy to say the whole word.[24] And on *Saturday Night Live*, Seth Meyers joked in a Weekend Update segment that retailers like Target, Costco, and Kmart were selling freshly cut Christmas trees online that could be delivered to people's homes. "And for just a few dollars more," Meyers cracked, "they'll put it up, they'll decorate it, unwrap all your presents, play with your new toys, and feel the joy that you and your family apparently no longer have time for."[25]

So much do we value busyness, researchers say they have found a human "aversion" to idleness and need for "justifiable busyness." Christopher Hsee, a psychologist and professor of behavioral science at the University of Chicago, gave ninety-eight students a survey to fill out. Then he gave them a choice. They could either sit idly and wait for fifteen minutes before taking a second survey. Or they could walk fifteen minutes round-trip to drop the first survey off—the equivalent of unnecessary busywork. Hsee found that the group that had busied itself with walking felt happier. "If idle people remain idle," Hsee wrote, "they are miserable."[26]

These days even the superrich and powerful are superbusy. No longer content to show status by lazing about in conspicuous idleness as in the past, elites today act more like the U2 mega–rock star, Bono, who jets off to Africa and global capitals to meet with world leaders and push for a cure for AIDS and debt forgiveness for impoverished countries—squeezing humanitarian work in between songwriting and concert dates. The Microsoft billionaire Bill Gates, a man who was once so busy he slept under his desk at work rather than lose a minute away from the office, is now so busy seeking cures for malaria and promoting innovation and education reform that he's hung up his golf clubs.[27] Celebrities, such as the star chef Marcus Samuelsson, stuff as much "wild and frenetic life" into their fifteen-minute window of fame to last a lifetime. Samuelsson cooks, runs six restaurants, has a cookware collection, a line of tea, deals with airlines and credit card companies, TV appearances, two websites, four cookbooks, and a memoir.[28] "In the contemporary money culture," wrote the columnist Daniel Gross, "to be at leisure, to be idle, is to be irrelevant."[29]

I met with a group of researchers at Leisure Trends, a consumer research and marketing company for the outdoor sports and recreation industry in Boulder, Colorado. They first noticed busyness creeping into the leisure industry in the 1990s with the dot-com bubble. "Leisure time became angst-ridden," said Julia Clark Day, vice president of sales and marketing. "There was so little free time and people were working so hard, they felt like they had to make the right choice for what to do in their leisure time." Since then, busyness has transformed the leisure industry. Years ago, she said, leisure retailers catered to consumers who could take weeklong backpacking trips. As people got busier, the industry's focus narrowed to selling equipment for activities people could do in a weekend, like a camping trip or a fly-fishing getaway. The focus shrank again around the time of 9/11, she said, to what people could do in a day. By 2010, she said, the time focus narrowed to what people could do in about four hours in an afternoon—a canoe trip, say, to a nearby stream with the family. The mind-set in the leisure industry soon became, what could people do closer to home? How could they reinvent their commute? "And now, the focus is on what you can do in forty-five minutes over lunch," she said. "Keen Footwear even pioneered the idea of taking a ten- to fifteen-minute Instant Recess. They want people to go outside and do something they love. Or just move."[30]

Life in the early twenty-first century wasn't supposed to be so busy. The economist John Maynard Keynes, in his 1930 essay "Economic Possibilities for Our Grandchildren," predicted a fifteen-hour week by 2030, an end to the human struggle to survive, and time to enjoy "the hour and the day virtuously and well." In the 1950s, some prominent thinkers predicted that the post–World War II boom in productivity and the ever-rising incomes and standards of living for Americans and the industrialized world could only mean that we were entering a new age of unprecedented leisure. All our basic needs would be met. Free from toil, we could begin to savor its fruits. True to the Greek ideal of the good life, we would spend our time cultivating the mind and the soul. Some economists, thinkers, and politicians like then–vice president Richard M. Nixon predicted that by 1990, Americans would enjoy a twenty-two-hour workweek, a six-month work year, or a standard retirement age of thirty-eight.[31] Many thought a four-day workweek was looming on the horizon. In 1959, Senator Eugene McCarthy chaired special hearings on shortening weekly work hours from the official forty, which had been enshrined in federal law since 1938.[32]

The idea that leisure was now meant for all was, truly, a radical notion. For most of human history, it was the kind of time available only to the wealthy and the powerful. An article in the *Harvard Business Review* in 1959 worried that "boredom, which used to bother only aristocrats, had become a common curse."[33] Thinkers worried about what workers unaccustomed to so much free time would do with it and whether they'd squander it in idle "loafing." In the early 1960s, CBS broadcast a year-end round table of commentators and asked: "What is the gravest crisis facing the American people in the year ahead?" One panelist said heightened cold war tensions. Another said revolutions in Latin America. Longtime TV journalist Eric Sevareid said the most dangerous threat to the nation was "the rise of leisure."[34]

In the purest sense, leisure is not being slothful, idle, or frivolous. It is, in the words of leisure researcher Ben Hunnicutt, simply being open to the wonder and marvel of the present. "The miracle of now," he calls it, to choose to do something with no other aim than that it refreshes the soul, or to choose to do nothing at all. To just be and feel fully alive. The high-minded Greeks called leisure *skole*. Like school, they considered it a time for learning and cultivating oneself and one's passions. It is a time not just for play, recreation, and connection with others but also for meditation, reflection, and deep thought.[35] Throughout the course of history, in this "leisure" time away from toil, elite men—the ones who, as Jonathan Gershuny explained over lunch in Paris, enjoyed true leisure for most of human history—came up with some of the most brilliant innovations, enduring art, and soaring discoveries humanity has ever known. The "leisure class," Bertrand Russell wrote, "cultivated the arts and discovered the sciences; it wrote the books, invented the philosophies, and refined social relations. Even the liberation of the oppressed has usually been inaugurated from above. Without the leisure class, mankind would never have emerged from barbarism." In his 1932 classic essay, "In Praise of Idleness," Russell heralded a coming time when modern technology would bring shorter work hours and time for leisure to be enjoyed equally by everyone. Work and leisure both would be "delightful," and the world would be the better for it. "Every person possessed of scientific curiosity will be able to indulge it, and every painter will be able to paint without starving . . . Above all, there will be happiness and joy of life, instead of frayed nerves, weariness and dyspepsia."

Throughout history, the uneducated poor and working classes had a measure of time that, if not dedicated to high-minded pursuits, was at least free from work. The economist Juliet Schor writes that in fourth-century Rome, there were 175 public festival days a year. In the Middle Ages, though peasants and serfs worked in the fields from sunup to sundown, they broke for breakfast, lunch, afternoon nap, dinner, and midmorning and midafternoon breathers. Church holidays, Sabbath days, saints' days, official rest days, public feasts and festivals, and weeklong "ales" to celebrate major milestones like births, marriages, and deaths took up about one-third of the year in England. In Spain and France, Schor estimates that even the hardest workers had nearly half the year off.[36]

What changed, she argues, was the introduction of the clock in the thirteenth century and the rise of manufacturing. Time became money and employers had the power to control both. Work hours climbed steadily until, at the turn of the twentieth century, workdays as long as fifteen hours, six or seven days a week, became the industry standard. The U.S. steel industry enforced a twelve-hour-a-day, seven-day-a-week schedule until 1923.[37] During a 1912 millworkers strike for shorter work hours in Lawrence, Massachusetts, the mostly women workers sang, "Yes, it is bread we fight for. But we fight for roses, too." "They were calling for time for family. Time for joy," said Ellen Bravo, who heads Family Values @ Work and lobbies for policies to support working families. "Rather than seeing leisure as a frivolous, privileged notion, they saw it as a very human and laudable concept. That we all deserve time for roses."

In the 1950s, work hours did finally begin to fall. Leisure time was on the rise.

"So my question," Ben Hunnicutt told me, "is what the hell happened?"

Some argue that today's knowledge economy professions—art, technology, engineering, communications, politics, think tanks, academics, and the like—are more like leisure pursuits of the mind that the Greeks envisioned, and that to be fully engaged in life through work is a good thing.[38]

But economists like Schor argue that a voracious advertising industry creates shiny new wants and that insatiable consumer spending now powers 70 percent of the U.S. economy. The astonishing rise in the cost of medical care, the cost of living, and ever-steeper housing prices for ever-larger homes have outstripped stagnant earnings. As a result, household debt has reached historic highs,[39] and people are drowning in stuff—caught up in what she calls a vicious cycle of "work and spend."

Hunnicutt sees something deeper happening, too. "Work has become central in our lives, answering the religious questions of 'Who are you?' and 'How do you find meaning and purpose in your life?'" he told me. "Leisure has been trivialized. Something only silly girls want, to have time to shop and gossip."

Even in academia, scholars confess they're sometimes embarrassed to say they study leisure, as, to be honest, I often was when I told people what I was researching for this book. Karla Henderson, who studies women's leisure at North Carolina State University, has been contemplating writing a paper with the title, "Don't Laugh When I Say Leisure." "I think my mother thinks what I study is kind of goofy," she told me. Henderson's own Leisure Studies department has been renamed the Department of Parks, Recreation and Tourism Management. "We live in a society that thinks work is far better than leisure. But when you really understand what leisure is, what it means to the quality of your life and the relationships you have, leisure is really, really important," she said. "Leisure is so misunderstood. That's what makes people feel guilty about it."

Without time to reflect, to live fully present in the moment and face what is transcendent about our lives, Hunnicutt says, we are doomed to live in purposeless and banal busyness. "Then we starve the capacity we have to love," he said. "It creates this 'unquiet heart,' as Saint Augustine said, that is ever desperate for fulfillment."


Ann Burnett hunches over a table across from me in a café on the North Dakota State University campus. Spread out before us are stacks and stacks of holiday letters we've brought from her office, arranged in manila folders neatly by year. A handful are marked with a big *A* across the top.

"*A* as in a grade? For a good Christmas letter?" I ask, waving one at her.

"*A* for authentic," she says. "Do these letters show people living authentic lives?"

"Meaning?"

"Do they recognize that life is finite," she says, "that they're going to die."

"That's pretty heavy for a Christmas letter, isn't it?"

"When you realize you're going to die, you value your time more," Burnett says.

"That's depressing."

"That," Burnett says, "is living honestly and courageously in the moment. You're able to step back, stop, and smell the roses. Or realize the roses are even there. You recognize the past is gone. The future's not set. You may still be busy, but you're savoring every second of it."

The German philosopher Martin Heidegger wrote that authentic living requires keeping both life and death in mind at all times, Burnett explains. He called it "*dasein*," literally, human be-ing. Few of us are able to do it. It is, perhaps, only human nature to avoid at all costs thinking of life's ultimate, unavoidable conclusion. Maybe that's the attraction of busyness, she says. If we never have a moment to stop and think, we never have to face that terrifying truth.

Burnett and her colleagues scrutinized a random sample of close to six hundred Christmas letters to look for signs of people living authentic lives. They found only thirty-two. Burnett shows me an example: "Dear Friends, Hither and Yon, In this, my 80th season, I'm learning that life is increasingly a process of LETTING GO of loved ones, family and friends who have been closer than family. Of special places I have loved to be and things it has been a joy to do." Another describes how a near-fatal accident made the family more aware of "the transience of this lovely life together."

The vast majority of the other letter writers, Burnett says, were living in what Heidegger called "forfeiture," a lack of self-awareness from being so distracted with the hectic busyness in everyday life. "Life is short," Burnett and her coauthors wrote in their analysis of the letters. "If we are unable to get off the gerbil's endless wheel, and appreciate what life is about, we may never be able to recognize fully life's meaning and ultimate happiness."[40]

I think with regret how, caught up in my own busy forfeiture, over the years my holiday greetings have diminished from thoughtful, handwritten notes to hastily signed photo cards to a Facebook post to, one recent year, nothing at all.

Burnett says it's time to go. Time for me to go to the airport and for her to go for her radiation treatment. Burnett has cancer. We carefully pack up the piles of Christmas letters. As she drives me back to the Radisson, she muses on how busy she herself has always been. There were years of going "one hundred miles an hour," teaching, researching, serving on statewide boards, getting her daughter to piano lessons, speech tournaments, band concerts, and throwing her "spectacular" birthday parties. At dinner the night before, Burnett's daughter, now twenty-one, explained that she, too, has always felt compelled to be busy. "I don't know what to do with myself with free time," she admitted. And neither, really, did Burnett. Before she got sick, Burnett says she felt exhausted, that she had no time for herself, that everyone wanted a piece of her until she was spent. She wonders, sometimes, if being that busy is part of what made her sick. If she had known more the toll it would take, would she have tried to change? Now, she says, her cancer treatments leave her so wiped out she has no choice but to slow down. "It's frustrating. And I feel a little guilty," she says. "There's so much more I want to do."

# 4

# THE INCREDIBLE SHRINKING BRAIN

To pay attention, this is our endless and proper work.
—Mary Oliver

Emily Ansell flips on her computer. We peer intently at what look like irregular yellow blobs encased in the dusky blue-black outline of a human skull. Ansell points to an oddly shaped yellow blip, an island of bright color in the blackness of the brain scan, nestled just behind what looks like the forehead and eye sockets.

The yellow blob, she explains, is the prefrontal cortex. It is the key to human intelligence. In its size and complexity, it is, in short, what distinguishes humans from animals and makes us who we are. And, Ansell says, what she and other neuroscientists are finding is that when a human feels pressed for time, rushed and caught up in the overwhelm, that yellow blob does something alarming: It *shrinks*.

Ansell, thirty-six, is an assistant professor of psychiatry at the Yale Stress Center, where the soothing waiting room has the plush purple velvet chairs, tinkling fountain, soft lighting, and basket of organic teas you'd find at a high-end spa. She has short brunette hair and a blissful smile. She herself works hard at *not* feeling stressed. Among other things, she gets enough sleep, eats right, exercises, stops to breathe, meditates, sets realistic expectations, and makes constant adjustments to her goals and her schedule—as life around her shifts. But she recognizes that she's in the minority. The American Psychological Association reports that Americans are chronically overstressed.[1] The World Health Organization found that Americans live in the richest country, but they are also the most anxious.[2] The average high school kid today experiences the same level of anxiety as the average psychiatric patient of the 1950s.[3] And perhaps most disturbing, scientists are finding that when children are exposed to stress—often stemming from the overwhelm of their parents—it can alter not only their neurological and hormonal systems but also their very DNA.[4]

As a clinical psychologist who has treated patients with high levels of daily stress, Ansell wanted to know what that was doing to the brain. After watching Ann Burnett drive off to her chemotherapy appointment, so did I.

Ansell explains that she and a team of researchers at Yale were among the first to put relatively healthy people into brain scanners to see what's happening to the brain on overwhelm. That they found the prefrontal cortex most affected is troubling, she says. The prefrontal cortex is the most recently and highly evolved part of the human brain. It regulates physiological functions like blood pressure, heart rate, and glucose levels. More, it governs our highest cognitive "executive functions": how we think and reason, how we learn, plan, concentrate, remember, judge, and control ourselves.

Ansell points to a little almond-shaped doodad on the brain scan—the amygdala. The amygdala, she explains, is the seat of negative emotions like fear, aggression, and anxiety. The rational prefrontal cortex controls the id-like amygdala, keeping it in check and presentable in civilized society.

When we're feeling stressed, other brain scan studies are finding, the amygdala flicks on like a lightbulb, Ansell says. We become emotional, angry, and frustrated. We yell at our kids, we can't find our #$(& keys, we flip off the snotty driver of the BMW that just cut us off in traffic when we're already running late, and we are sorely tempted to hurl something out the window on an ugly deadline. The prefrontal cortex acts like a patient yet controlling kindergarten teacher. "It tells the amygdala to calm down, that everything's going to be all right," Ansell says, gently waving her hands as if soothing a child's forehead. "The prefrontal cortex is what tells you you're going to be able to cope."

But when stress becomes more than an occasional burst, when it becomes a constant, grinding swirl of rushing, gulping for air, feeling behind and worried, jumping from task to task and never feeling there's time to do everything you have to do, then, Ansell and her colleagues are finding, the prefrontal cortex itself begins to shut down. The more stress, the scans show, the smaller the volume of neuron-rich gray matter in this key region of the brain.

That shrinkage, Ansell and her coauthors hypothesize, impairs our ability to keep our cool, think clearly, reason, plan well, organize, remember, make good decisions, or just calm down at the very explosive moments when we need to the most. And that loss of self-control, she says, could also heighten the risk of addiction and destructive behavior.[5] "The prevailing view for years was that once we reached a certain age, our brains would stabilize and never change," Ansell explains. "But now studies like ours are discovering that the brain is plastic, it's constantly changing—not just the neural connections and not just the functions, but the actual structure. This is brand-new science."

And operating under the weight of so much constant stress, the brain is not changing for the better.


In truth, the body was built for stress. A little stress is good for us. It's a part of the reason why humans exist today at all. When our ancestors were living on the veldt and out in the wild, they needed to be constantly on the lookout for danger, for man-eating tigers, poisonous snakes, and a host of other flora and fauna lying in wait to kill them. Then, as now, at the first sign of threat, the hypothalamus, a tiny region at the base of the brain, sets off an alarm, prompting the adrenal glands to release a surge of hormones, including adrenaline and cortisol, into the bloodstream. The flood of adrenaline drives up the heart rate, blood pressure, body temperature, and energy supplies. Muscles tense. Palms start to sweat. The heart races. Lungs, like bellows, begin to pump air. Cortisol, the primary stress hormone, floods sugary glucose into the bloodstream, to give muscles the boost to act fast. It shuts down any bodily functions not absolutely necessary for survival at that critical moment, including digestion and reproduction. Dopamine, the reward hormone, which is key in forming cravings, addictions, and habits, floods the deep-brain structure called the basal ganglia. The neurons in the thinking prefrontal cortex literally stop firing. The older, more emotional and automatic part of the brain takes over. All the better to put every ounce of your energy into full-on fight-or-flight mode as you turn from a hungry bear or a spear-wielding enemy and hightail it as fast as you can back to the safety of your cave.[6]

Within an hour after collapsing in relief in your cave, the heart rate slows, the muscles relax, and the body returns to a calmer state. Because running away from life-threatening danger is, ultimately, good for the survival of the species, the body adapted to handle cycles of occasional surges of stress and return to calm. Scientists have come to refer to this natural stress-recovery cycle as "allostasis," which literally means "achieving stability through change."[7]

Cortisol levels are designed to be at their lowest during sleep and to rise gradually through the morning to fortify you to brave the day before dropping again in the evening to calm you for sleep. The body has become so adapted to this cycle that researchers have found that, in animals, at least, those who experience the most debilitating post-traumatic stress disorder after a harrowing event are the ones who aren't producing *enough* fight-or-flight cortisol when they experience it.

So a little stress is good. Some excitement or a new challenge rewires the brain in positive ways to help you learn and acquire new skills. But if the body is repeatedly stressed-out and anxious, when it is continuously bathed in cortisol rather than just spritzed now and then, all the finely tuned systems designed to protect the body begin to turn against it. That's when it goes into what scientists call "allostatic overload."[8]

That overload is not only shrinking our brains, it's making us sick.

Researchers like Ronald Glaser, director of the Institute for Behavioral Medicine Research at Ohio State University, have documented how stress weakens the body's immune system, making it more susceptible to inflammation, cardiovascular disease, high blood pressure, type 2 diabetes, arthritis, osteoporosis, obesity, Alzheimer's disease, and other debilitating ailments.[9] Stress is connected to depression and anxiety, particularly for women, who are twice as prone to the conditions. One study found that men's brains produce 52 percent more mood-regulating serotonin than women's.[10]

Glaser and others have found links between stress and autoimmune deficiency diseases such as chronic fatigue syndrome and Epstein-Barr and between stress and delays in wound healing. And, because inflammation can encourage tumors to grow, survive, and spread, Glaser and other researchers have linked stress to cancer.[11]

Bruce McEwen, who heads the neuroendocrinology lab at Rockefeller University in New York, was among the first to find that stress can alter the actual structure of the brain. In a series of lab experiments,

McEwen put rats into restraints during their resting period for several hours a day for up to three weeks. Just being confined like that was enough to produce a state of constant stress, he found. Then he looked at their brains. The neurons of the prefrontal cortex and the hippocampus, areas that govern learning and memory, had atrophied and shriveled, while those of the amygdala, the home of negative emotions like anxiety and fear, actually grew. "The animals, not surprisingly, became more anxious and less cognitively flexible and showed a somewhat impaired memory," McEwen told me. "But what's interesting is, when we stopped the stress, these effects all disappeared."

McEwen found that age was a critical factor in the brain returning to normal. Young rats recovered fully within three weeks. Middle-aged rats recovered only partially. And older rats, not at all. "How this translates to humans is much more complicated. Some people take better care of themselves than others," he said. "And there are interventions, like getting a sedentary person to walk five out of seven days a week for an hour a day, that have shown that the hippocampus becomes larger and improves mental flexibility."

But McEwen is worried about this constant stress bath that modern humans are slopping around in. Studies have found that the more stressed-out medical students feel, the worse they do on tests measuring the mental flexibility of the prefrontal cortex. Stress can lead to sleep deprivation, which can lead to cognitive impairment, overeating, and addiction. Other studies have found that stress can, literally, age someone. Especially women. A study of more than 13,000 genes in four brain regions found that 667 were expressed differently in men and women. And of those, 98 percent led to more rapid aging in women, something researchers attributed to women's "higher stress load."[12] McEwen said researchers know that stress hits the bodies and brains harder in those with low socioeconomic resources, low self-esteem, tough childhoods,[13] little physical activity, and few friends. And, from functional-imaging studies, a seemingly simple task like counting backward can cause enough stress to make lasting neural changes in the brain.

"I think we're in a brave new world," McEwen told me. "I look at families where both parents are working, where they spend all their time carting their kids around. I look at my own family—how we spend a huge amount of time on our weekends at baseball, gymnastics, lacrosse games, rather than relaxing. There's pressure all the time, from work, from the family. You've got media coming at you, e-mail coming at you. You've got so many choices, so much pulling at your attention, and you feel you're being pushed from all sides."

Which is exactly why Ansell and her colleagues wanted to see what that overwhelming "everydayathon" was doing to the brain.

Ansell and her coauthors first had seventy men and thirty-three women volunteers between the ages of eighteen and fifty fill out an extensive questionnaire, called the Cumulative Adversity Interview checklist, about the stress in their lives. Had they ever experienced major stressful events, such as failing a grade? Or did their parents divorce or abandon them? Another set of questions asked about trauma. Had they been in combat, or a natural disaster, were they ever attacked? They were asked about recent stressful events—a death in the family, a breakup with a romantic partner, a serious injury, or a financial crisis. A final set of questions asked them to rate their perceived "chronic" stress level: "You're trying to take on too many things at once." "Your job often leaves you feeling both mentally and physically tired." Or "There is seldom enough time to complete the things you need to do."

Researchers have found that the way people *feel* about the stress in their lives is a far more powerful predictor of their general health— whether they're more likely to be depressed, anxious, smoke cigarettes, or overeat—than any other measure. The perception is more precise, even, than *actual* stressful life events. In other words, what we *think* about ourselves and our lives *is* our reality. Ansell and the other Yale researchers rated the answers, then put the volunteers into a Siemens 3-tesla scanner and took MRI scans of their brains.

For their study, Ansell and her colleagues weren't trying to capture how an individual's brain changes over time. Instead, they sought to understand how the cumulative effects of a lifetime of stress actually shaped it. In order to do so, they controlled for their subjects' varia-tions in head size, age, gender, and other factors to make all of their brains comparable. That's when they discovered that the combination of living through a number of stressful events and the strong percep-tion that life is stressful proved to be the most toxic for the brain. These subjects' brains were smaller than others' in four distinct areas—parts that help us make good decisions; pay attention; control our emotions,

our moods, our appetites, our anxieties, and our impulse for risky behavior; and govern whether we get a good night's sleep.[14] Compared to
the subjects who'd had fewer stressful experiences and didn't feel quite
as stressed-out by everyday life, Ansell said these "worst-case-scenario"
volunteers' gray matter brain volume was, on average, fully 20 percent
smaller.[15] "It's really clear. As your adverse life events increase, your
gray matter decreases. And if you feel really stressed as well, it decreases even more," Ansell says. "It shows how vulnerable we are.
Maybe our study volunteers don't have major anxiety or depression
now. But the next time they get really stressed-out and start feeling
overwhelmed, their brains may be more vulnerable to the pathways by
which major anxiety and depression can occur."

Huda Akil is a neuroscientist at the University of Michigan who has
spent her career studying the neurobiology of emotions and stress.
Every era, she says, has required humanity to adapt to the stresses of
the day—war, disease, famine, pestilence, revolution, industrialization,
the cold war, terrorism. Breakthroughs in technology throughout
history have made it seem like information is exploding and time hur-
tling too far forward, too fast: the clock, the pencil, the printing press,
and the electric lightbulb that divorced us from our natural circadian
rhythms.

Stress, she said, is no more and no less than the inability to predict
and control the forces that shape our lives. And those two factors are
exactly what makes this particular Age of Overwhelm so insane. We
have yet to learn how to control the unprecedented flood of information coming at us. And the nature of what we do and how we do it
has been completely transformed in less than a century: We've morphed
as a civilization from the hard physical labor of rural agricultural work
to the sedentary chair sitting of urban knowledge workers. That's a far
more stressful life.

"Think about the farmer," Akil tells me. "The farmer can't control
and predict very much either. So why is that any better or worse than
being on Wall Street? As a farmer, if there was a freeze that destroyed
your crops, that might've stressed you, but it wasn't your fault. But as a
knowledge worker, you're *expected* to be in charge of everything. And
when things go wrong, it *is* your fault. The thinking is, you could have

planned more, or you should have anticipated what went wrong. That combination of having a lot coming at you and of shifting away from physical work—which does help cope with stress—and not even being able to say, 'It's not my fault, I surrender to higher forces,' whether you believe it's weather or God—that's been taken away."

The human brain grew to its current size over millennia, largely, scientists surmise, because humans lived in social groups and needed to cooperate in order to survive. But Torkel Klingberg, a Swedish professor of cognitive neuroscience, writes in *The Overflowing Brain* that the human brain today is very much the same size and shape as it was forty thousand years ago when the world of Cro-Magnon humans was a much, much simpler place. The brain can still hold only about seven pieces of information in the working memory at any time. Beyond that, we're fried. These days, Klingberg writes, our Cro-Magnon brains are close to what he calls maximum "channel capacity."

In the early twenty-first century, researchers at the University of California, San Diego, estimate that global information consumption exceeds 9.57 *zettabtyes* a year.[16] These researchers calculated that in 2008, Americans gobbled up information for 1.3 trillion hours, mowing through 100,000 words and 34 gigabytes of data about 12 hours *a day*.[17] Every second, the world's e-mail users produce messages equivalent in size to more than sixteen thousand copies of *The Complete Works of Shakespeare*.[18] Studies have found that information workers have so much coming at them, they switch tasks every three minutes, making the workday fragmented and incoherent.[19] RescueTime, a program that follows customers' every move on computers, reports that people use seventeen different programs on a typical day and visit at least forty different websites, losing themselves in what RescueTime founder Tony Wright called "information porn."[20]

Jonathan Spira, author of *Overload!*, has spent the past twenty years studying information overwhelm. He found that just reading and processing the daily onslaught of e-mails can occupy over half a worker's day. His surveys have discovered that two-thirds of workers feel they don't have enough time to get all their work done and 94 percent have at some point felt "overwhelmed by information to the point of incapacitation."[21]

Trying to even *decide* what to pay attention to in all that noise, writes time management guru David Allen, not only taxes the brain but also wears down the willpower and leads to "decision fatigue." We can't decide what to think about, worrying about home stuff at work and work stuff at home, "so then we walk around with what I call the GSA of life—the Gnawing Sense of Anxiety that something out there might be more important than what you're currently doing," he told *The Atlantic*. If only we could remember what that something is.[22]

With the brain so overloaded and the willpower weakened, it's become hard to resist interrupting whatever it is you're doing to check the constant chimes and dings of the smartphone or the computer telling you a new e-mail or text has arrived, that someone has made a new Friend request or is now following you on Twitter. Neuroscientists have discovered that *anticipating* those electronic notifications triggers a sweet narcotic dopamine release in our brains much like any powerful addiction or craving. And when the text is short, the thought incomplete, or the message fragmented, which leaves us feeling slightly unsatisfied, the dopamine levels surge, rocketing through our systems, firing up the desire for more more more.[23]

But those constant interruptions strain the brain further and make a hash of our time. For every interruption, Jonathan Spira writes, it takes ten to twenty times the amount of the interruption time to return to the previous task: It can take five minutes after a mere thirty-second interruption to get back on track. Fully one-third of every worker's day, he reports, is taken up by these endless cycles of unnecessary interruptions. Even *Fortune* 500 CEOs, with the ultimate power to predict and control their own time, are not immune. One study found they averaged only twenty-eight uninterrupted, productive minutes *a day*.[24] "This overwhelm is not any one thing," Huda Akil told me. "It's not just technology. It's not just two-career couples. It's a thousand little stabs. You put that together and it's like being constantly slightly jet-lagged."

Pushing the brain's channel capacity to the breaking point is the modern predilection for multitasking. No two tasks done simultaneously, studies have shown, can be done with 100 percent of one's ability. Driving while talking on the cell phone slows reaction times and awareness to the same degree that driving over the legal alcohol limit does. And the distractions from too many things going on at once hamper the brain's "spam filter" and the ability to distinguish between relevant and irrelevant information.[25] Or, as one British study found, multitasking makes you stupid—dumber than getting stoned.[26]

Though it's a popular notion that women's brains are wired to multi-task and men's to compartmentalize, neuroscientists have found that's patently untrue.[27] And Barbara Schneider, a sociologist at Michigan State University who studies multitasking and time, reports that men and women actually spend about the same amount of time doing at least two things at once. She finds that both mothers and fathers now spend *more than half* their waking hours multitasking, double the multitasking they did in 1975.

Both men and women say they feel productive multitasking. But women report feeling more frustrated, irritated, and stressed by it. That, Schneider says, could be because fathers multitask more at work, juggling between different work-related activities, while mothers switch from work to kids to home and back again. That distracted role overload takes an emotional toll.[28] And contaminated time, ruminating over the endless to-do list streaming across the brain like CNN's ceaseless news ticker, saps mental energy.[29] "All those gear shifts women are expected to make in a day is mentally exhausting because everything requires attention," neuroscientist Huda Akil told me. "Part of what the brain does to manage stress is to constantly decide what merits attention now and what can be ignored. Not everything can be salient simultaneously and get your undivided attention."

But undivided is precisely what attention is not.

Take, for example, the controversial diagnosis of attention-deficit/ hyperactivity disorder. The condition was once solely associated with fidgety little boys. Now, adult women are the fastest-growing group not only being diagnosed with ADHD but also using mind-focusing medication to clear the jumble, soaring 264 percent between 2001 and 2011.[30]

Daniel Goldin, a California psychotherapist, has a different explanation for the explosion in adult diagnoses: modern life. "If you're feeling very anxious and doing one hundred different things at once, your attention is going to suffer, the ability to plan and be goal directed is going to become increasingly difficult," he told me. "All these women being diagnosed with ADHD are just overwhelmed." Joanna Moncrieff, a senior lecturer in the Mental Health Sciences Unit at University College London, has gone so far as to write in the prestigious *British Medical Journal* that ADHD does not exist at all in adults, calling the explosion in diagnoses the "medicalization of underperformance." "I am convinced," she wrote in an e-mail, "that the increase in women being labeled is because the drug companies are trying to tap the market for 'neurosis.'"

But Patricia Quinn, a medical doctor who has studied ADHD in women and girls for thirty years, says women have always had ADHD but went undiagnosed because they were better able to cope when they had fewer roles to juggle in simpler times. Modern life simply pushed them over the edge.

"Women come to me saying, 'I'm running as fast as I can to do what everybody else seems to do so effortlessly, and I can't keep up,'" said Quinn, who herself has been diagnosed with ADHD and, after a lifetime of losing her keys or getting locked out of her car, sometimes with her kids inside, proudly showed me her new Toyota Solara that doesn't require a key.

The renowned psychologist Mihaly Csikszentmihalyi was one of the first social scientists to document how human time was becoming fragmented and the toll that was taking on what he maintains is the "peak" human experience: a state he calls flow. Flow is a timeless space, where one becomes absorbed in the challenge of the task at hand—the surgeon in the middle of a complex procedure, the artist caught up in the act of creation, the child playing in her own imaginary world. In flow, humans lose themselves and feel most at peace. It is a state that he describes as greater than happiness. And it requires undivided attention and uninterrupted time.

I called Csikszentmihalyi. There is no question that the overwhelm and information overload are fracturing time for both men and women and splintering it into whirling bits of time confetti. But for years time studies have shown that women's time is more fragmented than men's time. Their role overload, juggling work and home, has been greater and their responsibilities and "task density" more intense. What, I wondered, does that mean for a woman's opportunity to reach this optimal human state of flow? And if fewer women spend uninhibited time in this thoughtful, creative, joyful space, the sort of timeless room of one's own that Virginia Woolf imagined, what is the cost? To themselves and their experience of being alive? To their families? To the world, even, for the ideas or creations that don't have the time and space to be born?

"You are definitely onto a rather large problem," Csikszentmihalyi told me. He has found discrepancies for women, not only in the actual *opportunity* to have time for flow but also for *allowing* themselves to get there in the first place. "When I lecture about flow, in the question-and-answer period, there is always the same question: 'But doesn't one feel guilty when you are in flow because you forget everything except what you are doing? Isn't that giving up on the rest of your responsibilities—giving in to total involvement in what you are doing and not caring about anything or anyone else?' That question, almost 100 percent of the time, is asked by a woman. It's clear that it's much more difficult for women to feel that they can get immersed in something and forget themselves, forget time, forget everything around them."

Csikszentmihalyi is the pioneer of a very different kind of time study, one that seeks to understand not only what people are doing in a given moment, like John Robinson, but also how they perceive it. He calls it the Experience Sampling Method. He has his subjects wear a pager and then beeps them at random times during the day and asks not only what they are doing but how they feel about it. When he asks people about their time in flow, most men report feeling captivated by an adventure or a rewarding experience. Women, however, tell him that they most often reach a flow state when they force themselves to transform a boring, mundane task that has to be done. "One of the first women I interviewed described flow as the feeling she got when ironing her husband's shirts," he said. "That was very strange to me. But I got used to it, because other women talked the same way about cooking, washing dishes, or doing housework."

In his studies, he usually finds men do one and a half things at a time. Whereas women, particularly mothers, do about five things at once. And, at the same time, they are caught up in contaminated time, thinking about and planning two or three things more. So they are never fully experiencing their external or their internal worlds. And if you are never really here or there, then what kind of life are you living? "It is a problem," he said. "It is often very difficult for women to be able to live in the moment."

The sociologist Christena Nippert-Eng has written that throughout history, women's time has always been subjected to unpredictable interruptions, while men's ability to experience blocks of unbroken time has been protected. The "good" secretary and the "good" wife were the ones guarding it. Uninterrupted time is the territory of the advantaged, she wrote. To be interrupted is to exist in a "state of dishonor."[31]

Time, I was learning, was not only money, as the saying goes. It was power.

When you are overwhelmed, when you can neither predict nor control the forces shaping your time, when you don't even have time to think about why you're overwhelmed, much less what to do about it, you are powerless. From the moment I began keeping my time diary, I realized that's how I'd felt. So this journey to understand the roots of time confetti and discover the secrets to time serenity was really about finding how to get a measure of that power back. There are good answers. But it would take me a while to find them.

I decided to start looking for them in the first great arena of life. I would go to Work.

# PART TWO

## WORK

# 5

# THE IDEAL WORKER IS NOT YOUR MOTHER

We work to have leisure, on which happiness depends.
—Aristotle

Renate Rivelli loved her job. The thirty-nine-year-old single mother of two loved her job in the Human Resources Department of the elegant four-star Brown Palace Hotel in Denver so much that she never minded working the occasional crazy hours, sometimes braving snow and ice and closed streets to come back after she'd tucked her kids into bed for the night to help get payroll out or, when the housekeeping staff couldn't make it, to snap on plastic gloves and clean rooms herself.

She loved walking through the kitchens because the smells reminded her of her Austrian grandmother's cooking. She found meaning and purpose in her work as the benefits manager. So many of the hotel's cooks and maids had such struggles. Some had lost a husband or children in a faraway genocide or war. Some labored mightily to make ends meet. It humbled her, as stretched as she herself sometimes felt, to be able to help someone on the verge of breakdown switch money from a retirement account for the future to pay for the heat he or she needed now. The staff, she said, was like one big family. And for seven years, the Brown Palace, simply, was home.

At the hotel, there was no such thing as flextime or telework, no family-friendly policies to help employees manage work and life demands. When her kids got sick, she said, the hotel didn't allow her to take sick days to care for them. Because she lived with her mother, a surgical technician who worked long hours herself, Rivelli was able to call on her for help. But a few times when her kids were older, her mother wasn't available, and Rivelli couldn't afford to take a day off—three sick days in a six-month period put one's job in jeopardy—she had no other option than to throw some movies in the DVD player, promise to call, and, seized with guilt, kiss her children goodbye and rush out the door.

Once, she herself was so sick she wound up in the emergency room. Doctors were pumping her with antibiotics at 3 a.m. But she was back at the office by 7 a.m. to run an employee orientation because no one else could do it. She stayed until midnight repeatedly for several months, doing the work of two people after a coworker left. It was that kind of total devotion to work that won her consistently high performance reviews and recognition in 2005 as Manager of the Year. "I always gave 150 percent," she says matter-of-factly over a cup of coffee in Denver, pushing her short dark brown hair out of her eyes and straightening her crisp gray wool business pantsuit.

So it came as a shock when hotel managers called her into their office in November 2008 and announced out of the blue that they'd created a new position in her department and she had a new boss—her younger, less experienced coworker. Rivelli had been on the job for seven years at that point. Her coworker, a young woman fresh out of college with no children, two.

Stunned, Rivelli protested they hadn't given her a chance to apply for it.

The new position, they said, would require fifty to sixty hours of work each week, lots of travel, and possibly relocation to another city. That, they told her, was "simply not possible" for her because she already "had a full-time job at home with her children."[1] She was a *mother*.

"I felt like I'd been kicked in the face. They obviously didn't realize I worked those kinds of hours anyway," Rivelli says. "I wasn't even given an opportunity to say, 'No, it sounds like too much work' or 'Let me talk to my family.' They decided *for* me, based on their assumptions about my life as a mother."

To soothe her, the managers said they'd give Rivelli a $38 a week raise to her $42,000 annual salary—30 percent of which typically went to cover the cost of child care. Instead, Rivelli called a lawyer and lodged a complaint with the Equal Opportunity Employment Commission.[2]

Rivelli would ultimately win a $105,000 settlement and a promise from the Brown Palace Hotel to refrain from gender discrimination. I had come to Denver to talk to Rivelli because, far from being another run-of-the-mill employment dispute, her case set a groundbreaking legal precedent. Hers became one of the EEOC's first test cases in a brand-new kind of law called family responsibilities discrimination. As I struggled to understand how work fueled role overload and overwhelm, this new type of law, I came to see, strikes right at the source.

In recent years, lawyers across the country have begun filing thousands of family responsibilities law actions in every state, in every industry, and at every level in organizations. They include cases of mothers, like Rivelli, who have been held back or demoted, had pay docked, or have been fired because of their perceived lack of commitment to the workplace. But as fathers who are more fully involved in family life find themselves passed over for promotion or stigmatized at work, and as both men and women begin caring more for aging relatives—which nearly half of all American workers expect to do in the coming years[3]—family responsibilities discrimination lawsuits climbed, mushrooming 400 percent from 2000 to 2010.[4]

The premise is simple. Today's workplace thinks and operates much as it did in the 1950s, when people expected the world to be neatly divided into two separate and unequal worlds: the man in the gray flannel suit who could devote himself entirely to work in one, and, in the other, his homemaker wife, taking care of everything and everyone else. But the worlds of work and caregiving have collided. The lawsuits show the workplace is harshest on those who try to live in both worlds at the same time. "Look, if you design work around someone who starts to work in early adulthood and works full force for forty years straight, who have you just described? Men," Joan Williams, the legal scholar who helped shape the new theory, told me. "We have organized the workplace around men's bodies and men's traditional life pattern. That's sex discrimination."

Williams runs a hotline for caregiver discrimination cases at the WorkLife Law Center at the University of California Hastings College of the Law. In testimony before the EEOC, she rattled off a list of the kinds of calls they routinely get:

- A woman at a law firm was given less client contact and work when she became a mother. When she announced her second pregnancy, she was fired, which, Williams said, is a "common pattern."
- An aircraft mechanic was disciplined and ultimately fired for "lack of dependability" after using some of the twelve weeks of unpaid leave guaranteed under the Family and Medical Leave Act[5] to care for his pregnant wife, who had gestational diabetes.
- A carpenter on FMLA leave to care for his father, who'd had a heart attack, was told that "no one wanted to work with him" and was terminated.[6]
- An employee who worked at Wendy's for four years notified her employer that she was pregnant with her second child and was told, according to court filings, that if she wanted to keep her job, she had to have an abortion, something "sadly common" for low-wage workers, said Cynthia Calvert, an attorney who works with Williams.[7]

Though Congress passed the Pregnancy Discrimination Act in 1978, EEOC records show pregnancy discrimination claims are actually on the rise.[8]

I spoke with a twenty-three-year-old mother named Laura from Napa, California, who works two jobs and earns about $1,000 a month, most of which goes to rent. When she was pregnant and began to have back problems, her doctor sent a note to her employer asking that Laura not be required to lift more than twenty pounds or bend over. Her supervisor, who had shifted duties for other employees with back problems and other ailments, refused to do the same for her. Instead, the supervisor forced Laura to take her twelve weeks of unpaid FMLA leave early, or face being fired. If Laura hadn't gotten help from her local Legal Aid attorney, who threatened to file a family responsibilities discrimination lawsuit, Laura's maternity leave would have been used up before her baby was even born.

EEOC general counsel P. David Lopez said stories like Laura's are run-of-the-mill. "It's overt discrimination," he told me, shaking his head. Employers don't think twice about punishing pregnant workers or making offensive remarks. Sometimes, Lopez said, neither do judges. "On one case, a judge referred to the plaintiff as, 'Oh, isn't that the woman who should be at home with her kids?'"[9]

After the win with Rivelli's case, another EEOC foray into family responsibilities discrimination litigation was not as successful. The EEOC sued Bloomberg LP, the global financial services and media company owned by the former New York mayor Michael Bloomberg, on behalf of seventy-eight women, some of them highly placed in the organization, charging that the top-heavy male company had a pattern and practice of discriminating against employees with family responsibilities. The women asserted in court filings that once they announced their pregnancies or returned from maternity leaves, they were demoted, their pay reduced, their responsibilities taken away, or they were marginalized—a step many feared would lead to their termination. Bloomberg denied the charges.

The EEOC alleged that bias against caregivers started at the very top, with the executives who set the tone for the rest of the company. Court documents allege that Lex Fenwick, who took over as CEO after Bloomberg left the company, once said, "I'm not having any pregnant bitches working for me." The head of news, court filings allege, derided women who take maternity leave, saying, "Half these fuckin' people take the [maternity] leave and they don't even come back. It's like stealing money from Mike Bloomberg's wallet. It's theft. They should be arrested."[10] U.S. District Court Judge Loretta A. Preska sided with Bloomberg and ruled against the EEOC, arguing that, while each woman may have valid individual claims, the EEOC had not proved that the company systematically discriminated against pregnant women and mothers. "In a company like Bloomberg, which explicitly makes all-out dedication its expectation, making a decision that preferences family over work comes with consequences," Preska wrote. "To be sure, women need to take leave to bear a child. And, perhaps unfortunately, women tend to choose to attend to family obligations over work obligations thereafter more often than men in our society. Work-related consequences follow."[11]

The EEOC appealed the judge's ruling.

I couldn't get Preska's comments out of my head. There is no doubt that women, even when they are employed, are still expected to be the primary caregiving parent. And there are consequences: fewer women leaders in virtually every field, harried mothers, those sidelined on the "mommy track," those who opt out when it becomes too much, bread-winning fathers pressured to work long hours to hold on to jobs that provide for families they rarely see. But with such rigid and work-devoted cultures, how much of a "choice" does any worker who wants a full life or a family really have? If we have designed workplaces around an ex-pectation of work without end, if those workplaces expect all-out dedi-cation of body, mind, and soul, then *no one*, male or female, has much of a choice. There is only one way to work to succeed or to survive: all the time.

As I sought to get to the root of how work contributes to the over-whelm, it became clear complicated factors are at play: extreme work hours,[12] rapidly evolving technology, information overload, globali-zation, changing demographics, shifting gender roles, the high status of busyness, economic anxiety, and cutbacks that "offload" more work onto the fewer remaining employees, not to mention the increased cost of living, stagnant wages, growing household debt, and the steep cost of child care followed by eye-popping college tuition bills—increasing 893 percent since 1980—that perpetuate the work-and-spend spin cycle.[13]

But as I read case after case of workers, both men and women, claiming they'd been discriminated against because of caregiving responsibilities, as I read studies on human performance and moti-vation that show our work culture is completely at odds with how we produce our best work, I came to understand that something deeper, and more insidious, drives us.

I was about to meet the Ideal Worker.

The ideal worker doesn't take parental leave when a child is born. He doesn't need a place or time to pump breast milk. He has no need of family-friendly policies like flexible scheduling, part-time work, or telecommuting. The ideal worker doesn't have to find babysitters, deal with school closures on snow days, or otherwise worry about child-care responsibilities. The ideal worker doesn't mop up after the child who barfs up her breakfast Cheerios or the green Saint Patrick's Day cookie of the night before. He wrinkles his nose, says, "Good luck with that," and waltzes out the door. The ideal worker doesn't get interrupted by repeated calls from the school because a child is acting out, like Rivelli's, or daily 3 p.m. calls from kids begging for playdates instead of the scheduled after-school program, like mine. The ideal worker never has to think about researching good assisted care facilities for Mom or Dad as they get older, whether they're getting the best treatment in ICU, or how to get his sister to her next chemotherapy appointment. It's simply not his job.

Instead, the ideal worker, freed from all home duties, devotes himself completely to the workplace. He is a face-time warrior, the first one in in the morning and the last to leave at night. He is rarely sick. Never takes vacation, or brings work along if he does. The ideal worker can jump on a plane whenever the boss asks because someone else is responsible for getting the kids off to school or attending the preschool play. In the professional world, he is the one who answers e-mails at 3 a.m., willingly relocates whenever and wherever the company directs, and pulls all-nighters on last-minute projects at a moment's notice. In the blue-collar workplace, he is always ready to work overtime or a second shift.

So tied to his job is the ideal worker that he works endless hours, even if it costs him his health and his family.

Obviously I'm exaggerating. This is a stereotype. But stereotypes reflect deeply held beliefs—accurate or not—and this notion of the ideal worker wields immense power in the American workplace. We are programmed to emulate him at all costs, or at least feel the sting of not measuring up.

Rivelli and I walk across the street to the company where she now works. In the two years that her case against the Brown Palace Hotel dragged on, Rivelli went back to school at night to earn the college degree she'd put off when she had her children. She began walking to deal with the stress. Sometimes, when things got really bad, she'd escape to housekeeping to help fold towels. As part of the settlement agreement, the hotel asked her to leave.

At her new job, Rivelli smiles and hugs coworkers as they pass. Most everyone has families. Telecommuting and working flexible hours is the norm here. Rivelli has more time with her children and her mother. In addition to her college classes, she's found time for true leisure—to garden, to cook, and to start writing, a lifelong dream. Still, she says, she misses the Brown Palace and the thrill of striving against all odds to be the ideal worker.

"Would you go back?" I ask her.

"In a heartbeat."

I have to admit, I was skeptical that the ideal worker still holds sway in the twenty-first century. I mean, come on, women and mothers have worked throughout history as domestics, teachers, nannies, nurses, and secretaries, in family shops and businesses, on family farms and ranches. Women have been working in fields traditionally dominated by men since the early 1970s, graduating from college and many graduate programs in greater numbers than men since 1985, and they now make up about half the workforce. In a majority of married American families, both mothers and fathers are employed.[14] About three-fourths of all mothers with school-age children work outside the home.[15]

Plus, the ideal worker is so *old*. He first surfaced at the dawn of the Industrial Revolution when work became something you left home to do, somewhere you *went*. And over time it became something that *men* did. Men had public lives; women, private. Men's labor was paid. Women's was not. Men's work was visible and valued as contributing to the work of society, the market, or the life of the mind. Women's labor was invisible, noticed only if it was done badly or not at all.

This "separate spheres" theory of specialized work in an ideal family was first described as an economic theory in 1981 by Nobel Prize–winning economist Gary Becker in his landmark book *A Treatise on the Family*. He called it the most "efficient" kind of family unit. But real life is so much messier than tidy stereotypes. From 1952 to 1966, the TV show *The Adventures of Ozzie and Harriet* burned the notion of separate spheres as best into the American psyche. At the same time, the percentage of American families living that breadwinner-homemaker ideal dropped dramatically. The number of mothers of young children going to work about doubled, from 20 to nearly 40 percent. By the time the iconic black-and-white sitcom was in reruns in the mid-1990s, the number of mothers working for pay had nearly doubled again.[16] A majority of African American mothers have always worked. Blue-collar families were able to afford the single-earner lifestyle only in the two decades of economic boom following the Second World War.[17]

Still, the notion stuck that separate spheres, with an ideal worker father and an ideal mother at home, was "best."

In a survey of more than two thousand supervisors, managers, and executives around the globe, WFD Consulting, a company that researches work and life conflicts, uncovered deep-seated "caregiver bias." More than three-fourths of these bosses thought the best and most productive workers "are those without a lot of personal commitments." Half thought that "men who are highly committed to their personal/family lives cannot be highly committed to their work." Even more thought the same of women.[18]

Research has found that mothers are seen as less committed to work than nonmothers.[19] Pregnant women are perceived as less authoritative and more irrational, regardless of their actual performance.[20] One family responsibilities discrimination case quoted an employer calling employed mothers "incompetent and lazy."[21]

To gauge how notions of the ideal worker and caregiver bias influence hiring, promotions, and pay, Shelley J. Correll, Stephen Benard, and In Paik, then all at Cornell University, wrote a fictitious résumé for a person applying for a marketing job.

They put male names on half the résumés and female names on half. They signaled parenthood on half the résumés by listing work in a parent-teacher association in the activities section. The other half listed work for a charitable organization instead. Other than that, the résumés were virtually identical.

The researchers gave the résumés to nearly two hundred students and asked them to judge which one, the mother, the father, the childless woman, or the childless man, was the best worker.

Fathers were considered equally competent as men without children but significantly more committed to work. Fathers were held to a lenient standard of punctuality. They were considered more hirable and promotable, and were recommended for management training more than men without children.

Mothers ranked at the very bottom. They were rated as significantly less competent, less intelligent, and less committed than women without children. Mothers were held to harsher performance and punctuality standards and had to score significantly higher on a management exam than nonmothers to be considered for the position. The recommended starting salary for mothers was $11,000 less than for nonmothers and far less than what students recommended fathers receive. The students also rated mothers as less promotable. In the end, they recommended that only 47 percent of the mothers be hired, compared to 84 percent of the nonmothers.

To test what the researchers came to call this "motherhood penalty" and "fatherhood bonus" in the real world—the first such study of its kind—they perused the newspaper help-wanted ads in a large northeastern city and sent out 1,276 résumés to 638 employers advertising entry- and midlevel marketing and business positions. Just as in the lab experiment, the researchers sent each company a pair of nearly identical résumés, save for one detail: One was a parent and one was not. Consistent with their lab findings, fathers were called back at a slightly higher rate than nonfathers. But mothers received only *half* the offers of nonmothers.[22]

Working mothers are judged unfairly not only as workers but also as mothers. Studies have found that employed mothers are seen as more selfish and less dedicated to their children than at-home moms, especially if they are thought to be working because they want to, rather than being forced to in order to make ends meet.[23]

No wonder just walking out the door in the morning as a working mother can be so fraught. Already, you're judged as guilty at best, a jerk, or worse. As Joan Williams told me, "You just walk around feeling polluted."

The ideal worker norm, Williams argues, is behind the all-too-familiar statistics of the dearth of women in upper management and political leadership: 4.2 percent of *Fortune* 500 CEO positions and 18.3 percent of the 535 seats in Congress.[24] It is also the unspoken specter behind the wage gap. Although there has been a rise in female earning power and economic independence, the Bureau of Labor Statistics consistently finds that men still outearn women at every age.[25] But what those statistics mask, Williams said, is that the wage gap is not so much between men and women, but between *mothers* and everybody else. Williams calls it the "maternal wall."

Michelle Budig, a sociologist at the University of Massachusetts, testified before Congress about just how high and wide that wall is.

- All else being equal—type of job, education, years of experience, and hours on the job—childless women earn 94 cents of a childless man's dollar. But mothers earn only 60 cents of a father's dollar.
- Fathers, in contrast get a "fatherhood bonus," earning as much as $5,000 more than men with no children.[26]
- Mothers' pay drops with the birth of each additional child, ranging from 15 percent per child among low-wage workers to 4 percent for high-wage workers.
- Even after controlling for interruptions like taking maternity leave or working part-time, Budig found a persistent and unexplained 5 percent wage gap between mothers and women without children.

Social patterns reinforce the gap. Men tend to marry or partner with younger women. When couples start a family and decide that they both can't work like ideal workers anymore, the men typically have been in the workforce longer and earn higher pay. So it's not much of a stretch to see, from both a financial and cultural perspective, why it's usually the mother who steps back.[27] Women are twice as likely as men to work part-time.[28] And because part-time pay tends to be crappy, with the average part-time worker in sales, for example, earning 58 cents for every full-time worker's dollar, the cycle of lower earnings for mothers becomes self-reinforcing.[29]

The ideal worker is a big reason why some educated mothers simply disappear from the workplace, more so in the United States than in any other industrialized country.[30] Jane Leber Herr, an economist at the University of Chicago, analyzed national surveys of college graduates and found that fifteen years after graduating, nearly all the childless men and women were still working. But close to 30 percent of women with MBAs who had become mothers were out of the workforce, as were about one-quarter of the lawyers and those with master's degrees who had become mothers. Around 15 percent of Ph.D. mothers were gone. The one outlier was mothers with medical degrees. Fully 94 percent were still on the job, largely because doctors have the power to control and predict their own schedules.[31] "You would think that, given the rise in education of women, their experience, their presence in high-investment, high-income, high-value fields, the proportion of those who leave the labor force would have gone down," Herr told me. "What's shocking is that it hasn't."

Some have called this disappearance of women "opting out" of the workforce and choosing to stay home, and they worry about the consequences if their marriages end: Divorced older women are more likely to live in poverty.[32] But Joan Williams said the ideal worker often gives women no choice. "Women are being pushed out both by gender discrimination and by this 'all-or-nothing' workplace," she said. "I don't call that choice. I call that lack of choice."

The all-or-nothing workplace is exacting a steep price on the future. Fertility rates around the globe have been falling since the late 1960s, when greater numbers of women began going to college, birth control became more readily available, and women began working in ideal worker jobs previously held only by men. Now 97 percent of the world's population lives in countries with declining fertility rates, writes Jonathan V. Last, author of *What to Expect When No One's Expecting*.[33] When men and women do have children, more are having them later in life. From 1970 to 2006, the proportion of first births to American women over thirty-five increased nearly eight times.[34] Families are smaller. Now more people feel the ticking of both the male and female biological clocks. Emerging research has linked the aging sperm of older fathers to a higher likelihood of passing autism, schizophrenia, and other developmental and psychiatric conditions on to their children.[35] For women, delay can lead to a greater risk of birth defects and infertility.[36]

Delay can also mean that women simply run out of time, what the economist Sylvia Ann Hewlett calls a "creeping non-choice." Twenty percent of American women between the ages of forty and forty-four have never had a child, double the number thirty years ago.[37] When Hewlett surveyed "ultra-achieving" men and women between the ages of forty-one and fifty-five, she found that only 19 percent of men were childless. But nearly half the women were, and not always by choice.[38]

Even when mothers do put in ideal worker hours like Rivelli did, many do not escape caregiver bias. Nearly one-third of the wives in dual-income couples now outearn their husbands.[39] So that bias has real financial consequences for working families.

Dawn Gallina was a corporate lawyer in Northern Virginia working for a senior partner at Mintz Levin. After their daughter was born, her husband, also a lawyer, had given up his practice to take care of her. Though Gallina put in the grueling 2,200 or more "billable hours" a year required of most lawyers at big law firms,[40] she deviated from the norm by working some of those hours at home to make time for her family.

While other associates stayed at their desks, eating the take-out meals ordered by the firm, Gallina tried to leave the office at 6:30 most nights to make it home for dinner and bedtime. Then she went back to work on her laptop, often taking client calls from the West Coast long after 11 p.m. She was always available; her BlackBerry was always on.

Her problems started, she said, when she put a photo of her two-year-old daughter on her desk. The partner she worked for had a wife at home and never saw his kids, she told me. "His perspective was, if I can't see my kids, why should you see yours?"

The only mother in the office, Gallina said she soon became targeted for extreme face time. "I was the only one who would get called into the office on Saturdays all the time, even when there was nothing to do. It was almost like being hazed." Her supervisor routinely FedExed her work on vacations, even though it wasn't due for months. He even asked Gallina, who has an MBA and a law degree from Drake University and a master's in law from Georgetown University, to make coffee. "I made it. I made it," she said, chagrined. "My thought was, 'Well, if this is a big test of my dedication, then I'm going to pass with flying colors.'"

The final straw, Gallina said, came when she was considering getting pregnant with her second child. Her boss told her, "Pregnant women don't make partner." When she complained to higher-ups, her work suddenly became suspect. She was denied a bonus, she said, while at the same time the firm raised her billing rate to clients. Then, when she was working at home one day when her daughter was sick, she was fired. By courier.

Gallina sued, citing family responsibilities discrimination, and settled with Mintz for half a million dollars.[41]

Gallina went on to have a second child. She now works for a French law firm in Richmond, Virginia. "It's not a face-time culture," she said. "People here have families and understand that if you want to catch your son's baseball game, you can do that and still do good work."

Mintz Levin has since been named to *Working Mother*'s Best Law Firms for Women, Yale Law Women's Top Ten Family Friendly Firms, and received gold standard certification by the Women in Law Empowerment Forum.[42] At which point, one might ask, what the . . . ? How can a firm be both the defendant in a high-profile family responsibilities discrimination case[43] *and* one of the best places for women to work?

But Mintz Levin is not alone. Of the one hundred companies listed in the 2012 *Working Mother* Best Companies, thirty-five have been sued in family responsibilities discrimination lawsuits, most within the past decade. Twelve companies have been sued more than once.[44] At the same time that the pharmaceutical giant Novartis was enjoying a prominent spot on the list, it, too, was being found guilty in federal court of a pattern of gender discrimination throughout the company. One manager demanded "two child-free years" of one employee, while another manager allegedly pressured a woman to have an abortion. The court awarded up to $250 million in punitive damages to thousands of female sales reps. "If this is what it's like to work for one of our country's 100 best companies for working mothers," Sharon Lerner wrote in *Slate*, "one shudders to imagine what it'd be like to work for one of the worst."[45]

Carol Evans, president of Working Mother Media, acknowledged that several firms on the list have had lawsuits filed against them for violating the very principles the magazine seeks to reward, though the cases are noted and, if the company loses, they're barred from the list for a period of time.

Ironically, Evans said, the discrimination lawsuits, or the threat of them, can force companies to change in ways that eventually land them on the coveted Best Places to Work list. "Sometimes a big lawsuit will be a wake-up call for them," she said. "And by the time it wends its way through the courts, the company's almost superlative because they've had this big slap in the face."[46]

I began to wonder about the flip side of the equation. What if a *father* doesn't want to be the ideal worker anymore? Does he, too, face caregiver bias?

Meet Ariel Ayanna. He asked that same question. In court. Ayanna accused his law firm of having a "macho culture." When he was fired just months after he took parental leave to care for his ailing pregnant wife and children, Ayanna sued, citing family responsibilities discrimination. Ayanna, thirty-one, is a corporate lawyer, though on the day we meet with his attorney in a quiet café in Boston, he's wearing khakis and a black T-shirt, and with his tousled brown hair, looks more like a tough but fair intellectual college professor.

He is one of seven children, he tells me, and has always been around kids or taken care of them. "I've been babysitting since I was eight." He laughs. "In college, I was a nanny. It's just second nature to me." Growing up, his father worked as an investment banker on Wall Street but still made more time for the family than his own father had. Ayanna sees himself as the next step in a natural evolution toward more equal parenting and work. He and his wife, a medieval historian, had their first child when Ayanna was still in law school. Because of his ease with children, Ayanna said it was never a question that he would be the one to assume primary responsibility for their son's care.

After graduating with honors, Ayanna got his first job as a corporate lawyer in the Boston office of big law firm Dechert. He loved the challenge of the work and won accolades and high performance evaluations, earning a $30,000 bonus in his first year. And all the while, he was regularly leaving the office in the evening to be home with his family, often cooking dinner, scheduling doctors' appointments and playdates, putting his son to bed, and then going back to work on his laptop and BlackBerry. Though he worked flexibly, he had no trouble meeting his target for billable hours or doing good work. Once, Ayanna says, when a senior associate asked for a last-minute project and wanted it on his desk by the next morning, Ayanna worked on it from home until late into the night. The senior attorney "said it was better than he would have done," Ayanna says, "but he still complained that I left the office 'early.' That was the culture."

The culture was reinforced, not in formal policies, he says, but in hallway chatter, raised eyebrows, pointed ribbing at lunches, and the ubiquitous meals ordered in and expected to be eaten at one's desk. Two male associates, "golden boys," Ayanna calls them, who were held up as model employees, were constantly competing over who worked longer and harder. One said he worked on his BlackBerry while his wife was in the hospital. He won. Another said he had the firm pay to fly his wife to visit her family across the country so she'd stop asking him to come home from work. He won.

Ayanna's troubles with the firm started, his lawyer, Rebecca Pontikes, says, "when he began acting like a girl," asking for a transfer to Munich when his wife won a prestigious Fulbright scholarship to study in Germany. In the world of the ideal worker, "trailing spouses," the ones who leave careers for the benefit of the other spouse, tend to be women.[47]

In Germany, Ayanna's wife became pregnant with their second child. When she was about to deliver, his wife, who suffers from chronic mental illness, had a serious breakdown and was hospitalized. With no family nearby and no other help, Ayanna asked to take parental leave to care for her, their son, and a few weeks later, their new baby. But at Dechert, it was rare for men to take parental leave, Ayanna argued in his brief.

When he returned to the Boston office following his leave, he was assigned to a partner who valued long hours of face time, Ayanna says. The partner refused to give him work if he wasn't physically in the office, Ayanna alleged in his case. Struggling to care for his family, yet unable to work at home as before, Ayanna failed to meet his billable hours target. He received a poor performance evaluation, despite partners noting his "intellectual horsepower," and he was fired.

Dechert, in its court filings, maintained Ayanna was fired for cause.[48] On the day the case was to be tried, in February 2013, lawyers for Dechert and Ayanna, who now works flexible hours for a different firm, signed a confidential settlement.[49] The "golden boys" at Dechert, Ayanna says, have since become partners.[50]

The case highlights what Joan Williams calls the "flexibility stigma." Just as Ben Hunnicutt told me that leisure has been lost because work now answers the religious questions of who we are and how we find meaning, Williams said that the total work devotion of the ideal worker has become a religion itself. "If you're not giving your all, putting work ahead of family or any other obligation, then you are violating the work devotion ideal. You become suspect. Lazy. Undependable. A slacker," she said. Women who request flexibility may be tolerated because of their historical caregiving role, but often sidelined at work, she added. But men like Ayanna, who seek to work a different way, can be harshly punished. "It challenges our deeply ingrained understanding of the 'proper' behavior for men," she explained. "Like, when I hear of a man staying home full-time to take care of kids, very often my initial reaction is, 'Well, he's getting a good deal,' or 'What kind of loser is he that he couldn't get a job and is sponging off his wife.' And I don't have that reaction when I hear a man is supporting a woman so she can stay home."

To test those kinds of automatic reactions, Laurie Rudman and her colleagues at Rutgers University asked 137 male and female study participants to rate a fictitious employee named Kevin Dowd. In one scenario, he requested caregiving leave. In another, he asked for more work hours. Although everything else about Dowd was identical, the participants rated the caregiving Dowd as a poorer worker and saw him as weak, less masculine, less intelligent, and less ambitious. They weren't as inclined to give him rewards or promotions and were more likely to think he ought to be punished. "We'd done previous studies and found a 'wimp' penalty for guys who are modest during a job interview. But that led to people not wanting to hire him," Rudman told me. "That's different from wanting to fire you or dock your pay or downsize you."

Rudman said she was startled to find that women judged the leave-requesting Dowd more harshly than the men did, a sign, she wrote, of the "extent to which women have been co-opted by [the] Ideal Worker."[51]

Although technology is making it easier, faster, and more efficient to work from anywhere, at any time—even at home between playdates and dinner—the power of the ideal worker keeps everyone stuck on their butts in their chairs at the office. Researchers at the University of California at Davis's graduate school of management and the London Business School found that, regardless of the quality of their work, people who work remotely, like Ayanna and Gallina did, are less likely to be seen as responsible and dedicated and more likely to get lower performance evaluations, smaller raises, and fewer promotions than their face-time warrior ideal worker colleagues.[52]

But isn't the ideal worker the best worker? The most productive? Most creative? Smartest?

Actually, he's not.

Workers caught up in the total work devotion standard of the ideal worker are mired in an unhappy and unproductive funk. A 2011 Gallup poll found that 71 percent of Americans reported feeling emotionally disconnected and disengaged from their workplace.[53]

Surveys are finding that people would gladly leave their jobs for one with more flexibility. Nearly *two-thirds* of all employed workers, both women and men, say they'd rather own their own business for the freedom that would give them to control their time.[54] Research shows that forcing long hours, face time for the sake of face time, and late nights actually kills creativity and good thinking, and the ensuing stress, anxiety, and depression eat up health-care budgets. Stretched by long hours and ideal worker demands, one-third of the civilian U.S. workforce doesn't get enough sleep, costing companies $63.2 billion in lost productivity every year. The writer William Chalmers, in his book *America's Vacation Deficit Disorder: Who Stole Your Vacation?*, estimates that the stressed-out ideal worker culture of no vacations, endless work, and exhausted butt-in-chair face-time "presenteeism" costs the U.S. economy as much as $1.5 trillion a year.[55] The single largest cause of burnout is lack of personal control on the job—expected to be the ideal worker with no life and free to satisfy the boss's every whim.[56]

In fact, a raft of new research is finding that better work gets done when workers have more control over and predictability about their time and workflow, and when managers focus on the mission of the job rather than the time in the chair and recognize that workers are more engaged, productive, and innovative when they have full lives at home and are refreshed with regular time off. Leslie Perlow and Jessica Porter, of the Harvard Business School, compared two groups of workers at a Boston consulting firm. One group worked fifty or more hours a week, didn't use all their vacation time, and were constantly tethered to the office with electronics. The other group worked forty hours, took full vacations, and coordinated time off and after-hours on-call time so clients' needs could be covered but people could regularly, predictably, and without guilt totally unplug from the office. Which group produced better work? The team with time off, not surprisingly, reported higher job satisfaction and better work-life balance. But they also increased learning, improved communication with their team, worked more efficiently, and were ultimately more productive than their ideal worker colleagues.[57] Other studies have found that employees who take full vacations are not only more likely to stay with the firm but also receive higher performance reviews,[58] and that workers are not only more creative but that turning off the constant barrage of e-mails and the ideal worker requirement to respond to them immediately enables people to concentrate and get more done with less stress.[59]

So given the weight of evidence *against* the ideal worker, that he *isn't*, in fact, the best worker, why is he so hard to shake?

Because, Joan Williams said, no one believes it. "The belief in the ideal worker way of working is so deep that even when you introduce evidence that contradicts it, people just don't buy it. It shows you that what's operating is much deeper," she said. "It's not about the rational weighing of evidence. We're talking about work as people's religion."

An intriguing set of studies suggests another reason: He's the boss. In studies of more than seven hundred married men, researchers from Harvard, New York University, and the University of Utah found that men in traditional marriages with wives at home tend to occupy powerful positions in the upper echelons of organizations. They also tend to think that workplaces with more women don't operate well and that organizations with female leaders are "relatively unattractive." These ideal worker bosses more frequently deny female employees opportunities for promotion, considering them less qualified than men, even when their résumés are virtually identical. The researchers dubbed these men powerful "resistors" to a more egalitarian—and realistic— way of working and living.[60]

Psychologists are discovering another reason for the staying power of the ideal worker: It's the way our brains are wired. Our brains, as Torkel Klingberg said, have evolved little beyond the hunter-gatherer days when, on the savannah, survival was a matter of quickly judging threat from nonthreat. Today, this instant sorting leads to the automatic, unconscious beliefs that we don't even realize we have, which helps explain why stereotypes, no matter how grossly inaccurate, can be so powerful.

Mahzarin Banaji, an experimental psychologist who studies this unconscious bias at Harvard, has explored the power of stereotypes through an anonymous online test she and her colleagues devised called the Implicit Association Test. In analyzing more than two million tests, Banaji and others have found large implicit biases favoring whites over blacks, heterosexuals over homosexuals, Christians over Jews, and rich over poor, even though many of the test takers professed they harbored no such explicit biases.

To study the ideal worker norm, Banaji and her colleagues have test takers sit ready at keyboards. They are told to sort male and female names like Sarah, Derek, Matt, and Tammy with concepts like career, corporation, dishwasher, or house. Using timers, researchers have found that large majorities of test takers are much more easily able to sort career-related words with male names and home-related words with female names, as if it's automatic. When asked to do the opposite, match career words with female names and home-related words with male names, most stumble, make mistakes, and require more time. Both men and women have to stop and think, a sign, she said, that they are struggling to override their innate, automatic bias.

In fact, women have to struggle more. Their research found that 77 percent of the male test takers showed strong unconscious bias for male = career, female = family. But how's this for cognitive dissonance? Fully 83 percent of the *women* showed that same unconscious bias, even though they professed to have none. Banaji argues that the tests are a powerful predictor of whether people will act in biased ways, even if they intend not to. The test, she told my colleague Shankar Ve-dantam in the *Washington Post Magazine*, "measures the thumbprint of the culture on our minds." And she has found that the ideal worker thumbprint—unless one becomes aware of it and actively works to change it—has left its mark on both men and women. So, both sexes tend to associate men with careers and women with home.[61]

To test her results for myself, I went back and crunched some more data in the General Social Survey. As late as the 1990s, nearly one in five Americans still disapproved of married women working, whether or not they had children. To the question, "Should a woman with a preschooler work?" half of the men surveyed in 2002, the most recent time the question was asked, said no, she should stay home. And four in ten *women* thought so, too,[62] percentages that hadn't moved much from when the question was posed in 1988 and in 1994.

The survey does not ask whether married men and fathers of pre-schoolers should work. The assumption is, clearly, they should.

About the time I was exploring the roots of the overwhelm at work, Facebook COO Sheryl Sandberg made a splash by admitting she left the office at 5:30 to be home for dinner with her two children. I'd heard about high-tech firms' famous flexible work styles—one former Google exec told me people could work from a beach in Hawaii as long as work got done on time. Sandberg's confession seemed a hopeful sign that perhaps the new economy jobs of Silicon Valley were liberated from the grip of the ideal worker. Could Silicon Valley, I wondered, lead the way for the rest of the work world?

It took less than a day of reporting to come to this disappointing conclusion: God, I hope not.

The young, testosterone-fueled geek culture has revved up the ideal worker standard to a superhuman level. Work hours are not just extreme, they eat you alive. Projects are so poorly managed, often by boy geniuses with few social skills, that work is routinely done in an exhausting last-minute, seat-of-the-pants, save-the-day "hero mind-set," according to the Anita Borg Institute for Women and Technology. That mind-set, they write, "is sending the message that those who have family responsibilities need not apply."[63]

Marianne Cooper, a sociologist who has studied extreme work hours in Silicon Valley, said that working to the point of collapse to meet impossible deadlines has become a way to prove manliness and status in the high-tech world. "There's a lot of . . . He's a real man; he works 90-hour weeks. He's a slacker, he works 50 hours a week," engineers told Cooper.[64] It's the kind of culture that applauded when pregnant Marissa Mayer announced she wouldn't take maternity leave after being appointed CEO and president of Yahoo!

Catherine Keefer, forty-two, reveled in the all-hours work culture when she first moved to the Bay Area and got a job where most women end up in high-tech: the "pink ghetto" of marketing. Work felt like the center of a very exciting universe. It was fun. There were Ping-Pong tables, upscale cafés serving specialty coffees, and valet dry-cleaning services so you'd never have to leave. And she never did. "Then the kids came," Keefer said. Unlike Sandberg, Keefer discovered that it was virtually impossible to walk out the door at 5:30. With a workaholic boss and often pointless meetings called at the last minute in the late afternoon, or projects dumped on her desk just as she was trying to get out the door, and being married to another techie who regularly worked until 2 a.m. for a start-up, life in the high-tech world was simply incompatible with having a family.

"I got run over," she says.

By the time I met Keefer, she, like many other mothers I met in the Bay Area, had quit her job and become a consultant. She was doing the very same work for the very same company, but in her own time and on her own terms. And for less pay, no benefits, and zero chance of promotion.[65]

I began to realize that I, too, had spent my entire career caught in the cult of the ideal worker. My mother stayed home. The only role model I had for what it meant to be a good worker was my dad, and he was always working. When he wasn't at the University of Portland, where he worked first as an accounting professor, then a dean, and later vice president, he was spending much of his evenings and free hours at university functions and fund-raisers, or teaching night classes to pay for braces and ballet lessons for his four daughters. We rarely saw him. And when we did, he was often distracted, deep in thought and worrying about work. He was always serious. Work seemed important and hard. So, when I started to work, I worked like he did. An editor once anxiously told me that I really should go home for the day. It was 10 p.m.

After Tom and I got married, I was absolutely terrified about how I would be able to fit children into this crazy work-focused lifestyle. I waited until it was almost too late. When we finally brought our miracle baby home, I was torn. The ideal worker in me now desperately wanted to be the ideal mother, too.

I sank into a deep depression when my son was seven weeks old, realizing we couldn't afford to keep our little bungalow in the close-knit community we loved if I didn't work. I made more money at the time than my husband, and my job provided our health care. We'd already lived in a cheaper place with bars on the windows in a scary neighborhood, and didn't want to bring a stroller into that anxious world. We could have moved to a town house in the exurbs, but that would have meant a hellish commute for Tom and turned him into an absent father. And I worried that if I jumped off the speeding train of work in the corporate world, even for a little while, I'd never be able to jump back on. And in truth, I'd always *wanted* to do both—to do good work and to be a really great mom. I just didn't know how. And it is only in retrospect that I realize that I never even *asked* Tom what he wanted. I just assumed he would keep working, like my father had.

When our son was six months old and my maternity leave was up—a patchwork of time I cobbled together from unpaid Family and Medical Leave, the paid maternity leave my company offered, sick time, vacation time, disability, and several weeks of unpaid leave—I felt increasingly sick about the long hours reporters like me typically worked. I loved journalism. With our bills, I knew quitting wasn't an option. But I desperately wanted time to be with my child. So I asked for a four-day workweek.

My boss at the time said no, even though another mother and a man nearing retirement worked that schedule.

I asked to work one day a week from home.

No.

I left that job as a national reporter to join the *Washington Post*'s Metro staff, so even if it was late, I could always be home for dinner and story time.

Two and a half years later, at nearly thirty-nine, I had our daughter. I spent much of my maternity leave with her working on two projects, my infant snuggled peacefully against my chest in a BabyBjörn. When I asked my new managers for a four-day workweek, one warned me that I would "ruin my career."

"Can't you just leave early every now and then?" he asked.

But I knew I never would. That's not what an ideal worker in an overachieving culture does. As much as I hate to admit it, my inner workaholic needed formal permission to cut back. Over the years, some managers, both men and women, were great. One fantastic woman editor told me, "I never care where you are or when you work, as long as you get your stories done." I happily worked twice as hard for her. But others, both men and women, clearly thought that working part-time made me a less desirable, less productive worker. One, after I turned in what would become an award-winning series, said, "She did *that* on a four-day workweek?" But when the time came for my performance evaluation, another manager compared the number of times my byline appeared in the paper with those of others who worked full-time. I obviously came up short.

Still, I loved what my kids came to call "Mommy Monday." For the six years I worked that schedule, I was so happy for that precious time with my children and felt so loyal to the editors that I was more than willing to do what it took to show it could work. I answered work calls while changing diapers or flipped my day off as news or story deadlines required. I felt strangely proud to tell the other mothers on the playground who had given up careers to stay home that I "only" worked part-time, as if to say, "See, I put my children ahead of my career, too!" I was fully aware, however, as I watched colleagues and my husband advance, take glamorous overseas assignments, sign book deals, and win awards, that in the demanding ideal worker world of daily newspapers, I might have hung on to the speeding train, but I wasn't going anywhere fast.

As I neared forty, I wondered if we would have a third child. I had saved all our favorite baby clothes, toys, and books and stored them in big Tupperware bins under the eaves just in case. A coworker urged me never to let corporate America dictate the shape of my life and family. But I already had.

I sit with Joan Williams, whom *The New York Times* has dubbed the "rock star" of work and family issues, in her spartan office at the WorkLife Law Center in San Francisco contemplating the ideal worker.

Right now, she says, we're all stuck.

Mothers who venture to work are on their own. At home, they're still considered primarily responsible for all things domestic and still defined in a way that men are not—by their children's achievements and the tidiness of the house. At work, most are at the mercy of their immediate supervisors. Sure, some companies have family-friendly policies like flexible and part-time work, many of which were put together as "women's initiatives" to stem the tide after human resources departments noticed how many were leaving after starting families. The policies may even look good. On paper. But let's face it, with the ideal worker culture so firmly entrenched, in many workplaces you know only mothers are expected to use them, and you're not going very far if you do. So you either choose the flexi mommy track, opt out, hire help, or gut it out.

To top it all off, the fact that many women haven't "made it," that so few women have climbed to the upper echelons of business, academia, politics, science, and other fields, is seen as a sign—not that there's something wrong with the workplace, but that there's something wrong with women. That women aren't as ambitious or smart or *something*.[66]

She's stuck.

Fathers are stigmatized when they seek to deviate from the ideal worker, to do more than just slip out under the radar to attend the occasional Little League game, to actually spend the time intimately caring for children and being an equal partner at home. "Men with children have a sharp choice," Williams said. "They can choose *not* to be equal partners with their wives, in which case having children will *help* their careers with the fatherhood bonus. Or they can choose to *be* equal partners and *hurt* their careers even more than women. As long as that's the case, we'll have a few brave souls, but that's it. Brave souls."

He's stuck.

With smartphones and Skype and e-mail and other fast-emerging technologies keeping us all tethered to work, the ideal worker is now expected to be on call and ready to roll all day, every day, all the time. And because the ideal worker is just that, a demanding, voracious ideal, no one can ever measure up. No matter how much you do, how hard you work, how much you sacrifice, how devoted you are, you can never attain that ideal. You will never be the ideal worker.

We're all stuck.

Williams, fifty-nine, knows the syndrome intimately. She began her own career as an environmental lawyer. "Then I had a baby." She saw her home life revert to traditional gender roles and fall out of balance.

"You want equality in the workplace? Die childless at thirty. You won't have hit either the glass ceiling or the maternal wall," she says. "People say there will never be equality in the workplace until there's equality in the home. But to me, it's really the reverse. There will never be equality at home until there's equality in the workplace, until we redefine the ideal worker. Because until then, men will feel they have no choice but to meet that ideal, even if they don't believe in it, because they want to be 'successful'."

Right now, she says, the only way to shake the hold of the ideal worker is to hit him with family responsibilities discrimination lawsuits. "It's extremely demoralizing how little progress we've made. The conversation today is very much the same as it was in the 1970s. We don't have social supports for working families. We don't have workers' rights. What do we have? Discrimination law," she says. "Family responsibilities discrimination lawsuits may not be the most important way to bring about change. But right now, it's the only thing we have."

That, and changing the conversation. Seeing that the overwhelm never was just a "mommy issue." That it's a father issue. A children's issue. A workplace issue. A household issue. A family issue. A human rights issue. It's an issue for society, especially one that purports to value families so highly. The overwhelm is an issue for everyone, really, living in a country whose very mission is to guarantee the right of its citizens to pursue happiness.

Williams, whose daughter teases her about working like an ideal worker so others won't have to, leans back in her chair. There was a time in America, she says, when things could have been different.

"You should go ask Pat Buchanan."

# 6

# A TALE OF TWO PATS

In one of the most dramatic shifts our society has seen, two-thirds of all moms also work outside the home. This changed world can be a time of great opportunity for all Americans to earn a better living, support your family, and have a rewarding career. And government must take your side. Many of our most fundamental systems—the tax code, health coverage, pension plans, worker training—were created for the world of yesterday, not tomorrow.    —George W. Bush at the 2004 Republican National Convention

Pat Buchanan greets me jovially at the front door of his big white house nestled in the woods off a winding lane in Northern Virginia, not far from the CIA. As a reporter, I covered Buchanan's populist campaign for president in 1996 and rode with him through the South as he vowed to take on the Republican establishment like an angry peasant. He'd dubbed his campaign bus "the Pitchfork Express." He is seventy-three now and a little grayer. But I am struck by how little he has changed.

The conservative firebrand had recently been fired from MSNBC after executives there said his latest book—which included a chapter entitled "The End of White America"—reflected an America of the 1940s, not the twenty-first century.[1] But I have sought him out for a very different reason. In the early 1970s, Buchanan orchestrated a campaign that overrode Congress, ignored polls showing strong public support, and so utterly obliterated a bill that would have created a high-quality universal child-care system in America that in forty years, the very *idea* has never surfaced for discussion again. Ever.

The veto of the child-care bill set the stage for unpaid medical leave and all subsequent U.S. family policy. Or really, the fact that other than a few targeted programs to help the very poor, there is *no* U.S. family policy that could help ease the overwhelm for working families. Instead, the United States ranks dead last on virtually every measure of family policy in the world. Unlike countries with high-quality, government-supported child care, the United States has nothing of the kind. It is one of only 4 of 167 countries in the world with no paid leave for parents—the others are Lesotho, Papua New Guinea, and Swaziland. Saudi Arabia, where women aren't allowed to drive, offers paid parental leave. China, India, Brazil, Mongolia, and Haiti offer paid parental leave. Even Togo and Zimbabwe pay 100 percent of a woman's earnings for 14 weeks.[2]

Workers in the United States have no right to flexible or short work hours, unlike in Belgium, France, Germany, and the Netherlands. The United States has no system to require benefits, fair pay, and advancement opportunities for part-time work, while the Dutch government is promoting the concept of the "daddy day," with each parent working overlapping four-day workweeks so that children are in care only three days a week.[3] The United States has no paid sick leave policy, unlike at least 145 other countries.[4] No paid vacation policy, while Europeans who get sick during vacation are legally entitled to take another.[5] And a tax policy that still favors families with one breadwinner and one homemaker. In other words, U.S. policy not only doesn't work for more than three-fourths of all U.S. families with children, it makes their lives worse.

Buchanan ushers me into a room with polished wood paneling, darkened from the bright morning sun by heavy shades. He offers me a seat on an overstuffed chintz sofa while he settles into a nearby red velvet chair. Directly behind him, a gold-plated pitchfork encased in glass stands against the wall like a grandfather clock. On the wall over his right shoulder, the Irish Catholic who grew up in Chevy Chase, Maryland, has hung a portrait of Confederate General Robert E. Lee.

To prepare for our meeting, I'd read up on the Comprehensive Child Development Act of 1971. As more women and mothers entered the workforce in the late 1960s, public opinion polls showed that majorities of both men and women favored setting up "many more day care centers" and felt that the government should provide them. "Maternal employment was regarded as either a social good or a basic reality of modern life," writes Kimberly Morgan in her fascinating history of the politics of child care.[6] President Richard Nixon, influenced by emerging research on the importance of early learning to shape a child's future, appointed a task force that ultimately recommended "a system of well-run child care centers available to all pre-school children" as well as after-school programs for older children.[7]

Buoyed by this declaration, a coalition of bipartisan lawmakers, early childhood educators, civil rights activists, feminists, and labor leaders came together to craft federal legislation to create a high-quality, universal child-care system for all Americans run by community organizations, much like federally funded Head Start preschool programs. Local Child Development Councils, which would include parents, were to set policy. The bill had broad bipartisan support. The Senate bill, led by Democratic Senator Walter Mondale, was cosponsored by moderate Republican senators Jacob Javitz of New York and Richard Schweiker of Pennsylvania. Idaho's Orval Hansen, one of a number of Republican cosponsors in the House, said the good that the "landmark" bill could do "can have a more far-reaching impact than any of the major education bills enacted during the past 20 years."[8]

But to Buchanan, the Comprehensive Child Development Act was nothing less than "a great leap forward into the dark" that threatened the very fabric of America—a view he holds just as strongly today. He sits up in his chair and begins speaking quickly, passionately and, perhaps accustomed to jousting in the arena of TV shout fests, without pause. "The way I and other Americans grew up, we weren't regimented. We went down and did what we wanted to do on the playgrounds. We set up our own games. We learned to do things together ourselves. You come home from school, your mom's got pie or cake . . . and that's the natural way to grow up," Buchanan, whose mother worked as a nurse before staying home to raise nine children, says. "It was a far better way than to put kids into these child development centers."

Like many conservatives then and now, Buchanan says he wanted to preserve this "natural" traditional family of the father as breadwinner and the mom at home. "We felt the individual, family-centered society was the way good, healthy Americans grew up," he tells me. "We didn't want this mammoth institution set up through which all these millions of children would go well before kindergarten."

As the child-care bill was wending its way through Congress, Buchanan says he had in mind a recent trip he'd taken to the Soviet Union. It was a tense period of cold war proxy wars, a nuclear arms race, and fears of godless communism. He was haunted by what he saw. "We went to see the Young Pioneers, where these little kids, four, five, and six years old, were being instructed in Leninist doctrine, reciting it the way I used to recite Catechism when I was in first grade . . . The liberal Democrats were as appalled as the conservative Republicans." He became determined that that dark vision of a soulless state, heartless absent mothers, and factory-raised automaton children would never come to pass in the United States.[9]

Buchanan quickly marshaled the support of conservative writers and activists who decried how the bill would "Sovietize" the American family. Some called the bill an experiment in Orwellian thought control and the first step toward totalitarianism. "Big Brother Wants Your Children," ran one headline.[10] Fresh from battles over forced busing and desegregation, conservatives railed against the "socioeconomic and race mix of students" these child-care centers would foster.[11] Phyllis Schlafly and others opposed to the women's movement used the bill to lobby for working mothers to return home, arguing, "There is no substitute for a mother's presence."[12] Radical feminists, with their calls for twenty-four-hour child care to dissolve the "oppressive" nuclear family and redistribute responsibility for children, only helped Buchanan make the argument that child care would destroy families.[13]

As the emerging right wing mobilized, the coalition that supported the bill began to fray. Lawmakers, who had been quietly working with Nixon's Health, Education and Welfare secretary Elliot Richardson and other administration officials to craft a bill, fractured over how big it should be and whether state governments and school districts should run the child-care centers instead of community organizations. The bill passed, but not with the enthusiastic bipartisan support it originally enjoyed.[14]

When the child-care bill hit the Oval Office, some of Nixon's advisers urged him to sign it, saying universal child care would appeal to working mothers, "a huge slice of the electorate" where Nixon's approval was weak.[15] But Nixon was in trouble with the growing right wing of his own party, who were unhappy with his moderate social programs and his trip to Communist China. They were already lining up behind a right-wing challenger in upcoming primary elections. "That strengthened my hand," Buchanan says.

Buchanan was prepared to go to war, he says. Instead, Nixon easily agreed to a veto. "Some of these battles, like forced busing, you have meeting after meeting and everyone's arguing. But what surprised me was the ease with which we won this battle," he says. "I not only got to write the veto and to make it not only on economic grounds—that we can't afford this—or on novelty grounds—that this is something new—but on philosophical grounds. And I think that was the shocker."

Buchanan wrote Nixon's veto message to Congress. He warned against the "radical" and "family-weakening implications" of the bill. The child-care centers, he wrote, would not only create an "army of bureaucrats" but also would diminish "both parental authority and parental involvement with children—particularly in those decisive early years when social attitudes and conscience are formed, and religious and moral principles are first inculcated." The bill was, simply, un-American. "For the federal government to plunge headlong financially into supporting child development," Buchanan wrote in the veto, "would commit the vast moral authority of the national government to the side of communal approaches to child rearing over against the family-centered approach."[16]

"We wanted not only to kill the bill," Buchanan tells me. "We wanted to drive a stake right through its heart."

On December 9, 1971, Nixon vetoed the bill. Twenty-four hours later, Congress sustained the veto. "That sucker was gone," Buchanan says of the idea of a universal child-care system in America. "Gone forever."


In the forty years since the veto, the number of children living in Buchanan's ideal breadwinner-homemaker family has dropped by more than half, to 20 percent.[17] Two-thirds of mothers with children under six work. Forty percent of mothers with children under eighteen are the sole or primary breadwinners of their families.[18] Instead of killing child care, the veto Buchanan wrote helped shape what would become: Child care in the United States today is a disaster.

While there is certainly good quality care, it is rare, wildly expensive, difficult to find, and even more difficult to get in to, with waiting lists that can last years.[19] In France, the teachers at the crèche and *écoles maternelles* are part of the same civil service as the teachers at the Sorbonne.[20] In the United States, child-care workers earn roughly what parking lot attendants and bellhops do.[21] A 2007 survey found that only 10 percent of what's available in the United States could be considered excellent. The majority of child care is "fair" to "mediocre." Ten percent is downright dangerous.[22]

American child care is largely unregulated. States set their own safety and quality standards, and they are all over the map. Only certain states require teacher training. In others, anyone who feels like it can care for as many as twelve unrelated children in her home without any background criminal or sex offender checks, no safety inspections, no monitoring, and no training in basic CPR, first aid, or safe sleeping practices to prevent sudden infant death syndrome.[23]

Though children develop best when they have the time to establish firm bonds with loving teachers and caregivers, child care in the United States is notoriously unstable: The often jury-rigged care arrangements of one-third of all parents with children under the age of six fall apart within three months.[24] Compared to what the American Academy of Pediatrics calls for to ensure the healthy development of children in these critical early years when their brains are growing like mad, Child Care Aware of America gives child care in most states a D or an F.[25]

Elly Lafkin, who lives in rural Shenandoah, Virginia, thought she'd done everything right when she looked for child care for her eight-week-old infant, Camden. The twenty-four-year-old mother's options were slim. She and her husband lived far from family who could help. There were only three accredited child-care centers within a thirty-five-mile radius of their house, and they closed before either Lafkin or her husband could get there in the evening from work. At $150 a week, the cost was more than they could afford. She worked in the billing department of a pharmacy. He managed the pools at a nearby resort.

The U.S. Department of Agriculture estimates that it will cost a middle-class family with two kids anywhere from $212,370 to nearly

$500,000 to raise an American child born in 2011 to age seventeen—and that doesn't include college. The cost of child care and education in a family budget is second only to the mortgage or rent.[26] In nineteen states, parents fork over more money to pay for child care than they do to a four-year public university.[27] The difference being, with college, parents have eighteen years to save for it.

Out of options, Lafkin called her local Department of Social Services. They gave her a list of unlicensed family care providers. Nine out of the ten numbers Lafkin called were disconnected. So she did what most parents do: She relied on the advice of friends and family. Two friends recommended a grandmother who charged $85 a week and had cared for children for seventeen years. The grandmother didn't have a license, but the state of Virginia allows anyone to care for up to six unrelated children without one. Lafkin's choice was hardly unusual: Half of the estimated four hundred thousand children in need of child care in Virginia are in such unlicensed care settings, advocates say.

Five weeks later, Camden was dead and the cause of her death and the grandmother were under investigation. Only then did Lafkin discover that the grandmother had a criminal felony record. I met with Lafkin shortly after what would have been Camden's first birthday. The nursery, with its pastel lavender walls and sprinkles of glow-in-the-dark stars on the ceiling, was untouched. The hamper was still filled with Camden's tiny clothes, the Diaper Genie still full of her diapers. "I know it's stupid. I just can't throw them away," Lafkin told me. She spends hours at the cemetery reading baby books to her daughter's grave. "We didn't realize that sending your child to an unlicensed, unregistered provider meant throwing her to the wolves."[28]

Betsy Cummings, a Navy boatswain in Virginia Beach, thought the Little Eagles Day Care was licensed and inspected when she put her seven-week-old son, Dylan, there. She thought the child-care workers had been trained in how to care for infants. She was wrong. Little Eagles was run by a church. Like a number of states, Virginia exempts child-care facilities run by religious organizations from meeting most safety or quality standards.[29] If Little Eagles hadn't been exempt, the workers would have known not to put Dylan down for a nap on his stomach on two foam pads with ill-fitting sheets in a hot, cramped utility closet with nine other babies. They would never have left the babies unattended for two and a half hours while they ate lunch two rooms away. They would have known how to perform CPR when they found Dylan had turned blue. Cummings would have known that the director of Little Eagles had been cited in the past for running a dangerous day care.

Local prosecutors charged three child-care workers with child neglect and the director with felony homicide. A judge later dismissed the charges. "The Commonwealth quite accurately argued that had Little Eagles Day Care been subject to the regulation and inspection required of secular day care centers, many of the [sudden infant death syndrome] risk factors would not have been present," Judge Charles E. Poston wrote in his decision. "While the Court is certainly sympathetic . . . the remedy for this situation lies in the sound discretion of the General Assembly, not with the judiciary."

"I figured they were licensed when we went to take a tour," Cummings told me. "They seemed like they knew what they were doing. They were mothers. They were grandmothers."[30]

In 1981, when some states were trying to set higher teacher-training standards for child-care workers, Ronald Reagan scoffed at the attempt. "Mothers and grandmothers have been taking care of children for thousands of years without special college training," he said.[31] In the minds of many, child care means little more than babysitting. And how hard can that be?

The *New Republic* writer Jonathan Cohn, in his sobering "The Hell of American Day Care," chronicled the deaths of four children in a family care home in Texas. The child care was run by a woman with a criminal record. One day, while the children were napping, she left them unsupervised to go shopping at Target. She also left a pan of oil on a hot stove that began to burn. When she returned, the house was on fire.[32] The Minneapolis *Star Tribune* won a Pulitzer Prize for its 2012 investigation into why children were dying of SIDS, asphyxiation, and unexplained causes in the state's unregulated family care homes at a rate of about one per week.[33]

Faced with a growing number of these damaging, high-profile media reports, in May 2013, the U.S. Department of Health and Human Services announced that it could no longer wait for Congress to act and proposed the first-ever federal safety standards for child-care facilities that accept government subsidies for the very poor.[34] "Fifteen years have passed since we last updated our child-care rules—years of tragic stories of children lost and families devastated because there were no safety standards in place to protect them," HHS Secretary Kathleen Sibelius said.

But the regulations will cover only the 1.6 million children poor enough to receive government subsidies. And the humiliating, bureaucratic, time-consuming process of trying to actually *get* one of those subsidies often defeats the very purpose of the subsidy in the first place.[35] Just spend time in line with the mostly single mothers applying for one. I arrived in one such line in Washington, D.C., at 6:30 a.m. with Andria Swanson, a twenty-three-year-old single mother of two who works and goes to college, as she sought to renew her subsidy. Though the doors wouldn't open for another hour, the line was already snaking down the block. The first person in line said she'd arrived at 3:45 a.m. Many, like Swanson, had spent hours, for three and four days in a row, standing in line, only to be turned away to get more paperwork. Once, Swanson missed so much work trying to get the child-care subsidy that she lost her job, lost her apartment, washed up at the local shelter, and found herself on welfare, a familiar story I was to hear up and down the line. "This process is hell," Swanson said. "H-E-L-L."

But she has no choice. At market rates, it would cost her nearly $40,000 to send her infant son and toddler daughter to a private child-care center in Washington.[36] She makes barely half that.

Because the quality of child care in the United States is so uneven, parents are justifiably uneasy about it. There is a distinct stigma to child care in America that is not present in other countries, no doubt made worse by the spate of bizarre and widely publicized abuse and devil worship scandals in the 1980s, which proved wholly untrue.[37] The uneven quality has led to wildly confusing studies about whether child care and "maternal employment" harm children the way Buchanan and other conservatives feared it would. It wasn't until 2010 that researchers sponsored by the National Institute of Child Health and Human Development controlled for the *quality* of child care and found that children in high-quality child care for a reasonably limited amount of time every week "did not develop differently" from children who were cared for exclusively by their mothers.[38] Reassuring, no doubt, for the 10 percent who can find it, get a coveted spot, and are able to pay the tuition.

I began to wonder if the crazy way the entire child-care system is organized is really one not-so-subtle message telling mothers to hang it up, quit, and go home where they belong. "We've heard that from policy makers," Michelle Noth, an advocate with Child Care Aware of America, told me. "That's what they had as children. With their wives at home, that's what they have now. They're not thinking about how employers can work with both mothers and fathers to figure out a way to support people who have children in this country."

It's clear that when it comes to women, industrialized countries and ever more of the developing world have come to agree that educating women, just like men, is a good thing. Large majorities around the globe agree that women can and should work in whatever profession they choose, just like men. More even say that they are happier in egalitarian rather than traditional relationships and marriages.[39] But once a woman has a baby, survey after survey continues to show we don't know *what* we think. More, we don't know what to do.[40]

That ambivalence about a mother's proper role has led to inertia. The prevailing view seems to be: Why promote policies and change cultures to *help* mothers work if we aren't so sure mothers should work at all?


Pat Schroeder arrived on Capitol Hill the year after Buchanan's successful drive to kill the child-care bill. She was thirty-two. When she was sworn in, she held hands with her two-year-old and her six-year-old, and carried a diaper bag slung over her shoulder.[41] Unlike Buchanan, whose mother didn't work outside the home, Schroeder spent part of her childhood, she tells me, along with more than 1.5 million other children, in one of the more than 2,500 high-quality child-care centers that were created under the Lanham Act during World War II so that Rosie the Riveter could go to work.[42]

"We did a survey and found that in society, only one in ten families could afford to have a full-time caregiver at home. But among our elected officials, it was just the reverse—there were just a handful with a spouse with a career outside the home," she says. "In the halls of Congress, the traditional Norman Rockwell family was alive and well. And when you would talk about child care, they would think babysitting so you could go play tennis. I would say, 'No, the woman is working outside the home, she needs child care so she can get to work.' But it wasn't real in their lives. I would have progressives say shocking things to me, like, 'If I do this, then our wives will want to go out and work.' And I'll never forget when George H. W. Bush was campaigning in New Mexico on a Sunday and he wanted to go to a child-care center. His campaign had to tell him, 'It's Sunday, they don't operate on Sundays.' Politicians are so protected from the real world. Half of them are millionaires. They just don't get it."[43]

I had called Schroeder, seventy-one and now retired in Florida, to hear from a very different Pat about the long reach of the veto Buchanan orchestrated. She spent her entire career in Congress trying to undo the damage, she tells me. She worked with Mary Rose Oakar and Geraldine Ferraro, who, like Schroeder, chaired subcommittees of what was then seen as the ultimate political backwater—the Post Office and Civil Service committee. "We would put all three of our subcommittees together for hearings and steamroller things through," Schroeder has said.[44] The idea was to turn the federal government into a model family-friendly employer. Schroeder attacked wasteful military spending and then channeled the "savings" into family programs. "I was on the Armed Services Committee, and I could stick all that stuff in and nobody paid any attention to it," Schroeder tells me. "All anybody paid attention to was how many weapons were being built and whether they were being built in their districts."

It was about this time, she said, that she noticed a mounting pressure for women to be not just good mothers, but supermothers. "You had to bake your own bread and look like a *Vogue* model," she says. "My friends found themselves doing things they would not have been doing if they hadn't been working. They'd say, 'Why am I baking bread?' But you were supposed to compensate your poor family for being neglected because you were gone at work. I used to make people furious when they asked me to contribute to recipe books. I'd send in a recipe for 'How to Make Ice.' But they wanted gourmet recipes. They'd write that someone in my office was trying to sabotage me. And I'd say, 'No, no, no. This is what my life is. You think I'm home making waffles and Eggs Benedict for the children in the morning? No way.'"

Because of Schroeder's under-the-radar maneuvering, the federal government has become a pioneer for flextime, compressed workweeks, and telecommuting. The government oversees more than two hundred highly regarded on-site child-care centers for thousands of federal workers' children that, with their long waiting lists, can't keep up with demand.[45] Thirty-three federal agencies offer child-care subsidies to help workers cover the cost of care.[46]

But perhaps her greatest achievement, Schroeder said, was transforming a "vast government-sponsored child-care system" (in Buchanan's words) into one of the best in the world: the Pentagon.

Until 1970, the Defense Department required women who became pregnant to quit. In 1982, after a highly critical GAO report found that only 1 percent of army child-care facilities met minimum standards, the military-run system was dubbed the "ghetto" of child care.[47] In 1989, Schroeder pushed through the Military Child Care Act, which set high safety and quality standards, called for teacher training and inspections and, far more than "babysitting," had an actual curriculum designed to teach children through play.

By 2012, the Department of Defense was spending more than $1 billion a year to provide care for more than two hundred thousand children[48] and now deems child care so critical to its mission—enabling parents to work free from worry about whether their children are safe, learning, and happy—that it is dedicated to providing the "best" child care in a "high-quality, developmentally appropriate, nurturing environment."[49] Nearly 100 percent of its early learning centers are accredited by the National Association for the Education of the Young Child and meet the highest standards. The teachers, despite a handful of high-profile lapses,[50] are among the best trained and highest paid of any in the country. The Pentagon shares costs with parents so that the care is affordable. They provide working parents a variety of choices, from child development centers either on base or nearby to family care in accredited homes and after-school programs. They are consistently held up by early childhood education advocates for creating the absolute "gold standard" of child care.[51]

Desiree Wineland, the first woman to command an Apache attack helicopter army unit, served in the military for more than two decades before retiring as a lieutenant colonel.[52] Her husband was a fellow army officer. Their two boys both grew up in the Pentagon's child-care system, which, she said, was "excellent." Providers always understood how crazy military family schedules can be, with deployments, single parents, and spouses who are assigned to different bases, as she and her husband often were, she said. One even offered to open up at 5 a.m. when necessary to accommodate Wineland's schedule. "The boys were always engaged, always learning, being read to," she told me. "They had cooking classes, their teachers taught them nutrition. The curriculum, even at age three and four, was about teaching self-reliance. I really felt they were doing all the things I would have wanted to do with them."

The military, the ultimate face-time kind of workplace, is also winning awards for its flexible work policies, providing enlisted and civilian workers with flexible work schedules, vacation, and time off.[53] The Pentagon also offers the most generous medical leave allowances in the country, giving up to half a year of unpaid leave to those on active duty, reservists, veterans, and family members caring for injured vets.[54]

But try to get anything like those family programs for the rest of the workforce, Schroeder says, and the rhetoric that Buchanan first inspired becomes deafening. "The equivalent of the Rush Limbaughs then were on the radio 24/7 saying we were trying to pull children out of people's homes in order to indoctrinate them," she says. The first Take Our Daughters to Work days were meant to show employers how many people desperately needed good child care, "but legislatively, you couldn't get people moving. The right wing had so convinced people that this was a Communist plot."

It took Schroeder eight years to get the Family and Medical Leave Act passed. And though she fought to make it paid leave and to extend parental leave to both mothers and fathers, the most lawmakers would agree to was twelve weeks of unpaid leave for any worker with medical needs. "It was so watered down and pathetically small," Schroeder laments. Because it applies only to large companies, full-time workers, and those employed for more than a year, FMLA does not cover 40 percent of the U.S. workforce. Government surveys have since found that the majority of people take leave because they themselves are ill.[55] Schroeder's attempt to get paid parental leave at least for federal workers was shot down. In 2012, when another effort was scuttled by conservatives, Darrell Issa, a California Republican and one of the wealthiest members of Congress, released a video on YouTube featuring North Korea's Kim Jong Il and Iran's Mahmoud Ahmadinejad among an array of other despots and the catchphrase: "Could these guys be wrong on paid parental leave?"[56]

Schroeder said she could never understand the peculiar schizophrenia in political minds when it comes to mothers: "If you're poor and a single mom, you damn well better get out there and work and don't expect us to help you, thank you very much. But if you're middle class and you can maybe afford to be home, then you should be guilty as hell if you're gone and should be running around trying to do fourteen thousand things to make up for it."

That double standard was on display in the 2012 presidential election when Republican candidate Mitt Romney, whose wife stayed home to raise their five sons, said at an NBC Education Forum that to have one parent that "can be at home in those early years of education can be extraordinarily important."[57] But a few months earlier, he had talked with pride about the tough work requirements he'd passed as part of welfare reform as Massachusetts governor: "I said, for instance, that even if you have a child two years of age, you need to go to work. And people said, 'Well, that's heartless,' and I said, 'No, no, I'm willing to spend more giving daycare to allow those parents to go back to work.' I want the individuals to have the dignity of work."[58] The "individuals," of course, being poor single mothers.

That economic conservatives, like Buchanan, who philosophically favor small government and private enterprise, would fight any kind of government-sponsored family policy like a universal child-care system is not unexpected. That social conservatives, like Buchanan, fought in the 1970s to preserve the breadwinner-homemaker model of the family, at least for the middle class, is also not a surprise. What is shocking, however, is that, despite massive global social, economic, and demographic shifts, Buchanan's traditional worldview, outlined in the child-care veto, exerts such power in America in the twenty-first century.

In talking to both Pat Schroeder and Pat Buchanan, I was struck not so much by the differences in their visions of what's best for American families and children but, at heart, how similar they are. They both have fought their battles in order to preserve sacred time for family outside of work and the sanctuary of the home. They both lament that children don't just run outside to play anymore. Pat Buchanan wants moms to be home at 3 p.m. with cake and pie because they've been there all day while Dad is at work. Pat Schroeder wants both parents to be able to have work that is flexible enough so that they, too, can be home, at least sometimes, at 3 p.m. with cake and pie. The point is, *nobody* wanted an America of the soulless homes and factory-raised automatons that Buchanan feared in the Soviet Union. But because we've been so busy shouting past one another since 1971 about the best way to protect the time it takes to create these havens at home, we've failed to protect that time or those havens at all.

The early 1970s were a singular moment in history as governments responded to social movements, such as the call for equal rights for women, that upended the old traditional order and set the stage for what was to come.

Shortly before Pat Buchanan would engineer the veto of the comprehensive child-care bill, Swedish prime minister Olof Palme gave a speech to the United Nations declaring that his government's top goal was to create a society of total gender equity that would enable men and women to both work and have time for family. He pushed sweeping policies to provide subsidized child care, early education, paid parental leave after the birth of a child for both mothers and fathers, paid sick leave, reduced and flexible work hours, good part-time jobs with benefits, and tax and labor policies that promoted women as financially independent breadwinners. He also ushered in programs that would begin to ensure that more women were elected to political office and appointed to cabinet ministries and corporate boards.[59] (At the other end of the spectrum, in 1971, some women in Switzerland had just been granted the right to vote.)

The Swedish government's push for gender equity was driven in part by a labor shortage and the desire to avoid importing immigrant workers.[60] Other countries, such as France and Germany, their populations decimated by world wars and flagging fertility rates, were similarly galvanized into pushing for "pro-natalist" policies.[61] Other smaller and more homogeneous countries, like Denmark, came to support family policies as a means of cementing national identity, even if it meant higher taxes and income redistribution.[62]

None of these programs were perfect, or perfectly embraced. For years, the generous policies in Sweden applied only to mothers. In West

Germany, mothers who worked continued to be called "*Rabenmutters*"—raven mothers—after the bird that lays her eggs in someone else's nest and blithely flies away.[63]

But while conservatives like Buchanan claim the programs are a drain on economies, a look at productivity measures tells a different story. True, the United States boasts enviable rates of economic growth and total productivity, but that's due in large part to the sheer amount of *time* Americans put in on the job, working long and extreme hours. Measuring productivity *per hours worked*, on the other hand, has in recent years put the United States behind such countries as France, Ireland, Luxemburg, the Netherlands, and Norway.[64]

When it comes to spending tax dollars on social programs, the United States is close to the bottom, twenty-third out of twenty-seven countries studied by the Organization for Economic Cooperation and Development. But add that public spending to all the money people pay out of pocket, and the United States leaps into fifth place in the world for spending on social programs, just behind Sweden.[65] In Sweden, everyone shares the cost of the health and welfare of society. In the United States, you pay for your own.

Like any other working parent, I felt the aftershocks of the child-care veto every single day once I had kids. You want to talk overwhelm? Try cobbling together preschool and child care at one place for your toddler, a nanny share with another family for your infant because there *is* no infant care in your neighborhood, and a babysitter to pick both kids up at the end of the day, because the long, traffic-clogged commute and late newspaper deadlines for both you and your spouse make a 6 p.m. pickup impossible. Then throw any one of those fragile pieces off—a preschool closure, snow, a car breakdown, a fever—and you have guilt-stricken and panicked chaos.

Summer break? Please. There is a good reason why many working parents pull out calendars, spreadsheets, and camp forms, rush to the mailbox, repeatedly call registration numbers for popular camps that can fill up within hours, stand in lines overnight to secure a spot for their child, and generally freak out every year in *February*.[66] It's called *ten weeks* with nothing for kids to do. I remember the shock, when my son was five, of discovering that a host of camps ran only from 9 a.m. until noon.

After-school care? When my son was eleven and hit middle school, I was wrapped in knots because there was practically *nowhere* for him to go after school, save a community program aimed at reducing drug use and teen pregnancy rates, which my wide-eyed, Age of Empires–playing son wasn't quite ready for. I wrote a piece for *The Washington Post* about the open secret that fifteen million kids in the United States—more than a quarter of all children[67]—are, like my son, latch-key kids. I wrote about how awful that felt. But instead of picking up on my suggestions to overhaul workplace culture to create more flexibility for parents to be home, to devise accessible neighborhood or community after-school programs for tweens, or to better match school schedules with parent schedules, anonymous online commenters called me a bad mother.[68] At 8 a.m. on the morning the piece appeared, the phone rang. An FBI agent was calling to sarcastically congratulate me for alerting "every pedophile within an eight-hundred-mile radius" that my son would be home alone every day after 3 p.m.

When my children were little, I, like many other Americans, felt so queasy about the notion of "day care" that I didn't even consider child-care centers. But when the nanny we shared with another family didn't show up one day, we didn't have a lot of options. I got a list of child-care providers from the city and started at the top of the list: *A. Abra-cadabra* is a licensed, accredited child development center in a cozy little house in our neighborhood filled with paints, crafts, costumes, and blocks, and surrounded by a big playground. It turned out to be one of the best things that ever happened to us. It was expensive. It was a near miracle they had an opening. But the tough, funny, and wise director became like a surrogate mother and one of my best friends. What I learned from her and the loving teachers, who have taught there for years, made me a better parent.[69]

Researchers have found that parents with stable child care are less stressed, better at coping, and more satisfied with their jobs.[70] Australian time-use researcher Lyn Craig found that formal child care, more than any other arrangement save shift work, leads to more gender equity at both work and home for both mothers and fathers.[71] Research has found that not only parents but also their child-free colleagues benefit when a company offers stable quality care because there are fewer disruptions, fewer absences, and higher productivity and morale: Childcare breakdowns that lead to employee absence cost businesses an estimated $3 billion every year.[72] "The bottom line," wrote Cali Yost, a consultant who helps companies devise business strategies for better work-life "fit," "is that you benefit when the parents you work with have support."[73]

A rich early learning experience with loving caregivers also sets children on a path to higher academic achievement and a better chance for success in life, research shows. The Nobel Prize–winning economist James Heckman argues that investing in high-quality early learning will yield a rate of return of 6 to 10 percent per year per child—higher than historic stock market returns—in higher academic achievement, greater productivity in the workforce, and fewer drains on society.[74]

In other words, children create the future. And their futures start early.

I'm not arguing for some vast government-run and government-funded program that resembles the DMV. But when it comes to child care, when it comes to U.S. family policy, there's *got* to be a better way.

At Pat Buchanan's house, his wife, Shelley, silently brings us coffee and disappears.

He's been talking with longing about the days when America was "the greatest country on earth," in part because it was "just normal, natural, and understood" for women to want to get married and stay home to raise kids. He clucks about how crime, drug use, and incarceration rates have soared and test scores have dropped since mothers went to work.

It's a sentiment that the federal government itself promoted in taxpayer-funded propaganda after World War II when Buchanan was growing up and the government wanted Rosie the Riveters to go back home so returning vets could have their jobs. "The family was solidly founded on father as patriarch and breadwinner and mother as cook, housekeeper, and nurse of the children," intones the sonorous narrator in one of the Office of War Information's *March of Time* newsreels.[75] The widely distributed black-and-white film warned that the economic independence of working women was one of the most "disturbing trends" in society and cut to an "expert" saying that working mothers had abandoned their feminine role, which had made women "unhappy because it has made them frustrated," that their children had "no maternal love," and that they had become, instead of partners, their husbands' "rivals." The film showed unsupervised young children playing with cigarettes and hooligan teens on the loose, all because their mothers worked.

"The whole idea of the '30s, '40s, and '50s, people were focused on the family," Buchanan says. "Now, people focus on the 'me' and 'I.' It's the me-centered society rather than the family-centered society."

"Let me ask you," I say, "do you think mothers should be in the workforce?"

"Are you talking about mothers who *have* to go into the workforce to support their kids, or they *want* to go?" he asks.

"Should it matter?" I respond.

Let me stop here for a moment. It is the queasy ambivalence about this very point—should mothers work?—that stops any meaningful national discussion about what policies that acknowledge how families have changed since 1971 could even look like. Advocates pushing for saner family policies typically talk about how both mothers and fathers *have* to work these days to support a family. That is absolutely true for millions of families. But once you get to a certain income bracket, that argument falls apart. Conservatives can point to nice houses, shiny new appliances, and big minivans, and say, in effect, you don't *have* to work. You can downsize. You can drive a used car. You can sacrifice. But since you're not willing to, since you *choose* to work, you are a greedy, selfish woman and a bad mother. And since you *choose* to work so you can afford that big house, why should my hard-earned tax dollars go to support your heartless lifestyle? If a mother who works feels over-whelmed, pressed for time, guilty, and worried about child care, tough. You asked for it; muscle it out. As Buchanan told me, "The idea that both husband and wife are going to go off to work and tell the taxpayer to take care of junior? I don't think so!"

But that narrow view reduces all of the very human yearning of both men and women to follow a passion, face a challenge, make a difference, or leave a mark in the public arena of life to a venal economic argument. Can the solution in the twenty-first century really be to return to the 1950s? I ask Buchanan. "What happens to the economy if all that brainpower goes home?"

Buchanan snorts. "I don't mean to be elitist, but only the top 5 to 10 percent are the ones doing the brain work in society. A lot of men and women are in the service industry," he says. "My mother stayed home and raised nine kids until they were all out of the house and out of school. Is that a better contribution to the country and society than a woman who says, 'I don't want any kids, I want to go out and get a job and go out and have a good life?' Now, she's free to make that choice. But ultimately, what is better for the country and the economy?"

Must it always be either-or?

A few months before I met with Buchanan, I sat in the car on a family trip with three generations of men in my family: my husband, Tom, my son and nephew, and my eighty-four-year-old father. I had been on my cell phone interviewing fathers who were fighting for parental leave or flexible work hours, or who wanted to stay home themselves as primary caregivers. My fifteen-year-old nephew, Wyatt, said, "Cool." Tom immediately said, "I'd rather work." My father couldn't even wrap his mind around the idea. "You've got to understand, Brigie," he said, getting flustered. "There comes a time in every man's life when he has to decide, 'Who am I? What am I going to be? Will I be a doctor? A lawyer? What will I do with my life?'"

I paused. "And do you think, Dad," I asked quietly, "that that moment never comes for women?"

Buchanan stirs his coffee.

"So your idea with the veto," I say, "was to protect the mom staying at home, the dad in the workplace—"

"The idea was to protect the traditional family," Buchanan interrupts.

"And did you?"

Buchanan bursts into bitter laughter. "The traditional family is disintegrating."

"Or it's different," I say, getting irritated. "I don't have a 'traditional' family. And I don't like to think that it's disintegrated."

He shrugs.

"I've deplored what's happening in society, which is why my books are so pessimistic," he says. "I don't know what the solution is."

As I get up to leave, I ask how he and Shelley handled their child-care responsibilities. He shakes his head.

"We never had children."

## BRIGHT SPOT: STARTING SMALL

> The equality we fought for isn't livable, isn't workable, isn't comfortable . . . We have . . . to get on to the second stage: the restructuring of our institutions on a basis of real equality for women and men, so we can live a new "yes" to life and love, and can *choose* to have children.
>
> —Betty Friedan, *The Second Stage*

When she was pregnant with her first child and losing sleep thinking that she'd have to return to work just weeks after giving birth, Dionne Anciano had no idea that the state of California is one of only three in the nation that offer paid parental leave. New Jersey and Rhode Island are the others.[1]

The California law, which passed in 2002, allows workers to take off up to six weeks a year to bond with a newborn, newly adopted child, or newly placed foster child, or to care for a family member. While on leave, workers draw 55 percent of their usual earnings, up to a weekly cap of about $1,000. Employers pay nothing. Neither does the government. Workers foot the entire bill: The funds come out of a state temporary disability insurance fund that all employees regularly contribute $3 a month to through a payroll tax.[2] New Jersey has a similar system. Washington state passed a paid leave law but has yet to fund it. Efforts to pass a national paid family leave law in Congress have gone nowhere since Pat Schroeder first tried in 1985.

"It was such a relief just to be able to *recover*," said Anciano, who found out about the policy only after a client asked her to design a brochure about it. Anciano married at forty-one and had her baby after extensive fertility treatments and a difficult pregnancy at forty-four. Instead of having to put her daughter in child care after only a few weeks, Anciano was able to stitch together four months of paid leave, vacation, and sick days. Her husband was doing the same when I visited her. And, with the help of their families, their daughter would be cared for by family members for most of the first year of her life. "I can't tell you how important that is to me," Anciano said.

Advocates and supporters of paid family leave, like Paul Orfalea, the founder and chair emeritus of Kinko's, who urged businesses to become "responsible corporate citizen(s),"[3] say the law acknowledges the simple fact that workers have families and provides companies with a uniform policy to plan for it. But opponents, like the California Chamber of Commerce, argued that absences like Anciano's are disruptive to businesses. They're both right, Anciano's employer, design firm owner Tia Stoller, told me. "As an employer, there was anxiety about how I'd deal with her being gone," Stoller said. "But as a mother, I wanted her to have as much time as possible with her new baby." When Stoller had her son twenty-two years ago, there were no family leave laws. "I would have loved to have had maternity leave," she said with a sigh.

But for all her anxiety about Anciano's absence, once Anciano was on leave, "it was really okay," Stoller said. "We didn't work longer hours, but we worked more intense hours. We were, like, 'Wow, look at what we can do in a day.'"

Stoller's experience is not unusual. Despite the chamber's fears, a majority of California businesses report that the paid leave law has had a positive or neutral effect on profits and productivity, and 99 percent said it boosted employee morale. Workers who'd taken leave reported feeling more bonded with their children and better able to care for them. More were breast-feeding for longer periods and they'd had more time to arrange for child care to return to work.[4]

Herb Greenberg, founder and CEO of Caliper, a Princeton recruiting company, is one of the biggest supporters of the New Jersey paid family leave law that passed in 2008. If workplaces and work policies make it too hard for a woman to both work and have time for family "then she's lost a lot in her own life, and the world has lost, too," he said. "Family leave isn't just about women. It affects men as well."

In fact, it was *men* who were instrumental in getting the California paid family leave law passed in only one year, said Sheila Kuehl, a former child actress and Harvard law grad who, as state senator, shepherded the bill through the General Assembly. "Fathers *wanted* time to bond with their children. If you have time in those first months, it changes everything," she said. Men showed up to lobby for the bill. Paper ties with copies of the bill on it were delivered to all the male lawmakers on Father's Day. "Men showed that this is really important to them."[5]

I asked Anciano if I could talk to her husband, Rich, who was currently caring for their daughter on his paid leave. It was close to 5 p.m. She picked up the phone to call and ask. "Oh. Okay," she said. "Don't worry about it."

She turned to me and in six short words conveyed the power of fathers taking solo parental leave and finally seeing for themselves how annoying it is when, at the end of an intense day with the baby, when you're exhausted, in a messy house with wild hair, no real clue where the day went save for clipping the baby's fingernails, and your partner, surveying the disarray, asks, "So what did you *do* all day?" Anciano smiled apologetically and shook her head. "He hasn't had a shower yet."


Joan Blades sits in front of her laptop at the dining room table in Berkeley, the San Francisco Bay sparkling in the distance. Blades, one of the cofounders of the progressive Internet phenomenon MoveOn .org, is now using the same organizing and Internet savvy to stir up a new movement to push both U.S. workplaces and U.S. family policy out of the deep freeze of the 1950s. Though she and her cofounder, Seattle-based Kristin Rowe-Finkbeiner, call their one-million-member group MomsRising and their agenda *The Motherhood Manifesto*, they seek to reshape policies and remake ideal worker workplaces not just for mothers but for everyone. The overwhelm, they want people to understand, is not an epidemic of personal failures, of whiny moms unable to juggle work and home efficiently. It's a massive structural failure in society, and it's holding everybody back. "Of the last four Supreme Court justices appointed, two men and two women, both the men had children and neither of the women did. This is not an accident," Blades says. "Look, 80 percent of women become mothers by the time they're forty-four,[6] which means the profound bias against mothers is a bias against all women," she tells me. "And having a family is kind of core to the human experience. If we want to continue as a society, we have to have families."

Using the Internet, MomsRising collects stories of outrage, frustration, and struggle: mothers who had to go back to work days after giving birth, families nearly broken by the cost of child care, unconscious bias breathtakingly deep. One oncologist's home loan was turned down when the bank discovered she was on maternity leave. Though she planned to return to work, the bank assumed she'd be quitting to stay home with her baby and wouldn't be able to afford the mortgage. She sued and won a $15,000 settlement.[7] "Our storybank lets our members know they're not alone," Blades says. "It lets reporters know that there are real people behind statistics. And, most importantly, it lets elected leaders know about issues that they may not have seen as actual issues."

"A lot of elected leaders have no clue what's going on with American families," Rowe-Finkbeiner agreed when I spoke with her later by phone. "Working families aren't telling them because the time you need policies like paid leave the most is often the busiest time of your life."

The MomsRising organizers know that their natural constituency—tired and overwhelmed families—is too tired and overwhelmed just trying to keep it all together to do much else. So rather than try to organize protest marches, they get people to push change in the space of a few minutes. Busy and distracted people can read a short e-mail and forward it to a lawmaker, click on a Twitter link, post a comment, or add their story to the bank on the website in a matter of seconds. "We know moms and dads are busy," Blades said. "Between work and raising a family, they have very little time to take action, much less comb their hair and brush their teeth."

MomsRising and other organizations are springing up to push forward where they say the mainstream feminist movement veered off course. Rowe-Finkbeiner interviewed more than five hundred women for her book, *The F-Word: Feminism in Jeopardy*, and discovered the majority felt feminism, in pushing them to be ideal workers, was out of touch with the complicated reality of their lives. Dina Bakst cofounded A Better Balance in New York to fight for better family policy after her own experience working for a traditional feminist legal organization left her disillusioned. The older, single feminists running that organization wouldn't let one young mother work from home. They refused to allow another to take extended maternity leave or for two young-mother lawyers to share one job. "They viewed it as detrimental to accommodate working mothers. They didn't want motherhood to 'hold women back,'" Bakst told me. "That's when I realized we had it backward. It was the law, the workplace, and these outdated family policies that need changing. The fact that we as a society fail to value the work of caregiving, that's what's really holding women back." And men.

"It's just wrong, the sense that it was up to us women, that we had a *duty* to be out there working and showing what we could do," Blades tells me. "The next wave of the women's movement has to include men. It has to include families."

Blades and Rowe-Finkbeiner sound an awful lot like . . . Betty Friedan. Friedan is most remembered for sparking the modern feminist movement with her book about the limited horizons and stultifying inner lives of middle-class 1950s housewives like her in *The Feminine Mystique*. But in 1981, Friedan looked at what the women's movement had wrought and became dismayed. She was distressed that radical feminists, who proclaimed "marriage constitutes slavery for women,"[8] had become so vocally antimother, antifamily, and antimale. Though the women's movement did so much to open doors to higher education and careers for women, Friedan was concerned that its attention was being diverted by "the emotion-ridden issues of sexual politics" and "abortion hysteria,"[9] and risked not only alienating women but failing to do the harder work of transforming the institutions and attitudes of society so that all people could do good work, share in raising families, and have time for life.

Friedan watched mothers trying to do it all, too exhausted to be angry. She spoke to fathers who longed to be more involved with their kids, who felt so tied to work that they didn't dare try. She saw how isolated and guilty everyone felt. So Friedan wrote *The Second Stage* and argued that *family* was the new feminist frontier. Radical feminists were apoplectic. The book was largely ignored.[10]

Friedan was ahead of her time. But now, the MomsRising leaders hope, the time is ripe for change. Their agenda is ambitious. The obstacles, Blades admits, are huge. Politics at the national level are fractured, divisive, and polarized. The economy is sluggish, the federal debt and deficit are enormous, and Americans hate taxes and distrust government social programs, especially ones that so easily pick at the scabs of the culture wars, the mommy wars, and the deeply divided and deeply held views about what's best for mothers and children.

So MomsRising is taking a different tack. They are politically agnostic. "Finding common ground is extremely important. I have friends in the Christian Coalition and we agree on all the *Motherhood*

*Manifesto* issues," Blades said. Nor are they dogmatic. "There are paid family leave policies in over 170 countries and no two are alike," Rowe-Finkbeiner said. "We're not arguing to import something from somewhere else. We want to come up with our own policies that work for our nation."

How?

By starting small.

Rather than seeking sweeping federal legislation, MomsRising has been involved in efforts to get city councils and state governments to pass paid sick days bills, like the ones in the cities of Seattle, Washington, D.C., Portland, Oregon, New York, and San Francisco, and the state of Connecticut.[11] They're writing letters and e-mails in support of local paid family leave laws and local telecommuting policies like those actively promoted in Atlanta, Dallas, Phoenix, Philadelphia, and Chicago.[12] They're hoping that once people see that the changes are easing the overwhelm for everyone, the movement will catch on. Blades looks up from her computer and smiles. "You just have to start wherever there's an opening."

# 7

# WHEN WORK WORKS

What if I hadn't worked so hard? What if . . . I had actually used . . . my position to be a role model for balance? Had I done so intentionally, who's to say that, besides having more time with my family, I wouldn't also have been even more focused at work? More creative? More productive? It took inoperable late stage brain cancer to get me to examine things from this angle.
—Eugene O'Kelly, former CEO, KPMG

While working on *The Last Supper*, Leonardo da Vinci regularly took off from painting for several hours at a time and seemed to be daydreaming aimlessly. Urged by his patron, the prior of Santa Maria delle Grazie, to work more continuously, da Vinci is reported to have replied, immodestly but accurately, "The greatest geniuses sometimes accomplish more when they work less."
—Tony Schwartz, *Be Excellent at Anything*

It's just after 10 a.m. on a Friday at the software design company Menlo Innovations in Ann Arbor, Michigan. Greg Haskins and his programming partner sit in front of a shared computer. They're engrossed in writing complicated code for a machine called a flow cytometer, crucial for AIDS and cancer research, that's sophisticated enough to make 180,000 cell measurements a second yet easy enough for any grad student to operate. Haskins is dressed in jeans and a blue plaid shirt. On his shoulder, he wears a white burp cloth. In his lap, he cradles his infant daughter.

Haskins hands the baby to his programming partner and, without a break in the conversation, moves to a whiteboard hanging on the wall. His partner, an older man with gray hair, takes the burp cloth and gives the baby a bottle.

Across the cavernous, 17,000-square-foot room, Kristi Trader works unperturbed in front of her screen while her two boys, eight and nine years old, grab a ball and race off to play hockey on the polished concrete floor. On the table next to her desk, the boys, who are on summer break, have set up a mound of crafts, crayons, and electronic gadgets behind a hand-lettered sign: NO GIRLS ALLOWED IN BOYS CAMP. MOM'S CAN CUM. Three dogs snooze quietly out of sight.

Rich Sheridan, Menlo cofounder and CEO, sits happily in the middle of the buzzing workspace. On his business card, he calls himself Menlo's "Chief Storyteller and Tour Guide." He is tall and white haired, with a deep, booming voice. He also smiles. A lot. Sheridan says he knew exactly the kind of work culture he wanted to create: the opposite of the miserable, soul-sucking places of the overwhelm where he spent most of his own career. The company, he says, was founded on one guiding principle: joy.

Sheridan says corporate America has it all wrong. Its leaders don't understand that what drives people to greater creativity and productivity is giving them autonomy, mastery, and a sense of purpose, not longer work hours and a smartphone that goes off in the middle of the night. "We spend too much of our work lives trying to deny our humanity. We have to deny the fact that we're parents, deny that we have aging parents," he says. "For me, this is personal. I have three daughters. I lived the death march life of corporate America. It was torturous. I loved what I was doing, but the hours left me so tired and worn-out. Or the boss would make some irrational, unreasonable demand on my time. I was in so much pain that I wanted to get out completely." He wanted so far out that after he lost his job in the dot-com bust, he thought of starting a canoe camp in the boundary waters of Minnesota.

Sheridan takes out a piece of paper. He draws a steep diagonal line from the bottom left-hand corner to the top right. "That was my career," he explains. For nearly twenty years in corporate America, he achieved greater success, power, prestige, and money. Then he draws a straight, flat line across the bottom. "That was how happy I was."

So he and two other refugees from the ideal worker culture sat around his kitchen table and dreamed up a company that would make them happy. And in doing so, Sheridan and his cofounders hit upon the very keys to wresting the moribund American workplace out of the 1950s: *Don't* just write a policy or spout off a slick-sounding mission statement yet still secretly expect people to work the same workaholic way. *Don't* come up with a program for flexible work or reduced hours to "help" working families but really expect only mothers to take advantage of them and, if they do, see them as less committed and less intelligent, and shunt them to the side. Instead, think big. Start fresh. Include everybody. The saner twenty-first-century workplace means total transformation. "If you have time for your life, you are joyful. And when you come to work in the morning, you're more creative, more imaginative, more excited to be here," he explains. "There is, in fact, a tangible business value to joy. You get better relationships. Better quality. More productivity. The fact of the matter is, software is everywhere and most of it sucks. Ours doesn't. And that's because of the culture we've created. Our strategy is to eliminate fear as a management tool. Eliminate ambiguity. Make everything transparent. Life's too short. This is a wild experiment about doing things a different way."

Behind its industrial-glass-door entrance in the basement level of a commercial building in downtown Ann Arbor, Menlo Innovations is big, noisy, and more than a little messy. The setup, which draws on neuroscience and human motivation research, is designed to promote concentrated work, collaboration, and creativity. So there are no private offices. No earbuds. Everyone, from "problem solvers" like Haskins to "high-tech anthropologists" like Haskins's wife, Katelyn, works in the sprawling din of creative chaos in teams of two, talking and laughing over each other. Every week, Sheridan matches up new pairs and assigns them new tasks on one of several ongoing software design projects. People work on one thing at a time, the better to focus. There is no multitasking at Menlo. The pairs set up at whichever computer they feel like in the morning. And workstations are set on long cafeteria-like tables on wheels that workers can move around and configure in whatever manner suits them. Change the routine, the owners like to say, and you change the thinking. New ideas emerge. Today the tables are arranged in two long, haphazard parallel lines, like picnic tables at a large family reunion.

Working in pairs and assigning tasks, Sheridan said, gives Menlo workers a sort of "freedom through tyranny": Because employees don't have to spend any time, willpower, or energy deciding what to do, when, or who with, their brains are freed of needless "decision fatigue,"[1] the better to think more creatively, take risks, and even fail spectacularly, because you never know when you might learn something cool in the process. MAKE MISTAKES FASTER! urges an enormous poster on the wall. Working in pairs also frees up time for everyone, Sheridan explains. Because people work with a partner and are constantly rotated through different projects and tasks, no one person is indispensable. So if someone wants a vacation, needs to take the day off because of a sick child, or simply feels like going kayaking with a friend, all he or she has to do is schedule it, he says. Menlo adjusts. And the work continues seamlessly.

The longest meeting lasts no more than ten minutes. Every Friday at 9 a.m., everyone stands in a circle. The pair partners each hold a horn on a goofy Viking helmet that has become Menlo's unofficial mascot and give a brief update. The only other meetings are "pop-ups." "Hey, Menlo!" someone will call out. The room quiets and whoever called out stands and speaks his or her piece.

At the end of the day, when work is over, it's over. It's time to live your life. Checking e-mail or making work calls at night or on the weekend is expressly frowned upon. By 6 p.m. the day I visit, the place will be empty. Lisamarie Babik was accustomed to logging seventy-hour weeks as a face-time warrior in corporate America. She had a hard time adjusting at Menlo. "I had that work-harder-and-harder-and-harder mentality. But the owners came to me and said, 'If you don't go home and stop working so much, we will *fire* you,'" Babik tells me, handing me a card that gives her job description as "Menlo Evangelist." "I had to relearn how to have a personal life."

Sitting around one of the cafeteria tables sharing Potbelly sandwiches for lunch, workers marvel at what a difference being part of this experiment in sane working has made in their lives. One woman has time to play sports like softball and hockey again. Another decided on the spur of the moment to take her son to the zoo on a beautiful day without an ounce of guilt. Another was able to take time off to tend to her husband after he'd had major surgery. A young man named Nate explains that he takes every Friday off to work on designing video games for his own start-up company.

Menlo has won awards for being among the most innovative, democratic, creative, and cool places to work. It even was honored by the American Psychological Association for having one of the most "psychologically healthy" workplaces. It's also making money. It's among the fastest-growing private companies in America, expanding from its original three cofounders in 2001 to as many as fifty permanent and subcontracted employees. While money is certainly essential to keeping Menlo going, Sheridan measures real success differently. "Do you hear any phones ringing?" he asks me. I prick up my ears and shake my head. "No one calls to complain. There are no problems or questions with our software. When we get calls, it's people thanking us."

On a tour of the workspace, Sheridan proudly shows me the Baby Room off the kitchen, with cushy rocking chair, dim lights, and portable crib. The kids playing hockey, Haskins's baby, Sheridan says, smiling, was all his idea. A few years ago, Tracy Beeson, a valued employee, was on maternity leave. Menlo had just landed a big contract that Sheridan thought Beeson would be perfect for. She, too, was ready to come back. But she had no child care. "That was probably the last moment of Old Corporate Rich," Sheridan says. "I had to squish that part of my brain for a long time before it died. I looked at her and said, 'Well, why don't you bring the baby to work.' She said, 'All day?' I said, 'Sure.' She said, 'Every day?' I said, 'Why not?' If this company is about innovation, why not experiment?"

Beeson sits down to tell the story. Before Menlo, she worked for high-tech firms that rewarded long hours of face time, not necessarily performance. When her oldest child, her son, Charlie, was young, she worked late every night. She worked weekends. And it wasn't until she received her annual evaluation that she found out her bosses didn't think that was enough. "They told me I hadn't worked enough overtime to deserve a bonus," she says. She was nervous about Sheridan's offer but decided at least to give it a try. She brought her four-month-old daughter, Maggie, to work and put her in a bassinet near her desk. No one quite knew what to make of the arrangement at first. But then people began to fight for the chance to hold Maggie while they were working. They noticed that visiting customers were on their best behavior. Sheridan even took client calls with the baby in his lap. Maggie was the first "Menlo baby." Greg and Katelyn Haskins's baby is now the eighth. "Frankly," Lisamarie Babik leans over to say, "having babies in the room makes people nicer."

The raucous boys are in "Menlo summer camp." When Kristi Trader and her husband, who live an hour away, couldn't swing an early afternoon camp pickup for their two sons, Sheridan says it wasn't much of a stretch to tell her to bring them in with her as well.

By 6:30 Friday evening, Tracy Beeson has ridden her bike home, helped her husband make a quick dinner, and seen her son and husband off to a Little League game. We sit on the front porch of their Arts and Crafts bungalow in their tree-lined neighborhood sipping lemonade. Maggie, the first Menlo baby, is now five. She wears a blue-and-green helmet and, tongue out in concentration, rides a little red bike up and down the sidewalk in front of the house. Beeson talks about how much she loves her work. That day, she'd been developing software to help a company better fit artificial limbs to the contours of the human body. She says her boss and coworkers are like family. Menlo, she says, is truly a joyful place. She no longer works impossible hours. She also no longer misses out on watching her children grow. With Charlie, she missed so much. "It feels like Menlo is the only place I've ever worked where it's okay to be human," she says.

"Mommy!" Maggie calls out excitedly. "Mommy! Mommy! Watch me!" The little girl teeters on the training wheels of the bike. "Do you see?" the girl calls out excitedly.

"I see you!" Beeson calls back, smiling. "I'm right here."

As I searched for bright spots, where workplaces are changing, the ideal worker norm being overthrown and people climbing out of the overwhelm to live saner lives at work, love, and play, I was heartened to find that there are actually a lot of bright spots out there. Their numbers are growing. And each one is different, designing systems that work for their industries, their people, and their cultures. Some companies are running bold experiments, like Menlo. Others are doing the hard work of reinventing themselves. Some, like Menlo, expect people in the office but put strict boundaries on their time there. Others exist virtually, bounded neither by time nor space. Some workplaces are motivated to change after seeing a flood of talented women leave when they start families. Others want to get the most out of highly motivated workers to create what Daniel Pink, author of *Drive*, calls motivation 3.0, built on autonomy, mastery, and purpose.

The way forward is not coming from on high, as people once thought, through government or corporate policy or legislation. The ground is shaking. But it's not just harried working mothers who are crying in the wilderness for bread and roses, for time for life. It's the millennials, the roughly eighty million Americans between the ages of eighteen and thirty-five coming into the workforce. Not only does this generation expect time to both work and live well, they're willing to take their skills and walk or start their own ventures if they don't get it. And who knows how pressures like a changing global economy, technology, an aging workforce, climate change, extreme weather, and public health scares will reshape work? When hurricanes, snowstorms, flu outbreaks, and freak weather shut down the federal government and local businesses, the work goes on at the U.S. Patent and Trademark Office in Alexandria, Virginia. Two-thirds of the eleven thousand employees work remotely at least one day a week, Danette Campbell, who directs the telework program, told me. Remote workers examine 3.5 more patents than their colleagues who work in the office, PTO studies have found, and they save taxpayers $22 million in avoided real estate and office costs every year. The attrition rate is lower because workers are happier. Roads aren't clogged because workers don't have to commute. And work goes on despite the weather.[2]

Alison Maitland, a British journalist and author of *Future Work*, predicts a coming revolution in work on par with the wholesale transformation that swept people off country farms and deposited them in urban factories in the industrial age. "If work can be done anytime, anywhere, and it's no longer tied to putting in long hours of face time at set times at an office, rush hour disappears!" she told me.

The brightest spots have some key ingredients in common: They bore deeply into their work cultures and, like Menlo, change their very DNA. The transformation is thoughtful, deliberate, and embraced from top to bottom. The best workplaces recognize that working in a new way requires learning new skills and not assuming people automatically just *know* how to work with flexibility. Employees are trained to understand their own work style: Do they do their best work with distinct boundaries separating work and home? Are they adept at integrating the two? Managers are trained to measure performance, not hours. The mission of the company and the scope and quality of work expected from each employee are clearly defined and communicated—none of the we'll-know-it-when-we-see-it ambiguity that, organizational psychologists have found, is the biggest workplace stressor.[3] The clarity of purpose helps people better answer the three questions that drive so much of the unending overwhelm:

- How much is enough?
- When is it good enough?
- How will I know?

Change is hard. Our very human nature pulls us back to the status quo, not because it's better, but because it's familiar. However, I learned a few things about change as I visited bright spots: The unspoken culture we operate in trumps any policy on the books or nice speech by the boss. We create that culture by the stories we tell ourselves. And change gets a little easier when it's visible. When we see that somebody's out there doing things differently, we begin to think that maybe we can, too. We start finding others like us and build networks to create our own bright spot in the darkness.

So that's what I'm going to do now. Shine a light on some bright spots. Change the narrative. And see what happens.

### Millennials Rising

Leslie Zaikis sounded like a lot of the risk-taking millennials I spoke with who want to live a life of passion. She left the grinding hours of corporate America to become one of the first employees at the start-up Levo League in New York, a millennial networking site for women. She sets her own work hours, with the proviso that she'll get high-quality work in on time. The morning we spoke, she got to the office at 11 a.m. after taking time to train for a half marathon. She planned to work later in the evening to finish a project. She sent me surveys showing that millennials would rather be unemployed than stay in a job they hate, that they expect to change jobs often and to work in more collaborative, democratic workplaces, not the command-and-control totalitarian regimes of the ideal worker.

Accenture, a global management consulting firm, has found that both men and women millennials have no plans to work themselves into the ground and to the nether edge of their fertility, like older generations. And millennials want to have it all. Increasing numbers of *both* young men and women say that time for *both* career and family is important.[4]

"People in my generation are really pushing back," Zaikis said. "We're already starting to see a shift on campuses, where the prestige of working for some big corporation with a big recruiting budget is no longer seen as worth it compared to the flexibility and the 'cool' factor of working for some of the newer organizations."

### *Technology Is Cool*

When I spoke to Teresa Dove, a teacher with a Ph.D. in math, she'd recently won a prestigious Teacher of the Year award for her work in Florida. Yet Dove lives in rural Tazwell, Virginia, in the Appalachian mountains. She is part of a rapidly growing movement of online virtual schooling that is using innovative software, interactive whiteboards, videoconferencing, and one-on-one tutoring on the phone, by video conference, and by e-mail to expand the notion of what it means to get a good education. Because she wanted both to live in the rural town where she grew up and teach sophisticated, high-level math, Dove used to be on the road four hours *a day* driving to and from a school district several counties away. Now, working virtually at home, she has time to do good work and have quality time with her children, family, and community.

The morning we spoke on the phone, she'd just returned from decorating her son's preschool classroom for an end-of-the-year celebration. "If I worked in a traditional school, I never would have been able to go unless I took a sick or vacation day," she said. Instead, she simply rearranged her work hours. "I feel so fortunate. I can go in and spend time with my son—this is the biggest part of his life right now. *And* I can chunk my time somewhere else and still support my students and get my grading done on time." As we spoke, she was hanging out at the park with her two children, taking a short break from grading. I sat in a doctor's exam room with a forest of acupuncture needles spiking out of a bum knee, both of us proving that, indeed, good work can be done just about anywhere, anytime, and virtually in any manner.

## The Power of Why Not?

While some places are creating new cultures from scratch, others are seeking to remake existing workplaces, which is trickier. Ernst & Young, a financial services company, initially offered flexible schedules to promote saner living in the 1980s. But those schedules were widely seen as off-limits for anyone but moms, which only fostered resentment. Working mothers worried they were being sidelined. Others groused they had to work longer hours to pick up the slack. "It didn't feel fair," Maryella Gockel told me. Gockel, now the company's flexibility strategy leader, was one of the first Ernst & Young employees to work a flexible schedule in the New Jersey office when she adopted her first child twenty-five years ago. That flexibility, she said, was largely due to the vision of her boss at the time. "He would leave the office at 3 p.m. to take a walk on the beach and always come back with great ideas," she said. "His firm belief was that you could take your brain anywhere, so you could work anywhere."

It wasn't until leaders saw the drain of talented young women leaving that the company decided to make a systemic change. What drove them, Gockel said, was discovering that the women who left weren't staying home with their children, as everyone assumed. They were still working, just in workplaces with more give. "So we changed," writes Ernst & Young CEO James Turley in the foreword to *Future Work*. Turley himself used to shift his schedule around to take his toddler to Gymboree every week. "If people wanted to work different schedules, we stopped asking them, 'Why?' and started asking their managers, 'Why not?'"[5]

## Rewire the Culture

Hannah Valantine, senior associate dean and professor of cardiovascular medicine at Stanford University Medical School, knew the workplace culture in academic medicine had to change. Despite generous family-friendly policies, few women held leadership positions and, after ten years, close to half of all women doctors, as well as more than one-third of the men, were gone.[6] When she didn't know *how* to change, she called a design strategy firm.

Jump Associates sent videographers and ethnographic researchers to observe a day in the life of several doctors. They discovered the family policies actually *violated* the core beliefs of the culture: Success comes only from working 24/7 and ascending a very narrow career ladder. Now Stanford is seeking to "rewire" those beliefs by changing the narrative of success. They have ambitious plans to remake their culture, to provide career counseling and multiple paths to success at various speeds. And they're starting by showcasing a different kind of role model, in prominent displays along corridors and on the university website, focusing on those who have achieved excellence at work *and* have a rich life outside of it. People like Hannah Valantine herself, said Jump cofounder Udaya Patnaik. "She grew up in Gambia, got her medical education in the U.K., came to Stanford to stay for a year twenty-four years ago, and now is a stunningly accomplished heart transplant surgeon,[7] an African American woman in the most testosterone-fueled, chauvinistic medical field you could possibly think of. And she's a mother of two beautiful girls. Her husband is also in the medical field. It took a lot of effort and she didn't always get it right. But she has elegantly found a way to live and work. If you were a young doctor, stories like Hannah's are an inspiration, that, 'Wow, Hannah did that. I could, too.' You need that sense of hope."

The designers also came up with a host of what they call Practical Home Rewards to help ease the time squeeze for everyone. Valantine arranged to put Zipcars on campus so faculty can more easily get on and off the notoriously overparked campus in the middle of the day for a preschool play or parent-teacher conference. Faculty can now bank the unpaid time they serve on university committees and trade it in for ready-made organic meals or services like yard work, elder care, or housecleaning. "We decided to include the housework benefit," Valantine said, "because when [molecular biologist] Carol Greider got the news that she'd won the Nobel Prize in Medicine, she was doing the laundry."[8]

### Flexible Work Works

Anthony Curcio, a principal at fast-growing Summit Consulting, a data analytics firm in Washington, has employees who work part-time, flexible hours, and remotely—even from several states away. He himself blocks off time on his calendar to have lunch with his son at his elementary school and takes his daughter to violin lessons every Friday.

"Sometimes I read these stories about companies cutting back on flexible work and I feel like I'm on another planet," he said. "From my perspective, I tend to think of them as poor profit maximizers and poor managers. Securing top talent is the coin of the realm. When someone comes to me and says, 'I've got all these skills and, by the way, I want to work from home one day a week,' my response is, 'Is that all?'"

The Cambridge Innovation Center in Massachusetts, the largest flexible office facility in the Boston area, houses more than four hundred start-ups, small business, and high-tech firms. People traipse in and out at no set time and sometimes don't come in at all. No one has office hours. No one has offices, even. People who want time to concentrate can work in quiet "huddle" areas. And people who want to share ideas, be inspired, or inspire others work in open areas with people from other disciplines, the free-flowing exchange sounding like the hash of conversations in the college commons with people from different backgrounds and with different majors. "What we're doing is time shifting," Innovation Center founder and CEO Tim Rowe told me. "This is all about what you produce, not some manager managing your life. And that's very freeing." And not just for work. When we talked, Rowe had worked late the previous evening when he was seized with an inspiration. He was time shifting this afternoon so he could take his son to a museum.

### Take a Break

Google, 3M, and other innovative companies give their employees 20 percent of their work time to noodle around and work on whatever project intrigues them. At Google, that's when workers have come up with some of the best ideas, including Gmail, Google News, and Google Translate.[9]

Alison Gregory, a mother of three who works three days a week for IBM in London, says the company has embraced both the power of time shifting—giving employees more control and predictability over their work—as well as the effectiveness of taking breaks. "A very wise client once told me, 'I pay you for three days, but you'll be thinking and solving problems all five.' And that's true. Something will pop into my head in the bath, 'Oh! How about this!' and I'll write it down and use it later. I'm a great believer in taking breaks."

Hillary Harding, one of the few working mothers in the outdoor industry, takes to heart Patagonia founder Yvon Chouinard's motto: "Let my people go surfing." I met up with her one day while she "worked"—taking her weekly hike up Green Mountain outside Denver. She has always done her best thinking outside, she explains, with skis, hiking boots, or snowshoes on. "I usually ponder one question as I climb," she said. "I find I can think more strategically, rather than just be stuck in the play-by-play. I have time and space to just let my brain *go*." As we neared the summit, Harding said she needed the hike that day to prepare for a big strategy session with a colleague the next day. They would meet outside. While rock climbing.

### Dumping the Ideal Worker Is Good for Your Health

Working in an ideal worker workplace that doesn't understand you have a life leads to spikes in the hormone cortisol, according to research from a massive $30 million study on work environments, chronic stress, and health by the National Institutes of Health. And not just for you. David Almeida and his colleagues at Penn State took saliva samples from hotel workers and their families and found that cortisol acts like a "contagion" and spreads to a stressed-out worker's spouse and even his or her *children*. Too much cortisol can lead to a weakened immune system, anxiety, depression, obesity, and cardiovascular disease. "That's why we're targeting businesses and trying to convince them that changing work culture is a smart thing to do," Almeida told me.

NIH researchers have also found that people who work for ideal worker managers sleep less than those who have open and flexible managers, and are more likely to be at risk for cardiovascular disease.[10]

What to do? Train the managers. Organizational psychologists Leslie Hammer and Ellen Ernst Kossek created a training program for the NIH project to teach managers at Midwestern grocery stores how to create a "family-supportive" culture. They found that employees began to sleep better, their blood pressure and heart rates came down, they were healthier physically and psychologically, and they were happier at work. "Managers are the linchpins to change," Hammer told me. "They are the ones who really need to *get* it."

### *Sludge Eradication*

NIH researchers also compared workers at Best Buy's corporate head-quarters who worked in an ideal worker corporate culture with those who were part of the company's new Results Only Work Environment program, or ROWE, designed to give employees radical independence over when, where, and how they worked, as long as they produced quality results on time. Sociologists Erin Kelly and Phyllis Moen found that ROWE workers were healthier, felt less stress and anxiety, slept better, had more energy, and reported being more loyal to the company than employees who worked in what Moen calls the "time cages" of traditional workplaces. ROWE workers reported feeling something that eludes most of us caught in the overwhelm: They said they had enough time in the day to do everything they needed and wanted to at work and in their lives. Researchers call this elusive state "time adequacy."[11]

How to break open the time cage? Sludge eradication. "Sludge is judging other people for how they spend their time," Jody Thompson, one of the pioneers of ROWE and coauthor of *Why Work Sucks*, told me. "When someone says, 'Where are you going? It's 3 p.m.,' what they're really saying is, 'Why do you get to leave early and go flouncing off? You're *supposed* to be here until 5, like me.'" But in a ROWE, results and performance matter. Not time. So Thompson, formerly of Best Buy, who now runs a ROWE training company called CultureRx, teaches people to use five magic words: "Is there something you need?" "Here's the beauty of the statement: If I need something from you,

I need to just ask you for it. That is respectful and human," she explained. "If I don't need anything from you, I'm a big fat sludger and I need to shut up. I'm not the keeper of you. We're all here to do a job. ROWE is about the work. Not where you were at 8 in the morning."

### Who Says There's No Flexibility in a Blue-Collar World?

More than half of the employees are paid by the hour at Hypertherm, a New Hampshire company that designs and manufactures sophisticated metal-cutting systems for shipbuilding, manufacturing, and auto repair. In addition to a culture that allows for informal flexibility for workers to get to doctors' appointments or school visits, the company's Flex-Friendly policy gives each employee the right to request a formal alternate work schedule—just like workers are allowed to do by law in the United Kingdom and other countries—and even provides a ready-made template to make it easy for employees to do so.

Software that finally is sophisticated enough to protect financial transactions through encryption, even when conducted on home computers, has enabled companies like TeleTech to "homeshore" call center jobs that had been going overseas and bring them into American homes. Now the company has more than five thousand employees who work out of their houses, called "at-home associates," many of them military spouses, mothers reentering the workforce, and seniors, all of whom set their own hours. "We offer a true alternative to people who don't have the ability to get in a car and drive to a fixed location every day," CEO Judi Hand told me.[12]

Internal surveys at BDO Financial Services found that a majority of employees felt conflicted between their work and home demands, and that those feeling the most stress, interestingly, were not mothers, as everyone assumed, but fathers and employees with no children. BDO adopted a company-wide flexibility policy that allows both day-to-day informal flexibility as well as the opportunity to craft a more formal plan. All workers are eligible. One group of administrative assistants created their own team and began rotating four-day workweeks.[13]

At Georgia's WellStar Health System, instead of being assigned twelve-hour shifts, employees now go online and pick the hours they want to work for the next month. "Our nurses love to be able to sit at home in their fuzzy slippers with their calendars and think, 'Okay, I have a teacher conference the third Thursday in June, so I'm not going to schedule work on that day,' " said Karen Mathews, director of Work-Life Services. "Others want to homeschool their children, so they can schedule to go in in the afternoon and work later. If you can produce the same or better results with a different schedule, we are now open to entertain any option."

WellStar's philosophy of giving workers more control has filtered all the way down to the laundry room, where the largely Hispanic and deeply devout employees were unhappy about working on Sundays instead of being at church. So the workers came up with a plan to build up enough inventory of clean sheets and towels throughout the week that they could take Sunday off and still have the same amount of fresh laundry ready to go on Monday morning. "They are ecstatic about that," Mathews said.

### It's the Performance, Not the Hours, Stupid

In 1914, Henry Ford, the politically conservative paragon of capitalism, cut work hours on his assembly line to no more than eight hours a day. Fellow captains of industry at the National Manufacturing Association screamed in protest. Factory workers in the United States and in the U.K. worked as many as sixty to seventy hours a week at the time.[14] But Ford drew on in-house research that found that after eight hours of work, the typical manual laborer was spent—working less efficiently and making costly mistakes. When Ford cut hours, errors went down, efficiency, productivity, and employee satisfaction went up, as did the company's profits. He shuttered factories on Saturdays in 1926 for the same reason, and the forty-hour workweek, enshrined in federal law since 1938, was born.

But times and work have changed. Unlike manual laborers, knowledge workers have about six good hours of hard mental labor a day, futurist Sara Robinson found in a review of research on work and work hours. Work late for too long, she wrote, and "people get dull and stupid . . . They make mistakes that they'd never make if they were rested; and fixing those mistakes takes longer because they're fried."[15] A study of medical interns found that those on long shifts made 36 percent more potentially serious errors than those who worked shorter shifts.[16] Research by the Business Roundtable in the 1980s found that companies can get short-term gains by pushing employees to work sixty or seventy hours a week, Robinson reports. But after two weeks at that pace, workers were not just fried—they were crispy. Microsoft, like most other high-tech firms, has a "churn 'em and burn 'em" long work hours culture. (Apple once made T-shirts for employees proclaiming 90 HRS/WK AND LOVING IT!) But in a 2005 survey, Microsoft employees reported that in a 45-hour workweek, they put in only 28 *productive* hours. That's 5.6 hours a day.[17]

Change is hard, so there are dark spots in these bright spots. In addition to Menlo's empowered full-time employers, the company hires temporary contract workers without benefits. Ernst & Young's Gockel said the company is nowhere near its target of 100 percent flexibility and equal numbers of men and women partners. In August 2012, Best Buy hired a new CEO, Hubert Joly. The following March, he put an end to ROWE, calling it "fundamentally flawed." Instead, he wanted all employees "all hands on deck," in the office.[18]

Women-owned businesses are among the fastest-growing sectors of the economy, expanding at twice the rate of businesses owned by men.[19] Some of those businesses are run by women like Jennifer Folsom, who, tired of being passed over for promotions in corporate America because her male bosses didn't think she could handle her work and her "family responsibilities," started her own recruiting firm to find jobs for people like her: dedicated workers who want to work in a flexible way. But women-owned businesses are smaller, and they receive only 10 percent of venture-capital money.[20] Many are derided as the pet project of a "mompreneur" who, say, makes quilts in the basement while her kids nap. Time-use studies have also found that women entrepreneurs who work at home are still caught in the double bind, doing more housework and child care than men who work at home.[21]

Sometimes good ideas, poorly executed, go wrong. The newly minted Yahoo! CEO Marissa Mayer banned telework at the struggling

Internet company, frustrated that it was a sloppy program. No one measured performance. No one had any idea what anyone was doing. The company felt disconnected and adrift.[22]

Companies like Google and Apple encourage time in the office to increase interaction and the chance encounters that can lead to innovation and breakthroughs.[23] But such environments can also be noisy, distracting, and a waste of time. Independent telework can give workers the uninterrupted time to concentrate on bringing a creative idea to life. Or unsupervised employees can spend their time farting around.

The key is defining the mission, then deliberately crafting the motivation 3.0 work environment to best accomplish it and establishing metrics to measure success and feedback loops to course-correct.

Walk into the sleek, modern offices of Clearspire, an entirely new kind of law firm, on Pennsylvania Avenue in the heart of downtown Washington, D.C., on a typical workday and this is what you might see: a friendly receptionist and 3,500 square feet of spare, sun-splashed offices enclosed in glass that are mostly empty. But it's what you don't see that counts. A host of highly educated, highly trained lawyers, many of them refugees from Big Law and the tyranny of the 2,200-billable-hours year, are all working diligently in high-tech wired offices in the comfort of their own homes.

They are connected to one another and to their clients in virtual "hallways" through a cutting-edge web environment called Coral. Based on some of the latest research on how to build meaningful communities on the web, Coral lives in the cloud and functions much like a coral reef in the ocean, as the nerve center and sustaining force for the firm. Like Facebook, lawyers' photos show up in Coral's metaphorical hallway. If a lawyer is on the phone, the photo changes to show the lawyer holding a phone. If a lawyer is in a meeting, a stop sign appears on top of the photo. Lawyers connect via instant message, web conference, Google docs, and even scheduled face-to-face meetings. In Coral, lawyers can press an "elevator button" that takes them on the screen to, say, the "5th floor" of the metaphorical building for the litigation hallway, or the "10th floor" for the corporate law department.

Sitting in the conference room of the virtually empty office, cofounder Bryce Arrowood explains that when a client comes in with a legal job, the entire project is delegated and scoped out. Attorneys who will be assigned to the project estimate the amount of time they'll need to complete their part of it. Clearspire calculates the cost of those hours and presents a client with a bill up front, unlike big law firms that typically ask for their often astronomical and mystifying fee at the end of the project. At Clearspire, if the job changes or expands along the way, they treat it much like a construction change order, with recalculated time budgets. The work is totally transparent. Clients can dip into Coral at any time to see the work as it progresses.

As each lawyer works, a little hourglass filled with shifting red sand on the right-hand side of the computer screen tracks the time they estimated they'd take on a project and how much they've used up. If lawyers take longer to finish a matter than they'd estimated, tough, they eat it. But if they finish early, then the savings are divided in thirds and shared among the lawyer, the firm, and the client. The new approach to work can yield big savings for clients. George Kappaz, CEO of the Astrata Group, one of the fastest-growing global telematics companies, which provides GPS, satellite, and other tracking services, estimated that by using Clearspire, his firm spent one-fourth of what they would have with a traditional big law firm and the work was just as good.[24] "Everything about big law is broken," Arrowood says. "It doesn't work for attorneys. Studies have found that lawyers are at the top of the list for suicide and depression. It's an incredibly beleaguered existence. People don't have latitude to work in a different way. And it doesn't work for clients, who pay way too much money and get too little value and have no say in the matter. We thought, 'There's got to be a better way.'"

Arrowood, a Harvard MBA, teamed up with his friend, the nationally recognized civil trial lawyer Mark Cohen, and, with $5 million in personal savings and outside investments, the two created Clearspire and opened for business in 2011. An arcane regulation in the United States prohibits nonlawyers from managing or owning part of a law firm, so Arrowood runs the business side of the company that is responsible for bringing in business, and Cohen manages the legal side of the firm, freeing up lawyers from the time-consuming pressure of rainmaking so they can do what they do best: practice law. The firm is growing, opening up offices in New York, L.A., and San Francisco, and hiring additional lawyers. Their clients include *Fortune* 1000 and international companies. Arrowood said revenue grew 85 percent in 2012 and is "well into" seven figures.[25]

Clearspire attorneys, far from suffering burnout and overwhelm, are living full lives, some for the first time. Arrowood himself works like the attorneys do, taking his three kids to school, stopping by the gym for a workout, and working from wherever he feels he will be most productive. His wife, Lee, is the firm's executive vice president. She tends to work earlier in the day, then picks up the kids in the afternoon.

It's close to 3 p.m. when I drop in on Catherine Guttman-McCabe's Clearspire "office" just inside the front door of her upscale bungalow in Arlington, Virginia. She's dressed in a business suit and heels, just as she had dressed in her previous job as general counsel to Strayer University, one of Clearspire's first clients. She finishes up a memo, logs on to Coral to check the red thermometer measuring her time, and pushes a button to show she is currently unavailable. Then she walks out the door to the end of the block, where she greets her third grader as she gets off the school bus. "The structure is so fair," she says of Clearspire's setup. "I'm doing work I want to do, and I'm here at the bus stop waiting for my daughter in the afternoon. How can you argue with that?" The power to control her time, manner, and place of work has also given her time to sleep more, join a book club with friends, read legal briefs by her koi pond, and plan for a month of work and play with her family in Italy.

Her daughter flies off the bus and into her arms. "What did you do today?" Guttman-McCabe asks. Her daughter chatters happily all the way home about her word study test and her math homework and what her friends talked about at lunch. By 6 p.m., most working parents know, all that happy babble will have evaporated and an eager query about the day will be met with a grudging "nothing." Children live in the moment. When it's gone, it's gone.

Guttman-McCabe peels and slices a mango as a snack. The babysitter arrives with Guttman-McCabe's older daughter, who had been at an after-school drama club. Mother and daughter chat about the sixth grader's choreography project for *The Pirates of Penzance*. The children go off to do homework. Guttman-McCabe returns to her own office and flips a sign hanging from the doorknob that her younger daughter made: QUIET PLEASE. MEETING IN PROGRESS. THANK YOU!! SHHHHH. XOXOXOXOXO. The break has taken a total of twenty minutes. The Harvard Law graduate returns to her work as Clearspire's lead education counsel. "Clearspire makes it easy to be authentic."

Making time for his life was a big reason why Bill Hagedorn left big law and became D.C.-based Clearspire's senior counsel for litigation and risk management—even though he lives in Portland, Maine. On the day I called, dogs barked in the background. And he'd sent a quick e-mail asking to postpone our interview for a few minutes because he was waiting for a refrigerator repairman who hadn't shown up yet. He said he tends to keep fairly regular work hours from his home office in Maine, but the Clearspire model allows him to easily shift his schedule around—running errands at lunch if he needs to, getting to his children's school events, coaching his son's T-ball team in the afternoons. And all without the stress, he said, of the raised eyebrows and tacit disapproval so typical in big law face-time culture. "Even when I'm busy at Clearspire, it doesn't feel like I'm busy."

When he was growing up, both his parents worked in the public school system and were home in the afternoons and all summer. That time together was so important to him that he always knew he wanted to be both a great attorney *and* a good husband and father. Indeed, in a move "unheard of" at the time, he was one of the first fathers at his law firm to take four weeks of parental leave for each of his children. "But there was always the stress of feeling that people were looking at you funny, like you were trying to sneak out. It's wonderful not to have that pressure."

Melvin White, a senior trial attorney with expertise in white-collar crime, intellectual property, and antitrust cases, was a partner with McDermott Will & Emery, a big international firm. He has been recognized as one of D.C.'s "Super Lawyers" and served as president of the D.C. Bar. White, who is not married, said he came to Clearspire after eighteen years of practicing traditional law. "Single people want lives, too," he told me.

While the seemingly endless hours he spent working for a traditional law firm were "fruitful from a financial perspective," he didn't have much time for anything else. "I think balanced people are happier, and happier people do better work," he said. "And they have better relationships and participate more in the community." Since switching to Clearspire, White, a graduate of University of Virginia Law School and Morehouse, said he starts his day with yoga and meditation, something that was unthinkable before. And at the end of the day, he still has the energy to go to dinner with friends, connect with his extended family, do pro bono work, serve on community boards, volunteer, and mentor others. He actually knows his neighbors now. "People who've known me in both settings take a look at me and say, 'Oh, God, you look so much more relaxed,'" he said. "And the work I'm doing is quite similar."

# BRIGHT SPOT: IF THE PENTAGON CAN DO IT, WHY CAN'T YOU?

When Robert M. Gates asked Michèle Flournoy to become his under secretary of defense for policy in 2009—the first woman ever to serve in the number-three spot in the Office of the Secretary of Defense—she had a candid discussion with him about time. Flournoy, a graduate of Harvard and Oxford, had been a confirmed workaholic in the days before she had kids. And she well knew the Pentagon proudly wore its culture of total work devotion like the colorful ribbons arrayed on a general's chest. In "the Building," you work long hours. You work in the office where everyone can see you. You travel at the drop of a hat. You don't see your family? Tough. No one else does, either. You feel burned out? Pain, as the Marines like to say, is weakness leaving the body. Suck it up.

Flournoy proposed something different. "In my interview, I said, 'I'm the mom of three school-age children. I will work my ass off for you and do my best. But I need flexibility,'" she told me when we met one morning for breakfast. "'And more nights than not, I need to be home to see them before they go to bed. I need touchstone time with them.'"

Not one to boast, Flournoy, fifty-one, tall, thin, and athletic from her years of rowing in college, her wavy brunette hair pulled into a ponytail, and dressed in an understated sweater set, doesn't mention that this job is considered the "brains" of the Pentagon. The under secretary of defense for policy is responsible for strategic thinking, for anticipating threats and the nature of future conflicts—both conventional and counterinsurgencies—and the military strength that will be required to meet them. Flournoy's predecessor, Douglas J. Feith, was a high-profile architect of the U.S. invasion of Iraq. In other words, this position is a big deal. And Flournoy was telling Gates she wanted to be home for story time.

Gates said, "Absolutely."

Gates made sure Flournoy had secure systems set up in her home so she would be able to do everything there that she could in what she called the "aquarium"—the secure office where she worked in the Pentagon. Most nights, Flournoy went back to work—at home—after getting the kids to bed. Gates himself was disciplined about his time, others at the Pentagon told me, and often tried to leave by 6 p.m. to send the message to others to go home and have a life. Flournoy paid for a car and a driver so she could work on her way to and from home. Flournoy said she made a point of checking with each child about when her presence was most important. Then she was disciplined about her time at work, set clear boundaries when she could, and made sure that her children had predictable mom time that they could rely on. "The fact that I felt so supported by him made me think, 'How can I turn around and support my staff?'"

Flournoy soon realized that political appointees like herself come in and, understandably, want to make the biggest impact in the shortest amount of time. In the process, they work to death the military and civilian workers who were there before and will stay long after the political appointees leave. Not only do people's personal lives suffer, but the work suffers also. "In policy, your only asset is people," she explained. "I told Gates, 'This is the staff to think about the future, to anticipate what you don't have the time to think about. If they're exhausted, spent, and demoralized, they're not going to be able to do the thinking that will really help.'"

She saw how for so many military personnel, an appointment to the Pentagon often came between intensive deployments overseas in combat zones. "This was supposed to be their downtime," she said. "If they are always working and never seeing their families, that is unacceptable." She read in business literature that the biggest jumps in performance come not from incremental time management or productivity tweaks, but from changing entire work cultures and investing in "human capital." So she began listening to people. She walked around to different offices and heard about how out of balance and out of time people felt. She was inspired by what technology could do: One senior State Department official, a father who insisted on being home for dinner, would conference in for evening meetings via secure videolink. "I knew we had to do something," Flournoy said, "but I didn't know how to do it."

Flournoy brought in a consulting firm and, starting with the two busiest policy offices in the Pentagon, began not just rewriting policies on the books but also rewiring the culture of the workplace by creating a top-to-bottom Alternative Work Schedule. She appointed two men with young families to spearhead the effort and found that men were among the most enthusiastic supporters. "I presented it not as a woman's issue, but as a morale and staff issue," she said. "Because this has never been just a woman's issue."

For the culture change to work, everyone, including her, participated in developing a new Human Capital Strategy that would shift mind-sets and work habits. The shift required managers to think more about what a good employee looked like. If someone wasn't in the office, coworkers and managers could no longer assume he or she was AWOL. Working smarter did not mean working *less*. It meant working *differently*. Managers were encouraged not to send out e-mails in the middle of the night but to schedule them to go out during work hours. Perhaps a manager hadn't expected an immediate response at 3 a.m., but the junior recipient might worry that the manager did—something that Leslie Perlow, Harvard Business School professor and author of *Sleeping with Your Smartphone*, calls part of the merciless "cycle of responsiveness" that makes work feel intense, unending, and all-consuming.

Under the new Alternative Work Schedule Flournoy pioneered, employees and managers worked together to clarify the expectations, goals, and mission of each job. Employees were held accountable for getting quality work done by certain deadlines. But they were given more control over their schedules, for when, how, and where they met those deadlines. That, in turn, helped them plan more predictable workloads. With work time more manageable, family time could be scheduled in, so people could, without penalty, volunteer in children's classrooms, get to the kindergarten play, take an elderly parent to the doctor, train for a triathlon, or just have a life outside the office. In any ten-day period, if someone had worked long hours, he or she got a day off. Unlike in the past, where one person was assigned responsibility for a certain subject, Flournoy asked managers to ensure people could work on a variety of portfolios so workloads could be shared and no one would be missed or work stopped if he or she was out. Workers were no longer seen as more valued if they were the first in and last to leave. Instead, performance reviews evaluated output, she explained, not hours put into face time. Flournoy held regular town hall meetings and took "pulse" surveys every six weeks to see how the shift was working—or wasn't. "Some managers had to be coached; others had to be moved," she said. A time audit found that workers were wasting hours on "stupid stuff," like formatting memos and correcting typos. So she recalibrated expectations—memos could come to her in their "lovely imperfection" as long as the content was good. "I wanted them to spend their time on strategic thinking, not correcting typos," she said. "Correct them in the memo to the Secretary, yes. To me, no."

Pretty quickly, the pulse surveys showed that morale was way up. And so was the quality of work. "Thinking was sharper," she said . . . "We created an environment where people were better rested and could bring a freshness and perspective to their work. Then [Gates] saw it."

Flournoy realized that the shift had finally taken hold when a retired Marine colonel accompanied her to a noon speech. She asked if he'd like a ride back to the Pentagon. He respectfully declined. He said he'd put in enough time at work that week and was using his Alternative Work Schedule to take his son sledding for the rest of the afternoon. "That's when I knew we'd arrived," Flournoy told me. "In the military culture, if a seasoned officer not only felt okay about going sledding with his son in the afternoon, but felt okay enough to announce it to his boss's boss, I thought, 'Okay, they're getting it.'"

Before she left the Pentagon, Flournoy sought to institutionalize the Alternative Work Schedule, embedding it in policy[1] and performance measures so that it would not atrophy. The experience left her convinced that if the two busiest offices in one of the most demanding work environments in the country could successfully shift to make time for life, so could everyone else. I would later meet with Dr. Kathleen Hicks, who worked under Flournoy on defense strategy. She said that despite the often heavy workload, the new management culture made the work more bearable. Hicks, who has three children, said that with Flournoy's leadership loosening the stranglehold of the face-time culture and with advances in technology, she was able to be home more for dinner and be more present with her family on the weekends. Even if she had to carry her BlackBerry around, she said, at least she wasn't in the office.

When I met Flournoy for breakfast in the summer of 2012, she had just left the Pentagon to "rebalance" her life and be more available to her three children under age fifteen. Her own career, she said, has always been a fluid "sine curve" of intensity and pullback, though she's never pulled all the way out of the workforce. After taking time with her family, Flournoy returned to the board of the Center for a New American Security, the influential defense think tank she cofounded, advised the Obama campaign, joined a management consulting firm as a senior adviser, and became a fellow at Harvard's Kennedy School.

The change gives her control and predictability over her schedule in a way that her position in the Pentagon could not. "There are still a lot of balls in the air, but I get to decide how to manage them," she said. "I'm the parent of a varsity football player, so there are days this fall that I have to be helping out at the football concession at 3 p.m. That time is already blocked on my calendar. I couldn't have done that with the same certainty at the Pentagon." Flournoy has always trusted that she will be able to jump back into the fray after stepping to the side, and she always has. Indeed, with her reputation for commonsense pragmatism and the principled use of force, she is often mentioned in defense circles as a potential secretary of defense. This stepping out, she explained, is just another cycle in the undulating arc of her career.

Why her? I ask. Why was she, like so many wives, the one to pull back and not her husband? "The decision was not based on gender." Her husband, Scott Gould, is a naval reservist and was serving as deputy secretary of the Department of Veterans Affairs. "Either one of us stepping back would have been great for the kids. But what drove the decision was who could get more done in the last year of the administration's first term. He was working to cut homelessness and increase services for vets—very hands-on important work that affected real people. And me? Ask anybody in Washington, in the last nine months of any administration, there are not a lot of new policy initiatives. It was me who finally said, 'The president can afford to lose you less than he can afford to lose me.'"

For as much as the Alternative Work Schedule has changed the workplace culture at the Pentagon, at least in the policy shop, Flournoy recognizes its limitations. The world is an unpredictable place. Crises flare up unexpectedly, and in a job like that, the first duty is always to serve the president. "The part that was difficult for me," she said, "is that the White House and the rest of the world are not on an Alternative Work Schedule." Flournoy came into the Pentagon as the highest-ranking woman fully mindful that younger women were counting on her to "open doors and blaze a trail for them," she told *The New York Times* in 2009. She left hoping that she showed that the trail doesn't have to be so narrow, that a career doesn't have to travel in a straight line, that while work is important, life is bigger. And she leaves behind a legacy of an entirely changed work culture in one key corner of the Pentagon, designed not only to help more women rise to the top but also to ensure that everyone has time for what's important in his or her life.

# PART THREE

# LOVE

8

# THE STALLED GENDER REVOLUTION

Over the years, many times I would say to poems, "Go away, I don't have time now . . . I did keep the house scrubbed and waxed and that sort of thing."
> —Eleanor Ross Taylor, poet and wife of Peter Taylor,
> the Pulitzer Prize–winning novelist and
> short-story writer

People are saying that all feminism ever got us was more work.
> —Heidi Hartman

It is 2 p.m. on Thanksgiving Day. In three hours, eighteen friends will arrive for the feast we've been hosting for years. In the previous days, while I worked full-time, I'd looked for recipes, planned the menu, put together a shopping list, and gone to the grocery store three times. I'd obsessed on finding a tablecloth and raced around on my lunch breaks to find one. I'd hauled folding tables and chairs from a friend's basement late one evening. I'd baked pies with all the children who would be coming over. I'd stayed up late several nights in a row chopping vegetables and prepping for the elaborate dishes I love to cook and get around to only once a year. That morning, I'd made a quick breakfast for friends before we all dashed off to run the neighborhood Turkey Trot. I am still in my sweaty running clothes. The twenty-pound turkey is still pink and raw, waiting to go in the oven. The table is still not set, and the kitchen, covered in pots and pans, mounds of vegetables, spilled flour, and all manner of foodstuff, looks like a bomb has gone off.

Tom strolls over to the refrigerator. I think he's about to start cooking the turkey. He pulls out a six-pack of beer.

"I'm going to go over and help Peter cook his turkey," he announces.

I raise an eyebrow. "Peter's putting his turkey in a *smoker*. So you're going to go and sit on the patio in the sun, drink beer, and *watch* Peter's smoker?" I ask in disbelief. Tom smiles sheepishly. And walks out the door.

I can't move.

All week long, I hadn't complained. I love having friends over and I love cooking Thanksgiving dinner. I hadn't nagged for help, because after nearly twenty years of marriage, it had never done much good and it had gotten really old. I was used to "doing" the holidays, which anthropologists say has always been the work of women—the holiday planning and "kin work" that keep family ties strong.[1] And Martha Stewart, that cultural icon of domestic perfection, with her intricately carved "starburst" pumpkin sconces that look like Tiffany lamps and handmade cornhusk dolls to set on the Thanksgiving table, makes sure we'll never feel like we've done it quite right.

As I slammed the raw turkey into the oven and scurried around the kitchen preparing dinner with, God bless her, the help of my sister Claire, who was visiting—just us "womenfolk" in the kitchen—I thought back in time. Tom and I had done pretty well dividing chores fairly when it was just the two of us. But once we had kids, the scales started tipping, and though we'd tried to right them every now and then, usually after I'd lost it, I always ended up feeling like I was in charge of everything. Forget having it all, it felt like I was doing it all. Even though we both worked full-time and earned about the same amount of money. "You are NOT the Lion King!" I would occasionally yell, usually after finding myself scrubbing an oven hood so clogged with grease that the smoke alarms wouldn't stop screeching while he watched TV. "You don't GET to laze around while I do all the work!" He'd shoot back that my standards were too high. "You're just like Marge Simpson. When her house was burning down, she found dirty dishes in the sink and stood there washing them," he'd say. "Guys will live in squalor."

If you had asked him, on this particular Thanksgiving Day, Tom would not have been able to tell you where the kids' dentist was. I could count on one hand the times he'd taken them to the pediatrician. And I was the one who reshuffled my schedule and tried to work from home when they were sick or it snowed and school closed. He was *supposed* to do the grocery shopping, but he refused to take a list, and staples like toilet paper seemed to make his brain freeze. I always wound up running to the store every week anyway to get all the stuff he forgot. At one time, he was *supposed* to do the bills, but when he kept paying them so late our credit rating took a hit, I accused him of doing it badly on purpose and took the responsibility back (not that I've done much better). When it was his turn to clean the kitchen, I often had to ask him if he thought pots and pans just washed themselves. He *did* help out, but only, it felt, when I asked, which didn't free up any space in my cluttered mind. It had gotten to the point where I didn't want to feel so hostile and resentful all the time, so I had made a weird lopsided bargain: I would do most of the kid, house, taxes, and drudge stuff. And all I asked for in return, I told Tom, was this: "I just want you to *notice*, and say 'thank you.' "

That bargain is a big reason why my life splintered into unsatisfying, distracted, and fragmented time confetti. Once, when I complimented a coworker on a brilliant story that, to pull off, had required the kind of extensive, uninterrupted time I never seemed to have, she looked at me with pity. "I feel so sorry for you single moms." And once, when Tom was reporting in Afghanistan for a month, he e-mailed a photo of himself in the dusty nowhere of Forward Operating Base Ramrod outside Kandahar. He was sitting in filthy clothes, holding a cup of watery instant coffee and a laptop outside his "bunk," a giant metal box like those stacked onto container ships. My reaction shocked me: I was jealous. Of course I missed him and worried about his safety. But in my world of crashing work deadlines, teacher phone calls, late Girl Scout forms, forgotten water bills, kids' stomachaches, and empty cupboards, all I could think was this: Man, all he has to do every day is go to work.

But today, this Thanksgiving takes the lopsided division of labor in our house to a whole new level. As Tom walks out the door, I am both livid and, deep in my bones, flattened by a crushing disappointment. When we got married, we promised to be partners. But like that frog in the science experiment who has the sense to jump out of a pot of boiling water, but when plopped in tepid water doesn't notice it gradually heating to roiling until he's cooked, our division of labor had become laughably, ridiculously, irrationally, frustratingly unfair.

How did it get this bad?

Honestly, before I stepped away from the spinning top of my life and began researching this book, I was simply too busy to think much about it. But I always had company. Grousing about how little husbands do at home is a regular and tiresomely predictable social exchange. "When *I* work at home, I do all the kid and housework stuff," one friend told me. "When *he* works at home, he doesn't even *think* to." "We get the balance okay, then he'll go through an intense period at work, or travel, and I pick up the slack," said another. "And we never seem to recalibrate." There is a *reason* that time studies have found that married women in the United States still do about 70 to 80 percent of the housework, though most of them work for pay, and that once a woman has children, her share of housework increases three times as much as her husband's.[2] And it's not because women will wash dishes in a burning house and men are Lion King slobs. But it took me more than a year of reporting and soul searching to begin to see past my rage to understand why, and then figure out what to do about it. And that didn't happen until I met Jessica DeGroot.

A few weeks after that fateful Thanksgiving, as I researched what social scientists call the "stalled gender revolution," I called Jessica DeGroot, who runs the ThirdPath Institute in Philadelphia. For more than a decade, DeGroot has worked to help families create something entirely new. Not the traditional 1950s "first path" families with one breadwinner and one homemaker, which requires an either-or choice and, for those who want to do both, lopping off a piece of themselves. Not the "neotraditional" "second path" families of dual earners or with one breadwinner, usually the man, and one flex- or part-time working spouse who also tends to be in charge of all the child care and domestic chores, like mine. The "third path," DeGroot explains, is for couples who want to share their work and home lives as full partners, each one with time for work, love, and play. She doesn't deny it's difficult. "Change is hard. The answers are not easy. They take work and sometimes they take awhile to put in place," she said. "But there really are families who are doing it differently and making it work."

I'd called DeGroot to interview her about her work. Unlike other organizations that push for flexible work or, like MomsRising, better family policy, DeGroot's is one of the few that looks at both sides of the work-life equation. Beyond that, with more than a decade of research, they've developed an actual curriculum to coach people on how to make changes. By the end of our conversation, I'd asked her to work with Tom and me, because I was out of ideas. So one morning, the three of us got on the phone. DeGroot asked us what we loved about each other—always a good place to start when you're seething. By the end of the call, we'd been reminded why we were together, but we hadn't broached the subject of our one-sided distribution of domestic labor. DeGroot asked Tom, who had been less than enthusiastic about the idea, if he saw the value in continuing coaching.

"No," he said. "We need to make more time for each other. But I think we're doing okay."

He hung up the phone.

I burst into tears.

Jessica DeGroot realized when she was getting her MBA at Wharton that she wanted for herself what *both* her parents had. Her father is an award-winning endocrinologist who wrote the definitive textbook on the subject, still in use today. Her mother raised five kids, cooked great meals, created a loving home life, and was active in the community. DeGroot wanted to live both lives, but without the overwhelm that typically comes with it. She decided to study not just the workplace, not just women, as most people were, and not just men, but how they all interact. She wanted to learn what kept most families stuck in the overwhelm, what allowed others to forge their own completely new third path, and how to bridge the gap between them.

For *both* men and women to have time for work, love, and play, she realized, the way most people work, their relationships and their attitudes about play would have to change. But with no real role models, she didn't know how. So she began to imagine: What if not just women, but *both* men and women, worked smart, more flexible schedules? What if the workplace itself was more fluid than the rigid and narrow ladder to success of the ideal worker? What if a performance-based instead of an hour-measuring work culture could more easily absorb *both* men and women "taking their foot off the gas pedal" for time to care for children or families or have lives, as well as ramping up again when that time had passed? And what if *both* men and women became responsible for raising children and managing the home, *sharing* work, love, and play? Could everyone then live *whole* lives?

She experimented with her own life. When she married and she and her husband, Jeff, started a family, they both wanted to work and to share the care of their baby daughter. So they both shifted their work schedules and swapped days being the primary caregiver. They had repeated conversations about what each expected when it came to work, kids, and home, agreed to common standards, and sought to divide the duties in a way that felt fair to both. Sharing fairly also meant clearing mental clutter. Once when Jeff asked what DeGroot wanted for dinner, she responded, "To not have to think about it." Then when it was her turn to cook, she gave him the same mental break. Twenty years later, Jeff, co-owner of a manufacturing company, has seen his small business grow to three hundred employees and DeGroot's nonprofit ThirdPath Institute has become an important voice in the growing national movement to ease the overwhelm and conflicts between work and life. They both have strong relationships with their two children, now seventeen and twenty-three. And sharing equitably gave them time for regular date nights. "We thought we made this decision for the good of our kids, but it turns out it was good for our marriage, good for our work, and good for ourselves," she said. "It was such a gift."

Traveling the third path herself helped her see that to right listing family systems like mine so precariously off balance requires challenging enormously powerful cultural expectations of who we are and how we're supposed to act: the work-devoted ideal worker, the self-sacrificing ideal mother, and the distant provider father. The norms are what get us into the overwhelm, she said. And the overwhelm keeps us from having the time to imagine a way out. "When couples are angry with each other, standing in their living rooms fighting about ways to create more time and not seeing any, they don't realize that there are these other invisible forces in the room with them," DeGroot said. The ideal worker, the ideal mother, and the provider father are right there, pulling the strings. "*They're* the ones creating the stress."

Talk to a father about cutting back on work hours to become more involved at home, and the ideal worker takes a tug. Both men and women instinctively know—as the social science in chapter 5 showed—that he would be far more punished in the workplace for flexible work than she would. And for so many people living on the edges of their budgets, the fear of taking a big financial hit stops all conversation right there. Talk to a mother about stepping aside to let the father do more with the kids, and all three cultural norms yank that chain and shut her up. Aren't women just naturally meant to be the better parent? Isn't it selfish for a mother to want to work? Won't he get grief? And if his work suffers, how can he provide? We've got bills to pay! "So they both end up taking the path of least resistance. They get stuck," DeGroot told me. "People feel like they don't have a choice, because choice requires having meaningful alternatives, and so many couples don't think there are any."

To start down the third path, DeGroot asks people to fight what she calls "the good fight" right when the overwhelm kicks into gear: when the first baby is born. That one event, as I had discovered in all the time-use research around the world, changes a woman's life profoundly and, until very recently, a man's life hardly at all. DeGroot knows that's a tall order. "I'm asking couples, at the moment they are most exhausted, to think differently," she said. "To ignore all their neighbors, colleagues, family members, and these cultural norms. To start to imagine their *own* way."

I thought of our friends, Peter, with the turkey smoker, and Jenny, my running partner and one of my best friends. They'd met and married while getting their Ph.D.s in physics and were living in Holland doing postdoctoral research when they had their two boys. Away from family, free from American cultural norms, yet not fully integrated into Dutch society and not knowing what else to do, they created what I'd wistfully come to think of as Their Own Private Netherlands. Since flexible work arrangements are common in Holland, they each worked four days in the lab, alternating so that each parent had a day alone in charge of the kids. A nanny watched the kids on three days. But the days weren't long, since work hours in Holland tend to be intense and short. They'd leave the lab in the late afternoon and one would grocery shop before the stores closed at 5 and the other would get the kids, pausing for a cup of tea with the nanny, before meeting at home for dinner. The family had weekends together. That equitable division of labor would shift when they moved back to the United States, as both Peter and Jenny found themselves at times caught up in ideal worker workplaces. But when things get too far out of whack, they have a sense of the possible and a touchstone to guide them.

Helping couples find Their Own Private Netherlands, so to speak, is a key mission of DeGroot's institute. Her approach includes three main elements: vision, space, and story. When she asks couples to fight the good fight, she uses a well-researched curriculum to help them see the powerful unconscious forces at work in their lives—the ideal worker, the provider father, and the ideal mother. Then in what she calls "active listening" sessions, she creates a regular and predictable space for couples ordinarily too overwhelmed to even think, so they can begin to sort through where they are and how they got there. It's a time to pause, to step outside the swirl and examine their own work cultures, work creep, how their own histories can unthinkingly shape their expectations, and how easy it is to fall into what she calls reactive, no-win "tangos" when those unconscious forces are pulling the strings. She asks couples to talk to each other about what they really want for their life together. She asks them to start to imagine how to get across the gap between where they are and the vision of what they really want. Then she tells couples to experiment and see what happens. Over and over. Until the vision gets clearer and the path to it better lit. And when they get stuck, when change seems impossible, like MomsRising, she, too, has a bank of stories, and connects couples, families, businesses, and leaders who are striving to remake their lives on the third path to those who already have. Like at Stanford, and in the bright spots workplaces, she is rewriting the narrative and rewiring the culture. At home.

Some couples figure this out on their own. Tom and I, obviously, hadn't. Feeling stuck, I asked to hear some of those stories of people seeking to change.

### Anna and James—The Unintended Slide into Traditional Roles

By the time DeGroot began coaching Anna and James, a couple in Minnesota, they had slipped into traditional gender roles despite their best intentions. Anna, who had an emotionally volatile childhood with parents who divorced early, was between careers when they had their first child. She grew to like the idea of devoting her full attention to the family for a few years. James became the breadwinner. With their first child, he took his company's maximum paternity leave: one week.

When their second child was born, James planned to take leave. But after just one day off, his extreme-hour company called in a panic and said if he didn't return immediately, his job would be on the line. A big house and mounting expenses pushed them further into their separate spheres as James began sleeping with his BlackBerry and handling work crises at all hours and Anna did the work of both parents. At home, James was exhausted, snappish, and distracted. "If the kids tried to say something, I'd be thinking, 'Don't talk to me, I'm thinking about work,'" James told me. "If I read them a story, I'd read them the shortest one I could find because I was so stressed-out." James became physically ill. Anna was lonely and miserable. This wasn't the life either of them envisioned.

With dedicated time and space with DeGroot to think about their work and lives, Anna came to see that, as much as she wanted James to be a coparent, she was too often undercutting him—criticizing what he did or scolding him for what he didn't do. Social scientists call this "maternal gatekeeping," a common but largely unconscious behavior that flares because the ideal mother norm that is nestled deep in a woman's psyche holds that mothers not only know best but should always be in charge. James, instead of backing down, as he usually had, began to tell her to back off. "And I did," Anna said.

Anna was shocked to discover that James really wanted to work a reduced schedule to have more time to be part of the family. "His own father died when he was fifty-five and James was worried that if he didn't de-stress his life, he'd die early, too," Anna said. "I realized we'd never talked in any great depth about what we really wanted." It took years of small, incremental steps, of trial and error and backsliding and a lot of talking, but they finally sold their big home and down-sized. James took a job with flexible hours, works from home, schedules travel around school events, and has become a much more active parent and partner. Over time, Anna found her passion as a parent educator and as a volunteer with the ThirdPath Institute. Both Anna and James ultimately aim to work about thirty hours a week. James cooks. Anna mows. They have found time to walk in the nearby woods, have dates with each other, and laugh with their children. "Sometimes, it looks weird on my résumé, I went up upupupup and then all of a sudden you see I'm an assistant engineer," James told me. "But the other day, the kids were listening to a silly song and I found myself singing along. That was an aha! moment for me. A year or two ago, I wouldn't have even known the words."

## *Marcee and Jon—The Pull of the Ideal Worker*

The power of the ideal worker keeps Jon and Marcee from sharing their work and home life more equally, even after making explicit promises to each other that they would. When their daughter was born, Marcee's progressive company allowed her to take six months of maternity leave; Jon had one week. So Marcee came to better understand what the baby needed and her routine and became the "expert" parent and Jon the backup. When Marcee returned to work—she was overseeing her global financial services company's transition to a 100 percent flexible workplace—she worked four days and had every Friday with the baby. Then Jon got a big promotion and the family moved from San Francisco to New York. Jon began working late nights and weekends, wanting to prove himself in the new job. Marcee, alone with no friends or family in the new city, struggled to work and take care of the baby. "That started the slippery slope" toward traditional gender roles, Jon said. Marcee was sleep deprived and spent. "I finally just said, 'I can't do this. This isn't what I signed up for,'" she told me.

The two began working with DeGroot. Their housework wasn't so much the problem—she bought the groceries online and cooked. He picked up the house, vacuumed, paid the bills online, and planned the vacations. They both did laundry. But caring for the baby clearly was an issue. Marcee felt she was doing it all. "I had tunnel vision," Jon said. "I don't think I knew how much this was bothering Marcee until she sat me down and told me." They started small, creating new routines. They began to rotate days for who was responsible for getting the baby when she woke in the morning. That gave Marcee the ability to go to the gym again, or to get more sleep every other day. Jon agreed that he would come home in time to relieve the babysitter one night a week, come home for dinner more often, and wait until their daughter was asleep before going back to work. He agreed to work only during her naps on the weekend. On Saturday mornings, Jon takes over as the primary parent. But the grip of the ideal worker still keeps them from living the third-path life they envisioned. "Most of my sense of self-worth, which pains me to admit, comes from being successful at work," Jon said. "That doesn't mean I want to be a deadbeat dad. But I have a ton of ego wrapped up in being successful professionally, unfortunately at the expense of other things. That's something I constantly struggle with." Life is better, Marcee said. "But," Jon allowed, "we're not there yet."

### Laura and Jim—Letting Go of the Ideal Mother

In creating their third path, Laura and Jim, a couple DeGroot met in Philadelphia, wrestled not with the ideal worker but with with the pull of the ideal mother on Laura. "There was this period at the very beginning that I felt like I really needed to do everything at home—all the shopping, all the cooking, all the things related to our kids—plus go to work. I was driving myself crazy," Laura told me. "It was Jim who stopped me. He said, 'It doesn't make you a perfect mother because you wash every dish and clean every piece of clothing. What makes us a great family is we help each other.'"

At work, Laura, a partner in a public accounting firm, learned early on how productive she could be on a flexible schedule when she cared for her mother. "So when we started a family, what really made the difference was just being very up front and honest with my employer about what I was going to need," Laura said. "And then being confident enough to say, in a nicer way, 'You owe this to me. I earned it.'" Jim, a senior vice president at Citibank, came up with his own flexible work plan and sold his boss on it. Work is important, he said, "but my kids are four and two only once. I wanted to see it." Now the two work out of their home two days a week and share caring for their two toddlers, who are in preschool or with a babysitter for the other three days. Both use their home office time for conference calls and tasks that require quiet and concentration. On the days Jim works in his Manhattan office, he uses his commute time to plan and his office time for face-to-face meetings. The couple plan their calendars on a whiteboard at least one month in advance, and send each other Outlook invitations as reminders for whose turn it is to take the kids to the doctor or the date of a teacher conference. They have regular date nights and get away for a few days alone as a couple several times a year. "Jim and I have become very, very clear about what's important to us," Laura said.

The third path isn't easy, DeGroot said. But then again, neither is living with regret or in the overwhelm. "There are always going to be 'code red' moments when work and life collide," she said. "There's a myth that you can have everything. You can't. But you *can* have time for the things that are most important to you."

International surveys have found that majorities of men and women in most Westernized countries say marriages in which both partners share work, child care, and household duties are the most satisfying.[3] Research has found that when men and women share the housework, they have more sex,[4] and that the more equitably they share duties, the happier they both are.[5] Still, the gaping domestic divide, what social scientists call the "gendered division of labor," persists. The gap is narrowest at the top of the socioeconomic scale, among couples who have the resources to hire others to do the drudge work for them, and widest among couples with few resources.[6] Though men today certainly spend more time caring for their children and doing more chores than their fathers did, it is still about half of what women routinely do. Even though women's paid work hours have been on the rise, as a whole they are still nowhere close to men's. And since the mid-1990s, nothing's budged: Married fathers, on average, aren't doing more housework and child care. The number of mothers in the workforce has dipped, despite increasing numbers of women graduating from college and getting advanced degrees. And attitudes about whether fathers should be more involved at home and whether mothers can both work and have warm relationships with their children have, likewise, flatlined. Social scientists puzzling over the trends call it the stalled gender revolution.[7]

And no one is very happy about it. A host of surveys have found that arguing over housework is one of the main sources of conflict in relationships.[8] One survey in the U.K. found that women spend as much as three hours a week *redoing* chores that they think their partners have done badly.[9] Time studies show women are two and a half times more likely than men to interrupt their sleep to care for others, and they stay awake longer when they do.[10] Stress research is finding that when women come home from a long day at work, their stress hormone levels fall if their husbands help with the chores. But how's this for a twist? The study found that husbands' stress hormone levels fall only when their *wives* do all the housework and they are *relaxing*.[11] Even during the Great Recession, when more men began losing their jobs and more women took up the mantle of family breadwinner, time-use studies found that the division of domestic labor became slightly more fair, but only because working mothers stopped doing as much, not because unemployed fathers did more. And what did those unemployed fathers do with that extra time? They relaxed.[12]

Which might explain why psychologist Mihaly Csikszentmihalyi's time studies have found that men feel happier when their wives are present, but that women do not necessarily feel the reverse.[13] It might also explain his finding that men feel happier at home, and women when they go to work. Women, he found, reported feeling happiest around midday, when most were at work, and felt the worst between 5:30 and 7:30 p.m.—which most families know as the "witching hour" of flying to child-care pickup and squeezing tired kids, homework, dinner, baths, the detritus of bills and home stuff, and the hope of making meaningful connections into the space of a few hours. Men, in contrast, felt crummiest first thing in the morning and happiest in the evening, when they were heading home from work.[14] The media latched on to the study as another example of selfish working mothers gleefully ditching their kids. But let's think for a minute. If work is something working fathers are *supposed* to do, nonstop, unending for forty-plus years because they are the "providers," the stakes are high for them at work. They are under pressure to perform and always be on their toes. Home is a place of refuge. And, Csikszentmihalyi's studies found, men tend to have a choice whether to be involved in domestic duties. They tend to do only chores they like and tend to care for their kids only when they're in a good mood. What's not to like? For women, however, home, no matter how filled with love and happiness, is just another workplace.

Men and women, it turns out, not only do different things with their time but experience time itself differently, so much so that the groundbreaking work on the phenomenon is called "divergent realities."[15] Research has found that even when a family is engaged in the same activity—eating dinner—the mothers tend to feel frustrated that they aren't doing enough, while the fathers are proud of themselves that they've managed to get away from work to be there at all.[16] Csik-szentmihalyi, using his Experience Sampling Method, or ESM, tech-nique of paging people randomly throughout the day and asking not only what they are doing but also what they are thinking and how they feel, was one of the first to uncover how women's time is "contaminated."

No matter where they were or what they were doing, the women in his studies were consumed with the exhaustive "mental labor" of keep-ing in mind at all times all the moving parts of kids, house, work, errands, and family calendar. That, he wrote, only intensifies the feel-ing of breathless time pressure for women.[17]

It's no small wonder, then, that in surveys around the globe, women are more likely to report more chronic stress and the feeling that life is out of control than men.[18] It is no wonder that economists Betsey Stevenson and Justin Wolfers have found that women are unhappier today than forty years ago and that it is men who are happier later in life, while women are left with unfulfilled desires.[19]

To get the stalled gender revolution moving again, heterosexual couples need look no further than gay couples. An emerging body of research is finding that, free from provider father and ideal mother expectations, gay couples share labor more fairly and split tasks based on what people like to do or are good at doing. Gay couples tend to re-solve conflicts more constructively. And research has found that, un-like in heterosexual couples, where one partner may be happier than the other, gay partners tend to be equally happy.[20]

I called Patrick Markey, a psychologist and director of the Interper-sonal Research Lab at Villanova University and author of many of these studies.

"The biggest difference we see between heterosexual and gay cou-ples is the trait of openness. And because of that, gay and lesbian couples tend to be more egalitarian. They're much more willing to *share* power."

I spent an evening in the toy-filled house of Bill and Andy, partners of ten years, and their nine-month-old twins born by surrogate. Both have cut back on their work hours, work flexible schedules, and share caring for the babies. Both do laundry. They take turns cooking. Andy does the long-range planning. Bill pays the bills. With the help of their mothers, who live nearby, each takes time for himself. "I can honestly say that I don't feel at all imbalanced or that I'm doing more than he is, or that there's any ill will," Andy says. Bill, swaying with a baby on his hip, nods in agreement. "With two men, there's just no expectation for who does what."


To understand what happened in my own life, I did the one thing that came naturally to me as a reporter: I took out my notebook and pen and began asking questions. I ranted through twenty years of pent-up anger in weekly "active listening" sessions with Jessica DeGroot. I took long walks with Tom. We both slowly realized that we never *had* talked about what we really wanted. When we said we wanted to be equal partners, we had only a vague notion of what that meant.

In truth, Tom was always much more disciplined about his work hours, working efficiently, leaving when his work was done for the day to come home and make time for the family, and never buying into the face-time ideal worker culture in even the most toxic work environments. I was the one with work creep.

But we both came to see that the pivot point that had shifted the balance of labor, power, and time in our relationship arrived, just as De-Groot finds, with the birth of our first child. We never fought "the good fight." We just took our assumptions and swallowed them like a bitter pill. I assumed Tom would take parental leave, so we could share parenting. He'd always talked about wanting to be more active and involved with our kids than his own father had been. Instead, he took a few days of vacation after the kids were born. And, perhaps feeling guilty himself, he'd always cut me off whenever I pressed him about why he wouldn't take more time off all those years ago. One day, my notebook in hand, I asked him what really happened.

"I thought I'd be an equal partner," he said. "But where I worked at the time, it was just understood that taking parental leave wouldn't be a good thing to do. Only one father had, and he was a 'star.' I was wary of my position. I would now, though. It's much more accepted and I see young fathers doing it all the time."

"I was mad at you for years," I said. "Were you aware of that?"

"Yeah. But I was working in a really toxic atmosphere. There was always a lot of pressure to do more."

So I took the long maternity leave. I got to know everything about the baby. I became the default parent and we both assumed it was just "natural" anyway—an assumption I investigate in a later chapter. I flexed my schedule at work and, since I was at home more anyway, I began taking charge of everything else, too. As we talked, we began to see how the rest of our lives tipped the fulcrum even farther: When our daughter was born, she barely slept for two years and hated everyone but me. The kids started school in a Spanish immersion program and, truly, I was the only one who could help them with homework. Tom began to travel overseas every year. We came to see that just as the ideal worker pulled his strings, the ideal mother, crabby, sleep deprived, and "gatekeeping," kept a tight grip on mine. Tom became the fun parent, wrestling with the kids, mugging for the camera, changing a few diapers. And I, always the one behind the camera and nowhere in all the photo albums, did the invisible drudge work. So invisible, in fact, that, as we unspooled our lives, I discovered that Tom thought we really *had* divided things fairly. He was angry that I was angry all the time and felt I didn't give him credit for what he *did* do, which was so much more than his father had.

"And the fact that you didn't know where the dentist was? Never took them to the doctor? That I stayed home when they were sick? Planned all the kids' activities and summer camp . . . ?" I started one day.

"But that's the kind of stuff mothers do anyway, right?" he'd said. "I mean, what man do we know who does any of that?"

On that infuriating Thanksgiving afternoon I described at the beginning of this chapter, truly, the ideal worker and the ideal mother were both right there in the kitchen with us, clouding our vision. "Let's face it," Tom said, "without thinking much about it, men expect women to do all the stuff with kids and home. It's just the role they've always had. I've probably always had it in the back of my mind, too."

And, I came to see, so had I. Never asking for help because I thought I should do it all. Always deferring to his career as more important. Always assuming that if people saw a messy house, I, the negligent housewife, would be blamed. Watching angrily as he went to the gym, read the newspaper, and worked in long, interrupted stretches, but both of us thinking the reason I didn't was that I just couldn't get it together. Never realizing that it would take *both* of us to crawl out of the overwhelm.

"Looking back," Tom said one day, "we should have worked this out a long time ago."

So we started, finally, to try.

Now we take turns getting the kids to the dentist and the doctor. We take turns driving Liam to his drum lesson and picking Tessa up from swimming. Tom puts his e-mail on all the PTA, Cross Country team, Girl Scouts, and other Listservs so we both know what's going on, not just me. We trade off checking homework. Even if it's in Spanish, he can see whether it's been done. He cooks every night and I clean up. I empty the dishwasher in the morning. He loads. Last one out of bed makes it. The kids have their own chores, so I don't have the mind clutter of keeping track in my head. We have family meetings. Everyone is responsible for putting his or her own activities on the family calendar. If we miss something, too bad. Write it down next time. Each child can choose one field trip a semester for a parent to attend, then we schedule it. No more last-minute, wrenching requests that can really ruin your day.

Tom still grocery shops, but I rarely shop after him. When we're out of something, we're out. Even toilet paper. I wash and sort the clothes, but everybody folds their own—sometimes we'll have a "folding party" when we watch our family movie on Friday nights. I've even called up YouTube and had everyone watch a video on how to fold fitted sheets. I've made my invisible work more visible—once leaving the mass of bills and paperwork that I manage all over the dining room table for days, then showing Tom the files where everything goes, the book where I keep all the passwords, and how to manage the online accounts. We both now pay bills. I stopped weeding, so he could see that without effort, the tranquil Zen rock garden he loves so much becomes a fuzzy, overgrown Chia Pet. Then he and the kids started to pull them, too.

We had to agree on common standards—no doing the dishes in a burning house. No *Lion King* slobbery. Making the bed means not leaving the pillows on the floor. Doing the dishes means washing the pots in the sink and wiping the counters. When Tom at first kept shirking on the standards, I didn't just do it for him, like I had for years, figuring I was more efficient. I took a photo on my iPhone and sent him a text instead.

And we had to take time to think about what we really *wanted*— how finally becoming equal partners and sharing the load more fairly would free us from our usual crouch of anger and defensiveness and give us *both* time to do meaningful work, share moments of connection with each other and the family—and play. For Christmas, we cut down on giving stuff and started giving each other little "gifts of time." Tom and Tessa got "T-time" in the park and an afternoon together in an art studio learning how to make stained glass. I gave Liam "A Day of Yeses," when he got to choose what to do. For our anniversary, I told Tom I didn't want flowers. I wanted a love letter. Tom and I now have "cocktail minute" (who has an hour?) to check in with each other alone at the end of the day. We talk. We fight. We get it wrong. We get it right. Life changes. We adjust. We've learned some lessons. There will be countless more to come. But we're finally starting to learn them together. Here are just a few:

The Lesson of the Twinkie: Like any ideal mother, I signed up to bring baked goods to sell at Liam's school band concert. Then I forgot to bake something. The realization stabbed me right as we were on the way to the concert. We pulled into a nearby grocery store and Tom ran in. He came out not with the pretty cupcakes from the bakery that I'd asked for, but with two boxes of Twinkies. My inner Martha Stewart was mortified. "Are you kidding me?" Tom said. "It's middle school. They'll sell out in a heartbeat." And they did. I had to let Martha go.

Sometimes, Just Leave: Traveling to research the book was, honestly, probably the best thing I ever did. For everybody. The kids survived without me. Tom was forced to learn how to be the primary parent, and I left the ideal mother in storage and got to be just myself again. At first, I left entire packets of phone numbers and notes with the kids' schedules and activities, which were all ignored. (How do I know? The frantic text message that came in the middle of an interview in Copenhagen asking for the drum teacher's phone number, which was in the unopened packet.) But over time, Tom became more confident running the show, even flying solo for parent-teacher conferences. I let go. If a kid missed a flute lesson, she missed a flute lesson. If no one scooped the kitty litter, the cat would survive. And the kids got to see their mother in a new light. "I think it's cool you go off and have adventures," Liam said.

Camp Del Ray: This past summer, a group of five working families in our Del Ray neighborhood, sick of high camp fees, the stress of running around, and overscheduled kids, came up with a plan: For one week, each family would alternate taking a group of five girls for the day, giving everyone else four days to focus on work. Without my even asking, Tom, who *never* used to interrupt his work time for domestic stuff, suggested he take our day. He made the arrangements with the parents. He handled the flurry of e-mails. He took the girls to visit NPR and the Newseum, and out to lunch. And I had time to write this book.

# 9

# THE CULT OF INTENSIVE MOTHERHOOD

I always think of a good mother as . . . someone completely other than I am.   —Jean-Anne Sutherland, "Guilt and Shame: Good Mothering and Labor Force Participation"

At eleven o'clock one morning, Karen Graf had been going full tilt on the fumes of five hours of sleep before she realized she'd run out of the house that morning without putting deodorant on. She'd been focused on getting her three kids out of bed, dressed, fed, and off to school with the lunches she'd packed; flying out the door to buy another lunch box for the son who'd already lost two; swinging by Staples to pick up printer ink, and then dashing to the dry cleaner. It wasn't until she'd planted campaign signs for her upcoming school board election and was ready to start knocking on doors asking for votes that she became aware of her pungent omission.

Home for a quick dab, Graf dove into the rest of a day of what she herself calls "hyperparenting," most of it lived in her silver VW Routan van. Graf, forty-two, has shoulder-length brown hair and dark brown circles under her eyes, a genetic condition that makeup would help hide, she said, but who has time to put it on? She wears a white T-shirt, running shoes, and jeans with a rip in the knee. By the end of the day that I spent with her, she had ferried children to and from school, tutors, the orthodontist, the playground, home, a playdate, and back home again, her bright orange campaign signs in the back of the van clanking with every turn. She had forgotten to bring snacks for the kids, checks for the preschool school pictures and the tutor, and to pull something out of the freezer for dinner. She'd realized somewhere along the way that the car's tax sticker had expired. She'd apologized profusely for the "disastrous" state of her house, with the breakfast dishes still on the table, the Barbies, board games, rumpled Boy Scouts uniforms, and plastic toy soldiers strewn about. Between trips, she'd read to her daughter and played a game of Space Faces with her younger son, resting her tired head in her hands. She'd mused aloud about the constant tension between wanting to expose her children to everything and worrying that if she pushed them too soon they'd fail. "Mom!" her oldest son had called from the back of the van. "You *have* to make mistakes. That's how you learn!" She'd offered to take another busy mom's daughter for the afternoon and even managed to pick up *my* son from his cross-country practice. She'd made chicken tenders with her daughter for dinner, gotten the kids to bed, watched the Giants game with one eye while studying for the school board debate with the other, printed more campaign labels with the new printer ink, and fallen into bed about midnight for another night of five hours' rest. Before she drifted off, she wondered if she could have done more.

"I don't feel I do enough," she had told me. "I say it out loud and it sounds crazy. I look at my kids. They look happy. Why do I wonder why I'm not doing science projects with them every week, or worry that we don't go to museums more? When I was out knocking on doors in the neighborhood this morning, I noticed these little handmade decorations, and all I could think about was how my daughter's been wanting to make decorations with me. I'm always beating myself up that I'm not being more craft-y. There's just a scale you're constantly trying to rate yourself on."

Graf has a master's degree. She had a successful career in business for years before children, then nursed for seven and a half years straight after they were born. Wanting to be involved in their education, she has volunteered in their classrooms, been active in the PTA, spent two years completely reorganizing the avalanche of books in their elementary school's reading room, and is now campaigning for a seat on the school board. "It's intense. I know," she told me with a touch of embarrassment. "Sometimes I wonder—is this an American thing? Or is it just my personality?"

Or is she just trying to live up to the time-devouring, insanely high standards we've set for mothers today?

I had asked to spend a day in Graf's life not because she is an extraordinary mother, though she no doubt is a good one, but because she is a modern middle-class American Everymom.

American mothers of every stripe—working, at home, single—have not only ratcheted up the amount of time they spend with their children since the 1960s, but have also increased the intensity of that time, tripling the amount of "quality" interactive hours spent reading, talking, and playing. And the higher the education, the more time is spent with kids. Time intensity sparked at the very same time that the number of mothers working in the labor force nearly *doubled*. Now America has among the highest percent of working mothers of any country. They work among the most full-time hours. They clock the most extreme paid work hours. They do so despite laboring in some of the most demanding and unforgiving workplaces with the most family-unfriendly policies of any developed country on Earth. And, compared to mothers in other countries, American mothers spend among the most time with their children, sacrificing sleep, personal care, and leisure time to do so. Working mothers, like me, today spend as much time taking care of their children as at-home mothers did in the 1960s—about eleven hours a week, time studies have found. The time at-home mothers, like Graf, spend in child care has mushroomed to seventeen hours a week. (Father time increased from two to seven hours a week in the same period.) And that's just time mothers spend actively giving care. Working mothers spend forty-two hours a week *with* their children, more than half of all their waking hours not at work; at-home moms, a colossal sixty-four hours.[1]

And still, mothers tell time researchers, they don't feel it's enough.

The media is filled with stories of the control-freak helicopter mom hovering over her precious genius of a child, like the mother who sued her $19,000-a-year-preschool in New York for not sufficiently challenging her four-year-old.[2] It's a caricature most of us can look at with relief and say, "Well, at least I'm not *that* bad." But you don't get those kind of time diary numbers with a handful of whack-job chopper moms flitting about. You get those time-sucking numbers only if the *entire society* is in the grip of intensive mothering. I am certainly no exception. I've read the books, like Judith Warner laying out the "cult of Perfect motherhood" in *Perfect Madness*. I've followed the plethora of mom blogs and waded through the mind-blowing studies about how crazy perfectionist American mothers can be. I've witnessed the mompetition on the playground and see it every day on my mom Listservs. "Anyone know where I can find art classes for my toddler?" "Should I put my three-year-old in Mandarin?" I feel it in even the most casual conversations. The other day, a friend told me she'd signed her son up for a renowned fencing camp. "This could get him to the Olympics," she said. I was immediately seized with a blind panic that neither of my children was on track to get to the Olympics, castigated myself for failing them, and wondered for a split second if it was too late to start now.

The intensity starts early, with Mommy and Me classes and rushing after toddlers in the park to prevent a fall. It continues on through the school years with packed schedules of sports—"travel" teams earn special bragging rights—and endless enriching lessons with the "best" teachers and the projects like the Popsicle-stick dioramas of Fort Ticonderoga lovingly built in the wee hours of the night. (No, I didn't do that, but I did see it in a display case at a school.) The intensity superheats as college approaches. A friend of mine in Saint Louis has already been in touch with an expensive college-prep consultant who advised her to get her daughter to join clubs now where she can assume a leadership role. My friend's daughter is twelve. And the intensity, like an exploding supernova of angst, culminates with frustrated college admissions officials fielding e-mails about grades and class schedules and job recruiters asking parents to kindly not write résumés or sit in on interviews.[3]

Academics say intensive mothering is a white middle-class phenomenon. Middle-class mothers, researchers contend, practice "concerted cultivation" and invest time in their children as if they were high-yield bonds with long-term payout. Working-class mothers parent in a more hands-off "natural growth" way.[4] But I wonder. Time studies make the compelling case that everybody's ratcheted up the time spent with kids. And some of my reporting was finding a more complicated picture. When I met Elizabeth Sprague, thirty-one, a single mother of four in Frederick, Maryland, she was getting by on about $1,700 a month from child support and food stamps and trying to make a few bucks selling ads on the Internet while her children napped. Sprague had tried working, but not only was the cost of child care for four kids "insane," she worried that working was not something a "good mother" did. "Everyone likes to have a little treat in your life, so you don't want to be poor," she told me, nervously tugging her long blond ponytail. "But you also don't want to wonder what your child's doing all day while you're gone." When she came home from work one day and her baby smelled of another woman's perfume, the guilt was too much. She quit.

For generations, large percentages of African American mothers always worked, as did the mother of a woman named Kesha that I met through Mocha Moms, a nationwide support group for mothers of color. Yet Kesha, an MBA, dropped out of the corporate world to stay home with her children for a while. She felt pushed out by an unforgiving face-time ideal worker culture with little flexibility—many of her co-workers had at-home wives—that didn't allow her the time to take care of her children the way she wanted. At times, she has also felt the pressure to meet what she calls the "unobtainable standard of momdom." "For the past twenty years or so, there seems to be this mantra that motherhood is the hardest, most important, the best job in the world," she said. "I don't know where it started, sitcoms maybe, or *Oprah*. You hear it when people stake out their positions on it: 'The best kind of mother is the kind that can show their child that women can have it all!' 'No! The best mother is the one devoted to her child, to be there for any scrape or boo-boo!' 'The best mother provides a healthy immune system for her children by breast-feeding for two years!' Everyone is trying to fit into that role now." She talked to her own mother one day about how standards for mothers are so much higher now. "As I told her about what people expected mothers to do to raise a well-rounded child, I could see her brow starting to furrow," Kesha said. "Then her eyes got squinty and she looked at me with an expression like, 'Huh?' Then she said, 'Who is it that's coming up with all these new standards?'"

I wanted to know *why*. Why had the self-sacrificing ideal mother cultural icon grown to such monstrous proportions? Why were we spending so much of our precious time impossibly striving to be more like her, and flogging ourselves for always coming up short? Why were mothers bloodying one another with the interminable mommy wars between working and at-home mothers?

Unlike in the days before the pill or fertility treatments, couples today have fewer children, have them later in life, spend more on them, and tend to plan them. "Smaller family size contributes to the idea that each child is more precious, so you become more invested that each one turns out well," University of Maryland sociologist Melissa Milkie told me. "It's the *worrying* about that that makes mothering so much more intense."

Cultural ideals, like the ideal mother, are by their very nature unattainable, Milkie explained. "But the gap has never been as wide as it feels now between what we expect of a good mother and who we are."

So powerful has the ideal mother become that even the academics who study intensive mothering are not immune from her demands. Social psychologist Carin Rubenstein admitted ruefully in her book *The Sacrificial Mother* that she tracked down a classics scholar for her third grader to interview for a class project. Rebecca Deen, the chair of the political science department at the University of Texas, Arlington, found herself spending hours baking cookies, serving on the PTA, and organizing the "Friday Lunch Bunch" at her son's school. "My husband tells me, 'You're too intensive a mother. Why do you volunteer so much at school?'" she said. "And I say, 'Because it's important that his principal sees me, that his teacher knows that I'm *that* mother, the one who is there, not one of *those* mothers, who isn't.'"

*That* mother, who, of course, does *not* work and does *not* need help from her partner, husband, babysitter, or family, casts a long shadow, Deen and her colleague Beth Anne Shelton, a sociologist, found. In their study of the mother culture in school communities, they describe working mothers acting like "chameleons" and seeking to "pass" in the full-time mother culture. They wear the full-time mom "uniform" of sweatpants, casual clothes, or jeans. No one talks about whether she works or the flexible schedules or extravagant shuffling necessary to be at the school or a PTA meeting in the middle of the day. (Dads at the school had their own organization, but they met evenings or weekends.) Sometimes, a working mother would be found out only if she sent an e-mail from a work address. "These mothers view themselves as full-time moms, and they just add on their work identity," said Shelton, who confessed to being a chameleon mom herself. "Which leaves no time for anything else."

Throughout the chaos of her day, I was struck by how Graf maintained an aura of calm. I also had a few stabs of guilt as I, a working mother, watched her, an at-home mother, devote herself to her children in a way I've never had time to. Perhaps, I told her, she appears calm because she's confident she's closer to what an ideal mother should be. She shook her head. "Working moms like you feel guilty, worrying, 'Am I a good enough mom? Do I spend enough time with my kids?' And at-home moms like me are always asking ourselves, 'Am I doing enough? Is it the right thing? Should I be working? What was all that education for?' We're all torturing ourselves." Each one of us is ensnared in guilt and compelled to compensate for the phantom life we've forgone.

A few months after I met Graf, after she'd not only won her election to the school board but had been elected its chair, she flies in the door, fresh from picking her kids up from their playdates, and takes a rare moment to sit at her kitchen table and drink a cup of tea. Her husband is in India for work, and her mother, Janet Wood, is visiting from Pittsburgh to watch the kids while she goes to a school board conference. Graf has a burning question for her.

"I feel like you look at me and think I'm nuts," Graf says.

Wood, seventy-one, a quiet woman with kind eyes, looks puzzled.

"I mean, motherhood is so anxious and breathless now," Graf continues. "I feel like I have to expose my kids to so many things. There's so much pressure to take *every* path and there's *so* many activities they could do. I worry about them getting into college. And it feels like people are panicked because they can't identify the formula for success anymore."

Wood shakes her head. "No, I don't think you're nuts. I think you're amazing. I always refer to you as 'the Earth Mother,'" she says. "But I didn't feel the same pressure you do."

Motherhood was different a couple of generations ago, Wood says. Most women she knew back in the early 1970s stayed home to raise their children, just as she'd quit teaching when Graf was born. So there was never any searing doubt about whether they'd made the "right" choice. It was just what everybody did. It's not like parents didn't do crazy things to give their kids a leg up. "When you were born, your father bought a kaleidoscope with lights and had you look through it," Wood says, rolling her eyes. "It was supposed to make you smart." Wood put Graf and her sister into a few activities for fun, she says, but didn't feel as if the future depended on their excelling at them.

"And that's what feels different, too," Graf says. "There's such a seriousness that goes into activities now. The boys can't sign up for basketball unless they can make every game. I mean, when they're older, yeah, but they're seven and nine. Every weekend we're double booked with sports, Scouts, birthdays, and classes. It's just all so damn serious."

Wood nods. Growing up in California, Graf and her sister roamed the neighborhood and nearby park. And even then, Wood says, their freedom was nothing compared to what she herself had growing up. "We lived one block from the foothills. We'd pack a lunch and wander all over the woods, play in streams, at Dead Man's Pass, and no one ever worried about it," she says. "I think it's a shame that kids can't do that anymore."

The cult of intensive motherhood, I was discovering, runs on guilt, fear, and ambivalence. Let's start with guilt. Why do so many mothers who work for pay—three-fourths of all mothers of young children—feel they can never spend enough time with their kids? Probably because so many people have been telling them that they don't. Working mothers, I'd read again and again, "abandon" their children, "dumping them in care facilities," one conservative writer put it, "the way one might board a poodle."[5] Susan Chira, in her 1998 book, *A Mother's Place*, cataloged the rain of headlines through the years that reinforced that notion: "The Myth of Quality Time: How We're Cheating Our Kids." "Can Your Career Hurt Your Kids?" "Working Parents' Torment: Teens After School."[6] President Bill Clinton in a 1999 speech lamented how parents spent twenty-two fewer hours a week with their children than in the 1960s.[7] And a few years earlier, in 1991, the conservative Heritage Foundation published an article warning that "the biggest problem facing American children today is lack of time and attention from their parents."[8]

But if time studies show clearly that that *isn't* the case, that mothers are, in fact, spending more time and more intensive time with their children, why do so many people believe that it *is*?

Many, under the spell of the ideal mother, just want to. And others, it turns out, were influenced by the time study by none other than John Robinson, the University of Maryland time-use researcher who'd told me women had thirty hours of leisure. Back in the 1990s, Robinson crunched numbers showing that between 1965 and 1985 mothers' time with children dropped an alarming 40 percent. The media went wild, citing the statistic in more than fifty articles and several books and essays bemoaning absent mothers, latchkey kids, and the unraveling fabric of society.[9]

The only problem? The calculations were wrong.

Robinson quickly issued a correction. *U.S. News & World Report* published a thorough investigation, "The Myth of AWOL Parents," saying, "The tale of parental time famine is built on mistakes and misunderstandings."[10] Yet years later, when the incorrect figure was still being circulated in conservative circles, Robinson complained to Ann Crittenden in her book *The Price of Motherhood* that his mistake was being used by ideologues whose "agenda is to get women back into the home."[11] But the damage was done. Time studies now show that mothers' time with children has been climbing steeply, at the expense of sleep, personal care, and leisure, ever since . . . 1985.[12]

That strong, insidious, and sometimes unconscious cultural belief, that working mothers are bad mothers, and the pressure mothers feel to prove they aren't, drives much of working mother guilt, said Jean-Anne Sutherland, a sociologist at the University of North Carolina, Wilmington. Just as the pressure for at-home mothers to live up to the ideal mother drives theirs. Sutherland began studying intensive mothers and guilt when she had her first child. "I felt so guilty all the time. Guilty for staying at home. Guilty for going to work," she said. As she began interviewing mothers, she realized that the lofty ideal mother standards they all sought to meet were so unattainably high, they were mired in guilt no matter what they did. "Everyone thinks that everyone else is pulling this off. It makes you just want to hold a group meeting and say, 'Look, there's only 2 percent of us pulling this off and we don't like them, they're not any fun.' The rest of us are just getting by," she said. Yet even now, fourteen years after she began her first studies, Sutherland is not immune. "I have a friend who has three kids. She has chickens in the backyard. Her kids are on roller skates in the house. She has nine cats. It's bedlam and really fun and free-spirited," she said.

"And I've got my one daughter. I'm a single mom. I watch movies. My house is clean. And I so often say, 'I should let go more. I should have chickens.'"

Growing up in the 1930s and '40s, my mother had *one* birthday party, and she missed it because she stayed too long at a double feature. When I grew up in the 1960s and '70s, my birthday parties were tame affairs of party games like pin the tail on the donkey, a few friends, deliciously lopsided homemade angel food cake, and simple gifts like a jump rope. But for my kids, growing up in the aughts, I threw birthday party *extravaganzas* that sometimes took weeks to plan. It started when my son was a baby and we were invited to a one-year-old's birthday party. In a dizzying flash, I learned how far the childhood world order had shifted. There were *ponies*. When my son's birthday came along, I felt compelled to hire a woman to sing songs and play instruments. Like I couldn't do that? I bought a cake from a bakery so it would look perfect with those gorgeous squares of frosting in the shape of baby presents. I know the toddlers would just as gladly have smooshed any manner of sweet confection, or fingers, or dirt, into their mouths. But I remember watching as if outside myself. On one level, I knew it was ridiculous. But on another, I couldn't seem to help myself.

The singer birthday party was followed by a spate of Moon Bounce birthday parties, gymnastics parties at a nearby rec center, astronaut parties, *High School Musical*–themed parties, go-kart parties, disco parties, tea parties, candy-making parties. The birthday mania reached its apex when I staged a full-out 101st Airborne D-day assault for my *Band of Brothers*–obsessed son when he turned eight, and borrowed plaster Ionic columns and turned the backyard into Mount Olympus for my daughter's Greek Goddess birthday.

I'm embarrassed to even be writing about what we—I—threw for our kids. At the time, the parties seemed so normal, right in line with the pirate or Hawaiian-themed parties, nature walks, and science experiments hosted by their friends. It's just what everybody did. Marketers figure the average parent spends hundreds of dollars to create "birthday magic" for a child's party.[13] The Learning Channel has even hosted a show called *Outrageous Kid Parties* that featured red carpets, spa treatments, Ferris wheels, circus clowns, aerial acts, fire trucks, and gatherings of 350 people that ran anywhere from $30,000 to $60,000. "I will do anything for my kids," announced one mother.[14] Karen Graf, too, has spent hundreds of dollars on her children's birthdays, only to have her son rave about a friend's party that was little more than a rousing game of tag. Perhaps we parents are reliving our own childhoods, as some academics surmise. Sociologists would argue that we're displaying our social status to one another. But honestly, it didn't feel like I was showing off, recapturing my youth, or keeping up with the Joneses. Rather, for me, it felt like I was "proving" to whoever was watching that I, too, was a good mother, even if I worked, wearing these birthday parties like the proud peacock feathers of mother love.

Then there is fear. Fear of the future.

To Margaret Nelson, a sociologist at Middlebury College in Vermont and author of *Parenting Out of Control*, the panic started creeping into mothering in the early 1970s, as stable, high-paying manufacturing and blue-collar jobs went overseas or industries shut down. As factories closed, studies began emerging showing that those with college degrees earn at least $1 million more over their lifetimes than someone with a high school diploma.[15] College became the only sure path to upward mobility, and, to nervous parents, the more elite the college, the better. "Middle-class and professional-class parents are desperately frantic. They want to make sure their children aren't left behind," she told me. "There's so much competitiveness because the stakes are so high."

And we're afraid of what we're doing, or not doing, to our babies' brains.[16] A baby's brain weighs three-fourths of an adult brain, but it is twice as active. Each neuron becomes stronger and more powerful, growing branching tendrils of axons and dendrites at warp speed and making as many as ten thousand new connections each. That's a *quadrillion* new connections—twice that found in an adult brain—by the time a child turns three.[17] All those tiny little neurons, we mothers were warned, needed to be properly "stimulated" or they would *disappear forever* before our babies could drink without a sippy cup. You could so easily be a bad mother, dulling your child's potential, if you didn't spend hours twirling those expensive black, white, and red mobiles over their heads, playing Mozart, or plopping them in front of those weird Baby Einstein videos that look like something out of an acid-tripping Grateful Dead concert.[18]

And we feel sheer terror about everything else. So much hover-inducing terror, in fact, that Eden Kennedy, a writer and librarian, satirized it in *Let's PANIC About Babies!* We worry that we're not forging the kind of close connections with our children that we wished we'd had with our own mother, so we spend countless hours with them, she said. We can't escape a gnawing distrust that the school system just isn't doing enough, so we have to make up for it at home. Dread seeps in with every new report of a child abduction[19] or school shooting. So we keep our kids inside, arrange playdates, go with them to the park, or fill their time with activities. And there's the apprehension that, as Karen Graf says, in an unpredictable world, no one knows the formula for success anymore. "I get the feeling that if I don't really prepare my child for all that he's worth, there's going to be nothing for him," Kennedy said. "It feels like there's no security. So if he needs to be able to stand on his own two feet and use his wits, I've just *got* to make sure he gets an A on that history test!"

She'd love to stop worrying. "But it takes courage," she said. "You get so criticized for that."


That criticism for daring to defy the ideal mother is the flying shrapnel of the bloody mommy wars, which are fought on the battlefield of ambivalence. The massive social upheaval of the latter half of the twentieth century that sent women to college and propelled them into the working world of men was so profound and came so fast that no one is sure what a "good" mother looks like anymore. Which mother represents the "right" family values? What's the "best" way to raise kids? The ambivalence keeps everyone looking over her shoulder, peering across her back fence, comparing, judging, competing, and running to check out the latest parenting fad in search of more certainty. Walk into any bookstore and you'll find shelves lined with twenty-five different books by twenty-five different authors urging you to parent in twenty-five different ways. Experts are followed with near fanaticism. I attended a class in Portland, Oregon, where an attachment parenting expert showed parents how to fashion slings, wraps, and carriers around their bodies to comfortably wear their increasingly heavy babies until the age of three.

How to potty train, whether to breast- or bottle-feed, which kind of diapers to use are all loaded subjects. Broaching them in public can be like taking the pin out of a grenade. You do so at the peril of ruining parties, destroying friendships, and seeing your confidence that you're doing the right thing utterly shredded. The combination of ambivalence and the American drive for success keeps everyone off-kilter. "We live in an achievement-oriented society," said Sharon Hays, a sociologist and author of the seminal book on intensive mothering, *The Cultural Contradictions of Motherhood*. "It makes perfect sense that you have to pay attention to every new fad, to have knowledge of all the BEST new ways to parent, to not just be as good as the Joneses, but to be *better* parents than the Joneses."

If working mothers are judged as selfish women who abandon their children, then mothers at home are criticized as bad feminists. Though they're praised as better mothers, the work they do, not only at home but also keeping schools, churches, and community organizations running, remains unappreciated and invisible. Both sets contribute to the cult of intensive motherhood. What researchers will tell you is that educated at-home moms have turned motherhood into a profession. And working moms overcompensate for their guilt by overdoing. Then both sides try to outdo the other (or at least keep up). And both get whipsawed by the culture's schizophrenic ambivalence. Sociologists analyzing mother magazines have found that while the articles tend to center on working mothers and dismiss at-home mothers as superficial, all the images glorify the domestic bliss created by the ideal mother.[20]

Just venture into the anonymous no-woman's-land of parenting Listservs and mom blogs on the Internet and it can sometimes feel as if you've landed in the middle of a brutal Mothering Civil War. Every new study is quickly devoured and used as ammunition to shore up one's position or hurl a new fusillade of abuse at the other. Working moms are happier![21] At-home moms cook, shop, and play more with their kids![22] Working moms are healthier![23] At-home moms' kids are exposed to fewer germs![24] Kathryn Masterson, a journalist and bewildered expectant mom, writing in D.C.'s *City Paper* brilliantly—and depressingly—captured this scarred landscape by tracking the anonymous mortar attacks on the popular Listserv DC Urban Moms over . . . *strollers*. "Bugaboo is rich and trend-oriented. Maclaren is highly-educated upper-middle class. Graco is low class," one mother wrote.

One self-described "highly educated" Tahoe-driving, quilted jacket–wearing Georgetown mother and Bugaboo owner let loose. "I don't give a damn if you all judge me," she wrote. "We probably wouldn't be friends if we met at the park and that's fine too."

And the flame war was on. In nineteen pages of comments, mothers hurled assumptions about others' class, education, income level, and the depth of their love for their children. Epithets began flying. Until the final death blow landed and silenced the stroller skirmish: "You are a planet killer, waste your money, and dress your kids funny. How can one not judge you?"[25]

The war of experts didn't begin with this generation. Consider this bit of expert advice from Granville Stanley Hall, the founder of child psychology, in 1899: "All that rot they teach to children about the little raindrop fairies with their buckets washing down the window panes must go. We need less sentimentality and more spanking." Luther Emmett Holt, one of the founders of pediatrics, said that the less playing with infants the better. Screaming, he wrote, was "the baby's exercise."[26] Up until the First World War, most middle-class households employed servants who, like Mary Poppins, did most of the child rearing—nearly half of all women who worked for pay at that time were domestics.[27] When working-class women went to work in factories and middle-class women were left to their own devices, experts warned that they were too emotional to parent and shouldn't "smother" children and should instead keep them to strict schedules.[28]

That impersonal parenting approach was followed by a more permissive era in the 1930s. That trend was quickly disparaged in Philip Wylie's bestselling 1942 book, *Generation of Vipers*, which warned that too much mother love would "infantilize" children. The pendulum swung back with the self-sacrificing, indulgent TV mothers of the 1950s like Donna Reed. Then came the "benign neglect" of the 1960s. Then the women's movement, parts of which denigrated marriage and motherhood as institutions of an oppressive patriarchy, and now intensive mothering.

These days, even as mothers put in extreme hours on the job, the New Domesticity movement urges the ideal mother to raise chickens, grow organic gardens, knit, can vegetables, and even homeschool her children.

The number of children being homeschooled in America—two

million—equals the number attending charter schools.[29] And now, homeschooling mothers are not just religious, as was the case in the past. A growing number are like Lisa Dean, who graduated from Vassar and Georgetown Law and gladly gave up a stressful sixty-hour-a-week job as a real estate lawyer to homeschool her two children. When Dean founded the Columbia Homeschool Community in Maryland in 1999, she had four members. By 2012, when she hit 225 families and 500 kids, she had to close the membership because the organization was getting too big. Homeschooling is a big industry now, with books, materials, and special days set aside for homeschooler field trips at places like Colonial Williamsburg. "Homeschooling sucks up every moment of your life," she told me. Dean recounted staying up until 4 a.m. preparing lessons. She's the kind of teacher who, when they were studying Rembrandt, sewed a mop cap for her daughter so she could look like someone he might have painted. She had her kids dissect a cow's eyeball in the kitchen and has turned every vacation into an educational experience, with daily journaling and creative essays due afterward. She organized monthly homeschool get-togethers, homeschool proms, homeschool field days, homeschool Christmas pageants. She took her children to mosques when they studied Islam, started classes at 11 a.m. when their teenage brains needed more sleep, and had days when they all stayed in their pajamas and just read. She organized summer camps where kids played in the creek behind her house and when the cicadas swarmed, baked insect cookies with them. "Perhaps I'm guilty of being the worst helicopter parent ever," she said. "But I don't think I could have found a way to spend my time in any way that was actually more valuable."

So who's right? What's best? More important, how do we stop this "perfect madness"?


A group of mothers sits around a long table at a busy café in Portland, Oregon. For more than a year they've been coming together, quietly seeking refuge from the cult of intensive mothering all around them, trying to answer those questions. As they order organic hors d'oeuvres and glasses of wine, they explain how they've been exhausted by the mommy wars. They've driven the car pools, raced children to and from lessons, worried over homework, and flown mission after mission as helicopter moms. They've known the fear, the guilt, the ambivalence. They've felt the competition from the parents who teach their sixth graders calculus to give them an edge. They've tried to be perfect. And they've had enough. They want to stop feeling, as one mother put it, that time is racing past "like a rabid lunatic," and figure out not how to live up to the unreachable standards of the ideal mother, but how to set their own.

Some mothers work full-time, others own their own businesses, work part-time, work at home, or care for their children full-time. They call their group Simplicity Moms, for yes, they, too, have been following an expert—one who advocates a style he calls Simplicity Parenting. But, really, the book is cover, a reason to come together and, if only for an hour a week, step out of the mothering madness long enough to see how they got in and help one another find a way out. The Simplicity Moms live far from their own mothers, grandmothers, sisters, aunts, and the wise older women who could look at them with squinty eyes and, like Kesha's mother, ask, "Who is it that's coming up with these standards?" Then tell them to breathe. So they're trying to do that for one another.

"Honestly, it's not all that hard to just give in and go with the inertia," one mother says.

"Inertia?" I ask. "Isn't that the force that keeps you from moving?"

"I mean the inertia of going along with doing what everyone else is doing," she says. " 'Have you signed up for this class?' 'Your children must do this.' 'They really should try that.' It takes so much conscious effort to pull back."

Another mother, Jen Yoken, admits it took a hurricane to make her realize how unlivable her life had become. For two weeks, the family lived without power, sleeping on makeshift mattresses on the laundry room floor and eating out of whatever cans they had in their pantry. "I thought I would have a nervous breakdown at first, but then I realized I'd never felt calmer," she says. "We lit candles. The kids set up a tent. We had no choice but to live simply." And she wanted to keep that spirit alive once the power returned.

Cassandra Dickson, a writer, attended Quaker schools, so she has always been drawn to the beauty of living a simple life. She was the one who first sought others who wanted out of intensive mothering. "It just seemed that there was this new kind of vertigo in the world and everyone was thinking it was just them. There was a bit of a code of silence so no one could talk about it," Dickson explains. "When you can share stories, when you can be vulnerable within a group, then you grow and feel stronger. There's an opportunity to make real change, even if it's small."

The Simplicity Moms will be the first to tell you they haven't figured it out yet. But they're trying. When I met with them, they had given one another an assignment to find time for themselves, which, most admitted, had never been a priority.

"I sat on the landing in the sun, just trying to be present. Then I started feeling guilty, like 'Oh, my gosh, I'm spending fifteen minutes trying to do nothing," says Megan Galaher. "But at least I got my fifteen minutes in this week."

"It was supposed to be fifteen minutes a *day*," says Dickson.

They've worked to create rituals like regular family dinners as predictable "anchors" in the chaos and "islands of calm" of unscheduled time for themselves, their children, and their families. Now that one of Dickson's daughters has become swept up in competitive gymnastics, Dickson makes sure the two have a quiet moment to share a pot of tea together. The mothers try to help one another see that the supercharged "special" moments they're always trying to pump up for their children are far less valuable than the beauty of the ordinary ones—the spontaneous dancing or the jokes that can break out while the family cleans the dinner dishes—moments of unadorned grace that unfold when you're not distracted and rushing into the next big thing.

Mary-Beth Frerichs was in the process of simplifying her entire life when she joined the group. She quit her corporate job to start her own business. She let her son cut his activities to just one sport that he really liked. The group helped her to stop and think before she acted: "Do I really *want* to bake these cupcakes, or am I just doing it so people won't think I'm a bad mom?" She began saying no to invitations that felt like obligations. Slowly, the family found themselves in the middle of lingering weeknight dinners and taking spontaneous ski trips on the weekend because they didn't have three other things on the calendar. "I'm *feeling* more than ever—more sadness, more joy. When I was on the treadmill, I just didn't have the time," she says, a little surprised. "I feel more . . . alive."

Kathy Masarie, a pediatrician and parent coach, has been meeting with the Simplicity Moms and urging them to keep on with their imperfect experiment, because taking on the ideal mother is hard to do alone. As social creatures wired to fit in with the crowd, sometimes the only way to push back against the craziness the crowd demands, she said, is to create a different, smaller crowd of your own. Do it, she said, to save not just your own sanity but also your children's. "What this intensive mothering culture *tells* us is valuable is at discord with what really *is* valuable: Love your kids. Keep them safe. Accept them as they are. Then get out of their way."

# BRIGHT SPOT: MOTHER NATURE

Women are just as prone as other apes to worry about the well-being of new babies. But what hunter-gatherer mothers do not do postpartum is refuse to let anyone else come near or hold their baby. This is an important difference . . . Babies are never left alone and are constantly held by someone, but that someone is not invariably the mother.

—Sarah Blaffer Hrdy, *Mothers and Others*

She [the Angel in the House] was intensely sympathetic. She was immensely charming. She was utterly unselfish. She excelled in the difficult arts of family life. She sacrificed herself daily. If there was chicken, she took the leg; if there was a draught she sat in it—in short she was so constituted that she never had a mind or a wish of her own, but preferred to sympathize always with the minds and wishes of others.

—Virginia Woolf, "Professions for Women"

I pull up to Sarah Blaffer Hrdy's walnut farm in the foothills of the Vaca Mountains in northern California and park near a grove of elegant cypress trees. The hacienda-like house is open, gracious, and filled with the colorful folk and tribal art she's collected during more than thirty years of fieldwork studying the mothering of monkeys, apes, and other primates in order to better understand the maternal behavior of our own primate species. Hrdy, a Harvard-trained evolutionary anthropologist, member of the National Academy of Sciences, professor emeritus at the University of California, Davis, and one of the world's foremost experts on mothering, leads me into her large farm kitchen. She corrals her enthusiastic Rhodesian ridgebacks, pours me a cup of coffee, and slides me a bowl of walnuts.

I had sought out Hrdy because, to be honest, after my afternoon with Pat Buchanan and my foray into intensive mothering, I was confused. Was it better, indeed "natural" as some argued, for mothers to stay home with their children? Were women, as one of my at-home mother friends liked to argue, simply biologically "wired" to be the primary caretaker, so why fight it? Should I, like the self-sacrificing "Angel in the House" from the popular Victorian poem by Coventry Patmore that Virginia Woolf railed against, just quit the job? Sit in the draft? Take the smallest serving? Eat the burned toast? Drive the car pool? Wear those helicopter wings with pride? Was this whole endeavor to understand time at work, at home, and whether I, as a mother, deserved to have time to play somehow just a futile and ill-advised upending of the natural order?

Tall, willowy, and soft-spoken, with a hint of her Texan upbringing, the sixty-five-year-old Hrdy wants me to look at a photograph of a !Kung woman. The woman, part of a hunter-gatherer tribe in the Kalahari Desert in Africa who live much like early humans did some two hundred thousand years ago in the Pleistocene era, is eight months pregnant. She carries a twenty-five-pound bag of mongongo nuts she's gathered and a five-pound bag of water and food. Her thirty-pound four-year-old son rides on her shoulders. Hrdy estimates the mother has carried the boy about forty-nine hundred miles so far in his lifetime.

"This is a working mother," she says. "The whole idea that mothers stayed at camp and the men went off to hunt? No way! These women were walking thousands of miles every year with their children. Or if it was not safe, they were leaving them back at camp." She pauses to drive that point home: Sometimes mothers *left their children back at camp.* The children were with their fathers, older siblings, grandparents, relatives, and other trusted, nurturing adults—people Hrdy calls "alloparents" ("allo" means "other than" in Greek). "It's natural for mothers to work. It's natural for mothers to take care of children," she says. "What's unnatural is for mothers to be the *sole* caretaker of children. What's unnatural is not to have more *support* for mothers." And not just mothers who work outside the home. "Moms who stay at home still need and deserve a lot of help," she says.

With so much support from alloparents early in human evolution, mothers' lives were more integrated between work and home, she says. "What's different today is that the workplace is no longer compatible with being a mother. It's as simple as that."

It's not so much that women are wired to be mothers—in fact, Hrdy argues in her pioneering book *Mother Nature* that women aren't. They are wired to have sex. And if there's enough fat on her and she's ovulating, she'll get pregnant. That's why human babies evolved to be born roly-poly and so darn cute, she says. That's why they are so good at staring deeply into adult eyes and reading emotions. To survive, human babies early on had to learn to counteract what Hrdy calls natural maternal ambivalence until they could latch on and breast-feed and the flood of milk-producing prolactin and feel-good oxytocin hormones coursed through a mother's body and bonded her to the baby.

And now, science is discovering that men, too, are wired to bond with and nurture babies. For years, the fact that some men gain weight and experience morning sickness while their wives or partners are pregnant—so-called couvade syndrome—was dismissed as psychosomatic. That is, until scientists found that primates like male marmosets and cotton-top tamarins do the same thing. Researchers are now finding that fathers, like mothers, produce high levels of the hormones cortisol and prolactin. Cortisol, the fight-or-flight stress hormone that, when it's constantly flooding the body, can cause so much damage, is also linked to infant bonding and empathy. Prolactin, which stems from the word "lactate," is what stimulates breast milk for a woman and, for a man, is associated with greater responsiveness to a baby's cry. A father's level of the aggressive male hormone testosterone drops by about one-third in the first three weeks after a child's birth. And brain studies in certain primates are finding that fatherhood enhances regions needed for planning and memory, two critical parenting skills.[1] What does that mean? Male parental care is so important that their bodies physically change to adapt to it. "Men," Hrdy says, "have tremendous capacity for nurture."

How is it, then, that mothers have come to be seen as the "natural" carers? Time, Hrdy says. There is no doubt that there are biological differences between men and women, though both have innate nurturing instincts that await "activation." Whatever brain gender differences may exist, solid neuroscience has found that it's not so much that men and women are *born* with different brain wiring but that, over time, the malleable brain is more likely to be shaped by *life experiences.*[2] Hrdy argues that with time and experience, what may start as slight differences between men and women—regardless of whether they're biologically innate or socially programmed—become magnified. And that was as true in the Pleistocene era when men left camps for extended periods to hunt as it is today, when men are still largely expected to be breadwinners going off to work.

Once a baby is born, Hrdy says, women don't just instinctively know what to do. But with extended time alone with the new baby—brought on typically because of breast-feeding, maternity leave, and custom—they learn through trial and error and experience. So they're able to clue in faster than men to what a baby needs. Most men simply have not had as much time on their own, she argues, to develop the same competence and confidence. And when fathers do have time and proximity to their children, they are far more likely to actively share in raising them. Researchers studying the Aka pygmies of Central Africa found that when a family lives near a mother's kin, her extended family helps so much that the father cares for his children only about 2.6 percent of the time. But when the family lives near *his* family, where she has less support and his becomes critical, he takes on nearly two-thirds of the care.[3]

To test the theory that time and experience are what magnify even small differences, Hrdy explains that social scientists timed response rates in new parents. Both mothers and fathers responded in a flash when they heard a recording of a wailing baby. Hrdy snaps her fingers. But if the baby was merely fussy, the researchers found mothers responded just a little bit faster.[4] (The opposite is true in the response times for primates like titi monkeys, Hrdy found, and titi infants "naturally" prefer their fathers.[5]) In humans, "the difference in response time is very small. The man has the capacity to respond, but her threshold is just a little lower," Hrdy says. "What this means over time is, the baby frets and Mom picks the baby up and soothes the baby. The baby gets used to Mom. So then the dad comes and, if Mom isn't there, picks the baby up. The baby is not quite as familiar with the father and keeps on fretting. And the dad starts to think, 'Why do I bother? The baby wants its mother.' As [biologist] Ed Wilson put it, 'At birth the twig is already bent a little bit.' But through experience, over time, the gender gap widens." Imagine, she says, if changing workplaces and gender norms enabled fathers to have more time alone early on with babies. "These are exciting times."

If humans are wired for anything, Hrdy argues, it's to trust and care for one another. Infants have evolved to instinctively scan the world for people they can count on, appeal to, and elicit care from—not just parents, but alloparents. It's an impulse, Hrdy says, born of a long human history of what she calls "cooperative breeding." In brain scans of adults looking at images of babies' faces, neuroscientists have found that reward centers and brain regions associated with communication, attachment, and caregiving instantly activate. And not just in parents' brains but also in the brains of adults with no children at all.[6]

Other primates that share so much ancestral DNA with humans—chimpanzees, gorillas, orangutans—leave the care of infants exclusively to the mother, as do about half of the 276 species of primates. So, since the time of Charles Darwin, mostly male scientists assumed the same was true for humans. But humans are different. Anthropologists studying primitive hunter-gatherer bands like the !Kung, Hazda, Aka, and Efe report that in every one, babies are passed around to others—both male and female—almost from the moment of birth. And everyone helps care for and feed the children. Among the Efe of Central Africa, researchers found that babies average fourteen different caretakers in the first days of life. By the time a child turns four, he or she will have spent 60 percent of his or her daylight hours in the arms of alloparents.[7]

How did that cooperation get started? Survival, plain and simple. "If mothers didn't have social support from alloparents, they didn't have children," Hrdy says, "because the children would be dead."

Cooperative breeding, Hrdy argues, is responsible for the uniquely long human childhood and a key reason why humans developed such an enormous brain. In short, it is this very novel drive for people to share in the care and feeding of the young that made us human in the first place.

She lays out her argument for me: No mammal in the world takes longer than humans to grow to adulthood. It takes more than thirteen million calories to raise a human child from infancy to independent adulthood. In the Pleistocene, as now with hunting-and-gathering societies, meat from the hunt accounted for no more than 30 to 40 percent of those calories. "Hunting was always a very dicey occupation," Hrdy says. "A man could go out for days and days and not come back with anything." And when the hunters did return, the meat was often divided up with politics in mind—currying favor with this powerful male, repaying that friend, forging ties with another. So for a child to survive—and nearly half did not—they needed to get 60 to 70 percent of their diet from foraging. There was simply no way one mother could supply all that food on her own, or even a mother and a father. They needed the help of alloparents. So much so that anthropologist Kristen Hawkes, who observed that older Hazda women past childbearing age were the hardest-working and most efficient gatherers of food, came up with the "grandmother hypothesis"—that human women, alone among primates, survive so long after menopause *because* they have been such valuable alloparents.[8]

Sharing care and staving off starvation are what enabled human childhood to become long in the first place, Hrdy theorizes, just as the young of other animals that share care have longer periods of dependency. And that longer childhood, she says, "was a wonderful opportunity for big brains to evolve." Sharing care may have also forced adult brains to become more sophisticated in order to cooperate and share information. Chimpanzees, with their mother-only care and shorter childhoods, she says, have brains that are two and a half times bigger than you'd expect, given the size of their bodies. Human brains are nearly seven and a half times larger.[9] "Somehow the early Darwinian models just assumed humans evolved to have big brains because the males were going to be better hunters. Or we evolved to have big brains because the males were going to be better fighters," Hrdy says. "What was going on with mothers and infants wasn't taken into account. Even though where the rubber hits the road is child survival. You could have all this mating and it doesn't matter if none of those offspring survive."

Hrdy takes me on a walk outside through the walnut farm. She explains that she began her own quest to understand motherhood after delivering the first of her three now grown children. She found herself torn between desperately wanting to succeed in her career, feeling a "whirring resentment" of her husband who left for long periods of concentrated work every day, and being desperate to give her "luscious" newborn the best care. Hrdy herself was raised by a series of governesses. But at the time, she was deeply influenced by psychoanalyst John Bowlby's new attachment theory—that the more responsive and consistent a mother is with an infant early on, the more secure the child will grow to be. (Bowlby later modified his view and came to realize, like Hrdy, the importance of alloparents.) Hrdy was worried. If she left her child to go to work and delegated care to others, would she be reverting to the unenlightened ways of her mother's generation or, worse, depriving her infant of emotional security? A nagging question lurked in the back of her mind: "Am I a bad mother?"[10]

Those conflicting feelings between wanting to work—in a demanding field with few women and fewer mothers—wanting a parenting partner in her husband, and wanting to give her children the emotional security they needed, propelled thirty years of research that is now considered unparalleled in redefining our understanding of human evolution and the roles of mothers and fathers. "Even what I failed to learn in time to help me rear my own three children, I could pass on to others," she writes in *Mother Nature.*

She's still a firm believer in attachment theory, but her own research, as well as her own experience with her husband and an array of loving child-care providers, nannies, au pairs, housekeepers, teachers, family members, and nurturing friends, showed her that infants and children develop emotional security from having close relationships to caring people around them. "It's like I had a community helping me raise my children," she says. As her children grew, her husband became the primary parent on the weekends, allowing her uninterrupted time to concentrate on her own thinking and writing. Her children did get the responsive and consistent care they needed, she says, they just didn't get it only from her. "She's a fabulous mother," her daughter, Katrinka, a history teacher and crew coach in upstate New York has said. "She feels bad about the time when she was busy with research, but I don't remember that."[11]

For people living far from extended family or a "tribal" network of supportive alloparents, Hrdy says, it's imperative to create your own.

Even conservative Phyllis Schlafly raised her six children—and got a law degree and traveled the country giving speeches urging mothers to stay home, railing against feminism and working mothers, calling child care "stranger care," and organizing protests against the Equal Rights Amendment—with the help of alloparents. "She had domestic help . . . She wouldn't have called them nannies, but she had people in her home," Schlafly's niece, writer Suzanne Venker, told the *Los Angeles Times.* "Did she mention that fact enough to get her point across to young people about how she managed to do it? No, she did not."[12]

# 10

# NEW DADS

Were I Queen, my principal affirmative action plan would have three legs. First, it would promote equal educational opportunity, and effective job training for women, so they would not be reduced to dependency on a man or the state. Second, my plan would give men encouragement and incentives to share more evenly with women the joys, responsibilities, worries, upsets, and sometimes tedium of raising children from infancy to adulthood. (This, I admit, is the most challenging part of the plan to make concrete and implement.) Third, the plan would make quality day care available from infancy on. Children in my ideal world would not be women's priorities, they would be human priorities.                              —Ruth Bader Ginsburg

Two dads sit on blankets with their toddlers in a sunny park in Albuquerque at 3:30 one Friday afternoon. Todd Stenhouse holds his squirming son, Rhys, in his lap and reads him a thick colorful board book. Howard Kaibel feeds his daughter, Iris, pineapple slices from a Tupperware container. A third father arrives, carrying a big pink diaper bag embossed with a giant purple elephant, and quickly drops the bag to run after his daughter, Lilly, as she totters toward the sandy playground and babbles gleefully about her new fuzzy hat.

Kaibel and Stenhouse share a look. "Lilly's quite a talker. And she's not yet two," Kaibel says with just a hint of both admiration and worry. "Iris isn't saying much yet." Stenhouse assures him it's absolutely normal for toddlers to develop verbal skills at different rates. "Want to stand?" Stenhouse holds fourteen-month-old baby Rhys by the arms and lets him march his fat toddler legs. Now Stenhouse is the one cha-grined. "He's not walking yet," Stenhouse says as he watches the girls wobble busily about the playground. This time, Kaibel is the one to offer assurance that that's normal. For the next hour, the men push their children on swings, follow them on tricycles, answer each incessant question with patience, catch them before they fall—"Gotcha!"—dust them off when they don't—"Baboom!"—and take their little ones on endless trips down the big red slide. With Kaibel, I stopped counting after seventeen. "Go down, Daddy! Go down!" Iris shouts again and again. Another father runs after his son, Benjamin. "Gotta make sure he doesn't crap in his pants."

The men are part of an Albuquerque Dads Meetup group that Kaibel organized. Some of the forty or so dads in the group work part-time, like Kaibel. Some work full-time or flexible hours, like Benjamin's dad. Some share equal loads of work and child care with their spouses, Kaibel says, like Lilly's dad. Some are at-home dads, like a gay dad with triplets, and like Stenhouse, who lost his job in the mortgage industry when the market crashed in 2008. Others are shift workers, like a fa-ther who takes over child care when his wife works her nursing shifts. The dads are casual, texting one another before they head to the zoo, perhaps. When they get together, the men don't talk a lot. The conver-sation usually drifts from what to do when there's no changing station in the men's bathroom to the latest hockey game. There is no competi-tion among them. Kaibel freely admits he's terrible at dressing Iris and, for the longest time, put her clothes on backward or inside out. None of the other dads even noticed. "We all know we're going to do this our own way," Kaibel says. Though there is nervous laughter as dads recount sons or daughters slinging purses over their shoulders, like their wives do, and announcing, "I go work!" They are in uncharted territory, cast-ing off the ideal worker and provider father roles. And everyone's a little off-balance. "It's one of the big reasons I started the group," Kaibel says. "I knew if I was having a tough time, others were, too."

Many of the men are flying blind, with no role models to guide them. When Kaibel was growing up in Minneapolis, his own father, a public defender and administrative law judge, worked constantly. Kaibel's mother took care of the kids. When Kaibel became Iris's primary caregiver, his father wasn't sure what to make of his son taking on something few men in his generation had. But as Kaibel became more assured—even getting written up by the local paper for hosting one of the first dads-only baby showers—so did his very traditional father. He posted that article all over his Facebook page, Kaibel says, and bragged about his son to his friends. When the dads of the Meetup come together, they share a sense of relief. "It's just nice to be with a group that encourages this behavior," Stenhouse says, "where we're more accepted and not so out of the norm."

Because they don't feel that they are just yet. "I was at a library with another dad, hanging out with our little girls on a Wednesday afternoon, and a mom came up to us and stared. She didn't know what to make of us. Then she asked, 'What do you call yourselves?'" Kaibel says, "Was I supposed to be something more than a dad? I just walked away." They get weird looks from moms and nannies on the playground and feel left out of all the Mommy and Me groups in the area. They bristle at the moms who try to make them feel guilty for not signing their toddlers up for "enriching" activities like a popular Spanish class for babies. And don't get them started on the latest attachment parenting craze of constant baby-wearing and breast-feeding. "In all the articles, where are the dads?" Kaibel says, outraged. "They're not even in the picture."

And men very much need to be in the picture if we are all to climb out of the overwhelm and redefine work, love, and play for everyone.

Howard Kaibel didn't choose to be a hands-on father. Kaibel, his ginger-colored hair cropped close, wears jeans, blue sneakers, a gray sweatshirt, and a small gold hoop through his nose. As he pushes Iris on a tire swing, she leans her head back and closes her eyes, giggling. Kaibel explains that after Iris was born, his wife, a teacher, stayed home to care for her during her first year. "I was noticing that Iris was getting more and more distant, that I was not one of the centers of her world. Mom was," Kaibel says. He began writing a journal of what little he experienced of Iris's life, so he wouldn't forget. "And I did what every dad in that situation does. I just said to myself, 'Well, this is how it has to be. This is the cost of providing for your family.' I had no idea my life would turn out so differently."

In 2008, Kaibel lost his job as the recession hit. So his wife went back to work as a teacher and Kaibel took over child care for Iris, continuing to search for a job during the baby's naptime. Though he has a master's degree and has held responsible positions in businesses for years, more than 150 applications were rejected. After a few months of fruitless job searching, he felt lonely and isolated. He spent the day distracted and depressed, doing housework, grocery shopping, and caring for the baby. Then, he decided, as he says, to come out of his fog. If he was going to be Iris's primary caregiver, he was going to embrace it wholeheartedly. He began a blog. He bought a bike seat and began taking Iris everywhere. He came up with little rules—for every errand, a fun activity for the two of them. He started taking Iris to the library and to other children's activities, but, as the only dad, he got tired of what seemed like the moms' constant grousing about how little husbands helped at home. On one level, Kaibel says he got it. As he took over more domestic chores, he found himself upset when someone left a dirty towel on the floor expecting that he'd be the one to pick it up. "It's disrespectful," he says. And he and his wife, Laura, are still struggling to find their footing—with her working mother guilt, his inadequate provider guilt, their imperfect division of labor and hesitation to ask each other for help. "The marital structure will *have* to adapt and learn how to do this better," he says. "And men will *have* to learn how to communicate better."

Though Kaibel continues to look for full-time work, he loves his new life. "Men are starting to realize, Wow, we lose this massive dimension of our relationship with our kids by just enslaving ourselves at work all the time," he says. "And we're starting to figure it out, that we need to have that connection, too."

Some men have always been involved fathers. Others yearned to be. But all the heat and light of the national conversation on changing gender roles in recent decades has always centered on women: women's education, women's opportunities for engagement in the wider world, and arguing bitterly about whether mothers should work and the impossible double burden they carry if they do. The animating question, "What do women really want?" has always been posed with an undertone of exasperation, as if women themselves didn't know. *The Bitch in the House* raged that her man wasn't sharing the load at home. But she assumed it was because he simply didn't want to and had the power not to. And while some of that undoubtedly was true, no one was looking at how perhaps men didn't even think they had a choice, stuck at work and expected to work all hours as ideal workers and providers. In other words, no one has spent much time asking, "What do *men* really want?"

The fact is, many men *do* want or need to be new dads. The U.S. Census Bureau reports that as many as one-third of all fathers with working wives—who are increasingly becoming equal earners if not primary breadwinners—routinely care for their children under age fifteen, up from one-fourth in 2002,[1] and half report taking an equal share of child-care responsibility, up from 41 percent in the 1990s.[2] Although they still make up barely 1 percent of all married couples, couples where the men stay home to be the primary caregiver have doubled in recent years.[3] What this all adds up to is the beginning of a potentially profound shift toward more equal parenting that could shake up calcified gender roles, topple the ideal worker, unstall the stalled gender revolution, and unwind the time bind.

For years, most of the research about fatherhood has centered on the consequences of its absence in low-income communities. Much of the policy debate has involved divorced fathers' custody rights. It wasn't until the late 1990s that scientists began to more intently study how fatherhood profoundly changes men physiologically, and social scientists began picking up on surveys that showed fathers yearned to spend more time with their children. Thus began the research into what they called the nurturing "new father."[4] Time studies began finding that fathers nearly tripled the amount of time they spend with their children from 1965 to 2000, and had done so even as the marriage rate fell and divorce rates and births outside of marriage soared.[5] By 2008, researchers were finding that fathers with working wives were consistently doing more solo child care and taking more full responsibility for children than fathers with nonworking wives, especially when the children were infants and toddlers and time demands were greatest.[6] By 2011, studies picked up on the fact that more fathers in the United States, Germany, Norway, and the United Kingdom were becoming nurturing "new fathers," but primarily on weekends.[7] A series of time studies began emerging in the Nordic countries that found that fathers who took solo parental leave were more likely to spend more time with their children and have close relationships with them as they grew, something I look at in chapter 11. The fathers were also more likely to cut back on their work hours and to spend more time on housework—the first steps toward true gender equity with their partners.[8]

Brittany McGill, as a Ph.D. student at the University of Maryland, studied time diaries and found that trying to be new fathers at home and live up to the expectations of the ideal worker provider at work was creating the very same time insanity for fathers that working mothers began experiencing in the 1970s. McGill found that fathers who considered themselves progressive, nurturing new dads spent the same amount of time on the job as traditional fathers, who saw their roles as providers. But the new fathers were spending as much as four more hours a week with their children, playing, taking part in "achievement-related activities," and taking care of them. To make that kind of time for their children, she found that fathers, like working mothers had for decades, were giving up sleep, personal care, and leisure time.[9] In other words, they were becoming . . . overwhelmed.

A Families and Work Institute survey found that not only had the number of fathers feeling stressed by the competing time demands of work and home increased, nearly doubling for fathers in double-earner couples from 1977 to 2008, but more fathers than mothers reported feeling conflicted about it. In their report, "The New Male Mystique," they declared that men now, too, are suffering from the burden of trying to have it all. In two national surveys, Boston College's Center for Work & Family found that a majority of fathers considered their role as a caregiver *as* important as being a breadwinner and that 53 percent would consider staying home to raise their children if they could swing it financially.[10] When the CDC asked people to respond to the statement in a national survey "It is more important for a man to spend a lot of time with his family than to be a success at his career," more men than women, 75 to 68 percent, agreed or strongly agreed.[11]

The new dad isn't hard to see. He's wearing his baby in a Snugli, like Will Arnett in *Up All Night* on TV, and marching through the park in a stroller brigade of dads, like in the movie *What to Expect*. By 2013, Meetup advertised four hundred different dad groups, like the one in Albuquerque, with close to thirty-five thousand members in ten different countries. And the web has exploded with daddy blogs where many now write of "daddy guilt."

The new dads are becoming influential voices for change. When Huggies aired a new ad showing an inept father trying to change a diaper, a group of very adept new dads organized a protest against the outdated stereotype until Huggies removed the ad and apologized. Matt Schneider, one of the leaders of the biggest Dad Meetup group in the country, with close to seven hundred dads in New York City, was chatting with the CEO of Meetup.com about how important solo parental leave is for fathers to bond with their children and to set the division of labor in the house on a more equal footing from the start. As a result, the CEO instituted a four-week paid parental leave policy for new fathers. "It's small compared to what mothers are getting," Schneider said, "but it's more than what other companies are offering."

These dads are also spreading the word on once obscure research that has found that preschool children with more involved fathers show more cognitive competence, more self-control, more empathy, and less gender stereotyping than preschool children with less involved fathers. Adolescents with more involved fathers are more likely to have better self-esteem, self-control, social competence, and life skills—provided the father is not overly controlling or authoritarian.[12] Surveys have found that girls are less confident than boys as early as in elementary school, and girls' self-esteem continues to drop throughout high school. But spending time with a loving father, researchers are finding, is an important factor in keeping a girl from losing her self-esteem and confidence once she hits puberty.[13]

Many new dads tell researchers that having grown up with aloof or distant provider fathers, they want to be the kind of fathers they wish they'd had. Charlie, a new dad I spoke with, said he wasn't sure what that would mean exactly, until he found himself all alone with a hungry, screaming baby. "When I first made the commitment to taking two months off for parental leave, it was really mostly for my wife. We'd agreed to try to share our lives as equitably as possible when we got married. It wasn't out of any sort of deep-seated feeling of, 'Oh, I want to spend all this time with my newborn,'" Charlie told me. The reality sank in on his very first day of leave. He'd already endured the pressure of having to ask for the leave from his boss. Though the new father parental leave policy had been on the books for years, Charlie was the first one ever to ask to use it. And now he couldn't get his daughter to take a bottle. "I called my wife about 3 o'clock, saying, 'If she doesn't take this bottle, she's going to starve!' My wife was on the verge of coming home." He felt out of his element and, after only seven hours on the job, like a complete failure. "I told my wife, 'Let me give it one more shot.' And by the end of the day, my daughter and I had figured out how to do this together. That was a *huge* moment for me. That's when it really hit. 'Wow! This is really *my* kid.' It was the start of something really special, a really close father-daughter relationship. And I have that with both my daughters now."

# BRIGHT SPOT: GRITTY, HAPPY KIDS

I would maintain that thanks are the highest form of thought, and that gratitude is happiness doubled by wonder.
—G. K. Chesterton

The days that make us happy make us wise.  —John Masefield

One afternoon, when Tessa was in third grade, I was stressed out of my mind, working on a deadline story about an alleged Somali war criminal, when our high school babysitter called at the last minute to say she couldn't pick up Tessa from school and get her to her ballet class. The class was at 4:30, an impossible time for most working parents. And, without giving it a second thought, I began making plans to take her myself.

By the time I'd rushed to get her from school, flew home, and threw a snack at her while frantically juggling my BlackBerry, we had all of about eight minutes to dash across town and get her to class. She sauntered down the stairs after taking forever to pull on her little pink tights and announced that her teacher now required her hair to be in a bun.

"I thought a headband was okay."

"My hair got too long last week."

"And you're telling me this now? We have to go! NOW!"

She crossed her arms and raised one eyebrow. "But the teacher said."

The BlackBerry started ringing again. My heart raced. My head hurt. I cursed. "Forget the teacher. Get in the car."

As I careened across town, I have to confess, I wondered for a millisecond if we could squeeze in a stop at CVS to buy hairpins. When we blew past it, she shot daggers at me from the backseat. I'd had it.

"Tessa! Your mother works for one of the best newspapers in the COUNTRY," I started in. "I am working on a FRONT-page story on DEADline. I am taking time out of MY busy day to get YOU to YOUR ballet class. I would think you'd at least be GRATEFUL."

Silence.

Then came a steely little voice from the backseat: "What about *The New York Times*?"

The story has gone down in family lore as an example of Tessa's pluck. But over time, I've become more disturbed by it. Not by her behavior. By mine. Why did I automatically assume that when the babysitter couldn't make it, *I* had to step in? Had my poisonous guilt, my desire to be the perfect mother, the blind panic not to disappoint my children or have them miss out because I wasn't home all the time so clouded my vision that I couldn't even *see* how insane that decision was? But more important, what was I teaching *her*? Beyond giving her a working mother role model of an angry, cursing, crazy harpy, I was teaching her that she was at the center of the universe. Far from the lesson I *thought* I was teaching her—to stick with something and not become a quitter—I was teaching her the opposite. I was teaching her that she was entitled.

When I began this search for time to work, love, and play, I ran into my friend Deb. She, like me, was tearing her hair out. She found herself driving car pools all over creation, pulled into the competitive world of her kids' travel sports teams, music lessons, and playdates, and caring for a special needs child. "All this rushing around," she said. "Just tell me if it's worth it."

So this is for Deb: No. No, the research shows, it's not worth it. Not if it's making everybody crazy, no one is having any fun, there's no time to connect, adults are losing their identities in the service of their children, children think the world exists to serve and entertain them, and there's no space for anybody to . . . just be. Middle-class parents are now so "child-centered" that they may be fostering a "dependency dilemma" and raising youths who can't think, make decisions, and venture out on their own. That's the conclusion of researchers at UCLA's Center on the Everyday Lives of Families after studying thirty-two dual-income, middle-class families in L.A. Both mothers and fathers felt guilty when work intruded on family life. They felt pressured to create "perfect" family time together. These parents, researchers observed, sought to make their kids happy by buying them a lot of stuff, giving in to their demands, and never asking them to help with chores. They're hardly the only ones. Economists have found that advertisers spent $16 billion a year marketing to guilty parents and acquisitive kids, and that the average American child receives about seventy new toys a year.[1]

"We may have reached a tipping point," anthropologist and study director Elinor Ochs has said. "Perhaps we've moved from being child-centered to being child-dominated."[2]

Research shows that encouraging kids to participate in activities they like is important, but that cramming more stuff onto the schedule is not better.[3] And there's good evidence that it makes things worse. And all that bright, zingy addictive technology we give them to make them happy, to keep them quiet when we're busy, that we ourselves are addicted to, is making us all more impatient, impulsive, forgetful, and self-centered.[4] "We're exhausting ourselves," pediatrician and parenting educator Kathy Masarie had told me, "and creating an inferior product."

For years, Suniya Luthar, a psychologist at Columbia University's Teachers College, and her colleagues have been tracking groups of children, from both the impoverished inner city and the affluent suburbs of New York City. What she found came as a shock: Affluent kids are two to three times more likely to suffer from depression, anxiety, and high levels of distress than kids living in harsh urban poverty. And wealthy kids were more likely to use drugs and alcohol.[5]

"I'm one of these parents," she admitted. (She texted me from the beauty salon where she'd taken her daughter to get her hair done for prom.) "So I'm certainly not going to be casting stones. But the subculture we live in can be very noxious." It's a fiercely competitive subculture, she said, that values material success and is convinced that means getting your kids into one of the handful of slots at an "elite" college. "We are manufacturing this madness."

In the process, time for many children has become structured, organized, and accounted for down to the minute. Free time has dropped from 40 percent of their day to 25 percent, and much of that is consumed with TV and electronic media.[6] Parents' hovering and fears of a dangerous world full of strangers have, researchers found, shrunk childhood "habitats." Where a generation ago, as Karen Graf's mother recalled, children may have roamed freely for miles and spent hours outdoors, making up games and playing pickup ball games, today, many children's zones of independence extend no farther than the end of the block,[7] and only 6 percent of children between the ages of nine and thirteen play outside on their own in a typical week.[8] Organized sports leagues have become so structured that there's little room for *fun*. Kid participation peaks at age eleven.[9]

Jean Twenge, a psychology professor at San Diego State University and author of *Generation Me*, has found in her research that five times as many high school and college students are depressed and anxious today than were youths during the Great Depression. Today's overhelicoptered children, bred on parental overpraise and the worship of self-esteem, are entitled, spoiled, self-centered, value being rich, have inflated egos, and feel . . . miserable.[10] They feel they don't have the power to control their own destiny, Twenge reports, so they tend to be cynical and feel easily victimized. And having been so programmed all their lives, they hit young adulthood and aren't even sure of what they like, much less who they are. All that schlepping around in the car, from voice lessons to the tutor to baseball practice, doesn't build the intimacy or the independence that gives rise to a quality that researchers are finding is key to both success and happiness. A quality they call *grit*.

Grit is the ability to set your mind to something and stick with it when the going gets hard. Studies have found that the more grit children have, the higher their grade point average, the more likely they are to get through a tough program, outrank others on competitions like the National Spelling Bee, be better educated, and have a more stable career. Grit is a better indicator of success, these studies found, than either SAT score or IQ.[11] The more grit, the more likely you are to follow a passion, persevere, and do the sometimes arduous work *on your own* to reach a goal. And the more you do that, research shows, the more likely you are to be happy.[12] And isn't that what we all say we want for our kids?

Christine Carter, a social scientist with the Greater Good Science Center at the University of California, Berkeley, is part of the growing Positive Psychology movement. She studies that ephemeral state we call happiness and how to raise happy children. In our single-minded focus on our kids' achievement, we have it all backward, she says as we watch the sun set over the San Francisco Bay from the window of her bungalow in the Berkeley hills. "The underlying American assumption is, if our kids get into a great college, they'll get a great job, *then* they'll be happy," Carter says. "But that's not necessarily true. What we need to be parenting for is happiness first. Focusing on grit becomes more about them fulfilling their *own* potential rather than honing showy skills that look spectacular on a college admission application."

That's because achievement, all that showy résumé building, does not necessarily lead to happiness. Instead, she says, feeling positive and happy in the first place is what fosters achievement. A meta-analysis of 225 studies on achievement, success, and happiness by the psychologist Sonja Lyubomirsky of the University of California, Riverside, found that happy people, those who are comfortable in their own skin, are more likely to have "fulfilling marriages and relationships, high incomes, superior work performance, community involvement, robust health and a long life"—in other words, success.[13] And that positive, happy state, she says, arises from grit.

Grit isn't something you're born with, Carter says. It's something you can learn and exercise, like a muscle. If you're a parent, you can teach grit. How? Let your children struggle. A little challenge, a little anguish, even, is good for them. When children learn to resolve their own conflicts, without Mom or Dad swooping in to the rescue, they build grit, self-confidence, and the creative problem-solving skills that lead to higher academic achievement.[14] Teach them to try new things, she says, to take risks, follow inklings, see if they turn into passions, work hard, maybe master something, maybe make mistakes, but love the journey itself, not the reward.

Carol Dweck, a psychologist at Stanford, has spent years studying mind-sets. In one experiment, she and her research team gave kids a short test and then praised them. To one group, they said, "Oh, you must be very smart," an attitude they said reinforces a "fixed mind-set"— that one's abilities are inherent and set in stone. To another group, they said, "You did really well, you must have worked really hard." That kind of praise, they said, reflects a "growth mind-set"—or someone who believes that success is a result of grit, effort, and hard work rather than innate aptitude. The researchers then offered the two groups a second test. The children could choose an easier puzzle or a harder one. The majority of kids who were praised as "very smart" opted for the easier puzzle. They were afraid, Carter explains, of making a mistake and being "found out" as not so smart after all. But 90 percent of the kids whose grit had been praised chose to tackle the harder puzzle and keep learning. "When you're growth oriented, you're driven by love, passion, and who you are," she says. "When you're in a fixed mind-set, you tend to perfectionism. You're driven by fear and who you think other people want you to be. And perfectionists, by definition, can never be satisfied. They're never happy."

To raise "gritty," happy kids, Carter teaches parents to first lose the self-sacrifice. Depressed parents have been linked to negative behaviors in their kids, she says, while positive emotions tend to be contagious.[15] So it's important that parents start by taking care of themselves and their marriages or partnerships. She advises families to become more mindful of how they spend their time and how they talk to one another, to build support networks, create easy routines, meaningful rituals, and savor the small moments of connection.

And most important, teach them *gratitude.* "Teach your kids to count their blessings," Carter says. Adults who often feel grateful are more generous, more empathetic, and "have more energy, more optimism, more social connections and more happiness than those who do not," wrote Melinda Beck in *The Wall Street Journal*, reporting on a decade of gratitude research. "They are also less likely to be depressed, envious, greedy or alcoholics. They earn more money, sleep more soundly, exercise more regularly and have greater resistance to viral infections."[16] And, Beck writes, researchers are beginning to find the same benefits in children. "Kids who feel and act grateful tend to be less materialistic, get better grades, set higher goals, complain of fewer headaches and stomach aches and feel more satisfied with their friends, families and schools than those who don't."

As we talk, Carter's two daughters burst in the door with Carter's parents. The divorced Carter says she works hard to create her own family's "happiness habits"—like sharing three good things that happened during the day before bed. Human happiness is built not on indulgence, she says, but on meaningful connections with other humans. And for kids—as well as adults—you develop those connections, you foster creativity, build grit, and become most fully yourself—in imaginative, joyful, unstructured free time devoted to . . . play.

# PART FOUR

## PLAY

# 11

# HYGGE IN DENMARK

The gross national product does not allow for the health of our children, the quality of their education or the joy of their play. It does not include the beauty of our poetry or the strength of our marriages, the intelligence of our public debate or the integrity of our public officials. It measures neither our wit nor our courage, neither our wisdom nor our learning, neither our compassion nor our devotion to our country, it measures everything in short, except that which makes life worthwhile.

—Robert F. Kennedy

It's 3:25 on a rainy Friday afternoon in Copenhagen. Vibeke Koushede leaves her office at the National Institute of Public Health and expertly steers one of the few small minivans in sight through the narrow medieval streets, wedges the van into a parking spot, and dashes across the street to pick up her five-year-old twins. The two go to a public kindergarten in the country about twenty miles outside of the city, where the children play all day in the forest and fields. Although the kindergarten after-care program is open until 5 p.m., most Danes work flexible schedules, as she does, Vibeke explains, and pick up their children between 3:30 and 4. Danes view the hours of 5 to 8 as almost sacred family time, she says. After that, kids go to bed and parents have evenings together or often fire up computers and do more work at home. "By 4:30, the little chairs have already been stacked on desks, the floors have been swept. There's never more than one or two kids left waiting. And you never want to be that parent."

Vibeke smiles and nods in greeting to the dozen or so other parents who stand on the sidewalk under umbrellas or, clad in Gore-Tex, lean on rain-soaked bikes. Half are mothers, half are fathers.

The kindergarten teacher, a male "pedagogue," leads the children off the bus. After quick hugs, Vibeke's twins, Gustav and Bertram, are soon strapped into their car seats and she's back at the wheel, wending through traffic to the school her seven-year-old son, Luca, attends. Today is her "short" workday. She and her husband, Søren, trade short and long workdays so that one parent can concentrate uninterrupted and the other can make sure all four kids are home by 4:30 p.m.

She arrives at Luca's school, finds another impossible parking spot, and begins to spring through the rain toward the school, leaving her twins behind in the car.

Vibeke, thirty-seven, dressed in tight black jeans and sparkly silver Converse sneakers, her curly long blond hair flying, looks back at me, where I hesitate near the car with the twins. "I'm sure, as an American, this seems pretty weird to you."

I nod uncomfortably. Images from the evening news flash before my eyes: the woman who left her baby in her car to dash in to the dry cleaner who wound up being dragged down the street when a carjacker took off with the car and the baby. Elizabeth Smart. Jaycee Duggard. The forlorn kids on milk cartons. The steely glare of Nancy Grace and the judgmental bad-mommy police . . .

Vibeke smiles. "It's okay. In Denmark, everyone does it all the time."

I notice an unattended pram with huge buggy wheels in a nearby doorway. Inside, under a plastic rain visor, a baby sleeps peacefully. It's a sight that would become familiar over the next few days. "We think it's better for them not to be disturbed and to get fresh air," one parent would later explain as we threaded our way into a restaurant for brunch through unattended strollers parked nonchalantly in front of the building like a row of oversize flowerpots. Inside Luca's school, the air smells wonderfully of cinnamon and apples. A teacher holds out a tin of blackened muffins the children have baked as part of the after-school program. "They're burned. But we had a lot of fun and laughed a lot," she says. "And they got to learn that some things in life don't always work out perfectly, but you can have a good time anyway." Luca, who had been lounging in a cushy loft with his best friend, Inez, asks for a playdate with her, so Vibeke stuffs two more children into the van and heads home.

Their apartment in an old factory building in the immigrant-heavy-turning-trendy neighborhood of Nørrebro, is like Ikea heaven. With floor-to-ceiling windows, it is airy and light filled. Footholds for rock climbing adorn one wall, and on another, whimsical silhouettes of animals and mythical creatures dance about above sayings like, "The future belongs to those who believe in the beauty of their dreams.—Eleanor Roosevelt." Scooters stand at the ready near a giant goose floor lamp. The apartment is open, compact, playful, inviting, immaculate, and *uncluttered*.

I am struck for the first but certainly not the last time as I began to visit more Danes' homes that there is no junk. Where are the cities made of paper towel tubes, cardboard, and tissue paper? The giant pink Barbie Dreamhouse? The snaking tracks of Thomas the Tank Engine? The glittery butterflies made out of coat hangers? The macaroni artwork? The balls of smelly socks by the door? I began to wonder if the Danes had figured out how to create black holes for all those plastic toys, childhood masterpieces, endless math worksheets, and streams of catalogs, credit card offers, and coupon inserts behind those minimalist cabinets. I was assured again and again that Danes simply do not buy, produce, or save as much stuff.

The children, with one look from Vibeke, set the table for a snack of apples and juice. When they're finished, they all, with one word, clear their plates and set them in the sink, then run off to build a giant fort with blankets and pillows. I raise my eyebrows, thinking of all the nagging I do to get my children to help with chores. "I've got four boys and this is what I'm teaching my sons—that helping out around the house is what you do when you have a family," she says firmly. A large chalkboard on one wall keeps track of the family schedule. There's a potluck dinner with friends in the neighborhood every Monday, swimming lessons for the young boys—when she and her husband usually go for a run or walk around a nearby lake—and volleyball practice that her teenage son gets himself to and from on public transportation. There isn't a whole lot else on it. I ask Vibeke if that means she has some time to herself. She said she and her husband keep to a strict 8 p.m. bedtime for the children in order to spend the evenings together. "And sometimes my husband will kick me out of the house and tell me to go for a run or take time for myself," she says, recounting how her husband really wanted to go on the boys' Boy Scouts camping trip one recent weekend and, when she didn't, encouraged her to go with a friend to a spa instead. Taking time for friends is a priority for both her and her husband, as is taking leisure time for themselves. They take a short trip together at least twice a year. "We both know that taking time for ourselves means we'll come back to the family refreshed. We're better parents when we have a break."

I have come to Denmark because the Australian sociologist Lyn Craig's time studies found that Danish mothers have the most leisure time of mothers in any country she studied—as much as an hour more leisure a day than mothers in the United States, Australia, and France and an hour and a half more than Italian mothers. At six hours and twelve minutes of leisure a day, Danish mothers have nearly the seven hours that Danish fathers have and *more* leisure time than the fathers in all the other industrial countries Craig looked at. One and a half hours of a Danish mother's leisure time every day is spent in "pure" or child-free time to themselves. That's more pure leisure than everyone else Craig studied, save Danish and Italian fathers. American mothers, who spend the most leisure time of any parents studied with their children, Craig found, spend the least amount of leisure time without them. American mothers, on average, have about thirty-six minutes a day to themselves.[1] And it's not like Danish mothers are bonbon eaters. Denmark has one of the highest maternal employment rates in the world, with more than 80 percent of mothers with children under fifteen in the workforce.[2] I came here to see just exactly how they do it and to find out what having leisure time means. Are mothers less overwhelmed? Is everyone happier? And, more important, is there anything to learn?

By 5:05, Søren walks in the front door. Søren is head of the Speaker's Office in the Danish parliament. He says he left work at 4:30 and cycled home about three miles in the rain just to be home in time.

In time for what? I ask.

"My favorite exercise class," Vibeke says with a smile. She kisses her husband and dashes out the door.

Søren changes into a gray T-shirt and black jeans, walks to the fridge in the large open kitchen, and pulls out a bowl of dough, which he'd made that morning at 5:45. He begins kneading it to make pizza for dinner. The kids are settled in front of the TV for their Friday afternoon hour of their favorite *Lucky Luke* cartoon. Nestled on the gray couch, seven-year-old Luca gives Inez a foot rub. Søren is tall and slim with soft brown hair. Cooking, taking care of kids, and working around the house are just natural for Danish men like him, he explains, as he adjusts his glasses with the back of his flour-dusted hand. Both his parents had careers, and his father spent more time in the kitchen than his mother. Plus, he's liked making pizza ever since he learned how in the home ec class that every Danish boy and girl is required to take in school. "I intuitively found it very natural to take part at home because that's what I saw," he tells me as he rolls out the dough and places pepperoni slices in a circle. "Growing up, I always imagined I would have a career. I always expected to have a well-educated wife who would have a career of her own as well. For me, it would have been very odd to have a wife who didn't have her own perspective or who didn't develop her own skills. I find it very much part of human nature—to want to achieve something. For me to do all the work and have a wife doing everything at home would be strange for me. And we know very, very few couples like that."

In an hour, the pizzas are warm and bubbling. The kids have set the table. Vibeke walks in, beaming and glowing, bike helmet under her arm. Over dinner, I ask them what it is, exactly, that enables Danish mothers—and fathers—to have more leisure time than parents in other countries, and more leisure time to themselves.

The Koushedes exchange a look. Well, first, they say, Americans seem to value achievement above all, and Danes make it a priority to live a good life. "Here, you get a lot of status from what you do in your leisure time," Vibeke says, pouring wine for the adults and milk for the children. "The papers are filled with stories about people doing interesting things with their leisure," Vibeke says. "Sometimes I look at Facebook and wonder if anybody ever works."

## *Work*

Danes don't live to work. Danes work hard, the Koushedes insist, but they work in a very focused way. Lunch is usually no more than half an hour, and many companies provide a healthy smorgasbord of dark bread, smoked meats, vegetables, fresh fruit, and salad for their workers. Most Danes work the standard thirty-seven hours a week, Søren explains, from 9 to 4:24 every day. "Which, if you multiply by five days, comes out to exactly thirty-seven hours." Long hours are actually outlawed for most workers under the European Union's Working Time Directive (executives, entrepreneurs, hospital workers, and others are exempt). Though Europeans worked longer hours than Americans until as late as the 1960s,[3] now, no European is allowed to work more than forty-eight hours a week.[4] (The French government cut work hours to thirty-five a week in 2000.[5] German unions have negotiated the right to shorter hours—the "work less, work all" *Kurzarbeit* philosophy—in order to cut unemployment and share work among more workers.[6] Only Britain has an exception to the directive, with the caveat that workers can't be *forced* to work more than forty-eight hours.[7]) In Denmark, there isn't a whole lot of joking around the watercooler or Facebook checking in the office, they explain. You do your work and you go home. "Some of my colleagues who are the highest achieving and most productive pick up their children at 4 or 4:30 every day," Søren says. "No one works at the office until 6, 7, or 8 o'clock just to show they're there. We tend to focus on what needs to get done and just do it."

Flexible work to fit around one's life, in the jobs where it's possible, is the norm, the Koushedes explain. Workplaces tend to be flat, without a lot of layers of management, which gives workers more autonomy.[8] Some companies send workers home with dinner or do laundry for them because, Vibeke says, the feeling is that if workers have a life and are happy, they do better work. Most Danes don't feel obligated to check their smartphones and e-mail after hours. In fact, they say, people who put in long hours and constantly check e-mail after hours are seen not as ideal worker warriors, as in America, but as inefficient.

Most Danes also have six weeks of paid vacation every year, one of the most generous vacation policies of any in the world,[9] and, unlike Americans, most people take every minute of it. The Koushedes go camping as a family the first week in summer after school is out. And they spend several weeks, as do many Danes, at a rustic summer cottage out in the country where the kids roam freely and pass long, lazy days in nature. Twelve public holidays, including General Prayer Day and Whit Sunday and Monday—or Pentecost—add two weeks of paid time off.[10] (The United States has eleven federal holidays, including July 4th, Veterans Day, and Presidents' Day.) "The feeling here is that people have a right to take vacation," Søren says. Adds Vibeke, "With only two weeks off a year, like some of our friends get in America, I would think you would just run down."

So do those short work hours and long vacations come at an economic cost?

No.

The Danish economy is one of the most competitive in the world, just a few rungs below the United States.[11] And it's one of the most productive, ranking just behind the United States, even though Danes work so much less.[12] Denmark has a low unemployment rate[13] and one of the highest standards of living in the world.[14] It has one of the smallest gaps between rich and poor of any country on earth, while the United States has one of the largest.[15] And only 6 percent of Danes find it difficult or very difficult to live on their current income, compared to 21 percent of Americans,[16] even though the United States ranks highest in the world on household income.[17]

## *Love*

When it comes to families, Danes see giving children a good start in life as good for the whole society. Denmark ensures one year of paid parental leave for parents to split after the birth or adoption of a child. Both Vibeke *and* Søren have taken long parental leaves—something that Denmark, Sweden, Iceland, Norway, and Germany are encouraging more fathers to do through new "use it or lose it" government policies. "Fathers describe the experience as life changing," the Swedish sociologist and *New Swedish Father* coauthor Thomas Johansson told me. "They become more involved in housework and child care. Their relationships are closer. And many have time to rethink the meaning of their lives."[18]

Time studies show that Danish men, like Swedish men—and unlike men in any other country in the world—do almost as much housework and child care as Danish women. In forty years, the time gap between men and women has dropped from four hours to forty-five minutes a day (mostly on weekdays; the gap is narrower on weekends).[19] "This is really unprecedented in human history, to go in one generation from distant, breadwinning fathers to fathers who are present in the delivery room, taking parental leave, and pushing strollers," said Svend Aage

Madsen, a psychologist at Copenhagen University Hospital who studies fatherhood.

Though Søren took only a few weeks off when Luca was born, he cared for the twins for four months on his own after Vibeke's leave. He says he learned the hard way just how getting to the grocery store can be a long and arduous process of diaper bag packing, changing, feeding, and fussy baby managing. "Now that more men are taking leave, they're starting to recognize how busy it really is to be home and understand why their wives are tired," Søren says. "And my relationship with my sons is so much stronger from taking care of them. That will make a difference as they grow up, that their father was there."

Denmark has both one of the longest paid parental leaves—fifty-two weeks paid at 80 to 100 percent of one's salary—and one of the highest rates of mothers who work in the labor market in the world. After six months, the government guarantees every child a spot in an early childhood development center and, for school-age children, in an after-school program. If there's a waiting list, which is usually no more than three months, the government will pay a parent to stay home, help hire a "child minder," or pay a parent who takes on the care of another infant at home in addition to his or her own.[20]

Søren worried at first that a long parental leave would hurt his career. Instead, he was promoted within a few months after he returned to work. "It's become so common for men to take leave, it doesn't tend to affect their careers," he says. "And we get the opportunity to be with our kids when they're young that we'd never get again." Now, Vibeke says, sometimes the boys go to Søren first because he responds to them faster than she does. As if on cue, Gustav, one of the twins, moves his chair and nestles in to be closer to his father.

European Union regulations and Danish labor union agreements ensure that every parent with children under eight will get two paid sick days to care for children, above sick leave parents have for themselves.[21] And each parent gets two "nurture" days a year per young child, which can be spread out and taken as half days. With three children under eight, that means that Vibeke and Søren each get six days off a year over and above their eight weeks of paid vacation and public holidays. "When the children have something going on at school, I can quite happily take that day as a 'nurture' day," Søren says.

But what about parenting standards? I mention the babies sleeping in strollers, unattended. "You know, a Danish woman got arrested and charged with child endangerment for doing that outside a restaurant in New York."[22] I mention the twins left in the car and all the young kids I'd seen in my time in Copenhagen by themselves, walking on the streets, crowding the already crowded commuter bike lanes, and flying on their scooters to the train and metro stations. Vibeke and Søren nod again. Denmark is a small country where people feel safe, they say. Parents are loving and family focused, but much more hands-off than in other countries. Kids are allowed to be more independent at young ages. And adults value adult time, separate from the family time with children that they also prize. There is a group of intensive mothers in Denmark who say mothers should devote themselves to their children and to living an all-natural, gluten-free, organic lifestyle. "We call them 'spelt mothers,'" Vibeke says, after the ancient grain that has become fashionable in health food circles. "But they are really on the fringe."

Mothers getting an education—Vibeke got her advanced degrees when her children were babies—and going to work in the labor force has become the new norm, she says. Tax policy promotes women's economic independence, she says, by treating men and women as individuals, rather than as part of a family unit, as in America.

And men increasingly are expected to share equally in the work and child care at home. (There's a reason both boys and girls are required to take home ec, they say.) In a study of attitudes in Scandinavia, Danish men and women showed the highest preference of all countries to be in fully egalitarian marriages and partnerships. Nearly 70 percent of Danish women and 60 percent of Danish men said they preferred equally sharing paid work, housework, and child care.[23] Danish sociologists and economists I spoke with looked puzzled when I told them that the U.S. General Social Survey still picks up deep ambivalence in America on the question of whether it would be better for a mother of young children to stay home than to work. "In Denmark," said one, "you would never even ask that question."

## Play

The very structure of Danish society is set up to support leisure, Vibeke explains. Many shops and stores generally aren't open on Sunday or much past 7 p.m., so everyone can be home with their families (though new laws now allow longer hours at larger stores and supermarkets). Government-sponsored mothers' groups put together by nurse educators in Denmark and Sweden to keep new mothers from feeling isolated and overwhelmed actually end up becoming the foundation for many mothers' leisure activities for years to come. I would later have dinner in Malmö, Sweden, with Catarina Ellehuus, an ER doctor originally from Denmark, and Malin Rutberg, a preschool teacher, who have been getting together for dinner, drinks, movies, and girl getaways since meeting in their mothers' group in Sweden in 2005. "Having a child is such a big event. It changes you. So it's really natural that these mothers become your friend base. And this is Scandinavia, where everything is equal, right?" Ellhuus told me. "Our husbands go out on Mondays. So it's only fair that we have another night to ourselves." Hanne Dühr, a nurse educator in the government health system who I met in Copenhagen, creates these mother groups and understands how powerful they can be. She still takes ski trips and gets together regularly with the same group of new mothers she joined when she had her children in the 1970s.

I tell the Koushedes that I've been reading that Denmark holds the world record, by some accounts, for having the most sports clubs, exercise facilities, and community recreation centers per capita, with long waiting lists to get into the one hundred or so winter ice-swimming/sauna clubs.[24] "Most Danes do belong to sports clubs," Vibeke agrees. "And we do, of course, have the catalog classes."

The catalog classes, I was soon to learn, are part of a long-standing Danish tradition of adult education. Unlike in America, where adult education often conjures up dreary images of remedial reading, the classes offered in Denmark are meant to tickle the fancy, expand the mind, refresh the soul and, catalogs attest, make Danes "wiser and healthier." Every fall, thick catalogs arrive at Danish households offering classes on everything from foreign languages to art to cooking to history to photography to acting to learning how to debate or build a pair of skis, and everything in between. The classes are affordable, since they're subsidized by either the government, unions, or community groups. And they're wildly popular.

I would later spend an evening wandering through the classes offered by AOF, a community association that has been organizing catalog classes since 1924. In an English-language class, the attendees, a mix of men and women of all ages, had taken a wide range of classes over the years, from badminton and ghost walks to a series of popular talks on positive thinking called, mysteriously, "Fucking Nice." I ask if people, if mothers, feel selfish or guilty for taking time for themselves, like many in America. They look at me as if not sure what to make of my absurd question. Then they all laugh.

With dinner over at the Koushedes', Vibeke and the children clear the table and Søren loads the dishwasher. To make time for themselves, for a social life, and for leisure, Vibeke says, they've also lowered their standards. Danish tastes tend to be simple to start with, she says. But they stopped caring about keeping up appearances. "It used to be that if you wanted to entertain, you needed to clean, prepare a three-course meal," Søren explains. But now, spurred by an iconoclastic friend, Michelle Hviid, who convinced a group of neighbors that it's more important to share a short but good time together every Monday night than stand on tradition, they no longer wait to get together until their apartments and menus are perfect.

A few nights later, I am invited to the neighborhood potluck at Hviid's place—another open, airy apartment decorated with circus rings, trapeze, basketball hoop, and brilliantly lit star-shaped lanterns hanging from the ceiling. Hviid, a writer, business owner, and single mother of two, puts everyone to work, including her towheaded five-year-old daughter, who uses a very sharp knife to chop strawberries with surprising skill. Hviid explains that friends gather from 6 to 8 p.m. and not a minute longer. No one bothers to tidy or worry about dust bunnies. "And sometimes the meals are spaghetti with ketchup," Vibeke says with a laugh, "because that's all we've got."

Over dinner, Vibeke says that though she grew up in Denmark and both her parents worked, her mother did all the housework and child care. Vibeke's father is English and very traditional. "I remember as a child thinking, 'This isn't fair. She's doing all the work and you're just sitting there,'" she says. Vibeke was much more drawn to the Danish couples she saw all around her, and how sharing the workload gave both men and women time for themselves. Not just, as in her parents' case, the men. That feeling was reinforced when she lived in England with her oldest son, from a previous relationship, as a young single mother. "In England, you could feel it, you were considered not as good a mother if you wanted to go out and do your own thing," Vibeke says. "But here, having leisure time for myself isn't something we even have to discuss. It's just natural."

And you don't feel guilty? I ask. Selfish? That you're neglecting your children? Worried about the to-do list?

The Koushedes and their neighbors give me a blank look. "I think Danish women," Søren says finally, "perhaps know their worth."

Denmark, home of the Vikings, the fairy tales of Hans Christian Andersen, and sweet, buttery pastries, is a happy country. Danes aren't skipping madly down the street with exuberant smiles plastered on their faces. But there's a deep *contentment*. And a reason why LEGO, from the Danish *leg godt*, literally means "play well."

The United Nations' first-ever *World Happiness Report* put Denmark at the top of its global list (the United States ranked eleventh).[25] The Danes also rank at the top of the OECD's Better Life Index for having both the highest life satisfaction and the best work-life balance (the United States ranked fourteenth and twenty-eighth respectively).[26] And in addition to a host of surveys, polls, and reports rating Danes the happiest people on earth,[27] Denmark has consistently ranked at the top of the European Commission's Eurobarometer of happiness and well-being since the measurement was created in 1973.[28]

Danish children, too, are among the happiest (ranking seventh to the United States' twenty-first),[29] even as Danes, perhaps to the surprise of some Americans, have the highest number of children enrolled in formal child care.[30] *The Economist* ranked Denmark fifth in its "Where-to-Be-Born Index" for 2013. (The United States, largely because of its yawning debt, fell from the number-one spot in 1988 to sixteen.)[31] UNICEF reports that, at 6.5 percent, Denmark has one of the lowest child poverty rates of any industrialized country—the result of a tax policy that redistributes wealth and funds a sturdy social safety net (the United States' child poverty rate is just behind Latvia's, at 23 percent).[32]

Despite a high tax rate, Denmark is the darling of the political left *and* the right. The Danish government is rated as among the most transparent, efficient, trusted, and least corrupt by civil society organizations.[33] Denmark is moving toward energy independence, with renewables accounting for 40 percent of the country's supply.[34] And its pro-business policies land Denmark in the top rankings of the conservative Heritage Foundation's global Index of Economic Freedom.[35] The same safety net, which funds universal child care, heath care, generous unemployment benefits, and a robust free public education system through college and graduate school, gives businesses enormous flexibility in hiring and firing workers, called the "flexicurity model."[36] That makes everybody happy. As Rikke, a teacher I met while she was on parental leave, put it, "I don't have to worry, whatever may happen to my job, my partner, or to me. I know I'll never have to say, 'Oh, too bad, I've got to go sleep in the park.'"

Denmark is also rated as one of the best places to be a mother (the United States ranks twenty-fifth)[37] and has one of the highest fertility rates in Europe.[38] It is one of the best places to be a woman, ranking in the top ten in the World Economic Forum's Global Gender Gap Index (the United States ranks twenty-second).[39] So important is gender equity that in 1999, the government appointed a cabinet-level minister for gender equality to monitor it. The minister enforces laws designed to ensure men and women have an equal footing in the workplace, equal pay, equal opportunity, equal influence in society, and are considered of "equal worth."[40] Denmark has shied away from requiring formal gender quotas, like other European countries. But Danish law does require that where possible, all boards, commissions, institutions, and other organizations that receive government funding, have equal gender balance. When a position becomes vacant, the law requires that equal numbers of men and women be suggested as replacements. With women making up nearly 40 percent of parliament, Denmark ranks in the top fifteen countries in the world with the most women in the national legislature (the United States, with 16.9 percent in 2011, ranked ninety-first).[41] Denmark's constitutional monarch is the beloved Queen Margrethe II, and, in 2011, the country elected its first female prime minister, Helle Thorning-Schmidt, who is a mother of two.

Linda Haas, a sociologist at Indiana University, has dedicated her life to understanding how it is that in the last decades of the twentieth century, Sweden, Denmark, and Iceland so profoundly shifted their views on men and women. Labor shortages as much as ideology sparked the drive to gender equity, she explained, as governments sought to have mothers fill the gap rather than import immigrant workers, as in America. Nordic political systems are also better designed to think broadly about social issues and build consensus. Since the 1920s, they've relied on commissions of nonpartisan academics, thinkers, and practitioners to work with trade unions and politicians to study and recommend family policy. "That thoughtful, pragmatic, think tank approach to develop social policy is *not* one that we have in the United States," she told me. Over time, the new policies have become self-reinforcing. "The Social Insurance Agency in Sweden that runs the parental leave system, for instance, has played a big role in shaping views that fathers can and should care for children," she said. "And it's done so in a very, very visual way, with posters in every well-baby clinic and prenatal center of men, like this big, brawny wrestler, on parental leave with his tiny baby. You can't miss that as a parent."

I had come to Denmark to see why Danish mothers have so much leisure time, and yet found I was spending most of my time with increasingly involved fathers. You can't have one, I was told again and again, without the other. I was struck by the sheer number of fathers in business suits pushing enormous prams through the streets in both Denmark and Sweden. Fathers traveling alone on trains, buses, and bikes with their kids. Fathers dominating sunny playgrounds on lazy weekday afternoons with their children. Even painted signs on pedestrian paths showed the outline of a father, not a mother, holding a child's hand. And a giant poster outside the popular Tiger retail store showed a smiling man wearing a green-and-pink apron that read THE APRON MAKES THE PERSON.

I met with Jens Bonke, an economist with the Rockwool Foundation in Copenhagen who gathers and analyzes Denmark's time-use data. He's finding that, with the country's emphasis on equality, not only do Danish men and women have about the same amount of leisure time, but they are moving toward what he calls total "gender convergence." Bonke predicts that by 2023, if current trends continue, Danish men and women will be spending an equal amount of time on housework. And by 2033, they will spend the same amount of time working for pay as well.[42] "That's not very far away," he told me. "In other countries, gender convergence will take as long as seventy to eighty more years."

If time is power, Danish women appear close to the break-even point. But just as Hrdy discovered in her studies of hunting-and-gathering societies, gender convergence in modern societies requires alloparents. In Denmark, that includes not just fathers but also a high-quality and trusted child-care system.[43] I met with a family with a five-month-old daughter, Mathilde. Camilla was just finishing her parental leave, and her partner, Jørgen, was about to start his. They'd found a neighborhood child development center around the corner from their apartment where Mathilde would go when she was nine months old. I told them that many Americans are mistrustful of child care and think it's better if mothers of young children stay home. They looked puzzled. "Even if we had the money for one of us to stay home, I'd want Mathilde in child care, because 98 percent of the other children are there," Jørgen said. "The pedagogues are well trained in child development. And that's where children learn how to interact with other children and other adults." Camilla, who was about to go back to work as a web master at a private company, furrowed her brow, perplexed. "If a parent wanted to stay home, people would say, 'How could you possibly stimulate your child at home all day?'"

Okay. Let's pause here for a little global reality check.

Denmark is about sixteen thousand square miles, a little less than twice the size of Massachusetts. Its population of 5.6 million is bigger than Los Angeles's 3.8 million but smaller than New York City's 8 million. Unlike the United States, one of the most racially and ethnically diverse countries in the world,[44] Denmark is one of the most homogeneous. Close to 90 percent of all Danes are of Scandinavian descent. And while the country has seen an influx of Somali, Iraqi, and Bosnian refugees in recent years, its largest immigrant groups hail from Turkey, Poland, and Germany.[45] No one political party has dominated its parliament since 1909. So the government is forced to rule from the center by consensus and compromise, through what they call "collaborative democracy."[46] Which is a far cry from the divisive, loud, passionate, money-soaked, and often hostile power politics in America, where the two dominant political parties have been deadlocked for more than a century in a fundamental philosophical battle about what a proper government should even do. Denmark's psyche is oriented toward the communal. The American psyche springs from the ideal of rugged individualism. Denmark is not vast, sprawling, chaotic, and enormously dynamic. Denmark is not the world's military, economic, and humanitarian superpower.

And Denmark is *not* perfect. Everything is crazy expensive. The recent influx of Muslim refugees has unearthed an ugly intolerant streak.[47] Reports have found anti-Muslim bias in the media as well as in housing, education, and on the job.[48] Drawings of the Prophet Muhammad in a Danish publication enraged Muslims around the world. That, in turn, only strengthened the growing power of the anti-immigrant Danish People's Party,[49] now one of the largest parties in parliament, whose leaders have compared Islam to a "plague."[50]

As in other Nordic countries, the teen binge-drinking rate is high, as is, ironically in such a happy country, the suicide rate.[51] As in other Nordic countries, Denmark has among the highest rates of cohabitation, births to single mothers, and divorce.[52] And again as in other Nordic countries, the initial push in the 1960s to support working families gave all the breaks—parental leave, part-time and flexible work—to mothers. That pushed women out of more demanding jobs in the private sector and into more forgiving government jobs and, unintentionally, left these countries with high rates of what's called "occupational sex segregation," with few women in traditionally male-dominated fields or in positions of power in the corporate and entrepreneurial worlds.[53] (That, in part, is what led Scandinavian countries to begin more recently to push for gender-neutral family policies like parental leave for both parents.) "We've created a society that has enabled a mother to have a full-time *job*. But the question today is, can she have a *career*?" Elisabeth Møller Jensen, director of KVINFO, the government-funded Danish Centre for Information on Gender, Equality and Diversity, told me. And some complain that Nordic countries can take gender equity *too* far, as when Swedes insisted on having only gender-neutral toys in preschools and created a new gender-neutral pronoun *hen* (it), to use instead of *han* (him) and *hon* (her).[54]

The point here is, the United States is not Denmark. Nor should it be. Far more useful, then, in this journey to understand leisure time and happiness, is to acknowledge the differences and look for the broader and more universal themes that could apply:

- Money really can't buy happiness. Or time.
- Trust is important to living a happy life, as is having a stable income, good health, peace of mind, and close connections with others.

- Fairness, effective government, and social equity in race, gender, and income are the foundations of a good society and the building blocks of life satisfaction.
- Meaningful work *can* be done without working all hours and sacrificing yourself, your family, or your life. Giving workers control and predictability over their schedules *can* lead to productivity and profits. Vacation and rest *can* make you a better worker and a happier person.
- Fathers and mothers *can* share their lives and work equally. Both *can* be economically independent and develop close relationships with their children. They can be loving parents by both holding their children close and giving them the gift of grit and the freedom to roam.
- Meaningful family time is as accessible as an evening of laughter and spaghetti with ketchup, because that's all that's in the cupboard.
- Making time for leisure to refresh your soul is critical for living a good life.
- There is extraordinary power in a small table covered with a fresh sheet of white butcher paper and set with a rough wooden dish of sea salt, one bright green lime, and a single white candle.

That final happiness lesson, in the very Danish aesthetic of embracing the beauty and warmth in the simple, clean present moment they call *hygge*, I was about to learn from an American.

As I wait at the chilly Skodsborg train station outside Copenhagen, Sharmi Albrechtsen pulls up in a sleek silver Audi convertible, wearing a white cashmere coat and an enormous smile. "I'm an American. I always drive," she explains in this country so wild for public transportation that trains have bike stands and cars are taxed at close to 200 percent.

Albrechtsen, a writer who works in marketing and public relations, grew up in Bethesda, Maryland, a tony suburb of Washington, D.C., the hard-charging daughter of hard-charging Indian immigrants. "I was brought up with the idea that I *must* be a straight-A student. I *must* go to a good college. I *must* make a lot of money. I *must* achieve. I must

must must," she says as we drive through the flat, marshy landscape. "Then I moved to Denmark and my world turned upside down. Being ambitious is not something people appreciate here."

As we settle in for a lunch of smoked salmon, fresh salad, and thick, dark rye bread at a whitewashed eighteenth-century carriage house in the country, she explains that she learned the hard way that if she really sold herself and her qualifications in interviews, as she was taught in America, it hurt her. She was violating the unspoken principle of the Danish Law of Jante—a cultural imperative that values the community, the conviction that no one person is better than anyone else. She learned that if she worked past 6 p.m., hers was the only car in the parking lot. If she worked past 7 p.m., she had to buy milk, bread, and bacon for dinner at a gas station, because the stores were already closed. When she had her daughter, she said she couldn't just "hang around" on her yearlong maternity leave, so she started a catering company. "My husband calls me a shark, that I have to keep moving all the time in order to breathe. But I have something inside that's driving me, that keeps me up at night." Part of the drive, she says, has always been to get the larger house, the nicer car, the newer Louis Vuitton bag, the next big thing. That—looking out to the horizon for something better rather than noticing what is right in front of her—cost her her first marriage, she says. "That's when I had to decide: Was I going to leave Denmark? Or was I going to change?"

She decided to stay, for her daughter. And so she began studying what makes Danes so happy and writing a blog, *Happy Danes*, to capture her sputtering and often hilariously imperfect attempt at trying to live differently. The first thing she found was more leisure time. She agreed to work with the coach provided by her employer to improve the number 3 item they evaluate on her performance review: work-life balance. She learned to leave the office between 4:30 and 5:00. She got remarried and began cooking dinner with her husband every night. She started lighting a candle to make the simple meal feel special. She began fighting the impulse to interrupt her daughter and read her five books to improve her mind when her daughter was already happily engaged playing on her own. She learned to pull out her own book instead. She began taking morning beach walks and swimming naked in the ocean in winter. In slowing down, she began to notice how she sometimes got in her own way. On a family trip to a cottage in Sweden, she had been so preoccupied with what a dump the cottage was and how ugly the landscape that she'd completely overlooked a long walk in the snow and what should have been an exhilarating ride on Icelandic ponies. "I was *there*, but I was so focused on how much I hated the cabin and how there must have been a better place to stay somewhere else that I missed it all."

And that was it, she realized, the key to Danish happiness. *Hygge*. The moment. When you're riding Icelandic ponies, *ride* Icelandic ponies. When you're drinking a cup of tea, *drink* a cup of tea. When you're walking past a fancy house and find craving and envy creeping in, remember how much you love your own. It's not so much about lowering your expectations, she says, it's more like keeping it real. "This is *hygge*," she says, pronouncing it "heu-guh" and gesturing around the simple carriage house with a clean light pouring in through the windows. "This table. The one green lime. The one white candle. The dish of sea salt. The small, simple things that make life lovely."

"So are you happy?" I ask.

She smiles sadly. "Yes and no," she says finally. "My husband is totally happy and so is my daughter. And I wish I had their contentment— not striving for anything more than they already have. I struggle. You can't suddenly just get rid of your culture, and I was programmed to work and taught to strive. But I'm trying."

# 12

# LET US PLAY

I don't think it is too much to say that play can save your life. It certainly has salvaged mine. Life without play is a grinding, mechanical existence organized around doing the things necessary for survival. Play is the stick that stirs the drink. It is the basis of all art, games, books, sports, movies, fashion, fun, and wonder—in short, the basis of what we think of as civilization.

—Dr. Stuart Brown, founder, National Institute for Play

The popular assumption is that no skills are involved in enjoying free time, and that anybody can do it. Yet the evidence suggests the opposite: free time is more difficult to enjoy than work. Having leisure at one's disposal does not improve the quality of life unless one knows how to use it effectively, and it is by no means something one learns automatically.

—Mihaly Csikszentmihalyi

I stand with my toes curling over the edge of a slip of a platform twenty feet in the air. I had climbed a narrow steel ladder to reach this platform, my head getting lighter and my arms weaker with every reach. As I grabbed on to the platform support and stepped through the air from the ladder to the platform, I had no time to remember how terrified I am of heights. How I hate amusement park rides and hitting turbulence on airplanes. How I have spent most of my life holding other people's combs and pocket change while they ride the roller coaster or Ferris wheel and I watch safely, timidly from the ground.

On command, I cautiously begin to thrust my hips forward. I realize that I am so precariously off-balance that were it not for an instructor's firm grip on the back of the safety harness cinched around my waist, I would certainly plunge headfirst into the billowing air mattress below. My knees tremble. I can't breathe. Sweat bleeds through the chalk I had generously applied to my palms just seconds before. With my right hand, I reach for the surprisingly heavy trapeze bar. With my left, I hold on to the platform support behind me with every fiber of strength I have left.

"Time to let go," the instructor behind me says gently.

"With my left hand?"

"Yes."

"Let go and grab the trapeze with my left hand?"

"Yes."

"Now?"

"Yes. Now."

I am standing on the tiny platform high in the air at the España-STREB Trapeze Academy in Brooklyn because Nadia Stieglitz and Sara Baysinger asked me to come with them on a playdate. The two women run an organization they call Mice at Play—as in what the mice do when the cat's away. The organization started in Nadia's living room in 1998 when, consumed by work, the drudgery of keeping house, and the hard joy of raising young children, she felt the life draining out of her. She had grown up active and playful in France. But she felt lost. "I found myself becoming boring. And sad. My life had shrunk to these two areas: work and caregiving," she told me in her soft accent. "I realized, this is not how I want to live my life. A big part of me was missing and I wanted to find it again." When her three girls were asleep—her husband was often traveling—she carved out time on Monday evenings and invited a group of women over for informal playtime. They played poker. They sat up late telling stories. They cooked exotic meals or painted their toenails wild colors. As the group's children got older, the women began to venture out, going to lectures, art galleries, classes, daring themselves to try anything new, whimsical, or fun that struck their fancy. The idea at first, Nadia said, was just to keep their brains stimulated. But they soon discovered that by making time to play, it was their souls they were saving.

With the zeal of missionaries, Nadia and Sara began researching the science of play and learning how women, in particular, don't allow themselves to. They organized a formal Mice at Play group for time-and-play-starved women, started a website and newsletter, and began planning regular "playdates" for anyone to join. Since 2010, the women have tried boxing and sailing and, with the help of experts, made their own perfumes, cocktail concoctions, and artisanal ice cream. They've given belly dancing, synchronized swimming, and rock climbing a whirl. They've gone on photography safaris, learned wilderness survival skills, and plunged into the icy waters off Coney Island with the Polar Bears on New Year's Day. The playdates are active and involving. They are designed to hurl women out of their heads and out of time, and to immerse mind, body, and soul in play, in the exquisite moments that psychologist Mihaly Csikszentmihalyi has called "flashes of intense living against the dull background of everyday life."

Before the España-STREB Trapeze Academy playdate Sara and Nadia invited me to join, I spent the afternoon with their families at Sara's Brooklyn apartment in an old clock-making factory. Their husbands had just returned from playing one of their regularly scheduled games of soccer all afternoon. The men have always made time to play, they said, going out for a beer after soccer, playing tennis, taking crazy spur-of-the-moment trips. As for most men, nobody had to form an organization to keep them playing. The children were engrossed in making a gooey mess of a gingerbread house with graham crackers, vanilla icing, and dishes of peppermints and chocolates. With a warm fire crackling in the corner, soft music playing, and the room filled with the buzz of easy talk and laughter, Sara and Nadia explained that human beings *need* to play. Research is finding that play is what enables humans to create, improvise, imagine, innovate, learn, solve problems, be smart, open, curious, resilient, and *happy*.[1] "We're in a society where we have to justify play," Nadia said. "But play reminds you of your better self and how happy you can be. In play, there's a wonderful lightness of being."

"It blows our minds, sometimes, what play can actually do for a person," Sara said. "It can totally transform them. And it reconnects them—with themselves, with others, with the possibilities of the world." Sara, a mother of two young boys, felt that transformation herself through play. Never particularly good at sports as a child, she said she'd slowly stopped playing as an adolescent. As an adult, the only time she moved her body was to dutifully get her exercise. "It was always very boring and very painful." Then, at one of the Mice's very first playdates a few years ago, she jumped from a tiny trapeze platform twenty feet above the ground—like the one I would soon be teetering on—and flung herself through the air. She found that not only did her adrenaline level spike, but so did her confidence. She could be terrified in one instant and overcome that fear the next. "Before that moment, I would never have called myself an athlete. And now it's one of my passions." She has gone on to compete in triathlons and half marathons. "It wasn't until joining with the Mice that I recaptured the joy that I had as a young child."

Nadia, too, has transformed herself, her family life, and, she hopes, her daughters' futures through play. Leisure researchers have found that daughters learn about leisure from their mothers. And since most mothers put themselves last and reach for the to-do list first, their example teaches their daughters to do the same.[2] Leisure researchers have also found that the more one plays in childhood, the more likely one is to play in adulthood, that trying a range of activities and experiences early on, when the stakes for failing or proving oneself are so much lower, makes it easier to return to them later, in adulthood.[3] Nadia wanted to show her daughters that by infusing her own life and work as a painter and designer with play, they could do the same with theirs. She wanted to teach them not to lose themselves, like she did. Nadia also wanted to teach her girls that it's in playing together that a family becomes truly close. The family has its own kind of to-do list: a jar they pull from, full of fun things they'd like to do. On the agenda one recent weekend: Find the best hot chocolate in Manhattan, visit the Doughnut Plant in the East Village and try a new flavor; go on a scavenger hunt; ride bikes; play a Scrabble-like game called Bananagram; see a movie (which was actually a dare to see how many movies they could sneak into in one day); plan the next family vacation: Name the country you most would want to visit, explain that country's history, and create a budget and figure out what the family could do on it. "Our mom is always the one to say, 'Let's try something new.' She brings adventure into our lives," said Nadia's sixteen-year-old daughter, Iliade. "I never know what to expect when I walk through the door," said her husband, Mackie, laughing. "It's wonderful."

In polls, surveys, and interviews, people the world over describe their lives as an overwhelming, crazed, and often punishing grind. They say they yearn for nothing more than time for joy. Time to play.[4] And yet, despite the rise of social networking, Meetups, and Groupons, many people don't make time for it. Nadia and Sara are finding that even with their enticing, well-organized, and relatively affordable, by middle-class standards, playdates (an evening of trapeze cost $62), women just can't seem to bring themselves to play. "We meet a lot of resistance," Nadia said. "I thought, at this stage of our business, we would be much more successful than we are."

But there's a reason why play is hard for women. Nadia and Sara are not just taking on America's worship of work, productivity, achievement, speed, and busyness. The two women are pushing against the freight of human history that can be boiled down into three powerful words: Women. Don't. Play.

Remember Thorstein Veblen's influential *Theory of the Leisure Class*? He dispensed with women on page 2, who, as part of the "inferior" class since at least barbarian times, were supposed to do the drudge work of society. Think of the Bible and the "good" wife of Proverbs 31: "She rises while it is yet night and provides food for her household . . . Her lamp does not go out . . . She looks well to the ways of her household, and does not eat the bread of idleness." And this, of course, is after she buys land, plants a vineyard, helps the needy, sews scarlet bedcoverings, sells linen clothes, and makes her husband look good. In the Middle Ages, sure, there were festivals, holy days, and celebrations. But who, leisure scholars ask, do you think cooked the feast? Throughout history, the ladies who lunch, the women with time on their hands, were part of the wealthy elite. Their "forced idleness," leisure scholars contend, came as not a conscious choice but rather an unconscious conspicuous display of the high social status of either a husband, a father, or some male relative. If time is power, *her* free time showed *his* power. And women without status had pots to scrub. A study of the leisure of working-class women in Germany in the 1920s found that women shunned the very *idea* of free time for themselves as "incompatible" with being respectable. Instead, they saw "constant readiness to work and unflagging concern for the welfare of others" as hallmarks of a proper woman. Leisure time was something men, regardless of their social status, got to have.[5] Siesta time in Spain? "Gosh, I never took siestas in my life," time-use researcher Almudena Sevilla-Sanz told me. "My mother didn't, either. She is a teacher. Growing up, she had a long commute to and from school. She'd rush home, make lunch, and do everything while my dad took his siesta. She still does. It never made sense to me. But for her, it's normal."

What about in retirement? One leisure researcher I spoke with, Heather Gibson, a sociologist at the University of North Carolina at Greensboro, sighed. Sure, some play golf, pick up a new hobby, or make time for friends. "But so many retirees have a hard time transitioning into leisure and taking time for themselves, because they feel people will regard them as lazy," she said. "So they fill their time with all this busy stuff." And many retired women *are* busy—still doing the bulk of the housework. Time studies find that if husbands retire before their wives, they often do more housework and domestic duties. But once the wife retires as well, his housework hours drop and his leisure time goes up, and she winds up doing most of the chores, repeating the same pattern set through life.[6]

A seminal work of feminist leisure research by Eileen Green is titled *Women's Leisure, What Leisure?* In her study of women's free time in Sheffield, England, in the 1980s, she and her coauthors found that women identified themselves as wives and mothers first and felt guilty about taking time for or spending money on themselves. "Their husbands, when we asked how they felt about their wives having independent leisure, said it was all right once in a while, but if she did it very often, they would feel there was something wrong with the marriage," Green told me. "But for the men, well, that was altogether different. The husbands said having leisure for themselves was part of what being a man was all about." When North Carolina State University leisure scholar Karla Henderson tried to interview rural farm women about their leisure, they all laughed at her. Whatever "free" time they had, they filled with enjoyable but productive quilting bees, knitting circles, canning, gardening, and talk with friends as they bustled about the kitchen. Henderson came to think of this as "invisible" leisure—and truly, it is the only kind of acceptable and industrious leisure time most women have ever known. Henderson and other scholars say women taking time for themselves, deliberately choosing leisure without children or family, is nothing less than a courageous—subversive, almost—act of resistance.[7]

True to form, the most popular playdates, Nadia and Sara have found, are always the more "productive"-sounding ones on nutrition, detoxing, or exercise. "It's much more difficult to promote something that's just pure play," Sara said. "There is just this huge guilt."

On my last day in Paris at the time-use conference, when I talked with the Australian time-use researcher Lyn Craig about her leisure studies, she beamed as she told me she'd indulged in a little leisure time for herself that morning and had just returned from shoe shopping and coffee with a friend. I told her, proudly, that I, too, had finally made time for leisure. I had gotten up at 5 a.m. and gone for a run on the Champs-Élysées and around the Tuileries Garden.

She wrinkled her nose. "Purposive leisure," she said with distaste. "How very American."

I wanted to protest. I enjoyed my early morning run. But Craig was right. I'd gone out specifically, purposively to get *exercise*. I was thinking about virtuously burning off that *pain au chocolat*, dutifully *training* for my first half marathon, shedding the jittery anxiety that clings to me like an aura. I hadn't gone running just for the pure joy of it.

To time-use researchers like John Robinson, who sparked this whole journey of mine, "leisure" is defined by a set of activities, like listening to the radio or getting some exercise. Robinson also counts as leisure any residual time that, like leftovers, doesn't fit neatly into other prescribed categories like "work" or "personal care." That's how he could analyze my weekly time diary and come up with twenty-seven hours of bits and scraps of crappy leisure time.

But talk to any leisure researcher, and he or she will say the true test of leisure is not *what* the activity is that fills a certain block of time but how that time *feels*. And different activities feel different to different people at different times in their lives. A carefree day at the beach with friends in your twenties can feel a whole lot different from a day with two toddlers prone to sunburn, who can't swim, need naps, and insist on painfully scraping the sand off their tiny feet on your bare legs. Just as the overwhelm is the result of unpredictability and a lack of control, true leisure, researchers say, is the result of feeling both a measure of control over the experience and also choice, free from obligation. "But women have more of a sense of obligation rather than a feeling of voluntary choice," Heather Gibson told me. Gibson chairs the World Leisure Organization's newly reconstituted Commission on Women and Gender (it had been defunct for years).[8] Leisure time for women, studies have found, often just means more work. Women are typically the ones who plan, organize, pack, execute, delegate, and clean up after outings, holidays, vacations, and family events. And in addition to being physically taxing, leisure for women can be mentally and emotionally draining, Gibson and other researchers have found, because women tend to feel responsible for making sure everyone *else* is enjoying the leisure activity and so are constantly taking the emotional temperatures of all involved. That strong, self-sacrificing "ethic of care," as leisure researchers call it, is also the reason women tend to have the ongoing tape loop of tasks yet to get done, responsibilities, and worries that play in the head like an annoying and hard-to-shake jingle, which contaminates the experience of any kind of time.[9]

What Nadia and Sara are confronting as they struggle to stir up a play revolution for women sounds as if it could be ripped straight out of the pages of academic feminist leisure research. Women tell Nadia and Sara that they have no time to play. They say they're too busy ferrying their kids around to their playdates. Working mothers and at-home mothers alike say they worry they aren't spending enough time with their children, so mothers feel they both need and want to spend nearly all their leisure time with them,—which helps explain why women's leisure often comes in interrupted scraps of time. One recent study of thirty-two middle-class families in Los Angeles found that most mothers experienced leisure "episodes" that lasted no longer than ten minutes.[10] But doing something for a longer, more refreshing period on their own, many mothers tell Nadia and Sara, would feel selfish or lazy. "When children are young, we find that women's leisure tends to be friendship and home based, so mothers can be around," Gibson told me. "And when the children are older, there's still a sense of guilt about leaving them, even if that's what gives women a sense of escape and release."

Women tell Nadia and Sara that they feel they aren't *entitled* to have leisure time. They feel they have to *earn* it first by getting to the end of the to-do list. Which never comes. "We see that a lot, that women say they'll get to leisure when everything else is done," Gibson said. Often, women tell Nadia and Sara that they're too exhausted to do much more than collapse at the end of the day and turn on the TV.

Ah, finally, the question of TV and leisure.

Watching TV is the industrialized world's main pastime.[11] Various time studies have found that American adults, on average, watch two to four hours of TV a day. Researchers have found that American children are exposed, on average, to four hours of "background" TV a day on top of the hour and a half they are glued to a TV directly. And when computers, smartphones, video games, and other devices are added in, one study found that screen time for American adults, not counting work on computers, can hit an astounding 8.5 hours a day, the most time sucking of any developed country in the world.[12] To time-use researchers like John Robinson, we are a nation of couch potatoes, addicted to spending our free hours lounging mindlessly with a bag of chips in front of the tube, which is, various studies have found, making us fat, depressed, socially isolated, and more prone to violence, lowering our self-esteem, disrupting our sleep, dulling our senses, fogging our mind, and shortening our attention and our life spans.[13] Indeed, research has found that, with the flick of the TV's remote, our thinking brains shut off. Within thirty seconds, we lose our sense of self, and our alpha waves become no more active than if we were staring at a blank wall.[14]

Yet the relationship between TV and leisure time is far more complicated than it looks. Yes, we watch a lot of TV. But time-use researchers who look not only at what people are doing but also how they're feeling and what else they're juggling at a given moment have found that people often turn on the TV because they feel too exhausted to do anything else. And for many people with a lot to do, TV really does function more like a blank wall, perhaps with a bit of distracting colorful wallpaper on it. Experience Sampling Method studies have found that women multitask like champs while watching TV—paying bills, folding laundry, checking e-mail, or, like me one evening, crunching General Social Survey data on my laptop while the kids watched *Journey to the Center of the Earth.*[15]

But TV brings up a deeper issue. If true leisure is all about choice, sometimes TV is simply the easy choice. It's right in your living room. It's cheap. Turning it on requires no effort. Yes, sometimes we choose TV because we're too tired for anything else. But sometimes, leisure researchers have found, we choose it because we're unsure of what we really would like to do in a moment of unstructured free time. Part of that uncertainty comes from living in a work-worshipping culture. And part from decision fatigue. I met a young, single woman who'd just returned from living in Italy, where long, lazy days away from the office were embraced as part of *il dolce far niente*—the sweetness of doing nothing. Living back in the United States, that kind of free time *felt* different. "You know, sometimes, on weekends, when I have nothing on my schedule, I feel anxious," she confessed. And, for women, part of the indecision about what to do comes from being conditioned to put everyone and everything else first. "Sometimes we find that women say they're too busy to come on a playdate, but they've just filled their schedules with all these kid activities and social obligations that may not be that satisfying. Then they talk like they're heroes when they tell people that they have no time for play," Nadia told me. "Maybe it takes too much effort to be a little uncomfortable, to learn something new, and they don't have the energy. But really, I think they're *afraid*. They're afraid of what having free time to themselves would feel like."

Was I afraid? Afraid, perhaps, that stripped of work, of the responsibilities of motherhood and family, and of the bustle of my to-do list, I didn't know who I would find? Was that part of what kept me spinning?

Sara and Nadia had been after me for months to come out and play. In my heart, I knew if I was going to write about why leisure time is important, what carving out time for it does for the soul, and how science is finding that play is central to being alive, I had to find time to *do* it myself. Yet I had all the same excuses for deferring it as women have for ages.

Could I come snowshoeing in the snow and ice? No time. A day of finger painting? Yoga on a mountaintop? 1940s dress-up? Too busy. An erotic scavenger hunt in Manhattan? Um, pass. How about flamenco dancing until we found *duende*, the mystical state of wild abandon? Beach volleyball? Stand-up paddleboarding? I had more important things to do. I kept putting off playtime. Until, with my manuscript deadline approaching, I simply could not put it off anymore. And the only playdate on the Mice at Play calendar before my deadline was . . . the Flying Trapeze.

I groaned.

"No, this is perfect," Nadia had insisted. "A big part of play is stepping outside your comfort zone. That forces you to be very present. Your mind becomes completely engaged in the moment. You tend to forget about all the worries in your life and all the things you have to do. That's flow. That's when things start happening. That's the eureka! moment."

At the España-STREB Trapeze Academy in Brooklyn's Williamsburg neighborhood, we ran through a few drills on the mats, removed earrings and jewelry, and were cinched tightly into safety harnesses. I nervously lined up with six other women to take my turn climbing to the platform high in the air. Nadia and Sara have a few unwritten rules for playdates to ensure that the women will get out of their heads and into the flow: no smartphones, or at least no incessant checking of them; no talk of work and networking—a playdate is not a place to think about advancing your career. There's also nothing to prove on a playdate. There is no talk about winning something, beating someone else, or accomplishing anything, which Nadia and Sara know goes against the grain for achievement-oriented Americans where even blissed-out yoga has become a competitive sport.[16] A playdate is a time to be open to trying something new and have some fun. So, like pure play, it doesn't matter, really, what happens. You swing from the trapeze and make the catch in midair? Great. You fall twenty feet and land on your face on the billowing air mattress below? No big deal. So drop the judgment—of yourself and everyone else. Nadia and Sara want their women to feel free, to be both their truest selves and part of a spirited and supportive group, no matter what happens.

Ahead of me in line, Moria Holland, a divorced mother, had signed up for this, her first playdate, after a conversation with her six-year-old son. "He said, 'Mommy, when you and your friends get together, you never laugh or run around. You never have any fun,'" she said. "I'm scared to do this. But the more I thought about it, the more I thought, 'He's right.' I had to try something different." Behind me, Gigi Branch-Shaw, another divorced mother and one of the original Mice, said she hadn't really understood what she was missing until she started to play. "When we went on the rock-climbing playdate, I was afraid at first. Then, when I started doing it, I remembered how much I loved climbing trees as a child. It's like I came back to myself," she said. "Time seems different when you play." Doing things she never thought she could has brought energy and freshness to her relationships and given her confidence to try new things—at work, in life, for fun. Now she makes an effort to find time to play—"even if it's just for twenty minutes"—to go on a bike ride for the fun of it instead of determined to get a workout, to hike with her fourteen-year-old son, to call a girlfriend for no particular reason. "Sometimes I really have to force myself to come to these playdates," she said. "But the more I play, the more I crave it."

"Are you ready?" the instructor holding me up by my harness asks softly. I can feel the sweat not only on my palms now but also on the bottoms of my feet. I have just watched Moria swallow hard, step off the platform, and swing through the air. Gigi is climbing up the ladder.

There is no time to worry about whether I look fat in the safety harness. No time to wonder what the kids are doing and whether Tom has checked their homework. No time to think about whether I've done enough work to deserve this moment of play. There is no turning back.

In what feels like achingly slow motion, I loosen the death grip of my left hand from the platform support and hesitantly reach for the trapeze bar.

"Ready!" the instructor on the ground yells. This is not a question. This, we've been taught, is a command. My heart pounds. I bend my trembling knees.

"Hep!"

And jump.


Active play, says Stuart Brown, is a state of being unlike anything else. It is timeless, like flow, and crucial to humans from the moment of birth to the last breath. Play is also a state of mind, an attitude of lightness, curiosity, wonder that can infuse any situation. Both are so essential to human evolution, development, innovation, and civilization that the Dutch historian Johan Huizinga maintained in 1938 that far better than *Homo sapiens*, the intelligent or rational human, our complicated species should be called *Homo ludens*, the playing human. And neuroscience, Brown argues, is beginning to show how true that is. Play, he says, is what builds complex, skilled, responsive, socially adept, and flexible brains, which in turn build complex, skilled, responsive, socially adept, and flexible people and societies.[17]

Stuart Brown is a psychiatrist, the founder of the National Institute for Play, and one of the most prominent lonely voices advocating for time to play in the wilderness of a serious and busy world. He knows most people feel too overwhelmed to play. He's made a career of treating people suffering from the effects of what he calls play deprivation, which, he said, tends to set in just as humans hit adolescence. Men tend to maintain at least a semblance of play through sports, he said, either actively playing or watching it. Women tend to lose it entirely. "There's just this huge sense of loss," Brown told me. "The lament is intense and almost universal, that there's no time to play. But when you don't make that time a priority, there are huge consequences, emotionally, spiritually, and physically. Most all of us have a play nature and it's within our capacity to get it back. But if your time is constantly fragmented and you're revving in high gear with the demands of the day, it's very, very tough."

Ask Brown why humans need to play—a subject that continues to puzzle scientists—and he'll show you a series of pictures of an enormous white polar bear cavorting on the ice with a much smaller sled dog. The powerful bear with one swipe could rip the smaller dog in half. Instead, the two bow, roll about, wrestle, jump, play bite, and generally goof around. The first point Brown makes is that both animals appear well fed, well rested, and not in stress. Having their basic needs taken care of enables them to be open and ready to play, which, he says, is also true in humans. The second point, he says, is that this kind of "rough-and-tumble" frolicking shows just why play is so important. Something special is happening, Brown maintains, that goes beyond mere exercise or the scientific view that play is practice, a means to prepare young animals for behaviors they'll need to survive as adults. "It's the exploration of the possible," Brown said. "Play takes one thing—a massive polar bear that could eat a little dog—and turns it into something else, something unexpected. A dance. It takes chaos and finds order. It's based on trust, that no one's going to get hurt. And it doesn't seem to have any point. They're playing for the sake of playing."

Lizards, turtles, rats, birds, primates, most mammals, and even some fish play in their youth. Researchers have found a direct correlation between animal play and the growth of the cerebellum, the most neuron-rich part of the brain that controls movement, balance, coordination, and key cognitive functions like language processing and attention.[18] Scientists are also finding direct links between animal play and the development of the prefrontal cortex, the "mind" of the thinking brain that controls emotions and impulses and leads to improved attention and decision making, all of which are critical to forming healthy social relations. The more play, the bigger the prefrontal cortex. Scientists say the finding likely holds true for humans as well: Children who have more time for free, unstructured, and rough-and-tumble play tend to be more socially and academically proficient as they grow.[19]

Few animals continue to play into adulthood. Humans do. Play sculpts the brain, Brown maintains. In horsing around, pretending, telling stories, moving our bodies, creating, making jokes, tinkering, being curious, competing in sports, daydreaming, and playfully exploring novel experiences—like soaring on a trapeze, or writing a book, even—the brain creates rich new neural connections that fire together in new ways. As a child, play is how we begin to understand ourselves and the way the world works, simulating experiences and emotions, learning skills without risk. As adults, play is what keeps our brains flexible. And that, Brown says, is what enables our species to innovate, create, solve old problems in new ways, and continuously adapt our behavior to thrive in an ever-changing and often dangerous world. Once managers at Caltech's Jet Propulsion Lab discovered that the best engineers had the richest play experiences—building soapbox derby racers, taking apart clocks, working with their hands—they began to include questions about a candidate's play history in standard interviews.[20] The Nobel Prize–winning physicist Richard Feynman was a master of "serious play," Brown says, who approached his work with a playful attitude. "I'd invent things and play with things for my own entertainment," Feynman wrote in his autobiography. In the same spirit, he watched students in the cafeteria goof off by spinning plates. "For the fun of it," he began to make calculations of the wobbles— "piddling around," he said, which led to developing the "Feynman diagrams" to explain quantum electrodynamics and ultimately resulted in his Nobel Prize.[21]

In animal studies, life without play is bleak. Scientists put young rats in cages only with adults, who don't play, and kept them away from other young, playful rats. They discovered that when deprived of play, the young rats' brains developed abnormally. So abnormally, in fact, that they looked just like the brains of rats with a damaged prefrontal cortex. In one experiment, when presented with a cat odor, both rats who played and rats deprived of play fled, their stress hormone cortisol levels spiking and their hearts racing. But only the playful rats slowly reemerged, began to poke around, and tested the environment again. "The nonplayers never come out of hiding," Brown explained. "Their cortisol levels don't come back down. They often die."[22]

Brown began his lifelong study of play by analyzing, in experiments like the rat study, the consequences of its absence. As a young psychiatrist, he was asked to investigate why Charles Whitman, who'd been an Eagle Scout, an altar boy, and a Marine, shot and killed seventeen and wounded forty-one people at the University of Texas in 1966. Yes, there had been abuse, a controlling father, and a lot of stress in Whitman's life. But what struck Brown most was that as a child, Whitman had never been allowed time to play. And that absence "left him without a repertoire of behaviors to handle high stress, particularly humiliation and depression," Brown said.

Brown has since taken more than six thousand "play histories" of people. And what he finds in those who do not make time for play—in either attitude or activity—is often joylessness, rigidity, addiction, workaholism, diminished curiosity, and, at the core, depression. To help people reclaim their playful natures, he takes them back to their earliest memories of play, to remember what they loved doing as children so they can begin to build on it and figure out how to use it as adults—to bring creativity and passion to their work, like Richard Feynman, to foster intimacy, connection, and playfulness in their relationships at home with their partners and children and to make time to just have lighthearted fun for the soul.

That's what Brown saw Barbara Brannen, a woman he met in Colorado, do.

Brannen was a successful executive in Denver with two kids and a busy life who, over time, found herself feeling increasingly overwhelmed, unsatisfied, sad, and so stressed-out from working all the time that she lost the use of her left arm. "A whole bunch of things in my life fell apart, and I decided it was because I'd stopped playing," she told me. "I decided that play was a gift, a gift that women, in particular, get the message very early on that they should give up. And they need to find it again."

I visited Brannen at her home office. She answered the door wearing a headband with sparkly red hearts bopping from two wires, gave out a great laugh as if she were utterly delighted to see me, and handed me a little pink plastic pig. "This is a shower pig," she said. "Taking a shower with a pig every morning is like deciding, 'Today is going to be a good day. A playful day.'"

Her office, which looks out onto the Rocky Mountains, is decorated with sock monkeys, Tiggers, rainbows, butterflies, purple pens, hula hoops, colored highlighters, and all manner of plastic toy trinkets and stuffed animals. Brannen explains that, in the process of recovering from major surgery on her arm, she began to find time to bring play back into her own life and that she, as a "play coach," running a business called Playmore, has helped others do the same. The key, she has found, is helping people remember what, as a child, made them feel so happy they couldn't wait to do it and, once they started, never wanted to stop. To help jog people's moribund and often embarrassed memories, she brings out giant pads of paper with wide lines, like a kindergartener uses, and a box of colored pencils and tells people to just start writing what she calls a "playlist."

That's what she herself began to do. She discovered she *did* have time for leisure. It just wasn't *her* kind of leisure. She'd fallen into doing all the things that her kids wanted or that her husband liked or that others expected of her—playdates, socializing, going to movies, or just waiting for vacation or holidays to come. She did enjoy the time, "but I wanted to feel my heart sing," she said. "I wanted something to grab hold of, that when you finish doing it, it doesn't matter if it tires you out, it rejuvenates you."

She began trying to recall what it was that she loved but had set aside. She began reading the comics again and sitting down to play the piano for a few minutes when she walked by it. She injected playfulness throughout her day, blasting music when it was time to clean out the closet or wearing head boppers at work. She stashed bubbles in the car for her kids when they got cranky and began carrying a wand in case she felt like waving it around when she was stuck in traffic. Over time, she remembered that what she loved most as a child and what she missed most as an adult was being outdoors. She loved to ski, to be out in the woods. She loved making mud pies. And most of all, she loved the water. She also realized that her husband did not love any of these things, and perhaps that was why it took her so long to remember. It was a scary realization. She loved her husband. Her challenge became, then, how to find time for her own play while preserving time for the things they loved to do together. She started small, planting a garden in the backyard and getting her hands dirty, like she had making mud pies. Then she found nearby hiking trails and took her dog or met a friend to walk. Over time, as her arm healed and her children grew up, on a wild hair, she found herself at REI, shopping for a kayak. Though she had no idea how to paddle, she found three little lakes within ten minutes of her house, and now she regularly goes out to splash around. "It is just really, really fun."

She looked at me. "When was the last time you played?" she asked. "I mean really played?"

I paused. It would be months before Nadia and Sara finally cajoled me into coming on a playdate. I put down the pen and notepad that I'd been using to take notes on our conversation and thought back. When did I stop building Barbie houses out of our old red encyclopedias? Climbing that enormous pine tree in our neighbor's yard? Turning cartwheels? Tossing a football after school with my friend Julie? When did the daring feats of capture the flag and the rough-and-tumble games of British bulldog out under the streetlights on warm summer nights turn into spin the bottle and truth or dare?

"Oooof. I don't know. When I was ten or eleven years old?" I said. "Maybe twelve?"

In midair, it's surprising how weightless a body feels. At the high point of the swing out, your legs almost float up and over the trapeze bar. And in the breath of a moment at the apex of the swing back, your hands easily come off the bar as you glide forward, hanging by your knees, like you did so naturally as a girl from the cool, hard metal bars of the playground.

By this time, you've jumped from the España-STREB platform a handful of times and survived. You've stopped screaming with every swing. Your hands tremble, not with fear anymore but with a weird excitement that feels like your *skin* has been drinking coffee all day. Upside down, whooshing backward through the air, you arch your back and reach out with your hands, as much from instinct as from any instruction shouted from the ground below. You've watched as Mouse after Mouse on this trapeze playdate has done the same and, the timing off by mere seconds, just missed the midair catch with the instructor hanging by his knees from his own trapeze. So you expect nothing.

The moment comes effortlessly. At the arc of the swing forward, hands clap onto your wrists. Catch.

So this is what it feels like to fly.

# BRIGHT SPOT: REALLY *PLAN* A VACATION

Every summer, as she prepares for vacation, Carolyn Semedo-Strauss stuffs her minivan with luggage. Next to the suitcases and duffel bags, she crams in bags of yarn and boxes of books, like a promise to herself, in the hopes that she'll actually spend time enjoying a quiet moment alone. Most years, the boxes come home untouched. She rounds up her three kids and all the electronic gadgets, music, books, crayons, games, and gear to keep them relatively appeased for the ten-hour drive from Virginia to Massachusetts. She kisses her husband goodbye and heads out for her family reunion. It's a sprawling African American family, with eleven siblings, and every year they converge from all over the country for a few brief days at their parents' home. With so much of her time taken up in the whirlwind of logistics, rushing to see everyone and making sure everyone *else* is happy, her vacation time leaves her mind in an exhausting "tangle" and doesn't *feel* very leisurely.

Roger Mannell, a psychologist at the University of Waterloo in Ontario, has directed perhaps the only lab studies of leisure time. His research has found that when people have a sense of *choice* and *control* over what they do with their free time, they are more likely to get into flow, that engrossing and timeless state that some call peak human experience. "Part of the problem with leisure is that people aren't quite sure what they really *want*. They don't know what leisure time is for them," Mannell said. "And they never slow down long enough to figure it out."

In his experiment, Mannell told his subjects they were participating in two different learning tasks. But the real experiment was what they did and how they felt during a thirty-minute period of "free" time between the two tasks. One group was given a *choice* about what to do; the other was *told* what to do. Mannell then asked each group to estimate how long they'd waited between tasks. Those who had no choice were almost uncannily accurate—reporting that twenty-nine excruciatingly boring minutes had passed. But those who were given free choice became so engrossed in what they were doing, in flow, they lost track of time altogether. On average, they felt the waiting period was only nine minutes long. Mannell did further studies and found that people who felt they naturally had more control over their lives also experienced more flow, while those who felt that external forces were more in control of their lives felt less.[1] To Mannell, consciously choosing leisure is the first step to reclaiming it. "The institutions we move in and out of in our daily lives have some responsibility for creating saner lives and need to change. But something in us needs to change as well," Mannell said. "If we are really serious about finding more free time and having control over it, then we need to make the choice to pursue things that are really meaningful to us."

I told Mannell that in conversations with dozens of women as I researched this book, many lamented that their sense of time pressure and mind clutter followed them on vacation. "You get in this frenzied state, so that when you do have time, you don't know what to do with it," one told me. Said another, "Even on vacation, I just haven't been able to feel unburdened, untroubled, and turn-yourself-inside-out joy." Many women said that whether it was a trip to an all-inclusive resort, a beach vacation, a camping trip, or a road trip to visit family, vacation often just meant more work for them. "Who decides, who plans, who organizes, who makes arrangements? Me. Me. Me. And me," said Mara. Time to let go? She laughed bitterly and described a resort vacation where even a swim with the dolphins was just one more item to be checked off her to-do list, along with getting up early to grab seats by the crowded pool, slathering sunscreen on kids, and constantly checking the lost and found for the stuff they kept losing. "I just perpetuated what I do at home," she said. "I was irritating even myself."

Mannell suggested I design an informal experiment and get a group of women to think about what they *really wanted* to experience during their time off and write it down. That, he said, would *force* them to make time to think about meaningful leisure so they could deliberately choose it. Carolyn Semedo-Strauss was the only one in the group who actually did. In the fall, I met Semedo-Strauss at a coffee shop. She ran a hand through her long, thin twists of dreadlocks and then pulled out a thick book where she'd listed what she wanted to do and how she wanted her time to feel: She wanted to read for pleasure, write, see a sunset, have quality time with her family, feel fully present and not so scattered, and create lasting memories.

"How'd it go?" I asked.

She didn't read and she didn't write. But making a list of what she did want made it much clearer what she didn't want: being in charge all the time. "So I sat back and enjoyed the hot dogs, like everyone else for once," she said.

One day at the beach, the kids were flying kites with the cousins, playing soccer, and searching for shells. She sat contentedly in the warmth of the sun, enjoying the rich aromas of the family cookout they'd just finished eating and the ease of being with her extended family. Around sunset, thick black storm clouds gathered on the horizon, casting shadows of the family all around her in sharp relief. She brought out her camera. *Snap.* "That's when it hit me—*this* is what I wanted," Semedo-Strauss told me, her eyes gleaming, smiling at the sunset, the family time, the presence, and the lasting memory she had, indeed, created.

# PART FIVE

# TOWARD TIME SERENITY

# 13

# FINDING TIME

*The way you live your days is the way you live your life.*
—**Annie Dillard**

I sit at a table with four other people, pencil in hand, paralyzed. In front of each of us lies a blank calendar for one week, starting on Sunday and ending on Saturday. Each day is broken into hourly grids, starting at 6 a.m. and ending at midnight. The task at this daylong Time Triage workshop sounds simple enough: Design Your Perfect Schedule. What would you do, say, on Tuesday at 10 a.m. or on Friday at 3 p.m. to make your life meaningful? What, when you really come down to the quotidian details, does it *look* like every day to have time to do good work, to spend quality time with your family and friends, and to refresh your soul?

I stare at the page.

And so does everyone else: a real estate agent who feels there's so much chaos between her work and life demands that it seems as if her time is "bleeding"; a man who just wants to figure out how to relax on the weekends without feeling guilty; his wife who wants the world to stop for a few days so she can get caught up; a young woman living on fast-forward who has burned through two marriages and snaps photos of beautiful sunsets to post on Facebook as she flies down the road on her way to somewhere else. "I just feel this tremendous sense of loss all the time."

We'd started the workshop that morning with a very different exercise in time: filling in a schedule of what we'd done in the past week. That was easy. Everyone jam-packed the little hour grids with so much stuff that the cramped handwriting spilled out into the margins of the page. Terry Monaghan, our no-nonsense leader and self-described "productivity expert," then asked us what we'd do if our schedules opened up and we suddenly found we had more time.

"Read," I said. The others chimed in: "Sleep." "Organize all the drawers." "Learn to sail." "Sew." "Pray." "Travel." "Be happy."

"Where is the time for that on your schedules?" Monaghan had asked. There wasn't any. That's when she'd given us these blank calendars and told us to *find* the time. We stare, stumped, for several more uncomfortable minutes.

Terry Monaghan's approach to time management is simple: You can't manage time. Time never changes. There will always and ever be 168 hours in a week. What you *can* manage are the activities you *choose* to do *in* time. And what busy and overwhelmed people need to realize, she said, is that you will *never* be able to do everything you think you need, want, or should do. "When we die, the e-mail in-box will still be full. The to-do list will still be there. But you won't," she told us. "Eighty percent of the e-mail that comes in is crap anyway, and it takes you the equivalent of *nineteen and a half weeks a year* just to sort through. Eighty percent of your to-do list is crap. Look, the stuff of life *never* ends. That *is* life. You will *never* clear your plate so you can finally allow yourself to get to the good stuff. So you have to decide. What do you want to accomplish in this life? What's *important* to you right now? And realize that what's important now may not be two years from now. It's always changing."

Monaghan looks at us staring forlornly at our blank Perfect Schedules. She sighs. "This is not rocket science here, people," she says. "Start with time for what's most important."

But that's where I got stuck. *Everything* seemed important. My work. My family. My friends. My community. Changing the kitty litter. Sorting my daughter's Barbie shoes. Keeping the incoming tide of clutter in the house at bay . . .

That, Ellen Ernst Kossek, an organizational psychologist and management professor at Purdue University, would later tell me, means I'm not only an "integrator" of work and home duties, but the kind of über-integrator she calls a "fusion lover." Unlike "separators," who keep their work and life separated with bright lines, I tend to do everything all at once, all the time. In her book *CEO of Me*, Kossek writes that some people thrive on integration, answering work e-mails from the side-lines of a child's soccer game or checking in with the babysitter in the afternoon at the office, juggling a hundred different balls with aplomb.[1] But if that integration was making me feel overwhelmed, then I wasn't doing it particularly well. The downside to being a fusion lover, she said, is that people like me tend to get confused over which demand is more pressing in the moment, so we don't have clear focus on what to do. We can't decide. So we end up doing both work and home activities in an *ambivalent*, halfhearted way, which produces mediocre outcomes and vague disappointment in both. Youch!

There it was again, that *ambivalence*.

In truth, I had always suffered from indecision. Burger with fries or without? Call high school friends or stay home and watch *Love Boat*? The indecision was compounded by gnawing self-doubt and only in-tensified when I tried to both work and parent. Time management gurus talk about clearing away any nagging "internal friction" that erodes the willpower and clouds the thinking before one can take off to superproductive heights. But honestly, in living in a stew of am-bivalence and self-doubt, crashing between the impossible pulls of the ideal worker and ideal mother, "internal friction" doesn't even begin to cover what's going on inside.

Sometimes the sheer agony of leaving the warm baby or the weeping toddler and walking out the door in the morning to go to an unforgiv-ing workplace was enough to sap my strength for the rest of the day. I can still remember watching my son's tiny hand, waving out the win-dow from his car seat, and the utter anguish I felt as Tom turned left to take Liam to Abracadabra one morning and I, driving the car behind them, turned right to face another long and unpredictable workday. I felt guilty and heartsick as I dragged into the office. Working from home or working flexible hours wasn't as much of an option then as it is now.

The minute I crossed the threshold into the office, the chatter would start in my head: "You left your children. You'd better do something extraordinary to make up for it." But I usually had just enough psychic juice to start the day with the easier, distracting flash fires on my to-do list, thinking I'd just clear my plate and *then* get to more important stuff. The heavy inertia tended to burn off about midmorning. Then I'd often get so wrapped up in what I was doing that I'd lose track of time. The guilty, sluggish start tended to make my workdays longer, the churn of pollution in my brain making it harder to think. Then I'd get stuck on deadline or in traffic and guiltily slink home later than I'd hoped.

It wasn't like this all the time. There were good days. Leaving in the morning did get easier, emotionally if not logistically, once the kids hit school age. But that ragged feeling of being neither here nor there and vaguely inadequate in both is what I remember most about being a working mother with little kids in the early twenty-first century. For years, I imagined myself sliding sideways into the day, reluctant and resentful, skulking like a crab.

Psychologists say that ambivalence is, literally, being of two minds. In their labs, they have found that that nebulous feeling is far more uncomfortable and stressful on the body and mind than either embracing one position over another or merely being neutral. But the discomfort of the ambivalent soul becomes unbearable if we are forced to make a choice.[2] In constant battle with yourself, you fight, not to truce but to a stalemate. There is no clear victor, no end in sight. It's like living life on hold. We distract ourselves from this uneasy internal landscape with busyness, with the bustle of our to-do lists. To be ambivalent, say the psychotherapists David Hartman and Diane Zimberoff, is to be preoccupied with both what is wanted and what is not. "The opposite of ambivalence is a rigid intolerance for ambiguity, nuance or paradox," they write. "The synthesis of the two is 'passionate commitment in the face of ambiguity.'"[3]

Ah, is that it?

Sitting in the Time Triage workshop, staring at my blank Perfect Schedule, I realized I would never be able to schedule my way efficiently out of the overwhelm. I had to face my own ambivalence about trying to live two clashing ideals at once. There would never be enough room in a day for both. As I had been on this quest to understand the overwhelm and the way out, I watched helplessly as Jeff, one of our best friends, died suddenly and inexplicably of stomach cancer. Life is so fragile. I simply couldn't wait, like so many people clucked, until the kids were grown and gone and the madness was over to live my best life. I couldn't wait for the ideal worker to retire, for businesses and governments to rewrite policies, for society to reshape its attitudes. I may not have the time. I had to figure out how to embrace my own life with that passionate commitment in the face of ambiguity, right here, right now.

I searched for people who had. That led me to Maia Heyck-Merlin and the group she put together called WoMoBiJos: Working Mothers with Big Jobs. The WoMoBiJos are women in their thirties and forties who live in different cities and have big careers in finance, the nonprofit world, medicine, and other fields. The ones who live near New York meet once a month for breakfast. The rest communicate primarily through the magic of Google Groups and the Internet. They love their work, yet they are not ideal worker warriors. They love their kids and families, yet they don't buy into the ideal mother's demands. "Good enough is the new perfect," is their mantra. They love their lives. And many have found a way to make time for themselves. Though each one lives a busy life, not one described herself as feeling overwhelmed.

In talking to them, it pretty quickly became apparent why: None of the WoMoBiJos felt ambivalent. Their lives certainly weren't perfect—living with a two-year-old, one said, is "like living with a bipolar drunken troll." They were tired. They worked hard to make things work. But without the fog of guilty ambivalence shrouding their days, each was able to embrace her life with passion.

"I don't describe my life as overwhelming. I see it as deeply rich and complex. I feel energized by the challenges I have to confront," said Heather Peske, a Boston WoMoBiJo with two daughters who travels frequently for her job but makes sure she has Fridays off at home. "I'm not being Pollyannaish and I'm definitely tired. There are compromises and tensions, but I like living that way. Balance is a simplistic formulation because my life is often not balanced. It tips in various directions at different times between my work, my kids, my partner, or myself. But I've found that rather than seek perfect balance, it's better for me to ask myself: Am I trying my best? Am I doing things for the right reasons? Do I make those I love feel loved? Am I happy? And then adjust as I go."[4]

"I don't feel conflicted. I feel like I'm making my own choices," said Melea, a chief operating officer at a nonprofit and mother of two who sets her own schedule and works from home two days a week. "But I know a lot of that is because of the supportive culture of my workplace. When you're in a churn-and-burn environment, like a lot of my friends are, you're in constant conflict."

Maia Heyck-Merlin loves her work as a chief talent officer for an education reform nonprofit in New York and running her own company, the Together Teacher, teaching time management and organization techniques to teachers. She assembled the WoMoBiJo group soon after giving birth to her daughter when she ran smack into the haze of ambivalence that hovers over the mommy wars. She joined one mothers' group of women whose husbands had big jobs and made a lot of money and, following in the ideal mother's footsteps, they were staying home with the children. "The thought of going to work every day makes me nauseous," one told her. She tried another group of working mothers. But most were lawyers or struggling to work in the time cages of demanding ideal worker workplaces. They were miserable. The first session started with cutting out magazine photographs of what they imagined would be better lives or wistfully looking for businesses they could start on their own. Heyck-Merlin couldn't relate to either group. She wanted to work. She wanted to be a good mom. She wanted to have time to live a good life. And she saw no reason *not* to do it all. And neither did the other WoMoBiJos she began to find.

"We're all in very mission-driven work. We feel we are doing good by making the world a better place—for our kids, for everybody," Heyck-Merlin said. "I feel like I'm a pretty good mother. I'm pretty good at my job. I can't be all things all days. But if I shoot for it in a monthlong period, then I do okay. I am into having little stress in my life, a big job, and a lot of fun."

The more I spoke with the WoMoBiJos it became apparent they were freed from the mire of ambivalence because the structures of their lives, like the best of the bright spots I'd found, fully support them in work, love, and play. They all work in incredibly flexible work environments. Many WoMoBiJos work compressed schedules or work regularly from home. They have worked their way into positions of authority, so their time is their own to control and is predictable. They are unapologetic. Once, when the men at Heyck-Merlin's organization wanted to meet regularly at 7:30 a.m., she matter-of-factly pointed out to her boss that, as the only executive with a full-time working spouse—her teacher husband—that was unworkable. They decided to hold meetings during regular business hours instead.

Their partners are, to greater and lesser extents, equitably sharing care of kids and domestic work. They automate, delegate, or drop everything else—shopping for groceries online, hiring help, or not caring if the house is less than perfect or if their husbands always make sandwiches for dinner. So none face the double time bind at home. Heyck-Merlin has no qualms hanging up chore lists at big gatherings of family or friends. "Why should someone be sitting on the couch while I do all the work? They can empty the dishwasher."

The WoMoBiJos are also ruthlessly clear about their priorities. They feel no compulsion to do or spend time on anything that feels obligatory. They are all disciplined and organized, and have learned skills to integrate their work and home lives. They have taken time, as Peter Senge preaches in *The Fifth Discipline*, to first get curious, figure out what's important to them, and make sure that gets scheduled first on their calendars. They carve firm boundaries to protect uninterrupted time at work, undisturbed time to connect with family, and guilt-free time to themselves to recharge, even if that means fully savoring the small moments of alone time that they used to take for granted, like getting a haircut.

More than anything, I was struck by how supremely confident all the WoMoBiJos are, in themselves, their skills, the decisions they've made, and the way they live their lives, cultural norms be damned. I wondered, Was that it? Their confidence? Were they able to create these rich, complex, and full lives and live them wholeheartedly simply because they *believed* they could? And if that were the case, could the WoMoBiJos, instead of being just a small group of admirable women in enviable special circumstances, really be pioneers showing us all the way? If they could believe their way into living unambiguously, could others? Could I?

"I actually really do not care, to a fault, what people think," Heyck-Merlin told me. "But I also don't believe anything is due to personality trait. Everything is learned. It's a mind-set. It's a skill that needs to be developed. It takes practice. And time."

That's the gospel that Kathy Korman Frey, whom some call the "Confidence Guardian," has been preaching. Frey, a Harvard MBA, is an entrepreneur, a mother of two, and a business professor at George Washington University who runs The Hot Mommas Project, the largest global database of business case studies written by women entrepreneurs about how they run their companies and manage their home lives at the same time. She is adamant that what keeps so many women running ragged and out of time is that most have yet to develop the skill of confidence, or what she calls "self-efficacy."

"Self-efficacy is really the final frontier for women," she told me one day as we sat on the back patio between her Washington, D.C., house and the outbuilding that serves as her office. The lack of self-efficacy, she said, is a big part of why women don't negotiate for better salaries, bigger positions, or flexible work arrangements that would give them more control over their time.[5] It's why many feel like impostors in class or at work and don't offer opinions or challenge decisions. It's what keeps many women from asking for or expecting help from partners at home. It's part of why so many get caught in the overwhelm and have a hard time imagining life beyond it. And it's a big reason why young women limit their own horizons. "For women, we begin to lose self-efficacy when we're teenagers. We become first in line to put ourselves down and put others first," she said. "Then we get so busy with all the demands of this crazy world that we don't have time to even think about it."

But self-efficacy, like grit, can be learned, she said. Like a muscle, it can be exercised and made strong. And she is devoting her life to teaching the four ways that famed psychologist Albert Bandura said people could learn it.[6] She calls them "Jedi Mind Tricks":

- Have "mastery experiences." The more you do some things well, the more you'll build the confidence to do other things well.
- Find role models and seek out mentors.
- Listen to and believe the positive and encouraging words people have for you.
- "Get a grip." Recognize that *perceptions* are what shape experience. And when it comes to negative and self-defeating patterns of thought, she advises, as Cher did in *Moonstruck*, "Snap out of it!"

"Look, we're in crisis. Women can deal with it in one of two ways: become stockholders in the companies that make antidepressants like Prozac, or do commonsense things like connecting with people in very specific ways, changing our mind-set and developing self-efficacy," she said. "I'm not saying it's not hard. But I am saying it's like you're wearing the ruby slippers. You have the power. You've had it all along."

I called Terry Monaghan. If I was really going to use what I'd been learning on this journey and knit together the shreds of far-flung time confetti, if I was ever going to allow myself a moment of peace, if I was to figure out how to embrace my life with passion in the face of ambiguity, I realized I needed self-efficacy boot camp.

Monaghan had a good track record. When I met one of her coaching clients, Liz Lucchesi, a real estate agent and mother of two, Lucchesi told me that she had been stuck in the overwhelm and "on" all the time. She slept maybe four hours a night, grinding her teeth. By the time she began working with Monaghan, she hadn't seen her kids in four days. "They'd be in bed by the time I got home," she told me. "My husband was furious, saying, 'You don't laugh anymore. You're not fun to be around.' We hadn't been to church in a while. I was always so tired I'd get emotional and take things personally. I'd get easily distracted."

At their first session, Monaghan started by asking Lucchesi what was most important to her. Lucchesi wrestled with her own ambivalence. She'd branched out on her own in real estate after working her tail off in an all-male property management firm and getting nowhere. She thought being her own boss would give her the time and flexibility her former firm wouldn't. Yet she found herself being even more inflexible and demanding than they ever had been. Lucchesi's story made me think of an older woman I'd met who'd just left a time-consuming job in corporate America only to lament, "I went to work for myself, and my husband said I went to work for a bitch. I work evenings and weekends, I never get time off, and my work is never good enough. Where is the time for me?"

Lucchesi realized that what she most wanted was not to be the ideal worker of her old property management firm but time to play with her kids and to concentrate on the best part of her job—building relationships with clients and writing contracts. Monaghan began working with her to create a system and routines that would help her do that. It's not so much that they scheduled everything down to the minute, but Monaghan forced Lucchesi to take the most important pieces of her jigsaw puzzle and fix them in time on her calendar first. Everything else flowed around those big pieces.

At work, as Lucchesi began to focus on doing what she really *liked*, her business grew and she was able to hire other people and delegate tasks like putting up the FOR SALE signs, staffing most of the weekend open houses, doing her books, and running her website. When I met her, Lucchesi's annual volume of sales had tripled from $15 to $48 million. She slept eight hours a night. She had time to play with her children and go to church. She'd become an active philanthropist in her community. She was running again and enjoying it, not just slogging through a workout. For fun, she was taking piano lessons and had just returned from a weekend camping trip. "The knots at the base of my neck and at the top of my shoulders are gone," Lucchesi said. She was put on this earth to live a good life, she told me. And she finally felt that she was.

At our first meeting, Monaghan asked me the same question: "What's most important to you right now?"

"Um, writing this book?" I answered. "And having time for my family?"

She cut me off before I could add anything. Then she asked me what I planned to do in the coming week to make time for both. I began rattling off an exhaustive list of just about everything that I needed to do, ever, in my life. By the following week, when we were scheduled to talk again, I was feeling guilty and defeated. I'd barely made a dent in all the tasks I'd assigned myself to do.

"So," she said wryly when she called, "how long did it take for you to figure out you couldn't do everything on your list in one week?"

In truth, I'd always known it.

"So much of our overwhelm comes from unrealistic expectations," she said. "And when we don't meet them, instead of questioning the expectations, we think that *we're* doing something wrong." Managing the overwhelm, she said, comes down to knowing the underlying story that's driving those unrealistic expectations.

"So what's my underlying story?" I asked.

"You want to write the perfect book," she said matter-of-factly. "And you think the perfect book is anything written by anyone *else*. Your ongoing conversation with yourself is: You're not enough. So whatever you do will *never be enough*. Every human being has some flavor of 'not enough.' You can either be stopped by it, or simply notice it, like the weather."

I began to try to just *notice* that stormy internal weather, instead of getting swept away in it. *Notice* how much I was unconsciously trying to live up to impossible ideals. *Notice* my ambivalence. And I began to more consciously grapple with the questions that daunt not only perfectionists but, really, anyone with a pulse: How much is enough? When is it good enough? How will I know?

We started small: by clearing my desk. "It gives your brain a rest from visual clutter." As we worked to build systems and routines into my days, we always seemed to be coming back to my brain, and how getting a handle on the overwhelm was not just about creating more space and order on my calendar and in my office, but doing the same in my mind.

When I would second-guess myself or become obsessed about not knowing what I was doing, she'd interrupt me brusquely. "Right now, you need to free up all this energy that's being consumed by worry." She told me to take out a piece of paper, set a timer for five minutes, and write furiously about absolutely everything that was bugging me. I didn't have to do anything about this "Worry Journal." Just getting the ambivalence out of my head and putting it somewhere would give my brain a rest. "It's a way off the hamster wheel."

We did the same with the enormous to-do list I carried around in my head like a mark of shame. Every Monday morning, I began to set aside time to plan the week. I began with a brain dump. It was the list of everything on my mind from here to eternity. The working memory can keep only about seven things in it at one time. And if the to-do list is much longer than that, the brain, worried it may forget something, will get stuck in an endless circular loop of mulling, much like a running toilet. The brain dump is like jiggling the handle. "If your to-do list lives on paper, your brain doesn't have to expend energy to keep remembering it," Monaghan said.

As I worked with Monaghan, I also interviewed productivity and time management experts, read books, clipped magazine articles, watched webinars, listened to podcasts, attended lectures, took my Time Perspective Inventory[7] to see if I viewed the past, present, and future in the optimal configuration for happiness, took an Energy Audit[8] to see if I was working at peak performance physically, mentally, emotionally, and spiritually, and reviewed dozens of different methodologies all aiming to relieve the time-sucking overwhelm. The essence of their advice all seemed to boil down to what my kids learned in preschool: Plan. Do. Review. Take time to figure out what's important in the moment and what you want to accomplish in life. If you're ambivalent, notice it. Pick something anyway. Embrace it. Play. Try one approach. Assess. If that isn't working, ditch it and play with something else. Keep yourself accountable but enjoy the process. There is no right answer. This is life.

Like Monaghan does herself, I began using bits of one method, pieces of another.[9] If they seemed to help, I kept on using them. If the methods were too complicated or took too much work, I moved on.

But by far, the one skill that I have learned that has transformed my experience of time is the power of the pulse.


"I'll bet you're writing your book the way I wrote my first three," Tony Schwartz told me. I'd called Schwartz, the author of *The Way We're Working Isn't Working*, to ask about the Energy Project, his company that draws on human performance science to transform work cultures from grueling time-starved ideal worker "survival zones" to what he calls fully engaged "performance zones."

"What do you mean?" I asked.

"Chained to your desk. Sitting in front of a computer for ten hours straight."

"Um. Yes."

"I write in three or four ninety-minute sprints now and I am 100 percent engaged. Then I take a break, I either eat something, take a run, or I meditate. I distinctly change channels," he explained. "My first three books took me at least a year each to write. My last two, I worked less than half the amount of time each day, but I finished each one in six months. It's all about using *rhythm*."

Human beings, he said, are designed to *pulse*, to alternate between spending and recovering energy. The heart beats. The lungs breathe in and out. The brain makes waves. We wake and sleep. Even digestion is rhythmic. We're built to work the same way, he said, alternating between periods of intense focus and time for rest and renewal. Because old ideal worker work is measured in hours, we tend to put in long ones, he said. We ignore the signs of fatigue, boredom, and distraction and just power through. But we're hardly doing our best work.[10] "We've lost touch with the value of rest, renewal, recovery, quiet time, and downtime," Schwartz told me. It's hardly a wonder, then, with the pressure of long hours, putting in face time, and the constant interruptions of the modern workplace, less than 10 percent of workers say they do their best thinking at work.[11]

In his book *Be Excellent at Anything*, Schwartz writes that scientists in 1957 discovered that humans sleep in ninety-minute cycles, our brain wave activity slowing and then speeding back up to near waking, only to begin the next sleep cycle. A few decades later, sleep researchers found those same ninety-minute oscillations from higher to lower states of alertness during the day and dubbed them "ultradian" cycles.[12] Schwartz's thinking was also influenced by Florida State University psychologist Anders Ericsson's research. Ericsson studied young violinists at the prestigious Academy of Music in Berlin to see what it takes to be the best. Ericsson is widely credited for coming up with the theory that it takes ten thousand hours of deliberate practice in anything to become an expert. "That led to the assumption that the best way to get things done is to just work *more* hours," Schwartz said. But that's only part of it. Ericsson's study found that not only did the best violinists practice more, they also practiced more deliberately: They practiced first thing in the morning, when they were freshest, they practiced intensely without interruption in typically no more than ninety-minute increments for no more than four hours a day. And, most important, Schwartz said, the top violinists *rested* more. They slept longer at night and they napped more in the day. "Great performers," Schwartz wrote, "work more intensely than most of us do but also recover more deeply."[13]

Working continuously, without breaks, is in fact a surefire way to produce subpar work. Scientists have long known that, during sleep, the brain consolidates new information and skills by making new connections between neurons, effectively rewiring the brain. Neuroscientists in Sydney have found that that rewiring happens during the day as well, when we take a break. In lab experiments, they discovered that students who studied, but took regular breaks, performed better on cognitive tests than students who studied continuously. Continuous practice, continuous study, continuous work, the scientists theorized, disrupts the natural, pulsing brain rewiring cycle.[14]

Pulsing—deactivating and reactivating the brain—actually makes it pay better attention. The brain evolved to detect and respond to change, always alert to danger. And once the novelty wears off and the brain becomes "habituated," it no longer notices the nonthreatening sights, sounds, or feelings that have been constantly present, much like how you no longer notice the sensation of clothes touching your skin after a while, or your son the boring math worksheet he's been staring at. University of Illinois psychologists gave subjects a fifty-minute task. The group that performed best, they found, was the one that had been given two short breaks.[15]

Breaks also inspire creativity. Scientists have found that people who take time to daydream score higher on tests of creativity.[16] And there's a very good biochemical reason why your best ideas and those flashes of insight tend to come not when you've got your nose to the grindstone, oh ideal worker, but in the shower.

In a series of tests using brain imaging and electroencephalography, psychologists John Kounios and Mark Beeman have actually mapped what happens in the brain during the aha! moment, when the brain suddenly makes new connections and imagines, Kounios has said, "new and different ways to transform reality creatively into something better."[17] When the brain is solving a problem in a deliberate and methodical way, Kounios and Beeman found that the visual cortex, the part of the brain controlling sight, is most active. So the brain is outwardly focused. But just before a moment of insight, the brain suddenly turns inward, what the researchers called a "brain blink." Alpha waves in the right visual cortex slow, just as when we often close our eyes in thought. Milliseconds before the insight, Kounios and Beeman recorded a burst of gamma activity in the right hemisphere in the area of the brain just above the ear, believed to be linked to our ability to process metaphors. A positive mood heightens the chances for creative insight, as does *taking time to relax*,[18] as Archimedes did in his bathtub before his eureka! moment about water displacement and as Einstein did when working out his Theory of Relatively while reportedly tootling around on his bicycle.[19]

Terry Monaghan sought to train me to work in pulses. The idea was to chunk my time to minimize the constant multitasking, "role switching," and toggling back and forth between work and home stuff like a brainless flea on a hot stove. The goal was to create periods of uninterrupted time to concentrate on work—the kind of time I usually found in the middle of the night—during the day. And to be more focused and less distracted with my family.

When it was time to work, I began to shut off e-mail and turn off the phone. When it was time to be with family, I tried to do the same. I began to gather home tasks in a pile and block off one period of time every day to do them. It was easier to stay focused on work knowing I'd given myself a grace period to get to the pressing home stuff later.

When I was having difficulty, procrastinating, avoiding a task, stuck in ambivalence, Monaghan had me set a timer for thirty minutes, then take a break. "Your brain can stay focused on anything, even an unpleasant task, if it knows it will last only thirty minutes," she said. Slowly, as I gained confidence and got a grip, as Kathy Korman Frey would say, I worked up to forty-five- and then ninety-minute stretches. I have been researching and writing most of this book in ninety-minute pulses. In the middle of the day.

Working in pulses, chunking time, the brain dump, and the Worry Journal have helped me begin to knit the scraps of my time together.

I've been practicing other skills:

• Making time to pause, and think about what is most important. From Peter Bregman's method,[20] I picked a handful of focus areas most important to me, which I eventually trimmed to just three: Write this Book, Have Quality Time with Family, and Be Healthy—which would help me do the first two better. Everything else went under a heading he calls "The Other 5 Percent," the garbagey stuff that shouldn't take more than 5 percent of your time and energy. That's been SO FREEING! More than anything, this shift in mind-set has helped me break the unsatisfying if-then cycle that I've been trapped in for so long: *If* I can get through everything on my to-do list, *then* I'll have cleared space for the important things or time for leisure. Now, the focus areas come first. I reserve a chunk of time for the 5 percent. My to-do list for the day is short enough for a Post-it note. Everything else goes into a master to-do list. I may never get to everything on it, but having it on paper gets the noise out of my head.

• I began carrying a small notebook around with me, as William Powers suggested in *Hamlet's Blackberry*, and using the Notes app on my iPhone to capture the stray thoughts, ideas, or anxieties that hit when you least expect them. Just knowing I have a place to put them, like the master to-do list, has helped break the polluting mental tape loop of contaminated time.

• I've tried to give my willpower more juice and avoid decision fatigue by creating rituals to make parts of my schedule so automatic that they require no decisions at all. I lay out my running clothes the night before so I don't have to decide in the morning whether to exercise or not. I've already decided.[21] Most mornings, as Tony Schwartz preaches, I try to choose ONE thing that is most important to do that day,[22] and I try to do it first, when, science is finding, the brain is most alert.[23]

• I try to check e-mail in batches during the day, if I'm not on deadline or expecting something urgent, and try to answer what I can immediately. I changed my settings so now I have to manually download my e-mail. I am no longer at the mercy of some server hurling info turds into my in-box every few minutes. Still, e-mail is very much a work in progress.

To be honest, this entire exercise in finding time, finding a way out of the overwhelm and beyond ambivalence, is all still very much a work in progress. For much of the time that I've worked on this book, I've been on leave and have had complete control over my time. When I returned to the hurly-burly of work at a newspaper and life as a small cog in someone else's much larger wheel, I was worried that I'd be flung right back to square one, my time shredded into confetti once again. That's certainly what it felt like those first few months. Caught right back up in the ideal worker world, I worked long. I worked late. I worked to the point of exhaustion, making stupid mistakes. But I began to realize that everything I'd learned, all the skills I'd been practicing, were still there. I still have focus areas, only one now includes doing good journalism every day. I still work in pulses. I have a Monday morning brain dump. I chunk my time. I take breaks. I still give no more than 5 percent to the endless stuff of life. I do ONE thing a day.

I try to be guided less by impossible ideals and unrealistic expectations and more by how I feel, whether I'm happy, if my work has made a difference, how connected I feel to my kids, to Tom, to my family and friends. I take time to understand why. I try to change. I no longer want to live someone else's life.

At home, Tom and I and the kids are getting better at sharing responsibility for the second shift. That has freed up time to play. I've spent entire days reading again. My good friend and running partner, Jenny, and I have now run several half marathons, one crashing through the woods on gorgeous forest trails and one silly one that gave out chocolate at mile 11. We even signed up and ran a crazy two-hundred-mile relay with ten other people, including Tom, and ran, sometimes in the middle of the night, ringed with so many pink, blue, green, and yellow glow-in-the-dark bracelets that we looked like festive party barges. We ate trail mix with abandon and I laughed like I hadn't in years. The Del Ray Moms that never got off the ground a few years ago has now become the Binders Full of Women, in honor of GOP presidential candidate Mitt Romney's famous line. It's not formal or organized, like the Mice at Play. But we've managed here and there to fit in an early morning canoe trip, a play, a circus silks class, making shaving cream art, and paddle boarding. Jenny also wrangled me into crew for a season. And there is, truly, nothing quite as good for the soul as seeing the stars and moon reflected on the quiet water as you catch your oar, press with your legs, and glide into the dawn.

Having a clearer sense of what's most important to do, having built up my self-efficacy muscles, I'm not as seized with the feeling that I haven't done enough and the urge to do "just one more thing." And so for the first time in decades I—sometimes—arrive places—shockingly—*on time*. Clearing the clutter in my head and the guilt that hung over every halfhearted decision has given me more peace of mind than any elaborate time management system. Time is still a struggle. I still work too much. I still don't sleep enough. I still worry. I haven't made much progress on a family budget. My weight's gone up and down. And I still have stupid days. But I am *learning*. Time *feels* better. Rather than ambivalence, what I feel most of the time is gratitude.

# BRIGHT SPOT: TIME HORIZONS

There does come a time when ambivalence comes to an end, when the choices are clearer and living with them is more comfortable. It has everything to do with time. Laura Carstensen, a professor of psychology and founding director of the Stanford Center on Longevity, spent years interviewing older people. She worried that aging people were lonely, anxious, depressed, or afraid of dying. She encouraged them to come to social gatherings or tried to get them to meet other people. "They would say, 'I don't have a lot of time for people.' And I would say, 'Looks to me like you have a *lot* of time.' It took me a long time to realize they weren't talking about time in a *day*; they were talking about time in their *lives*. They had a completely different perspective on time. A lot of things don't make sense anymore when time is running out."

She began to see that when a person's "time horizon" is short, if he or she has only five or ten years left to live, say, it becomes increasingly clear just exactly what is important. Ambivalence is replaced with a sharper sense of certainty. All of which makes it easier to decide how to spend the precious resource of time, now that you can see how finite it truly is. "Very open-ended, vast future time horizons turn out to be really hard on people emotionally. When I think about the childbearing years, you're anxious not only about yourselves and your own future, but you're very anxious about your children's futures. Are they playing with the right kids in preschool? Getting good enough grades? What's going to happen if they don't do well in math?" Carstensen told me. "But as our time horizons grow shorter, we start to see the world differently. We start to see that what matters most are often the simple things—the smell of roses, watching your grandchildren splash in a puddle, the smile on the face of an old friend you're meeting for coffee. It's those little moments that you start to focus on."

And by being focused on what's important and the beauty of the small moments, she said, older people are actually happier. To test her theory, Carstensen put young and old people into a brain scanner, showed them both positive and negative images, and registered how the amygdala, the area of the brain that controls emotions and fear,

responded. She found that young people showed heightened brain activity when shown both positive and negative images. But older people
registered responses only to the positive images, leading to what she
calls the "positivity effect."[1]

Collapsing one's time horizon is a skill, Carstensen said, that the
young can learn from the old. "My experience as a grandmother is,
when I'm with my grandchildren, I'm *really* with them. But when my
son was young, I was with him, but I was also working, preparing
something else, and trying to get him to do his homework," she said.
"It's hard to say this in a way that doesn't sound horrible, but if the
world as we know it were going to end in a year, you wouldn't be worrying about the homework."

I called Sue Shaw, one of the premier feminist leisure researchers.
Shaw had just retired and moved with her husband to a cottage by a
lake in Ontario, Canada. I was curious what a shortened time horizon
and the end of ambivalence meant for the experience of leisure. Shaw
no longer checks her e-mail much and has shed years of paperwork
and files. She spends her days walking in the woods, reading, and even
enjoying the cleaning and maintenance projects she and her husband
do together. "I have a fair amount of leisure time now and a fair bit of
freedom to do what I like with that time. But is it some exalted high
state?" she said. "Some people talk about flow as being a near mystical,
religious experience. Maybe they want to seek an altered state of consciousness. But for me, that sense of flow, being totally caught up in
the moment, I tend to find it in nature, in the countryside, or when I'm
having a good chat over a glass of wine with a friend. It's a fleeting
thing. It's not something I try and measure in time, because the hours
are almost irrelevant. There is a sense of peace associated with these
moments. A connection to a broader universe, to other people or the
world. I took my granddaughter out in the weekend to see the moon
and stars—the moon was really full—and she was awed by it. She's
only three. It's moments like these that just seem really important to
the quality of our experience of time."

However short or long the horizon.

# 14

# TOWARD TIME SERENITY

Whatever you're meant to do, do it now. The conditions are
always impossible.                                    —Doris Lessing

Tara Brach tells us to close our eyes and listen to our breath. Her voice,
calm and soothing, tells us to let go of the "ceaseless frenzy. Always
thinking we should be doing something else. Always thinking that
something is missing, something is wrong, and we need to be elsewhere."
She tells us to breathe. "Be here. Rest in your body. Your heart. This
moment. The earth. Be at home."

I drift off to sleep.

I had come to Tara Brach's daylong mindfulness meditation retreat
at the Insight Meditation Community of Washington, D.C., one Saturday morning as my journey to understand time was coming to a close.
A final lesson in learning how to climb out of that ceaseless frenzy of
the overwhelm, I was discovering, was learning how to master the
ceaseless clatter of your own contaminated mind.

Just as the neuroscientists at the Yale Stress Center that I visited
were finding that the overwhelm can physically *shrink* the thinking
brain, a different group of scientists, using brain scans and mindfulness
training—the process of learning to focus fully on the present moment—
were discovering that when we slow down, when we learn to pause and
notice where we are and feel at home, our complex brain literally *grows
bigger*. The fear center of the brain contracts. Neuroscientists at Harvard found that people's gray matter expanded after only eight weeks
of meditating, practicing yoga, or just noticing how their bodies felt for
as little as twenty-seven minutes a day.[1] "This is something that even a

few years ago we didn't think was possible," Britta Hölzel, a Harvard neuroscientist leading many of the studies and a mindfulness practitioner herself, told me. "I find it fascinating that in such a relatively short time, after a change in behavior and a change in the way you look at your life, we see the actual physical structures changing in the brain."

The point is, she says, the overwhelm never goes away. But you can change how you think about it: pausing and noticing it without judgment, not reacting to it. Changing your thinking makes your brain grow. And a bigger brain, more sizzling neurons snapping and firing in new ways, means more gray matter to think, remember, and make decisions more clearly, she said. A smaller amygdala from the older part of the emotional brain means fewer freak-outs, breakdowns, and episodes of paralyzing fear. So as the brain grows, the better you are able to *see* the swirl of the overwhelm without getting *swept away* by it. "I'm having a really stressful day today, so I can relate to this feeling of overwhelm very much," Hölzel said. "But with mindfulness, you realize you are already where you are. There's no need to rush to the next moment. It will come automatically. And you will probably get more done if you just concentrate on what's happening right now anyway. It's all about changing your perspective."

At the meditation retreat, the voice of Brach, a psychologist and Buddhist meditation teacher, wakes me. She's talking about space. Our brains, so unchanged from the days when we lived in hunter-gatherer bands, are wired to scan for threats and notice everything that's wrong, she says. So we can easily get stuck in what she calls a trance—of busyness, of unworthiness, of anxiety. "Then we find we're living in a world that's very much smaller than what we really are. We're a bunch of tense muscles, rerunning old patterns of speeding around, not able to enjoy the sunsets, really listen to the music, see the glow in a child's eye, listen to our children when they tell us stories," she says. "We are so riveted getting to the next thing that we miss out on life, miss out on love, miss out on being in the moment. I think it's worth challenging." And the way to do that, she says, is to find space to ventilate the overwhelm. "Open up some cracks."

So I try again. I shut my eyes. I take a breath. And a Boz Scaggs song I haven't heard since high school starts playing in my head. "Lido. Whoa-oh-oh-oh . . ." I think of Mihaly Csikszentmihalyi. When he first began randomly paging people throughout the day in his time studies and asking what they were thinking about, he expected they'd report contemplating great thoughts, planning new adventures, or lingering over happy memories. Instead, he found . . . chaos. "When left to itself, the mind turns to bad thoughts, trivial plans, sad memories, and worries about the future," he wrote. "Entropy—disorder, confusion, decay—is the default option of consciousness."[2] The only way to literal peace of mind, he said, was to either focus on a goal or train the mind through an internal discipline like meditation or mindfulness.

At the break, I approach Brach, a petite, serene woman with long brown hair and a beatific smile. How do you find this space, I ask, when so many people feel they have no time?

"You *don't* have to go on a monthlong meditation retreat." She laughs. "Maybe you take some time in the middle of the day to pause, for just three minutes, or five minutes. Maybe you pause for a few seconds after you hang up the phone before you go right to the next thing. You can change your perspective in fifteen seconds. If you sit with a slight smile for three minutes, you shift your biochemistry. It sends a message to the nervous system that you're not in danger. All you need is the *intention* to slow down. That's all it takes. Something that helps you leave the busyness of your thoughts and enter your body. The body will take you home."

When she had her son, she says, like so many parents she became pressed for time. She made a commitment to herself to meditate every day but gave herself a "back door": It didn't matter for how long. "Some days that meant I sat on the edge of the bed, took five deep breaths, offered a prayer to the world, and collapsed. That counted."

Getting out of the overwhelm, she says, means waking up. Waking up to life. Waking up to the fact that it's fleeting. That's why there's power in finding like-minded communities, like Jessica DeGroot and the ThirdPath has, like the Simplicity Moms, New Dads, WoMoBiJos and Hot Mommas. "Because when you forget, I'll remind you that life is going to be over quickly and that this is an amazingly beautiful day."

I remember one evening when I was growing up, looking out the window and seeing a brilliant sunset over the lush evergreen forest near our home. I was seized with one thought: If only I were somewhere else, somewhere better. Then I could really enjoy it. It was an unconscious theme that, looking back on my life, played like a broken record over and over, like the scrap of that Boz Scaggs tune I couldn't get out of my head at the retreat.

When I was thirty-four, I spent months helplessly watching my younger sister die of cancer.³ For the first time, I clung to each precious minute like a rare jewel. She had so few left. If she had to go down this awful road, then I wanted only to be right there with her, so at least she wouldn't have to travel it alone. In that singular focus, the smallest gesture, the quietest moment was transformed into an unimaginably exquisite gift of grace. Every detail presented itself in its aching fullness, the bright red Adriamycin dripping into her veins, the way we laughed like little girls who'd done something naughty when I combed her thick, wavy blond hair and a big chunk fell out, the quality of the fading light in her hospital room as evening gently softened to dusk. The single tear that rolled out of the side of her eye when it was clear that her life was at an end.

The Greeks called that kind of time *kairos*. When we live by the clock, the Greeks said, we are bound by *chronos* time. This is the time that races, marches, creeps, and flies. It is the life that T. S. Eliot measured out in coffee spoons and the thirty hours of leisure that John Robinson tallies on his spreadsheets. But kairos is the time of the "right moment," the eternal now, when time is not a number on a dial but the enormity of the experience inside it. On the day that I sought to write this chapter, I was caught in the gears of chronos, rushing from an early morning teacher meeting we'd forgotten to the shop to get Tom's rattling car. The dryer was broken. Soggy clothes were draped all around the house. My son had forgotten his big geometry project. And I'd had to physically remove the keyboard from the computer to keep my daughter from spending most of her waking hours on moviestarplanet.com. At a loss for what to write, I went for a walk. As I passed the park near our house, I saw a little girl wearing a bright pink paper crown and giggling with her friends. One asked, "What time is it?" The little girl, completely absorbed in the joy of walking home from school with friends on a gloriously sunny afternoon, started to laugh. "It's 200 o'clock!"

When my sister was gone, I thought, for her sake, I would remember to live the rest of my days with that same fragile and humble grace, as if it were always 200 o'clock, knowing that one day, I, too, would be gone. I even began to wear her watch every day to remind myself. I still do.

But I soon forgot.

I sit on one of the hard wooden chairs in the meditation room. Tara Brach is talking again. "Sometimes it's as if we're racing to the finish line our whole lives, skimming the surface and never dropping into life, as if life is a problem to be solved rather than a mystery to be lived," she says. The way back into life, she says, is, first, to breathe.

One evening when my kids were younger, I was outside weeding the infernal gravel while they bounced with sheer delight on the trampoline. "Mommy, come jump with us!" they'd cried. "In a minute," I kept saying. "Just let me finish weeding." It was a time, before this journey began, when I used to routinely ask myself, "What do I need to do before I can feel okay?" And then I'd run through a never-ending mental list. That evening, with a familiar sense of vague panic rising, I felt compelled to finish at least *one* thing, the weeding, on that long list. Lost in my churning thoughts, I didn't notice the sun go down. Or hear my kids go inside. When I looked up again, the sky was dark, the yard still covered in weeds, and I was alone. I have often thought back to that moment with such regret.

One rainy Sunday, not long after the retreat, the kids and I made soup together. The kitchen was a mess. I immediately began to tackle the sink, which was clogged with vegetable peels and dirty dishes. Tessa sat on the window seat in the family room to watch the rain pour down.

"Mom, let's have lunch," she said.

"I'm doing the dishes right now."

"Come on, Mom, let's take a break together."

"In a minute. Just let me get these dishes done."

"Mom. Come over."

It was the third time that hit me. Just stop, I thought. Stop right now. I took a breath. Now, I thought. I can feel okay right now. Here, I thought. Here is the best place to be. I keep forgetting, but right now I remember. I remember that life will be over quickly and that this is an amazingly beautiful day.

I poured myself some of the soup we'd just made, left the mess in the kitchen sink, and sat across from Tessa on the window seat. Liam came to join us. I didn't yip at them about chores or homework or things to do. We just sat together on the window seat. Eating soup. Watching the rain.

# APPENDIX: DO ONE THING

Time is the coin of your life. You spend it. Do not allow others
to spend it for you.                                    —Carl Sandburg

## *Work*

- Time is power. Don't give yours away.
- Doing good work, having quality time for family and meaningful
  relationships, and the space to refresh the soul is about having a
  good life. It has never been just a "mommy issue." And it's about
  so much more than getting the hang of the latest time management system. It's about equity. It's about quality of life. It's about
  state of mind. It's about human rights.
- Retire the ideal worker norm. Kiss nonproductive butt-in-chair
  face-time goodbye. Change workplace culture, performance standards, and the way we manage. Managing the overwhelm is
  about more than putting a few policies on the books or punting
  to the Human Resources Department or coming up with a new
  "women's initiative" to stem the tide of talented and educated
  women *and men* leaving rigid organizations because they want to
  do good work and *also* want to be active caregivers or live full
  lives. It's the antiquated organizations that need to change, offering
  flexible work arrangements for all, training managers in commonsense family-supportive behaviors, and leading from the top
  by example.
- Ambiguity is the enemy in the workplace that fuels the overwhelm. Define your mission. Set clear parameters and performance

measures to lay out how much is enough. When is it good enough? And how will you know? Communicate. Adjust.

- Reimagine career trajectories, replacing steep, narrow one-way ladders with lattices, broad fields with meandering paths that wind through them. Think fluidity. Could we create sine curves, career tracks of intensity and pullback, for both men and women? As a working mother friend of mine said, "If there are on-ramps back into the workplace for disgraced politicians like Eliot Spitzer, then why not for parents?"
- Understand the neuroscience of how humans work best: pulsing between periods of intense concentration of typically no more than ninety mintues, and breaks to completely change the channel.
- Embrace the restorative power of vacation. Allow knowledge workers to daydream or noodle around with an idea without fear of failure.
- Draw on the science of human motivation first by giving workers a fair salary and benefits, then allowing them to have greater autonomy, a sense of purpose, and the ability to become masterful at what they do.
- Working in a new way does not mean working *less*. It means working *smart*. It means a healthier work environment and healthier employees, reduced health-care costs, reduced turnover costs, and reduced absenteeism. It means more innovation, creativity and, heavens, even *profits*.
- Understand that implicit bias—that men = career, women = home—is alive and well in you and others and is simply the way your brain works. Train it to overcome automatic stereotypes by changing the story and exposing yourself to men and women who do good work, are loving caregivers, and make time to refresh their souls. Managers, understand the power of "micro-affirmations." Gestures of inclusion and caring, graceful listening, generosity, giving credit to others, and offering fair, specific, and timely feedback are small but effective measures to counter unconscious bias.
- Overwhelm is a product of lack of control and unpredictability and the anxiety that both produce. Learn from workplaces that have creatively embraced a new way of working and a healthier workplace culture. Find what works best for your organization,

whether it involves using scheduling software to give hourly workers more say in their work shifts, becoming a results-only work environment with Sludge Eradication sessions, instituting flexibility in time, manner, and place of work, or bounding work time with predictable hours. Use consultants. Use a design firm. Find a way to change.

- Know thyself. Even if your workplace culture isn't about to change, know how *you* work best. Are you a separator? Integrator? Segmenter? At some point we all switch from one to the other. Discover and refine your own "flexstyle." Create teams, networks, and islands of sanity and support within your organization. Clarify your own mission, battle ambiguity, and communicate it both up and down the line.

- Understand the story that drives your flavor of "not enough." Notice it. Get clear about how you define success, what you want, and *your* time horizon. As Steve Jobs said, "Your time is limited, so don't waste it living someone else's life."

- If you work in an insane ideal worker workplace and don't plan to leave, know that by not conforming, you are threatening. When others hurl sludge your way, remember the magic words: "What do you need?"

- What kind of family policies would work best for America? We don't really know. We've never had a substantive discussion. It's time to have one now. A good place to start: paid leave, short or flexible work hours, and good part-time jobs with benefits. A culture that expects *both* mothers and fathers to take parental leave. Affordable, accessible, high-quality early-childhood-education programs for all. Let's train the people who care for and work with our children and pay them more than parking lot attendants. School days, school years, and high-quality, creative before- and after-school programs that mesh more seamlessly with parents' work time, which, ideally and where possible, will be more flexible. Let's talk to one another across divides, let's listen, let's accept that there has never been one right way to do anything. And let's start small.

- Let's reclaim the phrase "family values" to mean families setting their own priorities about what's important and the lives they all want to lead together.

- Let's air out the word "feminist" and remember what it has always truly meant: a quest for the personhood of women.
- Take time to think about what you really want to accomplish in your life and what's most important to do. Schedule time for that in your day first.
- Remember most of your to-do list will never get done and a lot of it belongs in "the other 5 percent" column anyway.
- Plan. Do. Review. Find a system to manage the activities you choose to do *in time* that works for you. Create routines. Automate. Cut down on the number of small decisions you have to make in a day, reserving your willpower for the big decisions you really *do* need your full brain power to make.
- Choose ONE thing that's most important to do every day.
- CHUNK your time. Multitasking makes you stupid. Work in concentrated blocks of time with regular breaks, and fit in the 5 percent stuff-of-life crap after you've made time for what's important.
- Unplug. Set reasonable parameters for using instant communication and technology. Sometimes an e-mail at 3 a.m. is critical, but usually it's not. Stop the "cycle of responsiveness" that makes work feel intense and unending.

## *Love*

- Banish ambivalence. Know that society's ambivalence about working mothers, caring fathers, changing gender roles, changing workplace, and dismissal of leisure time feeds your own guilt and ambivalence. Know that humans have evolved to conform and fit in with the group. And know that right now, the group isn't clear on what it wants you to do. That means *you* have to be clear about what you want, make your choices, recognize when they're constrained, and own them. Embrace whatever it is you're doing, whatever you've chosen, with passion and see where it leads. Then adapt as you go.
- Let's be HUMAN, recognize that industrial-age gender roles are outdated, and agree that it's good for people, for society, for hu-

manity, for *both* men and women to be free to be educated, to work, to follow passions, and to raise children in whatever manner works best for each family.

- Check your unconscious bias. Are you favoring the male partner's career for fear he would suffer more if he left the workplace or cut back? Make the bias conscious. Question whether it's true. Talk. Fight. Make decisions *together*.
- Recognize that what happens when the first baby comes home from the hospital is critical: You will be setting patterns of living and being that will be harder to break later. This is when the demands of the ideal mother are tugging the hardest. This is when the gatekeeping urge to keep husband and others away is strongest. While your biology is indeed at work, so is your culture. Your partner or spouse's biology is just as clearly at work. Share care. That means Mom needs time away. And Dad needs to fly solo, not just be the "helper" or the "fun" parent. If solo parental leave is not possible, set up your own informal parental leave for Dad. Saturday morning. Sunday afternoon. And Dad, you do it all—diapers, dishes, bottles. The confidence and competence you develop will change your relationship with your children and your spouse, and your family's relationship with time.
- Find Your Own Private Netherlands.
- Recognize how critical involved fathers are.
- Create family systems and automate routines to cut down on arguing, nagging, and resentment. Share the load. As a family, figure out what needs to be done to keep the house and your lives running. Set standards that everyone can agree to. Then divide the load fairly, making sure your sons and daughters do equal work. Monitor. Assess. Keep working at it. Do NOT sigh, gripe, moan, and do it all yourself, muttering and resentful the whole time.
- Alloparents. Ask for and accept the help of loving alloparents. Create a network of support. Find creative solutions together.
- Park the helicopter. You don't have to do everything on your own and better than everyone else. As Kathy Maserie said, "Love your kids. Keep them safe. Accept them as they are. Then get out of their way."

- Seek not to hover and push achievement, but help your children develop resilience, perseverance, and *grit*. That means letting them follow little inklings that may—or may not—develop into passions. And letting them make mistakes.
- Happiness first. Happiness breeds success and achievement. The converse is not necessarily true.
- Teach your children to count their blessings, to be grateful.
- Give your kids time and space to do nothing, or just notice the shape of clouds. Get them outside. Let them, when you can, roam. And give yourself the same gift of time and space. Share moments of connection, have meals together, put the smartphone down and *be* there.
- Recognize that children do, indeed, grow quickly. And that the moment to stop and notice and enjoy is now. And now. And now.
- Keep it simple. Live within your means. Buy only stuff that you need, and find a place for it. (I know, I know, the budget. We're working on it.)
- Put down the expert books. Declare the mommy wars over—we've all been on the same side in search of the good life all along. Trust yourself. Create supportive networks of like-minded parents. As Dr. Benjamin Spock said, you know more than you think you do.
- Encourage your sons to babysit. Both men and women are, biologically, "naturals" when it comes to caring for children. It's just that the culture has always expected and given women the *time* to become good at it.

### Play

- Understand that, for women, there never has been a history or culture of leisure or play, unless you consider sweeping, making cheese, churning butter, quilting, and knitting your kind of fun. It will take effort and strain to allow yourself time to play. Make the effort. Find a group like Mice at Play or create your own. Try belly dancing. Take a walk. You'll be more likely to do it if you have a group or friends to be accountable to. Be subversive!

- Before vacation or a period of free, unstructured leisure time, really *think* about what you'd like to experience and how you'd like to feel, and even write it down. Being conscious of how you want your time to feel, and putting it on your agenda, makes it more likely that it will actually happen.
- Remind yourself that play is useful. Humans need it. Give yourself permission to do it. Take a playful state of mind with you to work and also have it at home. Be more curious than afraid. Find time to wonder and be in awe. Encourage your preteen daughters to stay playful.
- Light a candle. Like the Danes, bring some *hygge* into your life.
- Take a shower with a pink pig.
- Don't wait until the dust bunnies are gone and the fridge is full to share time with friends. Spaghetti and ketchup and good hearts will do.
- Be silent every day. Even if that means taking five breaths. Being mindful for less than a half hour a day will, literally, expand your brain.
- Try something new, get out of your comfort zone, and challenge yourself to get into *flow*.
- Believe in yourself. Practice the Jedi Mind Tricks: Have masterful experiences. Find role models and mentors. Listen to and be persuaded by positive words and encouragement. And get a grip. Cultivate a "growth" mind-set to try new things and believe in change.
- Not sure what you want or where you want to go? Find an active-listening partner. Take time to become clear about your current reality and your goals. Once you've become clearer about the gap between the two, let your brain go to work imagining creative solutions about how to bridge it.
- Carry around a notebook or have a note-taking function on a smartphone, to capture the inspirations and aha! moments that hit at the oddest times, when your nose is *not* to the grindstone.
- Give your brain a rest. Get out of your head and into your body, your breath, or the moment. Women, especially, are prone to ruminating and worrying. Notice the thoughts without judgment, choose to think in a different way, and rewire your brain. Ask for

help and delegate. Write the to-do list in an enormous brain dump, then give yourself permission not to do it all. Take five minutes to pour the clutter of anxieties into a Worry Journal. Uncontaminate your time.

- Shorten your time horizon. What if we really did live like we're dying? How would that change what you view as important and the choices you make for what to do with your time? Try it.
- Banish busyness.
- Live an authentic life.

# NOTES

## 1: THE TEST OF TIME

1. Brigid Schulte, "The Test of Time: A Busy Working Mother Tries to Figure Out Where All Her Time Is Going," *Washington Post*, January 17, 2010.
2. Benjamin Kline Hunnicutt, "Leisure and Play in Plato's Teaching and Philosophy of Learning," *Leisure Sciences* 12 (1990): 211–27. Hunnicutt, interview by author, October 21, 2009.
3. John P. Robinson and Geoffrey Godbey, *Time for Life: The Surprising Ways Americans Use Their Time* (University Park: Pennsylvania State University Press, 1997), 95.
4. Ibid., 43–56, 82–153.
5. Ibid., 236–38. See p. 237 for time crunch scale.
6. Ibid., 34.
7. Pauline Maier et al., *Inventing America* (New York: W. W. Norton, 2003), 693–94.
8. GPI Atlantic, *Developing a Community Genuine Progress Index: Materials for Community Development Planners*, vol. 2, "Appendix 3: Time Use & Health," 2003, 234–68, www.gpiatlantic.org/pdf/communitygpi/vol2appendix03.pdf. See also Jonathan Gershuny, *Time-Use Surveys and the Measurement of National Well-Being* (Oxford: University of Oxford, Centre for Time Use Research, 2011).
9. Robinson, interviews with author on phone, via e-mail, and in person in College Park, MD, from 2009 to 2011. Also Alexander Szalai, ed., *The Use of Time: Daily Activities of Urban and Suburban Populations in Twelve Countries* (The Hague: Mouton, 1973).
10. Robinson and Godbey, *Time for Life*, 323. For the detailed National Human Activity Pattern Survey (NHAPS) data-collection methodology, see J. Robinson and J. Blair, "Estimating Exposure to Pollutants Through Human Activity Pattern Data: The National Micro-Environmental Activity Pattern Survey," *Annual Report, Survey Research Center* (College Park: University of Maryland, 1995). See "The National Human Activity Pattern Survey (NHAPS): A Resource for Assessing Exposure to Environmental Pollutants," *Journal of Exposure Analysis and Environmental Epidemiology* 11 (2001): 231–52, doi:10.1038/sj.jea.7500165.
11. International Association for Time Use Research, www.iatur.org/.

12. Bureau of Labor Statistics, "American Time Use Survey," www.bls.gov/tus/. The study of time is an inexact science. Households that have been part of the Census Bureau's Current Population Survey for eight months are called and asked to recall what they did in the previous twenty-four hours, starting at midnight. Economists then extrapolate the responses to statistically represent an entire week of typical days, as if every Tuesday were like every Thursday and the reluctant slog of Monday were not an entirely different animal from every giddy Friday. Robinson said longer diaries would be more accurate but so burdensome no one would fill them out. Social scientists comb this time data for clues about the way we live, how we work, what kind of progress we're making toward gender equality, and how much time we make for leisure.

13. Suzanne M. Bianchi, John P. Robinson, and Melissa A. Milkie, *Changing Rhythms of American Family Life* (New York: Russell Sage Foundation, 2006), 53–58.

14. John P. Robinson, "Time Use and Qualities of Life," *Social Indicators Research: Special Issue* (IATUR Conference, Washington, D.C., 2007).

15. Kristen Gerancher, "The Economic Value of Housework: New Survey to Track Women-Dominated Labor," CBS.MarketWatch.com, 2001 (Washington, D.C.: Center for Partnership Studies, 2012), www.partnershipway.org/learn-more/ar ticles-by-riane-eisler/economics-business-organizational-development/the-eco nomic-value-of-housework. Also Janet C. Gornick and Marcia K. Meyers, eds., *Gender Equality: Transforming Family Divisions of Labor*, the Real Utopias Project, vol. 6 (New York: Verso, 2009).

16. Iatur.org. In 1995, the United Nations World Conference on Women called for national and international statistical organizations to measure unpaid work and reflect its value in satellite accounts to the GDP. As of 2013, few had. See also www.levyinstitute.org/pubs/wp_541.pdf.

## 2: LEISURE IS FOR NUNS

1. Peter Brown and Helen Perkins, "Fathers' Juggling Time Between Work, Leisure and Family" (lecture, IATUR Time-Budgets and Beyond: The Timing of Daily Life conference, Paris, 2010).

2. Linda Duxbury and Chris Higgins, *Work-Life Conflict in Canada in the New Millennium: Key Findings and Recommendations from the 2001 National Work-Life Conflict Study*, Report 6 (Health Canada, January 2009), www.hc-sc.gc.ca/ewh -semt/pubs/occup-travail/balancing_six-equilibre_six/sum-res-eng.php, 7. See pp. 19 and 21 for an outline of costs. Both men and women reported that leisure time had declined by 40 percent from the previous decade.

3. Nicole Samuel, ed., *Women, Leisure, and the Family in Contemporary Society: A Multinational Perspective* (Wallingford, CT: CAB International, 1996), 9.

4. Gladys Martinez, Kimberly Daniels, and Anjani Chandra, "Fertility of Men and Women Aged 15–44 Years in the United States: National Survey of Family Growth, 2006–2010," *National Health Statistics Reports* 51 (April 12, 2012): 1–29, www.cdc.gov/nchs/data/nhsr/nhsr051.pdf. On p. 5, the report shows that the U.S.

fertility rate is highest for men and women with no high school diploma or GED, 2.5 and 1.7 respectively, and lowest, around 1.0, well below the 2.1 rate that demographers call "replacement level," for men and women with a bachelor's degree or higher. For statistics on low birthrates around the world, see Steve Philip Kramer, "Mind the Baby Gap," *New York Times*, April 18, 2012.

5. Steven Philip Kramer, "Mind the Baby Gap," *New York Times*, April 18, 2012.

6. Bianchi, Robinson, and Milkie, *Changing Rhythms*, 55–57 (see chap. 1, n12). In terms of sheer time, employed mothers averaged a seventy-one-hour total workweek in 2000. That's a ten-hour workday *seven days a week* when you count paid work and unpaid domestic duties, an hour a day longer than in 1975. Single mothers' total workweeks were *two hours a day* longer in 2000 than in 1975. At-home mothers, too, saw their forty-seven-hour workweek in 1975 ratcheted up about an hour a day to fifty-two hours. Employed married fathers' total workloads have risen, though not by as much. They cut back their paid work hours from 1975 to 2000 but increased the time spent on housework and taking care of kids by forty-five minutes a day. The total workdays of both mothers and fathers in developed countries are getting longer. Parents in America and Australia, because of all the increasing time they spend with their children, have the longest workdays of all. See also Lyn Craig, "Parenthood, Gender and Work-Family Time in the United States, Australia, Italy, France, and Denmark," *Journal of Marriage and Family* 72, no. 5 (October 2010): 1344–61, doi: 10.1111/j.1741-3737.2010.00769.x.

7. Kerstin Aumann, Ellen Galinsky, and Kenneth Matos, *The New Male Mystique* (New York: Families and Work Institute, 2011). The institute found an increasing number of men in dual-earning couples experiencing conflict between the pressures of work and home, from 35 percent in 1977 to 60 percent in 2008, higher even than women, whose stress rose from 41 to 47 percent in the same period. http://familiesandwork.org/site/research/reports/newmalemystique.pdf. See also Brad Harrington, Fred Van Deusen, and Beth Humberd, *The New Dad: Caring, Committed, and Conflicted* (Boston: Boston College Center for Work & Family, 2011), www.bc.edu/content/dam/files/centers/cwf/pdf/FH-Study -Web-2.pdf.

8. Tom W. Smith et al., *General Social Surveys, 1972–2010* (machine-readable data file) (Chicago: National Opinion Research Center, 2011), www3.norc.org/GSS+Website/. I ran a table on the question, "In general, how do you feel about your time, would you say you always feel rushed, sometimes or almost never?" and sorted the data by sex and by number of children. The question was asked in 1982, 1996, and 2004.

9. Martha C. White, "Under the Covers, in the Tub: We'll Shop Anywhere," August 13, 2012, www.today.com/under-covers-well-shop-anywhere-938774?franchiseslug= todaymoneymain.

10. "Work-Life Balance," *OECD Better Life Index*, www.oecdbetterlifeindex.org/top ics/work-life-balance/. See also Steven Greenhouse, "Americans' International Lead in Hours Worked Grew in 90's, Report Shows," *New York Times*, September 1, 2001, www.nytimes.com/2001/09/01/us/americans-international-lead-in-hours-worked

-grew-in-90-s-report-shows.html. Greenhouse reports that the International Labor Organization found that Americans worked 137 hours more a year than Japanese workers, 260 hours more than British workers, and nearly 500 hours more than German workers.

11. Kenneth Matos, senior director of employment research and practice at the Families and Work Institute, provided the author with a report on overwork by worker demographics that he generated from their database.

12. Joshua Guryan, Erik Hurst, and Melissa Kearney, "Parental Education and Parental Time with Children," *National Bureau of Economic Research*, 2008, www.econ.umd.edu/media/papers/84.pdf.

13. Rebecca May, Milla Sanes, and John Schmitt, "No Vacation Nation Revisited," Center for Economic Policy and Research, May 2013, www.cepr.net/documents/publications/no-vacation-update-2013-05.pdf; "Expedia Vacation Deprivation 2012," Harris Interactive Inc., Banner Book #4, www.expedia.com/p/info-other/vacation_deprivation.htm; Harold Maass, "America's War on Vacation: By the Numbers," *The Week*, May 28, 2013, http://theweek.com/article/index/244771/americas-war-on-vacation-by-the-numbers; Derek Thompson, "The Only Advanced Country Without a National Vacation Policy? It's the U.S.," *The Atlantic*, July 2, 2012, www.theatlantic.com/business/archive/2012/07/the-only-advanced-country-without-a-national-vacation-policy-its-the-us/2559317.

14. Ellen Galinsky, telephone interview with author, September 2011. She quotes from the Family and Work Institute's 2002 and 2008 *National Study of the Changing Workforce*, as well as the 2004 report, *Overwork in America: When the Way We Work Becomes Too Much.*

15. Marybeth J. Mattingly and Liana C. Sayer, "Under Pressure: Gender Differences in the Relationship Between Free Time and Feeling Rushed," *Journal of Marriage and Family* 68 (2006): 205–21, doi: 10.1111/j.1741-3737.2006.00242.x.

16. Kim Parker, "The Harried Life of the Working Mother," Pew Research Center, October 1, 2009, www.pewsocialtrends.org/2009/10/01/the-harried-life-of-the-working-mother/.

17. Becky Pettit and Jennifer L. Hook, *Gendered Tradeoffs* (New York: Russell Sage Foundation, 2009), 75. For the international statistics on mothers returning to work full-time after childbirth, see Huerta, M. C., W. Adema, J. Baxter, M. Corak, M. Deding, M. C. Gray, W. J. Han, and J. Waldfogel, "Early Maternal Employment and Child Development in Five OECD Countries," OECD Social, Employment, and Migration Working Papers, No. 118, September 6, 2011, http://search.oecd.org/officialdocuments/displaydocumentpdf/?cote=DELSA/ELSA/WD/SEM(2011)3&docLanguage=En.

18. Kim Parker and Wendy Wang, "Modern Parenthood: Roles of Moms and Dads Converge as They Balance Work and Family," Pew Research Center, March 14, 2013, www.pewsocialtrends.org/2013/03/14/modern-parenthood-roles-of-moms-and-dads-converge-as-they-balance-work-and-family/. Pew researchers found that American mothers' yearning for part-time work declined slightly to 50 per-

cent in 2013 after the recession. The desire for full-time work grew, particularly among single mothers and mothers in difficult financial circumstances, from 20 to 32 percent from 1997 to 2012.

19. Ibid., 12.

20. Marielle Cloin, "How Busy We Are and How Busy We Feel: The Influence of Objective and Subjective Indicators on the Perceived Work-Life Balance in the Netherlands" (presentation, IATUR Time-Budgets and Beyond).

21. Robinson, *Time for Life*, 94–95.

22. Juliet Schor, *The Overworked American: The Unexpected Decline of Leisure* (New York: Basic Books, 1992), 1.

23. Jerry A. Jacobs and Kathleen Gerson, *The Time Divide: Work, Family, and Gender Inequality* (Cambridge, MA: Harvard University Press, 2005), 164. See p. 34 for the table of hours.

24. Ibid., 35.

25. John C. Williams and Heather Boushey, "The Three Faces of Work-Family Conflict: The Poor, the Professionals, and the Missing Middle" (Washington, D.C.: Center for American Progress, January 2010), www.americanprogress.org/wp -content/uploads/issues/2010/01/pdf/threefaces.pdf.

26. Michael Hout and Caroline Hanley, "The Overworked American Family: Trends and Nontrends in Working Hours, 1968–2001" (working paper, Survey Research Center, University of California, Berkeley, 2002), http://ucdata.berkeley.edu/rsf census/papers/Working_Hours_HoutHanley.pdf. Permission to cite work was given to author via e-mail January 15, 2013.

27. Bianchi, 115.

28. Bianchi, Robinson, and Milkie, *Changing Rhythms*. Fathers work an average of 46.5 hours a week, compared to a mother's 33 hours.

29. Suzanne M. Bianchi, "Family Time and Time Allocation in American Families," Workplace Flexibility 2010 Program Paper, http://workplaceflexibility.org/images /uploads/program_papers/bianchi_-_family_change_and_time_allocation_in _american_families.pdf, 8.

30. Leslie Stratton, telephone interview with author about her work with Elena Stancanelli, June 2012.

31. Italy: Carla Power, "Staying Home with Mamma," *Newsweek*, August 13, 2000, www.thedailybeast.com/newsweek/2000/08/13/staying-home-with-mamma .html; Japan and South Korea: Veerle Miranda, "Cooking, Caring and Volunteering: Unpaid Work Around the World," OECD Social, Employment, and Migration Working Papers, No. 116 (OECD Publishing, 2011), www.oecd-ilibrary.org /social-issues-migration-health/cooking-caring-and-volunteering-unpaid-work -around-the-world_5kghrjm8s142-en, 13.

32. Mario S. Floro and Hitomi Komatsu, "Labor Force Participation, Gender and Work in South Africa: What Can Time Use Data Reveal?" *Journal of Feminist Economics* 17, Issue 4, November 3, 2011, www.american.edu/cas/economics/pdf /upload/2011-2.pdf. The "onerous share" of domestic work, the researchers argue,

"influences not only women's availability for labor market work, but also their ability to seek employment, to take up learning, and/or to socialize outside the family." It is not surprising, the authors write, that women find fewer job options than men.

33. Sanjiv Gupta et al., "Economic Inequality and Housework," in *Dividing the Domestic: Men, Women, and Household Work in Cross-National Perspective*, ed. Judith Tres and Sonja Drobnič (Stanford: Stanford University Press, 2010), 105–24.

34. Katherin Barg and Miriam Beblo, "Does 'Selection into Specialization' Explain the Differences in Time Use Between Married and Cohabiting Couples? An Empirical Application for Germany" (paper presented at International Conference of German Socio-Economic Panel Study Users, June 30–July 2, 2010), http://ces.univ-paris1.fr/membre/seminaire/GENRE/Selection_into_Specialization.pdf.

35. Guryan, Hurst, and Kearney, "Parental Education and Parental Time with Children."

36. Suzanne Bianchi, Vanessa Wight, and Sarah Raley, "Maternal Employment and Family Caregiving: Rethinking Time with Children in the ATUS" (paper presented at the American Time Use Survey Early Results conference, Bethesda, MD, December 9, 2005, 13).

37. Lyn Craig, "Does Father Care Mean Fathers Share? A Comparison of How Mothers and Fathers in Intact Families Spend Time with Children," *Gender & Society* 20, no. 2 (April 2006): 259–81, doi:10.1177/0891243205285212.

38. Bianchi, Wight, and Raley, "Maternal Employment," 13. For the difference between employed and nonemployed mothers, see p. 15. See also Bianchi, Robinson, and Milkie, *Changing Rhythms*, 76–77. Bianchi notes that employed mothers in 2000 spent about eleven hours a week in primary child care, about as much time as nonemployed mothers did in 1975. Employed mothers spent about fifty fewer minutes a day caring for children than nonemployed mothers in 2000.

39. www.econ.umd.edu/media/papers/84.pdf.

40. Tamar Lewin, "Study Links Working Mothers to Slower Learning," *New York Times*, July 17, 2002; Bonnie Rochman, "Are Working Moms to Blame for Childhood Obesity?" *Time*, February 4, 2011; John Carvel, "Children of Working Mothers 'At Risk,'" *Guardian*, March 13, 2001.

41. Lyn Craig, Oriel Sullivan, and Kim Fisher interviews by author, Paris, July 2010.

42. Suzanne Bianchi, Sara Raley, and Melissa Milkie, "'What Gives' When Mothers Are Employed?: Time Allocation of Employed and Nonemployed Mothers: 1975 and 2000" (College Park: Department of Sociology and Maryland Population Research Center, University of Maryland, 2005), www.levyinstitute.org/pubs/CP/conf_oct05_papers/bianchi-paper.pdf. See tables 5 and 6. To understand how parental leisure varies with socioeconomic status, see also Almudena Sevilla-Sanz, José Ignacio Giménez-Nadal, and Jonathan Gershuny, "Leisure Inequality in the U.S.: 1965–2003" (working paper, Department of Sociology, University of Oxford, 2011), www.sociology.ox.ac.uk/documents/working-papers/2010/swp101.pdf.

43. Ibid. See also "Gender Brief," OECD Social Policy Division, March 2010, www.oecd.org/social/family/44720649.pdf, 16.

44. Bianchi, Robinson, and Milkie, *Changing Rhythms*, chap. 5.
45. Rachel Connelly, interview with author, fall 2009. Follow-up e-mail, fall 2009. Also Jean Kimmel and Rachel Connelly, "Mothers' Time Choices: Caregiving, Leisure, Home Production, and Paid Work," *Journal of Human Resources* 42, no. 3 (2007): 643–81.
46. John Robinson et al., "The Overestimated Workweek Revisited," *Monthly Labor Review* 134, no. 6 (June 2011): 43–53, www.bls.gov/opub/mlr/2011/06/art3exc.htm.
47. John de Graaf, *Running Out of Time*, VHS, (Portland: Oregon Public Broadcasting, 1994).
48. I am indebted to my friend Larry Robertson, who inspired me at breakfast one morning with these same two questions, which guided his own research and thinking for his book on entrepreneurship, *A Deliberate Pause: Entrepreneurship and Its Moment in Human Progress* (New York: Morgan James Publishing, 2009).
49. I am indebted to Dan Heath, author of *Switch: How to Change Things When Change Is Hard* (New York: Broadway Books, 2010), for suggesting looking for bright spots as I began my journey.

## 3: TOO BUSY TO LIVE

1. Focus group organized by Ann Burnett at the Radisson Hotel, Fargo, North Dakota, July 17, 2012.
2. Magali Rheault, "In U.S., 3 in 10 Working Adults Are Strapped for Time," Gallup, July 20, 2011, www.gallup.com/poll/148583/Working-Adults-Strapped-Time.aspx.
3. Ann Burnett's holiday letter collection archive shared with the author, July 18, 2012.
4. Ann Burnett et al., "Earning the Badge of Honor: The Social Construction of Time and Pace of Life" (paper presented at the National Communication Association meeting, Chicago, November 14, 2007), 4.
5. Ibid., 18.
6. Ann Burnett, "The Fast-Paced Lifestyle and Marriage: Cramming in Just One More Thing" (paper presented at the National Communication Association convention, Atlanta, 2001).
7. Ann Burnett, unpublished research material provided to author, July 18, 2012.
8. Sandra Blakeslee, "What Other People Say May Change What You See," *New York Times*, June 28, 2005, www.nytimes.com/2005/06/28/science/28brai.html. See also S. Gregory et al., "Neurobiological Correlates of Social Conformity and Independence During Mental Rotation," *Biological Psychiatry* 58 (2005): 245–53, doi: 10.1016/j.biopsych.2005.04.012. Also Elizabeth Landau, "Why So Many Minds Think Alike," CNN, January 15, 2009, http://articles.cnn.com/2009-01-15/health/social.conformity.brain_1_brain-images-opinion-new-study?_s=PM:HEALTH; "Dr. Greg Berns Answers Viewers' Questions on Conformity," ABC News, January 13, 2006, http://abcnews.go.com/Primetime/story?id=1504239#.UL427o5_Wol.

Berns told ABC, "What other people say they see actually gets inside your mind and can alter the information coming from your eyes—even before you are aware it is happening."

9. Darlene Bishop, "Too Busy for Life?" *The 13th Apostle;* www.the13thapostle.net /christian-articles/too-busy-for-life.htm. See also Douglas Todd, "Canadians Not 'Mad' at Churches, Just Too Busy for Them: Pollster," *Vancouver Sun* (blog), August 27, 2012, http://blogs.vancouversun.com/2012/08/27/canadians-not-mad -at-churches-just-too-busy-pollster/.

10. Susan Page, "Why 90 Million Americans Won't Vote in November," *USA Today,* August 15, 2012, usatoday30.usatoday.com/news/politics/story/2012-08-15/non -voters-obama-romney/57055184/1.

11. Elizabeth Cohen, "Do You Obsessively Check Your Smartphone?" CNN, July 28, 2011, www.cnn.com/2011/HEALTH/07/28/ep.smartphone.obsessed.cohen /index.html.

12. Lucy Waterlow, "How Work Colleagues Are Our Closest Friends Because We Are Too Busy to Keep in Touch with Old Mates," *Daily Mail* online, August 9, 2012, www.dailymail.co.uk/femail/article-2185991/How-work-colleagues-closest -friends-busy-touch-old-mates.html.

13. "Dating/Relationship Statistics," Statistic Brain, July 26, 2012, www.statisticbrain .com/dating-relationship-stats/.

14. Ian Kerner, "Are You Too Tired for Sex?" CNN, August 9, 2012, www.cnn.com /2012/08/09/health/kerner-too-tired-sex/index.html.

15. James Hall, "Busy Lifestyles Eat into Pudding Time," *Telegraph,* October 29, 2011, www.telegraph.co.uk/foodanddrink/foodanddrinknews/8856097/Busy-lifestyles -eat-into-pudding-time.html.

16. Statistics from 1968: James Gleick, *Faster: The Acceleration of Just About Every- thing* (Boston: Little, Brown, 1999). Statistics from 2000: Laura Miller, "Sound Bites Get Shorter," Center for Media and Democracy's PR Watch (blog), Novem- ber 11, 2000, www.prwatch.org/node/384.

17. "Americans Stressed-Out; 75% Too Busy for Vacation," Odyssey Media Group, September 14, 2010, www.odysseymediagroup.com/nan/Editorial-Hotels-And -Resorts.asp?ReportID=418924.

18. "Americans Too Busy for Lunch," Prepared Foods Network, July 25, 2005, www .preparedfoods.com/articles/americans-too-busy-for-lunch.

19. Tanzina Vega, "In Ads, the Workers Rise Up . . . and Go to Lunch," *New York Times,* July 7, 2012, www.nytimes.com/2012/07/08/business/media/ads-for-mcdonalds -and-las-vegas-aimed-at-harried-workers.html?_r=0. Also Stuart Elliott, "In New Ad Campaign, Orbitz Comes Out as Pro-Vacation," *New York Times* Media De- coder blog, May 4, 2012, http://mediadecoder.blogs.nytimes.com/2012/05/04/in -new-ad-campaign-orbitz-comes-out-as-pro-vacation/.

20. Dick Dahl, "The Tick-Tock Syndrome: How Your Clock Can Make You Sick," *UTNE Reader,* March/April 1997, www.utne.com/Mind-Body/Tick-Tock-Syn drome-Stress-Related-Illnesses.aspx#axzz2ZohTMLcS.

21. Burnett et al., "Earning the Badge of Honor," 13.

22. Jennifer Kunst, "A Headshrinker's Guide to the Galaxy," *Psychology Today*, September 23, 2012, www.psychologytoday.com/blog/headshrinkers-guide-the -galaxy/201209/are-you-too-busy-take-lesson-lucy. Henna Inam, "Leadership Practices for Work Life Sanity," *Glass Hammer* (blog), August 15, 2012, www .theglasshammer.com/news/2012/08/15/leadership-practices-for-work-life -sanity/. Inam writes, "For many of us (I'm on the list, too!) we associate our work with our worth as human beings. Unless we're really productive we're not feeling good enough about ourselves. So, while we're happy to blame our boss for sending an e-mail at midnight, secretly we feel quite proud replying to it at 12:01 am. I know this from personal experience." Inam goes on to write that she left a gathering of friends one Sunday morning after three hours. "I felt bad that I'd wasted all this time being unproductive."

23. Jennifer Soong, "When Technology Addiction Takes Over Your Life," WebMD, June 6, 2008, www.webmd.com/mental-health/features/when-technology-addic tion-takes-over-your-life.

24. Justin Ravitz, "Exclusive Video: Happy Endings' Casey Wilson Wants to Return to Saturday Night Live—as Host!" *Us Weekly*, April 6, 2012, www.usmagazine.com /entertainment/news/happy-endings-casey-wilson-wants-to-return-to-saturday -night-live-----as-host-201264.

25. Universal Television, "Saturday Night Live—Press Releases," December 5, 2011, www.nbcumv.com/mediavillage/studio/ums1/saturdaynightlive/pressreleases ?pr=contents/press-releases/2011/12/05/quotablesfromsa1323122223585.xml.

26. Christopher K. Hsee, Adelle X. Yang, and Liangyan Wang, "Idleness Aversion and the Need for Justifiable Busyness," *Psychological Science* 21, no. 7, June 14, 2010, http://pss.sagepub.com/content/21/7/926, 926–30.

27. Brent Schlender, "Bill Gates' Very Full Life After Microsoft," CNN Money, June 21, 2010, http://tech.fortune.cnn.com/2010/06/21/bill-gates-very-full-life-after-micro soft/.

28. Adrienne Carter, "Marcus Samuelsson, a Chef, a Brand and Then Some," *New York Times*, August 4, 2012, www.nytimes.com/2012/08/05/business/marcus-samuels son-both-a-chef-and-a-brand.html?pagewanted=all&_r=0.

29. Daniel Gross, "No Rest for the Wealthy," *New York Times*, July 1, 2009, www .nytimes.com/2009/07/05/books/review/Gross-t.html. Oriel Sullivan in Skype interview with author, December 16, 2011. See also Staffan Burenstam Linder, *The Harried Leisure Class* (New York: Columbia University Press, 1970). In her time diary study, Oriel Sullivan, a time-use researcher at Oxford, found that the higher the socioeconomic status of men, the busier they are, not just working longer hours than other men but also rushing from the golf course to the squash court to the theater to the latest charitable board they serve on. The appearance of being busy and important has become so desirable, and the choices of what to do with one's resources so infinite, she argues, that the wealthy and elite now make up an increasingly "harried" leisure class.

30. Keen Footwear, *Instant Recess Toolkit*, http://recess.keenfootwear.com/wp-content /uploads/2012/06/Keen_CorpToolKit_ALL_Download_11Jun.pdf.

31. Schor, *Overworked American*, 4. John de Graaf and David K. Batker, *What's the Economy For, Anyway?: Why It's Time to Stop Chasing Growth and Start Pursuing Happiness* (New York: Bloomsbury Press, 2011), 102.

32. McCarthy's hearings were tied primarily to easing the burden of unemployment—spreading it more widely, more workers, working fewer hours rather than the traditional economic model of fewer workers working more hours and reliance on overtime. He lost the argument, which has never been revisited. See William McGaughey Jr., "Shorter Workweek: History & Arguments For and Against," website, www.shorterworkweek.com/history&arguments.html. Statement by Juanita Kreps, Professor of Economics, Duke University, before the Subcommittee on Retirement and the Individual of the Species Committee on Aging, United States Senate, June 7 and 8, 1967, www.aging.senate.gov/publications/671967.pdf.

33. Reuel Denney, "The Leisure Society," *Harvard Business Review* 37, no. 3 (May/June 1959): 46–60.

34. Robert Lee, "Religion and Leisure in American Culture," *Theology Today* 19, no. 1 (April 1962): 39–58.

35. For more on *skole*, see Robert Lee, *Religion and Leisure in America: A Study in Four Dimensions* (Nashville: Abingdon Press, 1964), 42–43.

36. Schor, *Overworked American*, 6, 47.

37. Ibid., 60, 72.

38. Jonathan Gershuny, interview with author, Paris, July 2010.

39. Matthew Ruben, "Forgive Us Our Trespasses? The Rise of Consumer Debt in Modern America," ProQuest Discovery Guide, February 2009, www.csa.com /discoveryguides/debt/review.pdf.

40. Becky DeGreeff, Ann Burnett, and Dennis Cooley, "Communicating and Philosophizing About Authenticity or Inauthenticity in a Fast-Paced World," *Journal of Happiness Studies* 11, no. 4 (August 2010): 395–408, doi: 10.1007/s10902-009-9147-4.

## 4: THE INCREDIBLE SHRINKING BRAIN

1. American Psychological Association, *Stress in America,* "Our Health at Risk," 2011, www.apa.org/news/press/releases/stress/2011/final-2011.pdf. More than half of Americans surveyed report having stress-related health problems. More women routinely report feeling stressed-out than men. And everyone says they're too "busy" to make any effort to change.

2. Ronald C. Kessler et al., "Lifetime Prevalence and Age-of-Onset Distributions of Mental Disorders in the World Health Organization's World Mental Health Survey Initiative," *World Psychiatry* 6, no. 3 (October 2007): 168–76, www.ncbi.nlm .nih.gov/pmc/articles/PMC2174588/.

3. Robert L. Leahy, "How Big a Problem Is Anxiety? In Any Given Year, About 17% of Us Will Have an Anxiety Disorder," *Psychology Today Anxiety Files* blog, April 30, 2008, www.psychologytoday.com/blog/anxiety-files/200804/how-big-problem -is-anxiety.

4. M. J. Essex et al., "Epigenetic Vestiges of Early Developmental Adversity: Child-hood Stress Exposure and DNA Methylation in Adolescence," *Child Development* 84, no. 1 (January-February 2013): 58–75, www.ncbi.nlm.nih.gov/pubmed/21883162.

5. Emily B. Ansell et al., "Cumulative Adversity and Smaller Gray Matter Volume in Medial Prefrontal, Anterior Cignulate, and Insula Regions," *Biological Psychiatry* 72, no. 1 (July 1, 2012): 57–64, www.ncbi.nlm.nih.gov/pubmed/22218286.

6. Amy Arnsten, Carolyn M. Mazure, and Rajita Sinha, "Everyday Stress Can Shut Down the Brain's Chief Command Center," *Scientific American*, April 9, 2012, www.mc3cb.com/pdf_articles_interest_physiology/2012_4_10_Stress_Shut_%20Down_Brain.pdf.

7. The description of stress and how it impacts the body in this section is based on telephone conversations with Bruce McEwen, neuroscientist at Rockefeller University who heads the Harold and Margaret Milliken Hatch Laboratory of Neuroendocrinology, May 14, 2012.

8. B. S. McEwen, "Protection and Damage from Acute and Chronic Stress: Allosta-sis and Allostatic Overload and Relevance to the Pathophysiology of Psychiatric Disorders," *Annals of the New York Academy of Sciences* 1032 (December 2004): 1–7, www.ncbi.nlm.nih.gov/pubmed/15677391.

9. Emory University, "Stress Making Your Blood Pressure Rise? Blame Your Immune System," *Science Daily*, March 2, 2012, www.sciencedaily.com/releases/2012/03/120305103203.htm?utm_source=feedburner&utm_medium=feed&utm_campaign=Feed%3A+sciencedaily+%28ScienceDaily%3A+Latest+Science+News%29.

10. Larry Cahill, "His Brain, Her Brain," *Scientific American*, April 25, 2005, 44–46, www.scientificamerican.com/article.cfm?id=his-brain-her-brain.

11. For a list of Glaser's studies on the relationship between stress and physical health, see "Glaser, M. Ronald, Ph.D." on the Ohio State University's Department of Molecular Virology, Immunology, & Medical Genetics website, http://biomed.osu.edu/mvimg/1253.cfm.

12. Michael Slezak, "Women's Brains May Age Prematurely, Possibly Because of Stress," *Washington Post*, July 30, 2012, www.washingtonpost.com/national/health-science/womens-brains-may-age-prematurely-possibly-because-of-stress/2012/07/30/gJQAGdWvKX_story.html.

13. Rick Nauert, "Childhood Stress Can Result in Brain Changes," *PsychCentral*, March 1, 2010, http://psychcentral.com/news/2010/03/01/childhood-stress-can-result-in-brain-changes/11733.html.

14. Ansell et al., "Cumulative Adversity."

15. Ansell, e-mail message to author, June 18, 2012.

16. http://hmi.ucsd.edu/pdf/HMI_2010_EnterpriseReport_Jan_2011.pdf.

17. http://hmi.ucsd.edu/pdf/HMI_2009_ConsumerReport_Dec9_2009.pdf.

18. Mark Brownlow, "8 Email Statistics to Use at Parties," *Email Marketing Reports* (blog), www.email-marketing-reports.com/iland/2009/08/8-email-statistics-to-use-at-parties.html.

19. Victor M. González and Gloria Mark, "'Constant, Constant, Multi-tasking Craziness': Managing Multiple Working Spheres," Proceedings of ACM CHI '04, 113–20, http://citeseerx.ist.psu.edu/viewdoc/summary?doi=10.1.1.144.6988. For information on fragmented work, see also: Gloria Mark, Victor M. González, and Justin Harris, "No Task Left Behind? Examining the Nature of Fragmented Work" (paper presented at the Human Factors in Computing Systems conference, Portland, OR, April 2–7, 2005), www.ics.uci.edu/~gmark/CHI2005.pdf.

20. Roy F. Baumeister and John Tierney, Willpower: Rediscovering the Greatest Human Strength (New York: Penguin, 2011), 116.

21. Jonathan B. Spira, Overload! How Too Much Information Is Hazardous to Your Organization (Hoboken, New Jersey: John Wiley & Sons, Inc., 2011). www.basex.com/web/tbghome.nsf/23e5e39594c064ee852564ae004fa010/ea4eae828bd411be8525742f0006cde3/$file/costofnotpayingattention.basexreport.pdf.

22. www.theatlantic.com/magazine/archive/2012/11/busy-and-busier/309111/2/.

23. Susan Weinschenk, "100 Things You Should Know About People: #8—Dopamine Makes You Addicted to Seeking Information," The Brain Lady Blog, November 7, 2009, www.theteamw.com/2009/11/07/100-things-you-should-know-about-people-8-dopamine-makes-us-addicted-to-seeking-information/.

24. Dan Kennedy, No B.S.: Time Management for Entrepreneurs (Irvine, CA: Entrepreneur Media, 2004), 3. Kennedy also reports that Lee Iacocca figured top CEOs might average forty-five productive minutes a day and spent the rest of it "fighting off time-wasting B.S. like a frantic fellow futilely waving his arms at a swarm of angry bees on attack."

25. Torkel Klingberg, The Overflowing Brain: Information Overload and the Limits of Working Memory (New York: Oxford University Press, 2009).

26. "Emails 'Hurt IQ More Than Pot,'" CNN, April 22, 2005, http://articles.cnn.com/2005-04-22/world/text.iq_1_mails-iq-messages?_s=PM:WORLD.

27. Cordelia Fine, Delusions of Gender: How Our Minds, Society, and Neurosexism Create Difference (New York: W. W. Norton, 2010). The handful of studies that formed the basis for that common misperception were small, Fine writes, and studies with larger samples of men and women show more variation within each sex than across sexes.

28. Barbara Schneider, "The Human Face of Workplace Flexibility" (paper presented at Focus on Workplace Flexibility conference, Washington, D.C., November 29–30, 2010).

29. www.nytimes.com/2013/01/14/us/susan-nolen-hoeksema-psychologist-who-studied-depression-in-women-dies-at-53.html?partner=rssnyt&emc=rss&_r=2&.

30. "America's State of Mind: New Report Finds Americans Increasingly Turn to Medications to Ease Their Mental Woes; Women Lead the Trend; More Than One-in-Four Women Take Medication to Treat a Mental Health Condition; Women's Use of ADHD Drugs Surged 2.5 Times over Decade, Surpasses Men's Usage," www.prnewswire.com/news-releases/americas-state-of-mind-new-report-finds-americans-increasingly-turn-to-medications-to-ease-their-mental-woes-women-lead-the-trend-133939038.html.

31. Christena Nippert-Eng, "'Mommy, Mommy' or 'Excuse Me, Ma'am': Gender and Interruptions at Home and Work" (paper presented at the American Sociology Association annual meeting, Pittsburgh, August 1992).

## 5: THE IDEAL WORKER IS NOT YOUR MOTHER

1. Complaint and Jury Trial Demand, *Equal Opportunity Employment Commission v. Denver Hotel Management Company, Inc.* d/b/a Brown Palace Hotel & Spa, United States District Court for the District of Colorado, July 20, 2010, case 1:10-cv-01712-REB, 4. http://assets.bizjournals.com/cms_media/denver/pdf/EEOC %20v.%20Denver%20Hotel%20Management%20Co..pdf.

2. Renate Rivelli in two phone interviews with author, March 23, 2012, and in person in Denver, April 4, 2012.

3. Lynn Feinberg, senior strategic policy adviser, AARP Public Policy Institute, statement to the U.S. Equal Employment Opportunity Commission, *Unlawful Discrimination Against Pregnant Workers and Workers with Caregiving Responsibilities*, hearing, February 15, 2012. www.eeoc.gov/eeoc/meetings/2-15-12/fein berg.cfm. Feinberg referred to data collected in a Gallup Poll, "More Than One in Six American Workers Also Act as Caregivers; Low-Income, Less-Educated Americans More Likely to Be Caregivers," July 26, 2011, www.gallup.com/poll /148640/One-Six-American-Workers-Act-Caregivers.aspx. Feinberg also referred to the finding that 42 percent of all American workers reported caring for an elderly relative or friend in the past five years, and that with the number of aging baby boomers over age sixty-five projected to grow from forty to seventy-two million by 2030, she said caregiving demands on workers will only grow: Kerstin Aumann et al., *The Elder Care Study: Everyday Realities and Wishes for Change* (New York: Families and Work Institute, October 2010), http://families andwork.org/site/research/reports/elder_care.pdf.

4. Joan Williams, distinguished professor, University of California Hastings College of the Law, director of the WorkLife Law Center, statement to the EEOC, *Unlawful Discrimination Against Pregnant Workers and Workers with Caregiving Responsibilities*, hearing, www.eeoc.gov/eeoc/meetings/2-15-12/williams.cfm. See also Cynthia Thomas Calvert, "Family Responsibilities Discrimination: Litigation Update 2010," The Center for WorkLife Law, www.worklifelaw.org/pubs/FRDupdate.pdf.

5. The Family and Medical Leave Act, passed by Congress in 1993 and signed into law by Bill Clinton in one of his first acts as president, guarantees twelve weeks of unpaid leave every year to care for oneself or a family member. Business groups lobbied against making the leave paid, saying it would encourage employees to take unnecessary time off. The law covers only full-time workers employed for at least a year by firms with fifty or more employees. About 40 percent of the workforce is not covered. www.dol.gov/asp/evaluation/fmla/FMLATechnicalReport.pdf.

6. Ibid. Sharon Lerner also includes examples of pregnancy and caregiver discrimination in her book, *The War on Moms: On Life in a Family-Unfriendly Nation* (Hoboken, NJ: John Wiley & Sons, 2010), 27–29.

7. Joan Williams, statement to the EEOC. See also Opinion and Order, *Louisanna Hercule v. Wendy's of N.E. Florida, Inc.*, United States District Court Southern District of Florida, case 10-80248-CIV-MARRA, May 10, 2010, http://law.justia .com/cases/federal/district-courts/florida/flsdce/9:2010cv80248/351903/15. In the Wendy's case, when the employee refused to have an abortion, she alleges that her supervisor began to belittle her whenever they disagreed, telling her to "take your fat pregnant ass home." The employee later suffered a miscarriage and was fired for taking leave. Wendy's disputes the charges. Wendy's settled after mediation, and the case was closed in May 2011.

8. U.S. Equal Opportunity Employment Commission, "Pregnancy Discrimination Charges EEOC & FEPAs Combined: FY 1997–FY 2011," www.eeoc.gov/eeoc /statistics/enforcement/pregnancy.cfm, shows, for example, that the number of charge receipts filed with the EEOC and state and local Fair Employment Practices Agencies under Title VII of the Civil Rights Act of 1964 alleging pregnancy discrimination grew from 3,977 in fiscal 1997 to 5,797 in fiscal 2011. Monetary benefits, not including those obtained from litigation, rose in the same period from $5.6 million to $17.2 million. More than 50,000 charges were filed and more than $150 million paid in monetary awards in the first decade of the 2000s.

9. J. David Lopez, EEOC general counsel, in interview with author, Washington, D.C., March 15, 2012. Lopez said that unlike modern-day racial discrimination cases, which tend to be subtle and waged on the weight of circumstantial evidence, pregnancy discrimination is often blatant.

10. Memorandum of Law in Opposition to Defendant Bloomberg L.P.'s Motion for Summary Judgment as to EEOC's Pattern-or-Practice Claim EEOC v. Bloomberg, L.P., United States District Court Southern District of New York, 778 F. Supp. 2d 458. (No. 07-8383). More analysis of the case can be found in Joan C. Williams, "Jumpstarting the Stalled Gender Revolution: Justice Ginsburg and Reconstructive Feminism," *Hastings Law Journal* 63, no. 5 (2011-2012): 1290–97. See also Joan Williams, "Bloomberg Case: Open Season to Discriminate Against Mothers?" *Huffington Post*, August 26, 2011, www.huffingtonpost.com/joan -williams/bloomberg-case-open-seaso_b_934232.html. See also Sheelah Kolhatkar, "Mayor Bloomberg's Delicate Condition," *Upstart Business Journal*, Nov. 11, 2008, http://upstart.bizjournals.com/executives/features/2008/11/11/Gender -Discrimination-at-Bloomberg.html.

11. Opinion and Order, *Equal Employment Opportunity Commission v. Bloomberg L.P.*, United States District Court Southern District of New York, 07 Civ. 8383 (LAP), August 17, 2011, www.nysd.uscourts.gov/cases/show.php?db=special&id=124, 61.

12. Organisation for Economic Co-operation and Development, "Average Annual Hours Actually Worked per Worker, 2000–2012," http://stats.oecd.org/Index .aspx?DatasetCode=ANHRS. The table shows that the average worker in the United States worked 1,790 hours in 2012, higher than the OECD countries' average of 1,765. The OECD's *Better Life Index* also shows that more workers in the United States work "very long" hours of fifty or more each week, compared with

other OECD countries. "Work-Life Balance," *OECD Better Life Index*. www
.oecdbetterlifeindex.org/topics/work-life-balance/.

13. Chase Peterson-Withorn, "Rising Prices: College Tuition vs. the CPI," The Center
for College Affordability and Productivity. March 19, 2013. http://centerforcollege
affordability.org/archives/9623.

14. U.S. Census Bureau, "Married Couple Family Groups, by Labor Force Status of
Both Spouses, and Race and Hispanic Origin of the Reference Person: 2012," table FG1, www.census.gov/hhes/families/files/cps2012/tabFG1-all.xls.

15. Bureau of Labor Statistics, Economic News Release, "Families with Own Children:
Employment Status of Parents by Age of Youngest Child and Family Type, 2011–
2012 Annual Averages," April 26, 2013, www.bls.gov/news.release/famee.t04.htm.

16. Sharon R. Cohany and Emy Sok, "Trends in Labor Force Participation of Married
Mothers of Infants," Bureau of Labor Statistics Monthly Labor Review, February
2007, www.bls.gov/opub/mlr/2007/02/art2full.pdf. See Chart 1.

17. Schor, *Overworked American*, 114.

18. "Gender and Global Differences in Work-Life Effectiveness" (paper presented at
the Families and Work Institute/SHRM Work-Life Focus: 2012 and Beyond conference, Washington, D.C., November 8–10, 2011). In emerging markets like
China, Brazil, and India, 60 percent of the executives felt women who were committed to their families could not possibly be committed to work.

19. Shelley J. Correll, Stephen Benard, and In Paik, "Getting a Job: Is There a Motherhood Penalty?" *American Journal of Sociology* 112, no. 5 (March 2007): 1297–
1339, http://gender.stanford.edu/sites/default/files/motherhoodpenalty.pdf. The
authors write, "If work commitment is measured by the importance people at-
tach to their work identities—either absolutely or relative to other identities, such
as family identities—no difference is found in commitment between mothers
and nonmothers."

20. Ibid.

21. Mary C. Still, "Litigating the Maternal Wall: U.S. Lawsuits Charging Discrimination Against Workers with Family Responsibilities," Center for WorkLife Law,
University of California Hastings College of the Law, July 6, 2006, www.worklife
law.org/pubs/FRDreport.pdf, 5.

22. Correll, Benard, and Paik, "Getting a Job."

23. Madeline E. Heilman and Tyler G. Okimoto, "Motherhood: A Potential Source of
Bias in Employment Decisions," *Journal of Applied Psychology* 93, no. 1 (January
2008): 189–98. "Motherhood, it seems," the authors write, "can be hazardous in-
deed for a woman striving to get ahead." See also C. Etaugh and K. Nekolny,
"Effects of Employment Status and Marital Status on Perceptions of Mothers,"
*Sex Roles* 23 (1990): 273–80.

24. "Women CEOs of the Fortune 1000," Catalyst, July 1, 2013, www.catalyst.org
/knowledge/women-ceos-fortune-1000. "Women in the U.S. Congress 2013,"
Eagleton Institute of Politics, Rutgers University, November 11, 2012, www.cawp
.rutgers.edu/fast_facts/levels_of_office/documents/cong.pdf.

25. Philip N. Cohen, "Fact-Checking David Brooks, Citing Hanna Rosin Edition," *Family Inequality* (blog), September 11, 2012, http://familyinequality.wordpress .com/2012/09/11/fact-checking-david-brooks-citing-hanna-rosin-edition/. Cohen, a sociologist who studies gender and income inequality at the University of Maryland, quotes a Bureau of Labor Statistics July 18, 2012, news release on "Usual Weekly Earnings of Wage and Salary Workers, Second Quarter 2012." Cohen also notes that among young adults who have completed college and are working full-time, year-round, women make 80.7 percent of men's median earnings. "The gap includes discrimination in hiring, promotion, and wage setting, as well as women's family status, and occupational 'choices,'" Cohen explains. http://familyinequality.wordpress.com/2010/09/09/this-thing-about-young -women-earning-more/. Women between the ages of twenty-five and thirty-four earn 91 percent of what men earn. But for women ages thirty-five to forty-four, the gap widens to 79 percent and expands again for women forty-five to fifty-four to 73 percent, where it stays until age sixty-five. At that point, women earn about 85 percent of what men do.

26. Michelle J. Budig, professor of sociology, faculty associate, Center for Public Policy Administration, University of Massachusetts, Amherst, before the U.S. Joint Economic Committee hearing on "New Evidence on the Gender Pay Gap for Women and Mothers in Management," September 28, 2010, included in the report, United States General Accounting Office, *Invest in Women, Invest in America: A Comprehensive Review of Women in the U.S. Economy*, prepared by the majority staff of the Joint Economic Committee, Congress of the United States, December 2010, 124–42. A 2003 GAO report found a 2.5 percent pay gap between mothers and higher-earning childless women and a 2.1 percent bonus for fathers compared to childless men. The report also found a statistically significant 8.3 percent salary boost for married men over unmarried men, while marital status made no impact on women's earnings. *Women's Earnings: Work Patterns Partially Explain Difference Between Men's and Women's Earnings* (Washington, D.C.: United States General Accounting Office, October 2003), www.gao.gov/new.items/d0435.pdf, 32.

27. Philip N. Cohen, sociologist, University of Maryland, interview with author, September, 2012. His comments also appear in Brigid Schulte, "In Praise of the Male Biological Clock," *Zócalo*, September 9, 2012, www.zocalopublicsquare.org /2012/09/09/in-praise-of-the-male-biological-clock/.

28. "Women's Employment During the Recovery," United States Department of Labor, May 3, 2011, www.dol.gov/_sec/media/reports/FemaleLaborForce/FemaleLabor Force.pdf.

29. *Invest in Women*, 139–40.

30. Joan Williams, telephone interview with author, October 11, 2011.

31. Jane Leber Herr and Catherine Wolfram, "Work Environment and 'Opt-Out' Rates at Motherhood Across High-Education Career Paths," *National Bureau of Economic Research*, working paper 14717, February 2009, www.nber.org/papers

/w14717.pdf. Table 2, comparing mothers and men and women yet to have children, appears on p. 17.

32. www.ssa.gov/policy/docs/ssb/v72n1/v72n1p11.html.

33. Jonathan V. Last, "America's Baby Bust," *Wall Street Journal*, February 12, 2013, http://online.wsj.com/article/SB10001424127887323375204578270053387770718.html.

34. T. J. Mathews and Brady E. Hamilton, "Delayed Childbearing: More Women Are Having Their First Child Later in Life," data brief no. 21 (Hyattsville, MD: National Center for Health Statistics, 2009), www.cdc.gov/nchs/data/databriefs/db21.htm.

35. Augustine Kong et al., "Rate of De Novo Mutations and the Importance of Father's Age to Disease Risk," *Nature* 488 (August 23, 2012): 471–75, doi:10.1038/nature11396, www.nature.com/nature/journal/v488/n7412/full/nature11396.html. See also www.psychologytoday.com/blog/contemporary-psychoanalysis-in-action/201212/the-male-biological-clock.

36. "2010 Assisted Reproductive Technology National Summary Report," Centers for Disease Control and Prevention, December 2012, www.cdc.gov/art/ART2010/NationalSummary_index.htm. Women over age thirty-five accounted for about 60 percent of all women who underwent ART procedures in 2010. Although about half of all procedures with donor eggs resulted in a live birth that year, live birthrates with a woman's own eggs fell dramatically after age thirty-five, to, for women over age forty-two, 1 percent. See pp. 19 and 48.

37. Gretchen Livingston and D'Vera Cohn, "Childlessness Up Among All Women; Down Among Women with Advanced Degrees," Pew Research Center, June 25, 2010, www.pewsocialtrends.org/2010/06/25/childlessness-up-among-all-women-down-among-women-with-advanced-degrees/.

38. Sylvia Ann Hewlett, "Executive Women and the Myth of Having It All," *Harvard Business Review* 80, no. 4 (April 2002): 66–73. Michelle Budig has also found that women managers are far less likely to be wives and mothers than male managers are to be husbands and fathers.

39. "Wives Who Earn More Than Their Husbands, 1987–2011," Labor Force Statistics from the Current Population Survey. Bureau of Labor Statistics. The bureau reports that 28.1 percent of wives in dual-income couples outearned their husbands in 2011, up from 17.8 percent in 1987, www.bls.gov/cps/wives_earn_more.htm.

40. Yale Law School Career Development Office, "The Truth About the Billable Hour," brochure, www.law.yale.edu/documents/pdf/CDO_Public/cdo-billable_hour.pdf. Most law firms typically require attorneys to bill between 1,700 and 2,300 hours a year. But since billable hours don't include meetings, conferences, training, reading legal updates, networking, pro bono work, writing for law journals, and the like, the Yale Law School Career Development Office estimates that a lawyer wanting to make a 2,200-billable-hour target and take five weeks off a year would have to work twelve-hour days, three Saturdays a month, for ten months, and

take no sick or personal leave. "*You made it!*" the Yale brochure trumpets. "You have billed 2201 [hours]. However, you have been at 'work' 3058." That's a minimum sixty-five-hour workweek.

41. Dawn Gallina, telephone interview with author, March 1, 2012.

42. Vivia Chen, "Sued for Sexual Harassment, Yet Lauded for Being Family-Friendly," *The Careerist* (blog), May 2, 2012, http://thecareerist.typepad.com/thecareerist /2012/05/women-are-skeptical.html. Greg Walsh, "Mintz Levin Named Family Friendly Firm," *Boston Business Journal*, April 26, 2012, www.bizjournals.com /boston/news/2012/04/26/mintz-levin-named-family-friendly-firm.html.

43. Kamee Verdrager, telephone interview with author, May 1, 2012. Also David Lat, "I Suppose We Have Your Honeymoon to Blame for This?" *abovethelaw.com* (blog), March 21, 2008, http://abovethelaw.com/2008/03/i-suppose-we-have-your-hon eymoon-to-blame-for-this/. Kamee Verdrager, another breadwinner, was a lawyer in the Mintz Levin Boston office. She said her experience went downhill, culminating in her being demoted, just after she announced she was pregnant shortly after her wedding. "I suppose we have your honeymoon to blame for this," her boss said with a sigh, according to court filings. Verdrager's employers assumed she would take herself off the partner track, go part-time, or stay home. "It's so crazy," she said. "Even though I was willing to fit their ideal working model, to be on call 24/7, they still assumed I wasn't committed because I was a woman with children."

44. Cynthia Calvert, cofounder of the Project for Attorney Retention, phone interview with author, January 9, 2012, and an e-mail updating the figures, May 22, 2013.

45. Sharon Lerner, "How Could One of America's Most Sexist Companies End Up on Working Mother's Best 100 List?" *Slate*, May 24, 2010, www.slate.com/articles /double_x/doublex/2010/05/how_could_one_of_americas_most_sexist_compa nies_end_up_on_working_mothers_best_100_list.html.

46. Carol Evans, interview with author, April 30, 2013.

47. Sarah Jio, "Career Couples Fight Over Who's the 'Trailing Spouse,'" CNN Living, June 26, 2008, http://articles.cnn.com/2008-06-26/living/lw.men.v.women.career _1_couples-career-job?_s=PM:LIVING.

48. Defendant Dechert LLP's Memorandum of Law in Support of Its Motion for Summary Judgment, *Ariel Ayanna v. Dechert LLP*, 1:10-cv-12155-NMG, United States District Court for the District of Massachusetts, May 14, 2012.

49. www.americanlawyer.com/PubArticleTAL.jsp?id=1360503108457&slreturn=2013 0421172309.

50. Plaintiff's Response to Defendant Dechert LLP's Statement of Undisputed Facts in Support of Its Motion for Summary Judgment and Plaintiff's Statement of Additional Facts, *Ariel Ayanna v. Dechert LLP*, June 15, 2012.

51. Laurie A. Rudman and Kris Mescher, "Penalizing Men Who Request a Family Leave: Is Flexibility Stigma a Femininity Stigma?" *Journal of Social Issues: The Flexibility Stigma* 689, issue 2 (June 2013): 322–40.

52. Kimberly Elsbach and Daniel Cable, "Why Showing Your Face at Work Mat-

ters," *MIT Sloan Management Review*, June 19, 2012, http://sloanreview.mit
.edu/the-magazine/2012-summer/53407/why-showing-your-face-at-work
-matters/.

53. Nikki Blacksmith and Jim Harter, "Majority of American Workers Not Engaged
in Their Jobs: Highly Educated and Middle-Aged Employees Among the Least
Likely to Be Engaged," Gallup, Inc., October 28, 2011, www.gallup.com/poll
/150383/majority-american-workers-not-engaged-jobs.aspx. Likewise, Harvard
business professor Teresa Amabile's workplace study found that "a large percentage of employees at all levels feel dissatisfied with their organizations, apathetic
about their work, and/or unhappily stressed." See Teresa Amabile and Steven
Kramer, *The Progress Principle: Using Small Wins to Ignite Joy, Engagement and
Creativity at Work* (Boston: Harvard Business School Press, 2011).

54. David W. Moore, "Majority of Americans Want to Start Own Business: The Lure
of Entrepreneurship Is Especially Felt Among Young Men," Gallup World Poll,
April 12, 2005, www.gallup.com/poll/15832/majority-americans-want-start-own
-business.aspx.

55. Sleep deficit: Lauren Weber, "Go Ahead, Hit the Snooze Button," *Wall Street
Journal*, January 23, 2013, http://online.wsj.com/article/SB1000142412788732330
1104578257894191502654.html. Cost to U.S. Economy: Jodie Gummow, "America is No-Vacation Nation," *AlterNet*, August 22, 2013, www.alternet.org/culture
/america-no-vacation-nation.

56. WFC Resources, Work-Life and Human Capital Solutions, *Flexibility Toolkit*,
www.uky.edu/HR/WorkLife/documents/FlexibilityToolkit.pdf.

57. Leslie A. Perlow and Jessica L. Porter, "Making Time Off Predictable—and Required," *Harvard Business Review*, October 2009, http://hbr.org/2009/10/making
-time-off-predictable-and-required.

58. Gummow, "America is No-Vacation Nation."

59. *Economist*, Schumpeter Column, "In Praise of Laziness," August 17, 2013, www
.economist.com/news/business/21583592-businesspeople-would-be-better-if
-they-did-less-and-thought-more-praise-laziness.

60. Sreedhari D. Desai, Dolly Chugh, and Arthur Brief, "Marriage Structure and Resistance to the Gender Revolution in the Workplace," working paper, Social Science Research Network, March 12, 2012, http://papers.ssrn.com/sol3/papers.cfm
?abstract_id=2018259.

61. Shankar Vedantam, "See No Bias," *Washington Post Magazine*, January 23, 2005,
www.washingtonpost.com/wp-dyn/articles/A27067-2005Jan21.html. The online
test can be found at https://implicit.harvard.edu/implicit/demo/. Another test
has found that test takers more easily associate math and science with male
names and liberal arts with female names. Yes, of course I took the test. You
should, too. Mine registered no particular career and gender bias. It could be that
I was trying too hard. Or, as a result of this journey to the heart of the overwhelm, I'd begun to be exposed to some really different images of work, love, and
play, and old stereotypes were shaking loose.

62. National Opinion Research Center, *General Social Survey*, www3.norc.org/GSS

+Website/. I ran a table on the question "Should a woman with a pre-schooler work?" by sex of the respondent for each year the question was asked, 1988, 1994, and 2002.

63. http://anitaborg.org/files/breaking-barriers-to-cultural-change-in-corps.pdf.

64. For the quotations, which are from engineers Scott Webster and Kirk Sinclair, see Marianne Cooper, "Being the 'Go-to Guy': Fatherhood, Masculinity, and the Organization of Work in Silicon Valley," in *Families at Work: Expanding the Boundaries*, ed. Naomi Gerstel et al. (Nashville: Vanderbilt University Press, 2002), 7, 9. See also Joan C. Williams, "Jumpstarting the Stalled Gender Revolution: Justice Ginsburg and Reconstructive Feminism," *Hastings Law Journal* 63 (June 2012): 1267–97, www.hastingslawjournal.org/wp-content/uploads/2012/06/Williams _63-HLJ-1267.pdf.

65. Christine Keefer, interviews with author, January and February 2012.

66. Jane Seymour, "Women's Ambition: A Surprising Report," *More*, November 9, 2011, www.more.com/flexible-job-survey. *More*'s third annual workplace report found that 43 percent of women polled described themselves as less ambitious now than they were ten years ago and 73 percent would not apply for their boss' job. The magazine concludes that "women are sacrificing ambition" but does not point out that rigid workplace structures and ideal worker haven't changed, and the fight for mothers in particular to succeed is, simply, exhausting after a while. The issue of women's ambition was first raised by Anna Fels, "Do Women Lack Ambition?" *Harvard Business Review* 82, no. 4 (April 1, 2004), http://hbr.org /product/do-women-lack-ambition/an/R0404B-PDF-ENG. Fels argued that most women associate ambition with egotism, self-aggrandizement, or manipulation, that they demure when praised for their achievements, and do not seek to be recognized when competing with men. "The underlying problem has to do with cultural ideals of femininity," Fels wrote. "Women face the reality that to appear feminine, they must provide or relinquish scarce resources to others—and recognition is a scarce resource." Sociologists call that impetus the "ethic of care" that women are socialized to embody.

## 6: A TALE OF TWO PATS

1. Brian Stelter, "With Book, Buchanan Set His Fate," *New York Times*, February 26, 2012, www.nytimes.com/2012/02/27/business/media/with-book-buchanan-set -his-fate.html?pagewanted=all.

2. International Labour Office, Conditions of Work and Employment Branch, *Maternity at Work: A Review of National Legislation*, 2nd ed., (Geneva: International Labour Office, 2010): 17, 22.

3. Ariane Hegewisch, *Flexible Working Policies: A Comparative Review*, (Manchester: Equality and Human Rights Commission, 2009), www.equalityhuman rights.com/uploaded_files/research/16_flexibleworking.pdf. See also Katrin Bennhold, "Working (Part-Time) in the 21st Century," *New York Times*, Decem-

ber 29, 2010. www.nytimes.com/2010/12/30/world/europe/30iht-dutch30.html ?pagewanted=all.

4. Jody Heyman, Alison Earle, and Jeffrey Hayes, "The Work, Family, and Equity Index: How Does the United States Measure Up?" The Project on Global Working Families and the Institute for Health and Social Policy, McGill University, 2007. www.mcgill.ca/files/ihsp/WFEIFinal2007.pdf.

5. Paul Geitner, "On Vacation and Sick? A Court Says Take Another," *New York Times*, June 21, 2012, www.nytimes.com/2012/06/22/world/europe/europe-court -says-sick-workers-can-retake-vacations.html.

6. Kimberly J. Morgan, "A Child of the Sixties: The Great Society, the New Right, and the Politics of Federal Child Care," *Journal of Policy History* 13, no. 2 (2001): 222, doi: 10.1353/jph.2001.0005. Morgan writes that 68 percent of women and 59 percent of men told pollsters that the government should provide child care.

7. Sonya Michel, *Children's Interests/Mothers' Rights: The Shaping of America's Child Care Policy* (New Haven: Yale University Press, 1999), 248.

8. Edward Zigler and Susan Muenchow, *Head Start: The Inside Story of America's Most Successful Educational Experiment* (New York: Basic Books, 1994), 136.

9. Patrick Buchanan, interview in his home in McLean, Virginia, with author, May 24, 2012.

10. Morgan, "A Child of the Sixties," 234.

11. Ibid.

12. Ibid., 240.

13. Sonya Michel, *Children's Interests*, 251.

14. Morgan, "A Child of the Sixties," 224. See also Michel, *Children's Interests*, 250–51.

15. Morgan, "A Child of the Sixties," 232.

16. Richard Nixon, "Veto of the Economic Opportunity Amendments of 1971," speech, December 9, 1971, transcript at The American Presidency Project, www .presidency.ucsb.edu/ws/?pid=3251.

17. Council of Economic Advisers, *Work-Life Balance and the Economics of Workplace Flexibility* (Executive Office of the President, 2010), 2.

18. Kim Parker and Wendy Wang, "Breadwinner Moms: Mothers Are the Sole or Primary Provider in Four-in-Ten Households with Children; Public Conflicted About the Growing Trend," Pew Research Center, May 28, 2013.

19. Child Care Aware of America, *Parents and the High Cost of Child Care*, 2012, www.naccrra.org/sites/default/files/default_site_pages/2012/cost_report_2012 _final_081012_0.pdf, 7. The report says, on page 11, "In 40 states plus the District of Columbia, the cost of center-based care for an infant exceeds 10 percent of state median income for a married couple." For information on waiting lists, see Sue Shellenbarger, "Day Care? Take a Number, Baby," *Wall Street Journal*, June 9, 2010, http://online.wsj.com/article/SB10001424052748704256604575294523680479314.html. For waiting lists for child care subsidies, see Child Care Aware of America, "Number of Children on Waiting Lists for Child Care Assistance,"

April 1, 2013, www.naccrra.org/sites/default/files/default_site_pages/2013/waiting _lists_nwlc_2012.pdf.

20. Sonya Michel, phone interview with author, May 21, 2013.

21. Center for the Child Care Workforce, "Fact Sheet," www.ccw.org/storage/ccwork force/documents/all%20data_web(final).pdf.

22. www.nichd.nih.gov/publications/pubs/documents/seccyd_06.pdf.

23. Child Care Aware of America, *Leaving Children to Chance*, www.naccrra.org/about -child-care/state-child-care-licensing/2012-leaving-children-to-chance-child -care-homes; and We Can Do Better, www.naccrra.org/node/3025.

24. E. Galinsky and A. Johnson, *Reframing the Business Case for Work-Life Initiatives* (New York: Families and Work Institute, 1998).

25. Child Care Aware reports.

26. Mark Lino, *Expenditures on Children by Families, 2011*, U.S. Department of Agriculture, Center for Nutrition Policy and Promotion, Miscellaneous Publication No. 1528–2011, www.cnpp.usda.gov/Publications/CRC/crc2011.pdf. According to the USDA, "Child care and education expenses consist of day care tuition and supplies; baby-sitting; and elementary and high school tuition, books, fees, and supplies. Books, fees, and supplies may be for private or public schools."

27. Child Care Aware of America, *Parents and the High Cost of Child Care*, 7.

28. http://articles.washingtonpost.com/2013-03-09/local/37579999_1_unregulated -care-child-care-background-checks.

29. Compiled by Voices for Georgia's Children, updated June 27, 2011, and Child Care Aware of America.

30. http://articles.washingtonpost.com/2013-03-09/local/37579133_1_child-care -workers-day-care-centers-sudden-infant-death-syndrome.

31. Margaret Nelson, *Negotiated Care: The Experience of Family Day Care Providers* (Philadelphia: Temple University Press, 1991), 152.

32. www.newrepublic.com/article/112892/hell-american-day-care.

33. www.startribune.com/local/150283965.html.

34. Federal law requires states to do only three things when it comes to child care: prevent and control infectious diseases, make sure the premises are safe, and train the staff on health and safety. That's it. The law says nothing about a child's cognitive development or creating the kinds of high-quality programs with language, reading, and game playing that produce the best benefits. For more information, see "State Child Care Licensing," National Association of Child Care Resource & Referral Agencies, www.naccrra.org/about-child-care/state-child -care-licensing.

35. Helen Blank, interview with author, May 2012. Gina Adams, Urban Institute, interview with author, May 2013.

36. http://articles.washingtonpost.com/2013-05-15/local/39283045_1_child-care -centers-child-care-subsidy.

37. See Margaret Talbot, "The Devil in the Nursery," *New York Times Magazine*, January 7, 2001, http://partners.nytimes.com/library/magazine/home/20010107mag -buckey.html. Talbot writes: "Our willingness to believe in ritual abuse was

grounded in anxiety about putting children in day care at a time when mothers were entering the work force in unprecedented numbers. It was as though there were some dark, self-defeating relief in trading niggling everyday doubts about our children's care for our absolute worst fears—for a story with monsters, not just human beings who didn't always treat our kids exactly as we would like; for a fate so horrific and bizarre that no parent, no matter how vigilant, could have ever prevented it."

38. U.S. Department of Health and Human Services, *The NICHD Study of Early Child Care and Youth Development: Findings for Children up to Age 4½ Years*, National Institutes of Health, National Institute of Child Health and Human Development, January 2006, www.nichd.nih.gov/publications/pubs/upload/sec cyd_06.pdf#page=38.

39. Pew Global Attitudes Project, *Gender Equality Universally Embraced, but Inequalities Acknowledged* (Washington, D.C.: Pew Research Center, 2010), http://pewglobal.org/2010/07/01/gender-equality/.

40. Eileen Patten and Kim Parker, "A Gender Reversal on Career Aspirations: Young Women Now Top Young Men in Valuing a High-Paying Career," Pew Social & Demographic Trends, Pew Research Center, April 19, 2012, www.pewsocialtrends .org/2012/04/19/a-gender-reversal-on-career-aspirations/. The Pew survey on working mothers shows that only 21 percent of Americans say the trend toward more mothers of young children working outside the home has been a "good thing" for society. "Some 37% said this is a bad thing for society, and roughly the same share (38%) said it hasn't made a difference." Another Pew report found that when asked how they feel about their time, 40 percent of working moms said they *always* feel rushed, compared to "24% of the general public and 26% of stay-at-home moms. Only 25 percent of working dads said they always feel rushed." See Pew Research Center, "Women, Work, and Motherhood: A Sample of Recent Pew Research Survey Findings," April 13, 2012, www.pewresearch.org/2012/04 /13/women-work-and-motherhood/.

41. Thomas J. Noel, review of *Pat Schroeder: A Woman of the House* by Joan Lowy, *Colorado Book Review Center*, August 2004, http://games.historycolorado.org /publications/Lowy_Review.pdf.

42. Petula Dvorak, "Election Chatter Glosses Over Our Child-Care Morass," *Washington Post*, July 30, 2012, www.washingtonpost.com/local/election-chatter-glosses -over-our-child-care-morass/2012/07/30/gJQAnZ9RLX_story.html.

43. "Millionaire Freshmen Make Congress Even Wealthier," OpenSecretsblog, January 16, 2013, www.opensecrets.org/news/2013/01/new-congress-new-and-more -wealth.html. Pat Schroeder, phone interview with author, May 4, 2012.

44. Ann Allen and Jennifer Lyman, "Oral History of Patricia Schroeder," *ABA Senior Lawyers Division: Women Trailblazers in the Law*, August 1, 2006, July 15, 2008, 7.

45. U.S. General Services Administration, Public Buildings Service, Office of Child Care, *Starting a Child Development Center*, www.gsa.gov/graphics/pbs/startup guide.pdf.

46. U.S. Office of Personnel Management, *2009 Federal Child Care Subsidy Program Call for Data Results* (Washington, D.C.: Office of Personnel Management, June 2011), www.opm.gov/employment_and_benefits/worklife/familycareissues/child care_subsidy/2009_Federal_Child_Care_Subsidy_Program.pdf.

47. General Accounting Office, "Military Child Care Programs: Progress Made, More Needed," GAO/FPCD-82-30, June 1, 1982. For "ghetto" comment, see Linda D. Kozaryn, "DoD Child Care: A Model for the Nation," American Forces Press Service, April 25, 1997, www.defense.gov/News/NewsArticle.aspx?ID=40948.

48. Office of the Under Secretary of Defense (Comptroller)/Chief Financial Officer, *Fiscal Year 2013 Budget Request Overview* (Washington, D.C.: U.S. Department of Defense, February 2012), http://comptroller.defense.gov/defbudget/fy2013 /FY2013_Budget_Request_Overview_Book.pdf.

49. Elaine Wilson, "DOD Expands Community-Based Child Care Options," December 9, 2010, www.defense.gov/NewsArticle.aspx?id=62034.

50. Ernesto Londono, "Pentagon Begins Worldwide Probe of Daycare Hiring After Assault Allegations," *Washington Post*, December 19, 2012, http://articles.wash ingtonpost.com/2012-12-19/world/35929964_1_day-care-center-army-base -pentagon-employees.

51. "Learning from the Military Child Care System," Child Care Aware of America National Policy Blog, May 26, 2013, http://policyblog.usa.childcareaware.org /2013/05/. See also Linda D. Kozaryn, "DoD Child Care Cited as Model for Nation," U.S. Department of Defense, May 17, 2000, www.defense.gov/News/News Article.aspx?ID=45200.

52. "SU Army ROTC Hall of Fame: Featured Alumnus," Syracuse University Army ROTC website, http://armyrotc.syr.edu/featured.html#Anchor0.

53. *2012 Guide to Bold New Ideas for Making Work Work* (Alexandria, VA: Society for Human Resource Management, 2011), http://familiesandwork.org/site /research/reports/bold_guide_12.pdf, 143–44.

54. "The Family and Medical Leave Act: Proposed Rule," U.S. Department of Labor, Wage and Hour Division, RIN 1215-AB76, RIN 1235-AA03, www.dol.gov/whd /fmla/NPRM/FMLA_NPRM_2012.pdf.

55. Jacob Alex Klerman, Kelly Daley, and Alyssa Pozniak, "Family and Medical Leave in 2012: Technical Report," Abt Associates Inc., prepared for U.S. Department of Labor, September 7, 2012, updated February 4, 2013, 69–70.

56. Joe Davidson, "Federal Diary: Despite YouTube Tactic, House Passes Parental Leave Bill," *Washington Post*, June 5, 2009, www.washingtonpost.com/wp-dyn /content/article/2009/06/04/AR2009060404455.html.

57. Valerie Strauss, "Mitt Romney at Education Nation—Transcript," *Washington Post* (blog), September 25, 2012, www.washingtonpost.com/blogs/answer-sheet /post/mitt-romney-at-education-nation—transcript/2012/09/25/b03ebcd2-0741 -11e2-afff-d6c7f20a83bf_blog.html.

58. Ezra Klein, "Mitt Romney Flashback: Stay-at-Home Moms Need to Learn 'Dignity of Work,'" *Washington Post* (blog), April 15, 2012, www.washingtonpost

.com/blogs/ezra-klein/post/mitt-romney-flashback-stay-at-home-moms-need-to-learn-dignity-of-work/2012/04/15/gIQAhmbZJT_blog.html.

59. Linda Haas, "Work and Family in Sweden," *Network News* 12, no. 2 (Philadelphia: Sloan Work and Family Research Network, February 2010), http://workfamily.sas.upenn.edu/sites/workfamily.sas.upenn.edu/files/imported/archive/networknews/The_Network_News_Interview_68_Int.pdf. Also Haas, phone interview with author, January 2012.

60. Michel, *Children's Interests*, 285.

61. Ibid., 286–89. See also Katrin Bennhold, "Where Having It All Doesn't Mean Equality," *New York Times*, October 11, 2010, www.nytimes.com/2010/10/12/world/europe/12iht-fffrance.html?pagewanted=all; Bennhold, "In Germany, a Tradition Falls, and Women Rise," *New York Times*, January 17, 2010, www.nytimes.com/2010/01/18/world/europe/18iht-women.html?pagewanted=4&ref=thefemale factor.

62. Peter Abrahamson, "Continuity and Consensus: Governing Families in Denmark," *Journal of European Social Policy* 20, no. 5 (December 2010): 399–409, http://esp.sagepub.com/content/20/5/399.refs. See also Kristiana Brix, "National Identity Crisis: The Intersection of Gender Equality and Ethnic Minority Integration in Denmark," Claremont-UC Undergraduate Research Conference on the European Union, vol. 2009, article 4, doi: 10.5642/urceu.200901.04, http://scholarship.claremont.edu/urceu/vol2009/iss1/4/.

63. "Baby Blues: A Juggler's Guide to Having It All," *Economist*, November 26, 2011.

64. *OECD Factbook 2011–2012: Economic, Environmental and Social Statistics*, doi: 10.1787/factbook-2011-en, www.oecd-ilibrary.org/sites/factbook-2011-en/03/03/01/03-03-01-g1.html?contentType=/ns/StatisticalPublication,/ns/Chapter&itemId=/content/chapter/factbook-2011-25-en&containerItemId=/content/serial/18147364&accessItemIds=&mimeType=text/html. The report shows that workers in Korea, Slovenia, Chile, Japan, Turkey, and six other countries are outstripping U.S. workers in the rate of hourly productivity growth.

65. Willem Adema, Pauline Fron, and Maxime Ladaique, "Is the European Welfare State Really More Expensive? Indicators on Social Spending, 1980–2012; And a Manual to the OECD Social Expenditure Database (SOCX)," OECD Social, Employment and Migration Working Papers, no. 124, November 2, 2011, 9–10, table on p. 34.

66. Brigid Schulte, "It's February—Time for Summer Camp Madness," *Washington Post*, February 26, 2011, www.washingtonpost.com/wp-dyn/content/article/2011/02/25/AR2011022502639.html.

67. Afterschool Alliance, "Afterschool Essentials: Research and Polling," fact sheet, www.afterschoolalliance.org/documents/2012/Essentials_4_20_12_FINAL.pdf.

68. Brigid Schulte, "A Working Mother Finds Nowhere for Her Latchkey Kid to Go but Home," *Washington Post*, September 27, 2009, www.washingtonpost.com/wp-dyn/content/article/2009/09/25/AR2009092502013.html.

69. Brigid Schulte, "Parental Advisory," *Washington Post*, November 6, 2005, www .washingtonpost.com/wp-dyn/content/article/2005/11/03/AR2005110300127 .html.

70. Ellen Galinsky, James T. Bond, and Dana E. Friedman, *The Changing Work Force: Highlights of the National Study* (New York: Families and Work Institute, 1993).

71. Lyn Craig and Abigail Powell, "Non-standard Work Schedules, Work-Family Balance and the Gendered Division of Childcare," *Work Employment & Society* 25, no. 2 (June 2011): 274–91, doi: 10.1177/0950017011398894.

72. Karen Shellenback, *Child Care & Parent Productivity: Making the Business Case* (Ithaca: Cornell University, Cooperative Extension, Department of City and Regional Planning, December 2004), http://government.cce.cornell.edu/doc/pdf /childcareparentproductivity.pdf.

73. Cali Yost, "Think You Don't Benefit Directly from Childcare? 3 'What's In It for Me' That Will Change Your Mind," Work+Life Fit (blog), February 21, 2012, http://worklifefit.com/blog/2012/02/think-you-dont-benefit-directly-from -childcare-3-whats-in-it-for-me-that-will-change-your-mind/.

74. "Economic Return on Early Childhood Investment," YouTube video, posted by OklahomaHorizonTV, October 9, 2009, www.youtube.com/watch?v=sO2oFtY7tZA. See also James J. Heckman and Dimitriy V. Masterov, "The Productivity Argument for Investing in Young Children" (T. W. Schultz Award lecture, Allied Social Sciences Association annual meeting, Chicago, January 5–7, 2007), http://jenni .uchicago.edu/human-inequality/papers/Heckman_final_all_wp_2007-03-22c _jsb.pdf. Heckman's research shows that the yield from investing in early learning is far higher than the 5.8 percent seen in the stock market between 1945 and 2008. The only way America will remain competitive in the new global economy is by producing skilled workers who can do things that other people can't, he says. "Education is at the heart of the modern economy. And what's at the heart of a good education? A good start."

75. *The Life and Times of Rosie the Riveter*, directed by Connie Field (Berkeley, CA: Clarity Films, 1980). The documentary includes the *March of Time* newsreel "*Marriage and Divorce*," released February 20, 1948 (vol. 14, no.7).

## BRIGHT SPOT: STARTING SMALL

1. Eileen Appelbaum and Ruth Milkman, *Leaves That Pay: Employer and Worker Experiences with Paid Family Leave in California* (Washington, D.C.: Center for Economic and Policy Research, 2011), www.cepr.net/documents/publications /paid-family-leave-1-2011.pdf. As of early 2013, nine other states, Arizona, Illinois, Maine, Massachusetts, Missouri, New Hampshire, New York, Oregon, and Pennsylvania, are considering paid family leave laws. "The Need for Paid Family Leave," A Better Balance, 2013, www.abetterbalance.org/web/ourissues /familyleave.

2. Ibid.

3. Paul Orfalea, letter to the editor, *Santa Barbara News Press*, July 24, 2002.

4. Appelbaum and Milkman, 4–5. See also Linda Houser and Thomas P. Vartanian, *Pay Matters: The Positive Economic Impacts of Paid Family Leave for Families, Businesses, and the Public* (New Brunswick, NJ: Center for Women and Work, January 2012). The authors note that 72 percent of all children have their only or both parents in the workforce, and that women with paid parental leaves are more likely to be working nine to twelve months after birth than those who took no leave. They see their wages increase, and both low-income men and women are far less likely to require public assistance than families who return to work or take no leave.

5. Appelbaum and Milkman, *Leaves That Pay*, 18. The report found that the number of men taking paid family leave to care for a newborn or newly adopted child grew steadily over five years, from 17 percent to 26 percent.

6. U.S. Census Bureau, table 7, "Completed Fertility for Women 40 to 44 Years Old by Single Race in Combination with Other Races and Selected Characteristics: June 2010," www.census.gov/hhes/fertility/data/cps/2010.html.

7. Steve Vogel, "HUD Announces Agreement on Pregnancy Suit," *Washington Post* (blog), June 1, 2011, www.washingtonpost.com/blogs/federal-eye/post/hud-an nounces-agreement-on-pregnancy-suit/2011/06/01/AGXlgfGH_blog.html.

8. Sheila Cronan, "Marriage," in *Notes from the Third Year: Women's Liberation 1971*, Anne Koedt, Ellen Levine, and Anita Rapone, eds. (New York: Quadrangle, 1971), 65.

9. Betty Friedan, *The Second Stage* (Cambridge, MA: Harvard University Press, 1981), xvii.

10. Nan Robertson, "Betty Friedan Ushers in a 'Second Stage,'" *New York Times*, October 19, 1981, www.nytimes.com/books/99/05/09/specials/friedan-stage.html.

11. Caroline Winter, "Is Paid Sick Leave Good for Business?" *Bloomberg Businessweek*, July 20, 2012, www.businessweek.com/articles/2012-07-20/is-paid-sick -leave-good-for-business. "Current Sick Day Laws," Support Paid Sick Days, A Project of the National Partnership for Women and Families, http://paidsickdays .nationalpartnership.org/site/PageServer?pagename=psd_toolkit_laws.

12. Tilde Herrera, "Microsoft Tracks Telework Trends, Ranks Top Cities for Home Workers," *GreenBiz.com,* June 15, 2011, www.greenbiz.com/news/2011/06/15 /microsoft-tracks-trends-ranks-top-cities-home-workers.

## 7: WHEN WORK WORKS

1. John Tierney, "Do You Suffer from Decision Fatigue?" *New York Times Magazine*, August 17, 2011, www.nytimes.com/2011/08/21/magazine/do-you-suffer -from-decision-fatigue.html?pagewanted=all.

2. Danette Campbell, phone interview with author, March 6, 2013.

3. Russell Matthews, industrial-organizational psychology professor at Bowling Green State University, phone interview with author, May 11, 2012.

4. Eileen Patten and Kim Parker, "A Gender Reversal on Career Aspirations: Young Women Now Top Young Men in Valuing a High-Paying Career," Pew Social &

Demographic Trends, Pew Research Center, April 19, 2012, www.pewsocialtrends
.org/2012/04/19/a-gender-reversal-on-career-aspirations/.

5. Alison Maitland and Peter Thomson, *Future Work: How Businesses Can Adapt and Thrive in the New World of Work* (New York: Palgrave Macmillan, 2011), xi.

6. Association of American Medical Colleges, *Analysis in Brief* 8, no. 4 (June 2008), www.aamc.org/download/67968/data/aibvol8no4.pdf.

7. In 2010, Valentine pioneered the first blood test to diagnose organ rejection. See Krista Conger, "To Better Detect Heart Transplant Rejections, Scientists Test for Traces of Donor's Genome," *Stanford School of Medicine News*, March 28, 2011, http://med.stanford.edu/ism/2011/march/heart-rejection.html.

8. Londa Schiebinger and Shannon K. Gilmartin, "Housework Is an Academic Issue: How to Keep Talented Women Scientists in the Lab, Where They Belong," *Academe* 96, no. 1 (January–February 2010), www.aaup.org/article/housework -academic-issue#.UO4CrY7Zeok. In a study of women scientists and housework, Schiebinger and Gilmartin found that partnered women scientists do 54 percent of the cooking, cleaning, and laundry in their households, while partnered men scientists carry just 28 percent of the load.

9. Daniel H. Pink, *Drive: The Surprising Truth About What Motivates Us* (New York: Riverhead Books, 2009), 92–96.

10. Lisa F. Berkman, Orfeu M. Buxton, Karen Ertel, and Cassandra Okechukwu, "Manager's Practices Related to Work-Family Balance Predict Employee Cardio-vascular Risk and Sleep Duration in Extended Care Settings," *Journal of Occupational Health Psychology* 15, no. 3, July 2010: 316–29, http://psycnet.apa.org /journals/ocp/15/3/316.html. Orfeu M. Buxton, Keith Malarick, Wei Wang, and Teresa Seeman, "Changes in Dried Blood Spot $H_bA_{1c}$ with Varied Postcollection Conditions," *Clinical Chemistry* 55, no. 5, March 19, 2009: 1034-6, www.clinchem .org/cgi/content/full/55/5/1034.

11. Erin L. Kelly, Phyllis Moen, and Eric Tranby, "Changing Workplaces to Reduce Work-Family Conflict: Schedule Control in a White-Collar Organization," *American Sociological Review* 76, no. 2, April 2011: 265–90, www.ncbi.nlm.nih .gov/pmc/articles/PMC3094103/. Phyllis Moen, Erin L. Kelly, Eric Tranby, and Qinlei Huang, "Changing Work, Changing Health: Can Real Work-Time Flexibility Promote Health Behaviors and Well-Being?" *Journal of Health and Social Behavior* 52, no. 4, 2011: 404, www.flexiblework.umn.edu/publications_docs /Moen-Kelly-Tranby-Huang-2011-JHSB.pdf.

12. Judi Hand, phone interview with author, December 13, 2011.

13. Marcee Harris-Schwartz, flex strategy adviser for BDO, phone interview with author, March 20, 2012.

14. Schor, *Overworked American*, 51.

15. Robinson, "Bring Back the 40-Hour Work Week." Robinson based some of her conclusions on a white paper written by her computer game designer husband, Evan Robinson: "Why Crunch Modes Doesn't Work: Six Lessons," International

Game Developers Association, www.igda.org/why-crunch-modes-doesnt-work
-six-lessons.

16. Christopher P. Landrigan et al., "Effect of Reducing Interns' Work Hours on Serious Medical Errors in Intensive Care Units," *New England Journal of Medicine*
351 (2004): 1838–48, doi: 10.1056/NEJMoa041406.

17. Klint Finley, "What Research Says About Working Long Hours," *Devops Angle*,
April 18, 2012, http://devopsangle.com/2012/04/18/what-research-says-about
-working-long-hours/.

18. www.businessinsider.com/best-buy-ending-work-from-home-2013-3.

19. U.S. Department of Commerce, Economics and Statistics Administration,
"Women-Owned Businesses in the 21st Century," White House Council on
Women and Girls, October 2010, www.esa.doc.gov/sites/default/files/reports
/documents/women-owned-businesses.pdf. Sharon G. Hadary, "Why Are Women-
Owned Firms Smaller Than Men-Owned Ones?" *Wall Street Journal*, January 29,
2013, http://online.wsj.com/article/SB10001424052748704688604575125543191609632.html.

20. Meghan Casserly, "Female Founders: Overcoming the Cupcake Challenge and
'Mompreneur' Stigma," *Forbes*, March 22, 2011, www.forbes.com/sites/meghancas
serly/2011/03/22/female-founders-cupcake-challenge-gilt-groupe-learnvest-zipcar/.

21. Lyn Craig, Abigail Powell, and Natasha Cortis, "Self-Employment, Work-Family
Time and the Gender Division of Labor," *Work, Employment & Society* 26, no. 5
(October 2012): 716–34.

22. http://articles.latimes.com/2013/feb/26/business/la-fi-yahoo-telecommuting-2013
0226.

23. www.nytimes.com/2013/03/16/business/at-google-a-place-to-work-and-play.html
?pagewanted=all&_r=0.

24. "Bargain Briefs: Technology Offers 50 Ways to Leave Your Lawyer," *Economist*,
August 13, 2011, www.economist.com/node/21525907.

25. www.bizjournals.com/washington/print-edition/2013/02/22/upstart-law-firm
-expands-new-model.html?page=all.

## BRIGHT SPOT: IF THE PENTAGON CAN DO IT, WHY CAN'T YOU?

1. William E. Brazis, director of administration and management, Department of
Defense, "Overtime, Prescribed Hours of Duty, and Alternative Work Schedules
for Civilian Employees," Administrative Instruction 28 (January 5, 2011), www
.dtic.mil/whs/directives/corres/pdf/a028p.pdf.

## 8: THE STALLED GENDER REVOLUTION

1. Joan Williams, "Holiday Survival Guide for Women," *Huffington Post* (blog),
December 20, 2011, www.huffingtonpost.com/joan-williams/holiday-survival
-guide_b_1158828.html.

2. Lisa Wade, "Of Housework and Husbands," *Sociological Images* (blog), July 11, 2009, http://thesocietypages.org/socimages/2009/07/11/of-housework-and -husbands/.

3. Pew Global Attitudes Project, *Gender Equality Universally Embraced*.

4. Sue Shellenbarger, "Housework Pays Off Between the Sheets," *Wall Street Journal*, October 21, 2009, http://online.wsj.com/article/SB1000142405274870450060 4574485351638147312.html.

5. Matthijs Kalmijn and Christiaan W. S. Monden, "The Division of Labor and Depressive Symptoms at the Couple Level: Effects of Equity or Specialization?" *Journal of Social and Personal Relationships* 29, no. 2 (May 2012): 358–74, doi: 10.1177/0265407511431182.

6. Judith Treas, "Why Study Housework?" in *Dividing the Domestic: Women, Men and Household Work in Cross-National Perspective*, ed. Judith Treas and Sonja Drobnič (Stanford: Stanford University Press, 2010), 11. Treas notes that the wage gap in the United States, where women earn about 85 percent of what men do for equal work, is one of the larger gaps in the developed world, though it is by no means as gaping as in south Korea and Japan, where women earn, on average, about 65 cents for every man's $1, and women shoulder far more of the domestic burden.

7. David A. Cotter, Joan M. Hermsen, and Reeve Vanneman, "The End of the Gender Revolution? Gender Role Attitudes from 1977 to 2008," *American Journal of Sociology* 117, no. 1 (July 2011): 259–89, doi: 10.1086/658853.

8. "The Top 5 Things Couples Argue About," SixWise.com, www.sixwise.com /newsletters/06/02/22/the-top-5-things-couples-argue-about.htm.

9. Deborah Arthurs, "Women Spend THREE HOURS Every Week Redoing Chores Their Men Have Done Badly," *Daily Mail* online, March 19, 2012, www.dailymail .co.uk/femail/article-2117254/Women-spend-hours-week-redoing-chores-men -badly.html.

10. Charity M. Brown, "Women Are More Likely Than Men to Give Up Sleep to Care for Children and Others," *Washington Post*, February 14, 2011, www.washing tonpost.com/wp-dyn/content/article/2011/02/14/AR2011021405833.html?sid =ST2011021405945.

11. Darby E. Saxbe, Rena L. Repetti, and Anthony P. Graesch, "Time Spent in Housework and Leisure: Links with Parent's Psychological Recovery from Work," *Journal of Family Psychology* 25, no. 2 (April 2011): 271–81, doi: 10.137/a023048.

12. Gunseli Berik and Ebru Kongar, "Time Use of Mothers and Fathers in Hard Times and Better Times: The US Business Cycle of 2003–10," Levy Economics Institute of Bard College, working paper no. 696, November 8, 2011, http://ssrn .com/abstract=1956630.

13. Joel M. Hektner, Jennifer A. Schmidt, and Mihaly Csikszentmihalyi, *Experience Sampling Method: Measuring the Quality of Everyday Life* (Thousand Oaks, CA: Sage Publications, 2007), 165. The differing emotions, they wrote, "may be partly attributable to the fact that when both partners are home, the men are more likely to be engaging in leisure while the women work."

14. Ibid.

15. Reed Larson, *Divergent Realities: The Emotional Lives of Mothers, Fathers, and Adolescents* (New York: Basic Books, 1995).

16. Melissa A. Milkie et al., "Time with Children, Children's Well-Being, and Work-Family Balance Among Employed Parents," *Journal of Marriage and Family* 72, no. 5 (October 2010): 1329–43, doi: 10.1111/j.1741-3737.2010.00768.x. Milkie found that mothers felt best when they were paying focused attention to the kids, reading and talking to them. College-educated fathers felt best when they were engaged in routine care, perhaps, she said, because they did it so rarely they felt virtuous. Working-class men, particularly shift workers, however, have always done more routine care out of necessity.

17. Hektner, Schmidt, and Csikszentmihalyi, *Experience Sampling Method*, 150.

18. Harvard Health Publications, "The Many Faces of Stress," Helpguide.org, adapted from *Stress Management: Approaches for Preventing and Reducing Stress*, www.helpguide.org/harvard/faces_of_stress.htm.

19. http://link.springer.com/article/10.1007%2Fs10902-008-9106-5.

20. Lawrence A. Kurdek, "What Do We Know about Gay and Lesbian Couples?" *Current Directions in Psychological Science* 14, no. 5 (October 2005): 251–54.

## 9: THE CULT OF INTENSIVE MOTHERHOOD

1. Bianchi, Robinson, and Milkie, *Changing Rhythms*, 64–77.

2. José Martinez, "Manhattan Mom Sues $19K/yr. Preschool for Damaging 4-Year-Old Daughter's Ivy League Chances," *New York Daily News*, March 14, 2011, www.ny dailynews.com/new-york/manhattan-mom-sues-19k-yr-preschool-damaging-4 -year-old-daughter-ivy-league-chances-article-1.117712.

3. Jennifer Ludden, "Helicopter Parents Hover in the Workplace," *All Things Considered*, National Public Radio, February 6, 2012, www.npr.org/story/146464665.

4. Annette Laureau, *Unequal Childhoods: Class, Race, and Family Life* (Berkeley: University of California Press, 2003).

5. Tony Snow, "The Lewinsky Principle," *Jewish World Review*, March 8, 1999, www .jewishworldreview.com/tony/snow030899.asp.

6. Susan Chira, *A Mother's Place: Taking the Debate About Working Mothers Beyond Guilt and Blame* (New York: Harper, 1998).

7. The Council of Economic Advisors, "The Parenting Deficit: Council of Economic Advisors Analyze the 'Time Crunch,'" May 1999, http://128.121.176.141/Parenting DeficitCEA-May99.html#Anchor8.

8. David Whitman, "The Myth of AWOL Parents," *U.S. News & World Report*, June 23, 1996, www.usnews.com/usnews/culture/articles/960701/archive_033795 _3.htm.

9. Ann Crittenden, *The Price of Motherhood: Why the Most Important Job in the World Is Still the Least Valued* (New York: Henry Holt, 2001), 19; also 277n12.

10. Whitman, "The Myth of AWOL Parents." Chira, *A Mother's Place*, 160–62.

11. Crittenden, *Price of Motherhood*, 278.

12. Bianchi, Robinson, and Milkie, *Changing Rhythms*, Table 5A-1. But far from acknowledging how insane a life with those kinds of time demands can be, those in the grip of the ideal mother view harried working mothers as deserving their hair-on-fire lot. They made "adjustments," and rightly so, conservatives like Gary Bauer have said, "to ensure that, even with jobs outside the home, they provide what only mothers can provide." See Robert Pear, "Married and Single Parents Spending More Time with Children, Study Finds," *New York Times*, October 17, 2006, www.nytimes.com/2006/10/17/us/17kids.html?pagewanted=all&_r=0.

13. Punchbowl, *Birthdays by the Numbers: 20 Facts and Figures* (Framingham, MA: Punchbowl, Inc., 2010), www.punchbowl.com/trends/thanks/birthdays-by-the-numbers-20-facts-figures.

14. Janet Bodnar, "Outrageous Kid Parties," *Kiplinger* (blog), March 28, 2011, www.kiplinger.com/columns/drt/archive/outrageous-kid-parties.html.

15. Anthony P. Carnevale, Stephen J. Rose, and Ban Cheah, "The College Payoff: Education, Occupations, Lifetime Earnings," Georgetown University Center on Education and the Workforce, August 5, 2011.

16. Glenda Wall, "Mothers' Experiences with Intensive Parenting and Brain Development Discourse," *Women's Studies International Forum* 33, no. 3 (2010): 253–63, http://dx.doi.org/10.1016/j.wsif.2010.02.019.

17. Kim John Payne and Lisa M. Ross, *Simplicity Parenting: Using the Extraordinary Power of Less to Raise Calmer, Happier, and More Secure Kids* (New York: Ballantine Books, 2010), 177.

18. Alex Spiegel, "'Mozart Effect' Was Just What We Wanted to Hear," *Morning Edition*, National Public Radio, June 28, 2010, www.npr.org/templates/story/story.php?storyId=128104580. And mothers weren't the only ones. So eager to give kids an edge, the governors of Georgia and Tennessee even started giving out a free Mozart CD to every baby born in their states. The "Mozart effect" was based on a small study of thirty-six college students. Those who listened to Mozart for ten minutes performed better on a spatial-reasoning test than students who listened to silence or a monotone speaking voice.

19. Payne and Ross, *Simplicity Parenting*, 179. They report that more than 95 percent of missing children are runaways who return within a few days, the rest are largely the result of custody disputes, and only a tiny percent are the truly horrific nightmare disappearances that every parent fears.

20. Deirdre D. Johnston and Debra H. Swanson, "Invisible Mothers: A Content Analysis of Motherhood Ideologies and Myths in Magazines," *Sex Roles* 48, no. 1–2 (July 2003): 21–33.

21. Lisa Belkin, "(Yet Another) Study Finds Working Moms Are Happier and Healthier," *Huffington Post* (blog), www.huffingtonpost.com/lisa-belkin/working-mothers-happier_b_1823347.html.

22. HealthDay News, "At-Home Moms Cook, Shop, Play More with Kids: Study," *U.S. News & World Report*, September 16, 2012, http://health.usnews.com/health-news/news/articles/2012/09/16/at-home-moms-cook-shop-play-more-with-kids-study.

23. University of Akron, "Work Has More Benefits Than Just a Paycheck for Moms: Working Moms Are Healthier Than Stay-At-Home Moms," *Science Daily*, August 19, 2012, www.sciencedaily.com/releases/2012/08/120819153843.htm.

24. HowStuffWorks.com Contributors, "Does Being a Stay at Home Mom Benefit Your Kids?" *TLC*, http://tlc.howstuffworks.com/family/stay-at-home-mom-ben efit-kids.htm.

25. Kathryn Masterson, "The Mommy-Fight Site," *Washington City Paper*, January 21, 2011, www.washingtoncitypaper.com/articles/40290/dc-mommy-fight-site/.

26. Lisa Wade, " 'Too Much Mother Love': Proving the Necessity of Nurture," *The Society Pages*, September 5, 2012, http://thesocietypages.org/socimages/2012/09 /05/too-much-mother-love-proving-the-need-for-nurture/.

27. Sharon Hays, *The Cultural Contradictions of Motherhood* (New Haven: Yale University Press, 1996), 40. An expert no less august than the U.S. Children's Bureau advised in the 1920s that toilet training could begin as early as the first month with the goal of establishing "absolute regularity."

28. Ibid., 35.

29. Jay Mathews, "Hidden Rival of Charter School Growth," *Washington Post*, October 7, 2012, www.washingtonpost.com/local/education/hidden-rival-of-charter -school-growth/2012/10/07/f236c20a-0a99-11e2-a10c-fa5a255a9258_story.html.

## BRIGHT SPOT: MOTHER NATURE

1. Emily Anthes, "Stretch Marks for Dads: What Fatherhood Does to the Body and the Brain," *Slate*, June 14, 2007, www.slate.com/articles/health_and_science /medical_examiner/2007/06/stretch_marks_for_dads.html. See also Peter B. Gray and Kermyt G. Anderson, "The Evolving Father: How Fatherhood Differs Across Cultures and Through Time," *Psychology Today* (blog), July 2, 2012, www.psy chologytoday.com/blog/the-evolving-father/201207/prolactin-is-men-too.

2. Lise Eliot, "Girl Brain, Boy Brain?" *Scientific American*, September 8, 2009, www .scientificamerican.com/article.cfm?id=girl-brain-boy-brain. Neuroscientists have indeed found structural differences in male and female brains. But experiments looking at male and female brain structures at various ages and taking different personality traits into account point to life experience shaping much of those differences.

3. Sarah Blaffer Hrdy, "Cooperative Breeding and the Paradox of Facultative Fathering," in *Neurobiology of the Parental Brain*, ed. Robert Bridges (Burlington, MA: Academic Press, 2008). Aka men take on 62 percent of the care in such instances.

4. Sarah Blaffer Hrdy, *Mother Nature: Maternal Instincts and How They Shape the Human Species* (New York: Ballatine Books, 1999), 212.

5. Ibid., 213.

6. Morten L. Kringelbach et al., "A Specific and Rapid Neural Signature for Parental Instinct," *PLoS ONE* 3, no. 2 (2008), doi: 10.1371/journal.pone.001664. Andrea Caria et al., "Species-Specific Response to Human Infant Faces in the Premotor

Cortex," *NeuroImage* 60, no. 2 (April 2012): 884–93, doi: 10.1016/j.neuroimage .2011.12.068.

7. Sarah Blaffer Hrdy, *Mothers and Others: The Evolutionary Origins of Mutual Understanding* (Cambridge, MA: Harvard University Press, 2011), 78.

8. Enrico de Lazaro, "New Study Supports 'Grandmother Hypothesis,'" *Sci-News*, October 24, 2012, www.sci-news.com/othersciences/anthropology/article00678 .html. For the study, see Peter S. Kim, James E. Coxworth, and Kristen Hawkes, "Increased Longevity Evolves from Grandmothering," *Proceedings of the Royal Society B* 22, no. 279 (December 2012): 4880–84, doi: 10.1098/rspb.2012.1751.

9. Michael Balter, "Why Are Our Brains So Ridiculously Big?" *Slate*, October 26, 2012.

10. Hrdy writes movingly of her own motherhood and the beginnings of her search to better understand it in *Mother Nature*, xi–xix.

11. Claudia Glenn Dowling, Jenny Gage, and Tom Betterton, "The Hardy Sarah Blaffer Hrdy," *Discover Magazine*, March 1, 2003, http://discovermagazine.com/2003 /mar/feathrdy#.UL-FAo5_Wok.

12. Megan Daum, "Phyllis Schlafly: Back on the Attack," *Los Angeles Times*, March 31, 2011, http://articles.latimes.com/2011/mar/31/opinion/la-oe-daum-column -schlafly-20110331.

## 10: NEW DADS

1. Susan Gregory Thomas, "Are Dads the New Moms?" *Wall Street Journal*, May 11, 2012.

2. "The 21st Century Dad: Happy Father's Day!," Visually, accessed July 25, 2013, http://visual.ly/21st-century-dad-happy-fathers-day.

3. U.S. Census Bureau, "Families and Living Arrangements," Table SHP-1, "Parents and Children in Stay-at-Home Parent Family Groups: 1994 to Present" (Washington, D.C.: U.S. Department of Commerce, 2011), www.census.gov/population /www/socdemo/hh-fam.html.

4. Kathleen Gerson, *No Man's Land: Men's Changing Commitments to Family and Work* (New York: Basic Books, 1993).

5. Gretchen Livingstone and Kim Parker, "A Tale of Two Fathers, More Are Active, but More Are Absent," Pew Research Center, June 15, 2011.

6. Rong Wang and Suzanne M. Bianchi, "ATUS Fathers' Involvement in Childcare," *Social Indicators Research* 93 (2009): 141–45.

7. Jennifer L. Hook and Christina M. Wolfe, "New Fathers? Residential Fathers' Time with Children in Four Countries," *Journal of Family Issues* 33, no. 4 (April 2, 2012): 415–50, doi: 10.1177/0192513X11425779.

8. Ann-Zofie Duvander and Ann-Christin Jans, "Consequences of Fathers' Parental Leave Use: Evidence from Sweden," *Finnish Yearbook of Population Research* 2009, 49–62.

9. Brittany S. McGill, "Navigating New Norms of Involved Fatherhood: Employment, Gender Attitudes, and Father Involvement in American Families" (Ph.D. dissertation, University of Maryland, 2011).

10. Brad Harrington, Fred Van Deusen, and Beth Humberd, *The New Dad: Caring, Committed and Conflicted* (Boston: Boston College Center for Work & Family, 2011), www.bc.edu/content/dam/files/centers/cwf/pdf/FH-Study-Web-2.pdf. "Men are feeling a sense of loss at what they're not able to do," said Brad Harrington. A survey by A Better Balance, a nonprofit research group, found that 75 percent of fathers worried that their jobs prevented them from having the time to be the kinds of dads they wanted to be. "Now, there's not just mommy guilt, there's daddy guilt," copresident Dina Bakst told me. "Dads are feeling pressure to live up to this new ideal of what a good dad is."

11. "Key Statistics from the National Survey of Family Growth," Centers for Disease Control and Prevention, updated July 27, 2012, www.cdc.gov/nchs/nsfg/abc_list_a.htm#work.

12. Scott Coltrane, "Fathering Paradoxes, Contradictions, and Dilemmas," in *Handbook of Contemporary Families: Considering the Past, Contemplating the Future*, ed. Marilyn Coleman and Lawrence H. Ganong (Thousand Oaks, CA: Sage Publications, 2003), 394–410.

13. Chun Bun Lam, Susan M. McHale, and Ann C. Crouter, "Parent-Child Shared Time from Middle Childhood to Late Adolescence: Developmental Course and Adjustment Correlates," *Child Development* 83, issue 6 (November/December 2012): 2089–2103.

## BRIGHT SPOT: GRITTY, HAPPY KIDS

1. Payne and Ross, *Simplicity Parenting*, 57.

2. Wendy Soderburg, "How Working Parents Cope," *UCLA Today*, April 26, 2005, www.today.ucla.edu/portal/ut/050426news__howworking.aspx.

3. Joseph L. Mahoney, Angel L. Harris, and Jacquelynne S. Eccles, "Organized Activity Participation, Positive Youth Development, and the Over-Scheduling Hypothesis," *Social Policy Report* 20, no. 4 (2006): 3–19, www.srcd.org/press/mahoney.pdf.

4. www.nytimes.com/2010/06/07/technology/07brainside.html?_r=0.

5. Suniya S. Luthar and Bronwyn E. Becker, "Privileged but Pressured? A Study of Affluent Youth," *Child Development* 73, no. 5 (September/October 2002): 1593–1610.

6. Christine Carter, *Raising Happiness: 10 Simple Steps for More Joyful Kids and Happier Parents* (New York: Ballantine Books, 2010), 137.

7. David Derbyshire, "How Children Lost the Right to Roam in Four Generations," *Daily Mail* online, June 15, 2007, www.dailymail.co.uk/news/article-462091/How-children-lost-right-roam-generations.html#ixzz1ywZBP0EF.

8. Cheryl Charles et al., "Children and Nature 2008: A Report on the Movement to Reconnect Children to the Natural World," January 2008, www.childrenandnature.org/uploads/CNMovement.pdf.

9. Payne and Ross, *Simplicity Parenting*, 153–61.

10. Associated Press, "Study: Students More Stressed Now Than During Depression?" *USA Today*, January 12, 2010, http://usatoday30.usatoday.com/news/education

/2010-01-12-students-depression-anxiety_N.htm. See also Jean M. Twenge, "The Narcissism Epidemic," *Psychology Today*, www.psychologytoday.com/blog/the -narcissism-epidemic.

11. Angela L. Duckworth et al., "Grit: Perseverance and Passion for Long-Term Goals," *Journal of Personality and Social Psychology* 92, no. 6 (2007): 1087–1101.

12. Carter, *Raising Happiness*, 171–72.

13. Sonja Lyubomirsky, Laura King, and Ed Diener, "The Benefits of Frequent Positive Affect: Does Happiness Lead to Success?" *Psychological Bulletin* 131, no. 6 (2005): 803–55.

14. Carter, *Raising Happiness*, 27.

15. Ibid., 5.

16. Melinda Beck, "Thank You. No, Thank You," *Wall Street Journal*, November 23, 2010.

## 11: HYGGE IN DENMARK

1. Lyn Craig and Killian Mullan, "How Mothers and Fathers Share: A Cross-National Time-Use Comparison," *American Sociological Review* 76, no. 6 (December 2011): 834–61.

2. "Maternal Employment Rates," OECD Directorate of Employment, Labour and Social Affairs, May 13, 2012, www.oecd.org/els/familiesandchildren/38752721 .pdf.

3. Alberto F. Alesina, Edward L. Glaeser, and Bruce Sacerdote, "Work and Leisure in the U.S. and Europe: Why So Different?" in *NBER Macroeconomics Annual 2005*, vol. 20 (Cambridge, MA: MIT Press, 2006).

4. "Directive 2003/88/EC of the European Parliament and of the Council of 4 November 2003 Concerning Certain Aspects of the Organisation of Working Time," *Official Journal of the European Union*, November 18, 2003, http://eur-lex .europa.eu/LexUriServ/LexUriServ.do?uri=OJiL:2003:299:0009:0019:en:pdf.

5. Antoine Mariotti, "French PM Stirs Controversy Over 35-Hour Work Week," France 24 website, October 30, 2012, www.france24.com/en/20121030-france -prime-minister-ayrault-controversy-suggests-open-revising-35-hour-work-week.

6. Markus Dettmer and Janko Tietz, "Germany's Massive Job-Saving Program Could Still Fail," *Spiegel* online, December 30, 2009, www.spiegel.de/international /business/betting-on-an-upswing-in-2010-germany-s-massive-job-saving-pro gram-could-still-fail-a-669502.html.

7. "Guide: Maximum Weekly Working Hours," Gov.uk website, December 3, 2012, www.gov.uk/maximum-weekly-working-hours/overview.

8. "The Danish Work Culture," Copenhagen Capacity website, www.copcap.com /content/us/living_working/working_in_copenhagen/the_danish_work_culture.

9. Janet C. Gornick and Marcia K. Meyers, "Institutions That Support Gender Equality in Parenthood and Employment," in *Gender Equality*, ed. Gornick and Meyers, 3–64.

10. "Public Holidays," Visit Copenhagen website, www.visitcopenhagen.com/good-to-know/practical-stuff/public-holidays.

11. World Economic Forum, "Table 3: The Global Competitiveness Index 2012–2013 Rankings and 2011–2012 Comparisons" (Geneva: World Economic Forum, 2012), www3.weforum.org/docs/CSI/2012-13/GCR_Rankings_2012-13.pdf.

12. Bureau of Labor Statistics, "International Comparisons of GDP Per Capita and Per Hour, 1960–2011," Division of International Labor Comparisons e-newsletter, November 7, 2012, www.bls.gov/fls/intl_gdp_capita_gdp_hour.pdf.

13. "OECD Unemployment Rate at 7.9% in August 2012," news release, Paris, October 9, 2012, www.oecd.org/std/labourstatistics/HUR_NR10e12.pdf.

14. Central Intelligence Agency, "Denmark," World Factbook, updated July 10, 2013, www.cia.gov/library/publications/the-world-factbook/geos/da.html.

15. www.oecd-ilibrary.org/docserver/download/8111041ec016.pdf?expires =1354825701&id=id&accname=guest&checksum=1D1F01F471772BFFAC7BEA B473892BE9. The United States has one of the largest income equality gaps of wealthy countries, ranking just above Turkey, Mexico, and Chile. World Economic Forum, Global Gender Gap Report 2012, www.weforum.org/issues/global-gender-gap.

16. www.oecd-ilibrary.org/docserver/download/8111041ec018.pdf?expires=1354827 710&id=id&accname=guest&checksum=28799B2F2C1DB17F4349A61C19419 ABE.

17. "Income," OECD Better Life Index, www.oecdbetterlifeindex.org/topics/income/.

18. These European countries tried offering fathers more money to take parental leave. They offered them more paid time off. But it wasn't until they passed laws reserving a portion of the family's parental leave for fathers only—and stipulated that if fathers didn't use their portion, the family would lose the time—that the number of fathers taking parental leave began to rise, Thomas Johansson told me in an interview.

19. Jens Bonke and Bent Jensen, "Paid and Unpaid Work in Denmark—Towards Gender Equity," Electronic International Journal of Time Use Research 9, no. 1 (November 2012): 108–19, www.eijtur.org/pdf/volumes/eijtur_9_1.pdf.

20. "Education in Denmark," FYI Denmark website, www.fyidenmark.com/education-in-Denmark.html.

21. Summaries of EU Legislation, "Parental Leave and Leave for Family Reasons," Europa website, updated April 27, 2010, http://europa.eu/legislation_summaries /employment_and_social_policy/employment_rights_and_work_organisation /c10911_en.htm.

22. Benjamin Weiser, "Danish Mother's Claim of False Arrest Is Rejected," New York Times, December 15, 1999, www.nytimes.com/1999/12/15/nyregion/danish-mother -s-claim-of-false-arrest-is-rejected.html?ref=annettesorensen.

23. Anne Lise Ellingsæter, "Dual Breadwinner Societies: Provider Models in the Scandinavian Welfare States," Acta Sociologica 41, no. 1 (1998): 59–73, doi: 10.1177/000169939804100105.

24. Jennifer Buley, "A Celebration of Ice-Cold Water," *Copenhagen Post*, January 11, 2012, http://cphpost.dk/culture/culture-news/%E2%80%9C-celebration-ice-cold-water%E2%80%9D. See also *The Sport for All Committee Report—Conclusions and Proposals*, summary, 2009, http://kum.dk/Servicemenu/Publikationer/2009/The-Sport-for-All-Committee--Conclusions-and-Proposals.

25. John Helliwell, Richard Layard, and Jeffrey Sachs, eds., *World Happiness Report* (New York: Earth Institute, Columbia University, 2012), www.earth.columbia.edu/sitefiles/file/Sachs%20Writing/2012/World%20Happiness%20Report.pdf.

26. "Denmark," *OECD Better Life Index*, www.oecdbetterlifeindex.org/countries/denmark/.

27. "Denmark 'Happiest Place on Earth,'" BBC News, July 28, 2006, http://news.bbc.co.uk/2/hi/5224306.stm. See also Ray Clancy, "People Living in Denmark Are the Happiest, Europe Wide Study Shows," ExpatForum.com, December 29, 2011, www.expatforum.com/general-considerations/people-living-in-denmark-are-the-happiest-europe-wide-study-shows.html. Emily Alpert, "Happiness Tops in Denmark, Lowest in Togo, Study Says," *Los Angeles Times* (*World Now* blog), April 2, 2012, http://latimesblogs.latimes.com/world_now/2012/04/happiness-world-bhutan-meeting-denmark.html. Dan Buettner's *Blue Zones* highlights Denmark as a "blue zone," where people are healthier, happier, and live longer than in other areas: Buettner, *Thrive: Finding Happiness the Blue Zones Way* (Washington, D.C.: National Geographic Society, 2008), excerpted in "Lessons from Denmark," *Blue Zones*, February 7, 2012, www.bluezones.com/2012/02/lessons-from-denmark/.

28. "Happiest in the World," Official Website of Denmark, http://denmark.dk/en/meet-the-danes/work-life-balance-the-danish-way/happy-danes/.

29. "Dutch Kids Are the Happiest in Europe," *Dutch Daily News* (blog), January 16, 2010, http://www.dutchdailynews.com/dutch-kids-happiest/.

30. "PF3.2: Enrolment in Childcare and Pre-Schools," OECD Family Database, June 14. 2012, www.oecd.org/els/familiesandchildren/37864698.pdf.

31. Laza Kekic, "The Lottery of Life: Where to Be Born in 2013," *Economist*, November 21, 2012, www.economist.com/news/21566430-where-be-born-2013-lottery-life.

32. UNICEF Innocenti Research Centre, *Measuring Child Poverty: New League Tables of Child Poverty in the World's Richest Countries* (Florence: UNICEF, May 2012), www.unicef-irc.org/publications/pdf/rc10_eng.pdf.

33. *Corruption Perceptions Index* (Berlin: Transparency International, 2012), www.transparency.org/cpi2012/results. The U.S. ranks 19th.

34. Danish Energy Agency, "Renewables Now Cover More Than 40% of Electricity Consumption," news release, September 24, 2012, www.ens.dk/en/info/news-danish-energy-agency/renewables-cover-more-40-electricity-consumption.

35. The Heritage Foundation, "Denmark," *2012 Index of Economic Freedom* (Washington, D.C.: Heritage Foundation, 2012), www.heritage.org/index/country/denmark?src=next.

36. "Flexicurity: A Model That Works," *Economist*, September 7, 2006, www.economist.com/node/7880198.

37. Save the Children, *State of the World's Mothers 2012: Nutrition in the First 1,000 Days* (Westport; CT: Save the Children, May 2012), www.savethechildren.org/atf /cf/{9def2ebe-10ae-432c-9bd0-df91d2eba74a}/STATEOFTHEWORLDSMOTH ERSREPORT2012.PDF.

38. World Bank, "Fertility Rate, Total (Births Per Woman)," databank, http://data .worldbank.org/indicator/SP.DYN.TFRT.IN.

39. Ricardo Hausmann, Laura D. Tyson, and Saadia Zahdti, eds., *The Global Gender Gap Report 2012* (Geneva: World Economic Forum, 2012).

40. Maria Carbin, *Report Analysing Intersectionality in Gender Equality Policies for Denmark and the EU* (Vienna: QUING Project, Institute for Human Sciences, 2008), www.quing.eu/files/results/ir_denmark.pdf.

41. Jennifer L. Lawless and Richard L. Fox, *Men Rule: The Continued Under-Representation of Women in U.S. Politics* (Washington, D.C.: Women & Politics Institute, American University, January 2012), www.american.edu/spa/wpi /upload/2012-Men-Rule-Report-web.pdf.

42. Bonke and Jensen, "Paid and Unpaid Work in Denmark." "We shall have to wait 70–80 years until women and men quantitatively have the same amount of working time inside and outside the home" (p. 109). They give projections for gender convergence in Denmark and the projection that "women and men will also spend the same amount of time in paid work in 2033, while this happens already in 2021 for unpaid work" (p. 116).

43. Baby Blues: A Juggler's Guide to Having It All," *Economist*, November 26, 2011, www.economist.com/node/21539925. Amelia Gentleman, "'We Lost the Focus on Emotional Warmth,'" *Guardian*, April 20, 2009, www.guardian.co.uk/society /2009/apr/21/child-care-europe. Danish studies have found that child care benefits children, particularly from disadvantaged backgrounds, and leads to higher academic success. Jane Greve found that, unlike in the United States, maternal employment and child care are not associated with child obesity: Greve, "New Results on the Effect of Maternal Work Hours on Children's Overweight Status: Does the Quality of Child Care Matter?" *Labour Economics* 18, no. 5 (October 2011): 579–90, http://ideas.repec.org/a/eee/labeco/v18y2011i5p579-590.html. Jens Bonke told me that when Danish researchers find positive effects of child care, they have a difficult time getting their articles published in English-language journals. "There's always the question, 'How can it be so?'" he said. "Every time we send articles to American journals, they say, 'You should explain that it's different in Denmark and why it's so different.' There's a real bias, an unwillingness to understand another system." A more comprehensive review of the child-care literature and Denmark can be found in Rachel Dunifon et al., "Maternal Employment and Child Achievement in the Danish Context" (working paper, Cornell University and the Danish National Center for Social Research), https://espe.conference-services.net/resources/321/2907/pdf/ESPE2012 _0395_paper.pdf.

44. Peter H. Schuck, "Diversity and Candor: How Should We Talk About Our Differences" (speech presented at "Ethics at Noon," Santa Clara University, Santa Clara,

CA, October 24, 2004), www.scu.edu/ethics/publications/submitted/schuck /diversity-and-candor.html.

45. Statistics Denmark, "Population and Elections," *Statistical Yearbook 2012*, www .dst.dk/pukora/epub/upload/16251/02pop.pdf.

46. "Political Structure," Danishnet.com, www.danishnet.com/info.php/government /political-structure-31.html.

47. Philip Reeves, "Muslims in Denmark Face a Wave of Intolerance," *All Things Considered*, National Public Radio, February 6, 2012, www.npr.org/2011/06/28 /137480110/muslims-in-denmark-face-a-wave-of-intolerance.

48. For more on the media bias, see Hasan Cücük, "Study Highlights Anti-Islam Bias Seen in Danish Media," *Today's Zaman*, December 9, 2012, www.todayszaman .com/newsDetail_getNewsById.action?newsId=300585. For housing, education, and job discrimination, see "Islam in Denmark," Euro-Islam.info website, 2012, www.euro-islam.info/country-profiles/denmark/.

49. For the DPP's anti-immigration position, see Dansk Folkeparti website, "The Party Program of the Danish People's Party," www.danskfolkeparti.dk/The_Party _Program_of_the_Danish_Peoples_Party. It says, "Denmark is not an immigrant-country and never has been. Thus we will not accept transformation to a multi-ethnic society. Denmark belongs to the Danes and its citizens must be able to live in a secure community founded on the rule of law, which develops along the lines of Danish culture. It ought to be possible to absorb foreigners into Danish society provided however, that this does not put security and democratic government at risk. To a limited extent and according to special rules and in conformity with the stipulations of the Constitution, foreign nationals should be able to obtain Danish citizenship."

50. Tasneem Brogger, "Danish Support for Anti-Immigration Party Rises, Poll Shows," *Bloomberg*, February 27, 2006, www.bloomberg.com/apps/news?pid=newsarchive &sid=aYsZDc.NNfM0.

51. "Suicide Rates Per 100,000 by Country, Year, and Sex (Table)," World Health Organization website, 2011, www.who.int/mental_health/prevention/suicide_rates /en/. For more on teen binge drinking, see "UK Teen Drinking Is Serious and Chronic, Study Suggests," *Science Daily*, April 2, 2009, www.sciencedaily.com /releases/2009/04/090401102944.htm.

52. For Nordic divorce rates, see Ingrid Spilde, "Increased Divorce Rates Are Linked to the Welfare State," *ScienceNordic*, October 18, 2012, http://sciencenordic.com /increased-divorce-rates-are-linked-welfare-state. For international comparisons of marriage, divorce, and single mother rates, see U.S. Census Bureau, "International Statistics," *Statistical Abstract of the United States: 2012*, tables 1335, 1336, and 1337, www.census.gov/compendia/statab/2012/tables/12s1336.pdf. The Census Bureau reports that Denmark's marriage rate, 10.3 per 1,000 people in 2008, was almost on par with the U.S. 10.4 rate. But at 4.1, Denmark's divorce rate was not as high as the U.S. rate of 5.2. For cohabitation rates, see "SF3.3: Cohabitation Rate and Prevalence of Other Forms of Partnership," OECD Family Database, January 7, 2010, www.oecd.org/els/familiesandchildren/41920080.pdf.

53. "Women at Work: Who Are They and How Are They Faring?" *OECD Employment Outlook, 2002*, chap. 2, www.oecd.org/els/emp17652667.pdf.

54. Nathalie Rothschild, "In Sweden, a Debate Over Whether Gender Equality Has Gone Too Far," *Christian Science Monitor*, April 7, 2012, www.csmonitor.com /World/Europe/2012/0407/In-Sweden-a-debate-over-whether-gender-equality -has-gone-too-far.

## 12: LET US PLAY

1. Stuart Brown, *Play: How It Shapes the Brain, Opens the Imagination, and Invigorates the Soul* (New York: Avery, 2009), 11. Brown outlines the biology and brain science behind play as well as its benefits. "There is a kind of magic in play. What might seem like a frivolous or even childish pursuit is ultimately beneficial. It's paradoxical that a little bit of 'nonproductive' activity can make one enormously more productive and invigorated in other aspects of life."

2. Charlene S. Shannon and Susan M. Shaw, "Mothers as Leisure Educators: Lessons Daughters Learn" (paper presented at the Eleventh Canadian Congress on Leisure Research, Nanaimo, British Columbia, May 17–20, 2005), http://lin .ca/Uploads/cclr11/CCLR11-134.pdf. They write, "Many mothers' behaviours did not provide examples of personal leisure time, but rather the implicit message was that family leisure becomes the priority once a woman becomes a mother."

3. Heather Gibson, phone interview with author, March 23, 2012.

4. Margaret Beck and Jeanne Arnold, "Gendered Time Use at Home: An Ethnographic Examination of Leisure Time in Middle-Class Families," *Leisure Studies* 28, no. 2 (April 2009): 137.

5. Christina Bennighaus, "Mothers' Toil and Daughters' Leisure: Working-Class Girls and Time in 1920s Germany," *History Workshop Journal* 50 (2000): 45–72, doi: 10.1093/hwj/2000.50.45.

6. Catherine M. Richards, "Gender and Housework: Postretirement Change" (master's thesis, Oregon State University, July 14, 2000), http://ir.library.oregonstate .edu/xmlui/handle/1957/33064. For a fascinating look at how retired men and women fill the hours on an average day, see Rachel Krantz-Kent and Jay Stewart, "How Do Older Americans Spend Their Time?" U.S. Department of Labor, *Monthly Labor Review*, May 8, 2007, 8–26. The time-use data show that women fifty-five and older still spend far more time doing housework and far less time in leisure than men, with the biggest gap coming for those age sixty-five to sixty-nine: Men spent seventy hours a week in leisure and sports activities, according to the study, while women averaged about forty-six hours.

7. Nicole Samuel, ed., *Women, Leisure and the Family in Contemporary Society: A Multinational Perspective* (New York: Oxford University Press, 1996), 9.

8. Karla Henderson, phone interview with author, August 10, 2011.

9. Some of the best feminist leisure research is summed up in two anthologies: Karla A. Henderson, ed., *Both Games and Gaps: Feminist Perspectives on Women's*

*Leisure* (State College, PA: Venture Publishing, 1999), and Samuel, *Women, Leisure and the Family.*

10. Beck and Arnold, "Gendered Time Use," 139. The study found that fathers, too, experienced short leisure episodes, but fathers were still more likely than mothers to have some leisure episodes that lasted as long as 120 minutes. And fathers had more "pure" leisure time to themselves—as much as thirty minutes more a day. Mothers, on the other hand, spent almost all of their free time with their children.

11. *Society at a Glance 2009: OECD Social Indicators,* www.oecd.org/berlin/42675407 .pdf, chap. 2.

12. Americans and three to four hours of TV a day: Bureau of Labor Statistics, "Table 1: Time Spent in Primary Activities and Percent of the Civilian Population Engaging in Each Activity, Averages per Day by Sex, 2011 Annual Averages," news release, June 22, 2012, www.bls.gov/news.release/atus.t01.htm; Nielsen Company, *The Cross-Platform Report: Quarter 3* (New York: Nielsen Company, 2012), www.nielsen.com/content/corporate/us/en/insights/reports-downloads/2012 /cross-platform-report-q3-2011.html. Viewing rates higher among the older and those with less education: Catherine Rampell, "The Old and Uneducated Watch the Most TV," *New York Times* (*Economix* blog), June 26, 2012, http://economix .blogs.nytimes.com/2012/06/26/the-old-and-uneducated-watch-the-most-tv/. U.K. and four hours of TV a day: Mark Sweney, "TV Viewing 'Peaks at Four Hours a Day,'" *Guardian,* January 24, 2012, www.guardian.co.uk/media/2012 /jan/24/television-viewing-peaks-hours-day. Screen time up to eight hours a day: Brian Stelter, "8 Hours a Day Spent on Screens, Study Finds," *New York Times,* March 26, 2009, www.nytimes.com/2009/03/27/business/media/27adco.html ?_r=0. TV and four hours of background TV for kids: Alice Park, "Background TV: Children Exposed to Four Hours a Day," *Time,* October 2, 2012, http://health land.time.com/2012/10/02/background-tv-children-exposed-to-four-hours-a -day/. U.S. has highest rates of TV watching/screen time in the world: "Boxed In: Who Watches Most Television?" *Economist,* September 23, 2009, www.economist .com/node/14252309.

13. TV and obesity: Q. Qi et al., "Television Watching, Leisure Time Physical Activity, and the Genetic Predisposition in Relation to Body Mass Index in Women and Men," *Circulation* 126, no. 15 (2012): 1821–27, doi: 10.1161/CIRCULATIONA HA.112.098061. TV and depression: Emily Main, "Too Much TV Can Make You Depressed," Rodale News, updated April 9, 2010, www.rodalenews.com/watching -too-much-tv-0. TV and isolation: David S. Bickham and Michael Rich, "Is Television Viewing Associated with Social Isolation? Roles of Exposure Time, Viewing Context, and Violent Content," *Archives of Pediatrics & Adolescent Medicine* 160, no. 4 (2006): 387–92, doi: 10.1001/archpedi.160.4.387. TV and self-esteem: S. P. Tin et al., "Association Between Television Viewing and Self-Esteem in Children," *Journal of Developmental & Behavioral Pediatrics* 33, no. 6 (July 2012): 479–85, doi: 10.1097/DBP.0b013e31825ab67d. TV and violence: Rosie Mestel, "Adolescents' TV Watching Is Linked to Violent Behavior," *Los Angeles Times,*

August 5, 2008, www.latimes.com/features/health/la-hew-kidviolence2002,0
,2251451.story. TV disrupting sleep: Randy Dotinga, "Using Electronics Before
Bed May Hamper Sleep," *U.S. News & World Report*, March 7, 2011, http://health
.usnews.com/health-news/family-health/sleep/articles/2011/03/07/using-elec
tronics-before-bed-may-hamper-sleep. TV and shortened attention span: Iowa
State University, "ISU Study Finds TV Viewing, Video Game Play Contribute to
Kids' Attention Problems," news release, July 4, 2010, http://archive.news.iastate
.edu/news/2010/jul/TVVGattention. TV and shortened life span: Jeannine Stein,
"Watching TV Shortens Life Span, Study Finds," *Los Angeles Times*, January 12,
2010, http://articles.latimes.com/2010/jan/12/science/la-sci-tv12-2010jan12.

14. Herbert E. Krugman, "Brain Waves Measures of Media Involvement," *Journal of
Advertising Research* 11, no. 1 (February 1971): 3–9, www.thedryingroom.com/tv
/Brin%20Wave%20Measures%20of%20Media%20Involvement%20-%20Herbert
%20E.%20Krugman.pdf. See also Thomas B. Mulholland, "Training Visual Attention," *Academic Theory* 10, no. 1 (1974): 5–17, www.thedryingroom.com/tv
/Training%20Visual%20Attention%20-%20Thomas%20B%20Mulholland.pdf. A
sharp argument on TV as an addiction can be found in Wes Moore, "Television:
Opiate of the Masses," *Journal of Cognitive Liberties* 2, no. 2 (2001): 59–66, www
.cognitiveliberty.org/5jcl/5JCL59.htm.

15. Shira Offer and Barbara Schneider, "Revisiting the Gender Gap in Time-Use Patterns: Multitasking and Well-Being Among Mothers and Fathers in Dual-Earner
Families," *American Sociological Review* 76, no. 6 (December 2011): 809–33, doi:
10.1177/0003122411425170.

16. William J. Broad, "How Yoga Can Wreck Your Body," *New York Times*, January 5,
2012, www.nytimes.com/2012/01/08/magazine/how-yoga-can-wreck-your-body
.html?pagewanted=all. Robin Marantz Henig, "Taking Play Seriously," *New York
Times*, February 17, 2008.

17. Sara Beck, "Even Smiles Count, However Exacting the Competition," *New York
Times*, March 4, 2012, www.nytimes.com/2012/03/05/sports/national-yoga-com
petition-tests-even-the-audience.html?pagewanted=all.

18. Henig, "Taking Play Seriously."

19. "Dr. Sergio Pellis," University of Lethbridge, Research & Innovation Services
(biography), www.uleth.ca/research/research_profiles/dr-sergio-pellis. Brown,
*Play*, 33–42.

20. Brown, *Play*, 9–11.

21. Rebecca Abrams, *The Playful Self: Why Women Need Play in Their Lives* (London: Fourth Estate, 1997), 190–91. A hilarious video of Feynman playing the
bongos with abandon will make you smile: "Richard Feynman Playing Bongos,"
YouTube.

22. Stuart Brown, interview with author, March 9, 2012. Brown also referred to the
experiment in his talk at the Aspen Ideas Festival in 2010, "The Neuroscience of
Play: What Play Does for You and Your Brain, and What Happens to You if You
Don't Play," www.aspenideas.org/session/neuroscience-play-what-play-does-you
-and-your-brain-and-what-happens-you-if-you-dont-play.

## BRIGHT SPOT: REALLY *PLAN* A VACATION

1. Roger Mannell, interview with author, May 22, 2012. See also Douglas A. Kleiber, Gordon J. Walker, and Roger C. Mannell, *A Social Psychology of Leisure* (State College; PA: Venture Publishing, 1997). Roger C. Mannell, Jiri Zuzanek, and Reed Larson, "Leisure States and 'Flow' Experiences: Testing Perceived Freedom and Intrinsic Motivation Hypotheses," *Journal of Leisure Research* 20, no. 4 (1988): 289–304.

## 13: FINDING TIME

1. Ellen Ernst Kossek, *CEO of Me: Creating a Life That Works in the Flexible Job Age* (Upper Saddle River, NJ: Prentice Hall, 2008).
2. Frenk van Harreveld et al., "Ambivalence and Decisional Conflict as a Cause of Psychological Discomfort: Feeling Tense," *Journal of Experimental Social Psychology* 45, no. 1 (January 2009): 167–73, doi: 10.1016/j.jesp.2008.08.015.
3. David Hartman and Diane Zimberoff, "Existential Resistance to Life: Ambivalence, Avoidance & Control," *Journal of Heart-Centered Therapies* 7, no. 1 (2004): 3–63.
4. Peske said she adopted these big-picture questions after reading a blog post by Dr. Claire McCarthy, "Work and Life Aren't About Balance," *Thriving: Boston Children's Hospital's Pediatric Health Blog*, September 27, 2011, http://children shospitalblog.org/work-and-life-arent-about-balance/.
5. Joan Williams, "Women Don't Negotiate Because They're Not Idiots," *Huffington Post*, January 31, 2013, www.huffingtonpost.com/joan-williams/women-dont -negotiate_b_2593106.html.
6. Albert Bandura, "Self-Efficacy," in *Encyclopedia of Human Behavior*, vol. 4, ed. V. S. Ramachaudran (New York: Academic Press, 1994), 71–81, www.uky.edu /~eushe2/Bandura/BanEncy.html.
7. Philip Zimbardo, "Zimbardo Time Perspective Inventory," The Time Paradox website, www.thetimeparadox.com/zimbardo-time-perspective-inventory/.
8. "The Energy Audit," The Energy Project website, http://theenergyproject.com /tools/the-energy-audit.
9. I use part of the Pomodoro Technique to help my kids get caught up with their homework if they fall behind. They write every assignment for every subject that they have to do on a list. They set a timer for twenty-five minutes and start at the top, work for twenty-five minutes, then take a break, work for twenty-five minutes, then take a break, and so on until they've worked their way to the bottom of the list and the homework is done. See "The Pomodoro Technique," developed by Francesco Cirillo, www.pomodorotechnique.com/.
10. Phyllis Korkki, "To Stay on Schedule, Take a Break," *New York Times*, June 16, 2012, www.nytimes.com/2012/06/17/jobs/take-breaks-regularly-to-stay-on-schedule -workstation.html?_r=1&.

11. Judy Martin, "Employee Brain on Stress Can Quash Creativity and Competitive Edge," *Forbes*, September 5, 2012, www.forbes.com/sites/work-in-progress/2012/09/05/employee-brain-on-stress-can-quash-creativity-competitive-edge/.

12. Schwartz, Gomes, and McCarthy, *Be Excellent at Anything*, 61, 67.

13. Ibid., 4.

14. Nicky Phillips, "Taking a Break Is Secret to Success," *Sydney Morning Herald*, August 16, 2012, www.smh.com.au/national/education/taking-a-break-is-secret-to-success-20120815-24951.html.

15. Atsunori Ariga and Alejandro Lleras, "Brief and Rare Mental 'Breaks' Keep You Focused: Deactivation and Reactivation of Task Goals Preempt Vigilance Decrements," *Cognition* 118, no. 3 (March 2011): 439–43, doi: 10.1016/j.cognition.2010.12.007.

16. John Tierney, "Discovering the Virtues of a Wandering Mind," *New York Times*, June 28, 2010, www.nytimes.com/2010/06/29/science/29tier.html?pagewanted=all.

17. John Kounios, "The Neuroscience Behind Epiphanies," *TED Talks Talent Search*, video, http://talentsearch.ted.com/video/John-Kounios-The-neuroscience-b.

18. John Kounios and Mark Beeman, "The *Aha!* Moment: The Cognitive Neuroscience of Insight," *Current Directions in Psychological Science* 18, no. 4 (2009): 210, doi: 10.1111/j.1467-8721.2009.01638.

19. Legend has it that when the Greek mathematician Archimedes sank into his bath and saw his body displacing the water in the tub, he suddenly realized he could measure the volume of gold the same way. He is said to have famously yelled, "Eureka!" and run through the streets naked. See David Biello, "Fact or Fiction? Archimedes Coined the Term 'Eureka!' in the Bath," *Scientific American*, December 8, 2006, www.scientificamerican.com/article.cfm?id=fact-or-fiction-archimede. Legend also has it that Einstein came up with the Theory of Relativity while riding a bike. See Dennis Overbye, "Brace Yourself! Here Comes Einstein's Year," *New York Times*, January 25, 2005, www.nytimes.com/2005/01/25/science/25eins.html.

20. Peter Bregman, "18 Minutes: Find Your Focus, Master Distraction, and Get the Right Things Done," http://peterbregman.com/18-minutes/.

21. For a powerful exploration of the science behind habits and how to change them, I am deeply grateful for the work of Charles Duhigg, *The Power of Habit: Why We Do What We Do in Life and Business* (New York: Random House, 2012).

22. This idea is outlined in his videoblog: Tony Schwartz, "Develop Productivity Rituals," *HBR Blog Network*, video, January 3, 2012, http://blogs.hbr.org/video/2012/01/develop-productivity-rituals.html.

23. Sue Shellenbarger, "The Peak Time for Everything," *Wall Street Journal*, September 26, 2012. Science is finding that cognitive work is best tackled in the morning, as body temperature starts to rise and working memory, alertness, and concentration are at their peak. (This is, of course, assuming that you've had the requisite seven or eight hours of sleep the night before—something that many of us don't.) Although certainly not true for everyone, alertness tends to slump after

a meal. Sleepiness sets in around 2 p.m. And we tend to be more easily distracted from noon to 4 p.m.

## BRIGHT SPOT: TIME HORIZONS

1. Laura L. Carstensen, "The Influence of a Sense of Time on Human Development," *Science* 312, no. 5782 (June 30, 2006): 1913–15, doi: 10.1126/science.1127488.

## 14: TOWARD TIME SERENITY

1. Britta K. Hölzel et al., "Mindfulness Practice Leads to Increases in Regional Brain Gray Matter Density," *Psychiatry Research: Neuroimaging* 191 (2011): 36–43.
2. Hektner, Schmidt, and Csikszentmihalyi, *Experience Sampling Method*, 279.
3. I will always be eternally grateful to my former employer, the Knight-Ridder Washington Bureau, for generously granting me time to be with her under the Family and Medical Leave Act, and extended unpaid leave.

# ACKNOWLEDGMENTS

When I finished the manuscript of this book and pressed the send button to e-mail it to my magnificent editor, Sarah Crichton, I sat down on the couch in my office and began to think of all the other magnificent people who helped bring this book into being. I sat there for more than two hours.

In a time-starved world, I am humbled, grateful, and awed by the sheer number of people who so generously gave me theirs, returning endless e-mails, patiently answering persistent questions, sharing fascinating research, explaining it to me when I didn't get it, and letting me into their lives and trusting me to tell their stories. For reading crappy drafts and asking me pointed questions until the fuzzy, confused outlines of inklings sharpened into more defined thoughts. And for holding my hand when I worried I had nothing worthwhile to say or should really be writing about war or politics or something "important," and reminding me, with varying degrees of firmness, to snap out of it, that this, too, is important.

This book's journey began when Bob McCartney and R. B. Brenner at *The Washington Post* put me on the Women Readers' Committee after one of the few times I've ever spoken up publicly, albeit after the meeting was over. I am grateful to them and to John Robinson for answering the phone, issuing me the time diary challenge, getting me to Paris and outside my own overwhelm for the first time, being good sports, and ultimately spurring me to change my life. The journey would never have gotten off the ground had not my friend and gifted editor Sydney Trent told me to take Robinson's time diary challenge and write about it. I am grateful to her; to my research partner, Amy Joyce; to Lynn Medford, for whom I would walk through fire; to Frances Stead Sellers, Marcia Davis, Sara Goo, and the many smart and thoughtful women on the oasis of that committee. To Marc Fisher, one of the best in the business, for helping me find coherence in what was initially a rant, to Deb Leithauser for publishing it in *The Washington Post Magazine*, to Janet Michaud for believing I was on to something and for finding the right images to illustrate it, and to the literally hundreds and hundreds of readers who, when I worried I would only be exposing my own neuroses and personal failings, instead wrote long, impassioned e-mails saying, in essence, "You climbed into my head and wrote about my life." That gave me the courage to take the first steps to try to understand why we all felt so crazed and what could be done about it.

Tom Shroder was instrumental from the earliest days of brainstorming to writing the proposal to becoming one of the toughest and most clear-eyed readers and critics, catching flabby prose, marking clichés and lazy thinking with an "Ugh," and always pushing me to be better. In the midst of a grand mal overwhelm panic as deadline loomed, he gave me the best advice: "You don't have the time to indulge in freaking out." Tom also introduced me to Gail Ross, agent extraordinaire, for which I owe an enormous, happy debt. Gail listened to my rambling and rage and immediately got what I was trying to do before I did—"You want to write a game changer." I am grateful to her for being my rock, and to Anna Sproul-Latimer and the rest of the team at Ross Yoon. I am grateful that Gail always signs off her e-mails with XXs, which brightens even the gloomiest and most confusing of days.

Gail led me to Sarah Crichton, who I was lucky enough to have as a hilarious, brilliant, and beloved teacher at the Columbia Graduate School of Journalism. I admired her from afar for years and am still in a bit of a besotted daze that she saw the promise in this book and offered unwavering support, got just as excited about what I was finding as I did, patiently granted me the time I needed to sort it all out, and edited the book with precision, wisdom, and grace. I am grateful to Lottchen Shivers, Nick Courage, Tobi Haslett, and the entire team at Farrar, Straus and Giroux for believing in and expertly shepherding this project from idea to bookshelves and e-readers.

I am grateful to the editors and my colleagues at *The Washington Post*: to Don and the rest of the steadfast Graham family and their belief in journalism and journalists; to the editors Marcus Brauchli, Liz Spayd, and Raju Narisetti, who graciously gave me the time to take this journey; to Peter Perl, mensch and the man with the kind ear and Kleenex box, who arranged it; and to Vernon Loeb, whose infectious energy, unconditional support, enthusiasm, admonishments to go for a run, and the occasional mental-health lunch kept me going. And to Marty Baron, Kevin Merida, Lynda Robinson, Sydney, and my friends and colleagues on the enterprise and social issues teams for their goodwill in covering for me while I was out and graciously welcoming me back. It is a privilege to work with them and for *The Washington Post*, which is indeed, as I told my daughter, one of the best newspapers in the country.

Dee Cohn helped me get started finding the right research. Chris Davenport offered sage advice about the writing process and graciously read drafts. I am grateful to David Rowell for sharing his love of narrative writing, to Petula Dvorak and her awesome Mothers on the Hill network, to Ian Shapira and his connections to millennial culture, to Shankar Vedantam for his wise advice to report like hell first, then write only once the contours of the book have become clear. To Carlos Lozada, Rachel Dry, and Zofia Smardz for pushing me to write Outlook pieces.

I am indebted to Steve Coll, Andres Martinez, Rachel White, Faith Smith, and the board, the fellows, and the staff of the New America Foundation for wholeheartedly and generously supporting me and giving me a thought-provoking, intellectual home throughout the research and writing of the book. To Caroline Esser for her thorough and probing help with research, and to the indefatigable Becky Shafer, Lucy Shakelford, Kirsten Berg, and the crack team of fact-checkers who helped keep me honest. Any mistakes or misstatements are mine and mine alone. To Andrew McLaughlin and Karen Kornbluh for helping me see a more global picture. To Rosa Brooks, Sheri Fink, Amanda Ripley, Liza Mundy, Annie Murphy Paul, Jason DeParle, Tamar Jacoby, Louie Palu, Reniqua Allen, Christopher Leonard, Frank Foer, Katherine Mangu-Ward, Christine Rosen, and the other fellows for their invaluable support and advice on everything from public speaking to formatting endnotes. To David Gray for advising me early on to think about how men figure into the overwhelm, to Phil Longman for educating me about global fertility rates. And to Lisa Guernsey, who brought me to New America in the first place, and who, along with Konstantin Kakaes, read the policy chapter when it had the heft of a clunky *War and Peace*. Both offered expert guidance. Thanks, too, to Alex Sorin and Liam Malakoff for help transcribing interviews.

For the shape of both the journey and themes in the book, I am forever grateful to my friend Larry Robertson, who shared the guiding principles he used to write his own book on entrepreneurs, *A Deliberate Pause*, that became the twin beacons of my own search for time serenity: Why are things the way they are? How can they be better? To Martin Seligman, for the TED Talk I watched one day while I was sick, which gave me the idea of investigating time pressure in the three great arenas that make for a good life: work, love, and play. And to Dan Heath, who, when I confessed I wanted to find hope without resorting to treacly platitudes, suggested I concentrate on looking for real-world Bright Spots.

I owe more than I can say to the generosity of all the people and researchers who shared their time, many of whom are mentioned in the book or cited in the notes and many others who played crucial roles in the reporting. A special thanks to Lyn Craig, for her good humor and generosity, Kimberly Fisher, Almudena Sevilla-Sanz, Melissa Milkie, Barbara Schneider, Jonathan Gershuny, Liana Sayer, Oriel Sullivan, Linda Haas, Marielle Cloin, Mariam Beblo, Laurent Lesnard, Leslie Stratton, Catherine Sofer, Elena Stancanelli, Rachel Connelly, Kathleen Gerson, Betsy Thorn, Brittany McGill, Maria Stanfors, Max Haller, and the many researchers with the International Association for Time Use Research who generously shared their work. I am so grateful to have learned from the masterful Suzanne Bianchi before she died.

I am thankful to Laura Carstensen, Chandra Mason, Tim Elmore, Yelizavetta Koffman, Kim Parker, Anne McMunn, Michelle Budig, Tom Smith, Jane Waldfogel, Stephanie Coontz, Sharon Hays, Philip Cohen, Kei Nomaguchi, Jen Hook, Patrick Markey, Laurie Rudman, Linda Duxbury, Stephen Sweet, Russell Matthews, Claire Kamp Dush, and Sarah Schoppe-Sullivan. To the researchers who shared their groundbreaking work on the connections between the overwhelm, work culture, and health with the Work, Family & Health Network, I am grateful to David Almeida, Rosalind King, Ellen Ernst Kossek, Leslie Hammer, and Erin Kelly, and to Lisa Buxbaum, Jennifer Coury, and Mary Sawyers. I am grateful to Dan Pink for generously connecting me to Christena Nippert-Eng and Mihaly Csikszentmihalyi.

For educating me on the brain and overwhelm, I am indebted to Emily Ansell, Rajita Sinha, Tara Chaplin, and Keri Tuit of the Yale Stress Center. I want to thank Huda Akil, Brue McEwen, and Ronald Glaser. And Britta Holzel's work on mindfulness expanding the brain structure is beyond hopeful and just very cool.

I am grateful to Ellen Galinsky and Ken Matos for sharing their data and for their expert guidance not only in understanding overwork but in connecting me with companies and individuals actively seeking to change it. To Ellen Bravo for reassuring me that people, regardless of their socioeconomic level, want time for bread and roses. And to my friend Krishna Leyva, who got struggling immigrant families to trust me with their stories because they trusted her. To Kathleen Christensen, Cali Yost, and Judi Casey of the Work and Family Researchers Network, whose rich archive led me to Ann Burnett when my original idea for chapter 3 fell apart. I am grateful to Ann and the holiday letter archive she so generously shared, and to Edson Rodriquez, Lynne Casper, John De Graaf, and Ben Hunnicutt for their thoughtfulness on the meaning of time and busyness in modern life.

I am indebted to the brilliant Joan Wiliams, Cynthia Calvert, Manar Morales, and the Center for WorkLife Law, David Lopez, Sharon Terman, Renate Rivelli, Rebecca Pontikes, Ariel Ayanna, Dawn Gallina, Kamee Verdrager, Calla Rubino, Leslie Zaikis, Theresa Dove, Sarah Bailey, Alison Gregory, and Ellen Grealish and Sheila Murphy of Flexforce Professionals. Jenn Folsom is an amazing ally and all-around utility player. I am grateful to Jody Thompson for explaining sludge. And to Christine Keefer and the amazing, hardworking women in high tech whom I met with in Silicon Valley. I want to thank Bryce and Lee Arrowood for giving me such open access to Clearspire and all the attorneys there. And I am grateful to Rich Sheridan and everyone at Menlo Innovations for an inspiring and invigorating visit. For helping me understand how—and how hard it is—to rewire workplace culture, I want to thank Udaya Patnaik of Jump Associates, and Drs. Hannah Valantine and Ewen Wang of Stanford University Medical School. Alison Maitland's enthusiasm in a coming revolution of Future Work is infectious. A special thanks to Michele Flournoy.

I am grateful to Pat Schroeder for giving me so much of her time, to Pat Buchanan for welcoming me into his home, and to both for sharing their opposing views on the history and philosophy behind U.S. family policy. I'd also like to thank Andrea Camp, Edna Ranck, Patty Siegel, Mary Ignatius, Arianne Hegewisch, Dina Bakst, Susan Labin, Danelle Buchman, Desiree Wineland, Grace Reef, Michelle Noth, Elly Lafkin, Andria Swanson, Eileen Appelbaum, Jenya Cassidy, and Netsy Firestein. I am grateful that Netsy connected me with Tia Stoller and Dionne Anciano.

This book would simply not exist in its current form without Jessica DeGroot and the ThirdPath Institute. Jessica listened hard, asked tough questions, helped me see my own blind spots, and pushed and pushed and pushed me to think harder and go deeper to understand the way things are and to reach higher in the search for solutions. Along the way, as she made the book better, she helped my family make our lives better. I am grateful for her insight, her humor, her honesty, and her friendship.

And I am grateful to Catherine Birndorf for sharing her relationship equation. It is, indeed, true in an $A + B = C$ equation that if A changes and becomes A-prime, then C, the relationship, will also change. And eventually, so will B.

I want to thank MomsRising, the Hot Mommas Project, the WoMoBiJos—Good Enough Is the New Perfect!—Mocha Moms, the Enterprising Moms, Success in the City, the Wednesday Morning Group, the Montgomery County Women Entrepreneurs' Group, Melanie Meren, DC Urban Moms, Alexandria's OldTownMoms, Working Moms Against Guilt, Working Mawma, Mompetition, Eden Kennedy, Kathy Masarie, Jean-Anne Sutherland, Wendy Donohue, Andrea O'Reilly, M. K. Countryman, Georgi Laufenberg, Mararget Nelson, Lauri Teagan, Lisa Dean, Lea, Rebecca Deen, Rayna St. Pierre, Melissia Larson, Barbara Almond, and Beth Anne Shelton. To the deeply thoughtful Cassandra Dickson and the Simplicity Moms, and to Kitty Eisele for introducing me to them in the first place. To Christine Carter and Suniya Luthar. I am grateful to Karen Graf, for her generosity and honesty and for the serendipity of running into her one morning at the VW service center when both our cars had broken down. I'd run out of ideas on how to write about intensive mothering, and she invited me to spend a day in her life. And a shout-out to Sarah Blaffer Hrdy and a magical day on her walnut farm.

I am indebted to Brad Harrington, Matt Schneider, Howard Kaibel, Hogan Hilling, and Warren Emerson. And to the support and inspiration of the Journalism & Women Symposium, including Mary Kay Blakeley, Phuong Ly, Amy Alexander, Lisen Stromberg, and Lauren Whaley.

For helping me understand the history of women and leisure, I am grateful to Karla Henderson, Sue Shaw, Heather Gibson, Roger Mannell, Eileen Green, and Tess Kay. Thanks to Stuart Brown and Barbara Brannen, and to Julia Day and the staff at Leisure Trends Group for sharing their research on play. To Ali Sacash and Hilary Harding for showing me how mothers can still play outdoors, and to Jessica Haney and Jen Kogod for sharing the work of their mothers' self-renewal group, though I never did make it there. I still can't believe Nadia Stieglitz and Sara Baysinger got me on a trapeze. I am eternally grateful to them for opening up their Mice at Play group to me and for helping to reignite a passion for play.

The entire journey to Denmark began over a cup of coffee at the Caboose Cafe with my Norwegian friend Heidi Vatanka, who knew Rachel Ellehuus, who put me in touch with her Danish sister-in-law, Catarina Ellehuus, and their friends Vibeke and Søren Koushede. Vibeke introduced me to Michelle Hviid and Søren Broenchenburg, who arranged for me to meet with a host of other families. I am grateful to them all, as I am to Sharmi Albrechtsen for sharing the story of her life and her quest to understand Danish happiness, to Jens Bonke for sharing his time-use research and a delicious smorgasbord. I'm grateful to my friend Riikka Noppa for sharing her insights about Finland, and to fatherhood researchers in Denmark and Sweden and the fathers' playground in Copenhagen. And I cannot begin to thank my dear friends Fran Schwartzkopff and Eric Guthey for graciously opening their home and opening a wider window into Danish culture.

I'm grateful to Terry Monaghan for teaching me to clear the clutter in my head and to Tony Schwartz for teaching me how to work in waves. I want to thank Carolyn Semedo-Strauss, Ellen Ostrow, Michele Woodward, Cosper Scafidi, Pontish Yeramyan, Marlene Caroselli, Rick Hanson, Whitney Johnson, Christine Hohlbaum, Liz Lucchesi, and Tara Brach.

With a thousand kindnesses, my friends have sustained me and helped me every step along this journey. I am grateful to Marcia Call, who read draft after draft, offered keen insights, taught me the difference between kairos time and chronos time, and brought me white roses. And to her husband, Lonnie Rich, who enthusiastically spurred me on with his near-daily question, "What chapter you on now?" To Molly Sim, for the privilege of sharing her story, and to her sister, Elizabeth Wash, who offered me a weekend away at her house in rural Virginia, where I finally had the time and quiet to put together the book proposal. To Trudi Schraner, Elaine Bergmann, Angelika Olsen, Meg Connelly, Deb Riley, Leslie Turley, Amy Young and David Malakoff, Kathryn Klvana, Kathy Poor, Mark Sullivan, Nancy Needell, Lisa Shuchman, Fara Courtney, Wendy Moniz, and MOAB, the Mothers of Abracadabra, for reading drafts, letting me pick their brains, connecting me with others who became instrumental for the book, and offering truthful and invaluable feedback. To Jon Tilove and Jo Ann Moriarty, who fed me bagels and lox when I got stuck. To Ann Killion and Matt Gillespie, who not only connected me with high-tech workers but graciously let me and my "sewing machine" of a rental car crash at their beautiful house in the Bay Area. To Matthew Hirschmann and Lisa Carey for offering insights on cover design. To the Ragnar Van on the Run crew, the Binders Full of Fun Women, Alexandria Community Rowing, and Sandy Timmons and the B & RB group, for keeping my head clear, and the Del Ray Dads. To Stephen Baranovics, Peter Heimberg, Sharon Frances, and Philippe Depeyrot for getting me—reluctantly—camera ready. And to Sara Schroerlucke for transforming my home office into an oasis of "flow." And for all the miles and miles that my great friend and running partner Jenny Heimberg has patiently run with me as I sorted out the threads of this book, listening graciously as I wondered how to weave them together and offering wise and gentle counsel when I'd gotten them twisted in knots. God knows, this book is as much hers as it is mine.

And finally, to my family, without whom I couldn't breathe. I am grateful to my parents, Ruth and Arthur Schulte. My cousin Maura Youle, who opened her home to my family and opened my mind. And to my sisters, Claire Schulte and Mary Nelson, who are more than sisters—they are my best friends. To Tessa Schulte, who I wish was still here. To my beautiful daughter, Tessa Bowman, who came into my office one day with a sugar cookie on a pink plastic Easy-Bake Oven tray as I struggled to pound out my daily thousand words. For the wisdom beyond her years when she took my worried face into her hands and said, "It's okay, Mommy, sometimes you have to take risks." To my son Liam, my miracle child, who makes every day a gift. And to my husband, Tom, who has taken this journey with me, and who makes mine not only a Good Life, but a great one.

# INDEX

## A Note on the Author

Brigid Schulte is an award-winning journalist for the *Washington Post* and the *Washington Post Magazine*. Born and raised in Portland, Oregon, she has won numerous writing awards, including the Pulitzer Prize. She is also a fellow at The New America Foundation. She lives in Alexandria, Virginia, with her two children, Liam and Tessa, and her husband, Tom Bowman, Pentagon correspondent for National Public Radio.

@BrigidSchulte
brigidschulte.com